Narrating Practice with Children and Adolescents

Edited by Mery F. Diaz and Benjamin Shepard

Columbia University Press
New York

Columbia University Press
Publishers Since 1893
New York   Chichester, West Sussex
cup.columbia.edu
Copyright © 2019 Columbia University Press
All rights reserved

A complete cataloging-in-publication record is available
from the Library of Congress.
ISBN 978-0-231-18478-6 (hardback)
ISBN 978-0-231-18479-3 (paperback)
ISBN 978-0-231-54567-9 (e-book)
LCCN 2019002486

Columbia University Press books are printed on permanent and durable acid-free paper.
Printed in the United States of America

Cover design: Milenda Nan Ok Lee
Cover art: Randy Duchaine / © Alamy

—To Eloise, Emile, Stephen, Mami. And to Peter, who I know would be proud

—For Scarlett and Dodi

—This text is for Emma G. and every kid who ever "called BS"
on oppressive systems, took control of their own stories,
and pointed to something better

—For Bert Cohler

CONTENTS

ACKNOWLEDGMENTS   xi

Introduction: On Narrating Practice with Children and Adolescents
MERY F. DIAZ AND BENJAMIN HEIM SHEPARD   1

PART I: Ethnographies, Narrative Inquiries, and Life Stories

Chapter One
From Disempowerment to Self-Belief: A Center of Hope
for Vulnerable Youth in Cape Town
SHARON JOHNSON   31

Chapter Two
Aging Out and on My Own: Stories of Youth Transitions
Out of Foster Care
SABRINA GONZALEZ   48

Chapter Three
Dreaming Despite Status: Immigrant Youth
in Contingent Migration Contexts
STEPHEN RUSZCZYK   66

Chapter Four
"Hear Me": Collaborating with Youth to Address Sexual Exploitation
MARGOT K. JACKSON, VERA CAINE, JANICE HUBER,
AND MUNEERAH AMIN VASTANI   84

Chapter Five
In Between Worlds: Narrating Ecological Heritage
Practices for Teenage Wellness
KRISTINA BAINES   102

Chapter Six
Neighborhood Surveillance and the Prison Assembly Line
TREVOR B. MILTON   118

Chapter Seven
Considering Inequalities: Experiences in Part-Time
Youth Work
YASEMIN BESEN-CASSINO   133

PART II: Autoethnography and Storytelling

Chapter Eight
Finding Justice: Transforming Schools with the Children We Serve
MERY F. DIAZ   149

Chapter Nine
Fitting In, Letting Go, and Other Common Concerns
for Children with Disabilities
SHERRI L. RINGS   171

Chapter Ten
Between Life Stories and the Struggle for Homeless Youth
BENJAMIN HEIM SHEPARD   188

Chapter Eleven
Childhood and the Politics of Care
ELIZABETH PALLEY   214

Chapter Twelve
Living on the Frontline: Reality-Based Drug Education
in the Era of Black Lives Matter
JERRY OTERO   231

Chapter Thirteen
Poor Mothers, Poor Children: The Feminization
of Poverty in Rural India
GRETTA M. FERNANDES   247

PART III: Practice Reflections and Case Narratives

Chapter Fourteen
Understand the Brain, Understand Our Children
DEBORAH COURTNEY   263

Chapter Fifteen
Beyond Deficits: Shifting Perspectives in Child
and Youth Mental Health
MARGOT K. JACKSON   281

Chapter Sixteen
Shifting Identities, Shifting Meanings: Adolescent Siblings and Grief
ERICA GOLDBLATT HYATT   298

Chapter Seventeen
Creating Spaces for Sam: A Story of Healing Trauma
Through Narrative Means and Art Therapy
SUSAN MCDONALD AND STEPHANIE WISE   313

Chapter Eighteen
Stories of Youth and Family Navigating a New Frontier of Social Media
REBECCA G. JUDD AND BENJAMIN T. MAY   331

CONTRIBUTORS   351

INDEX   355

ACKNOWLEDGMENTS

We would like to thank the contributing authors, the storytellers of this text, for their commitment to this project. Each author persisted through the challenge of constructing meaningful stories about the significant lived experiences of children and youth. It was not an easy undertaking and at times was daunting. Nevertheless, every author rose to the challenge. We owe special thanks to Craig Hughes for his support throughout this project.

NARRATING PRACTICE WITH CHILDREN
AND ADOLESCENTS

INTRODUCTION

On Narrating Practice with Children and Adolescents

MERY F. DIAZ AND BENJAMIN HEIM SHEPARD

"Why are there so many stories?" one of our undergraduate students asked in a college-level human services community organizing class, where we were reading case histories full of personal accounts of individuals and groups creating change.

"Great question," we replied in a minor understatement. The other students jumped in.

"People learn from stories," one student explained.

"I liked the stories," another added.

"They bring you into other worlds."

"People explain themselves through stories."

We sat listening as other students chimed in, describing what was at stake with the narrative turn being acknowledged in our classroom. Why there are so many narratives is a question we have been asking for years. People's lives are grounded in narratives. Creation stories help us find reality. A visceral feeling colors stories that connect individual lives with larger social forces. They allow us into other people's lives in ways that other forms of data simply do not, enabling us to contemplate experiences of those we are trying to understand, in this case, the lives of children and adolescents.

From the moment we humans were able to communicate through gestures and sounds, and eventually spoken and written words, we have told stories (Jones 1996). Notes novelist Amy Hoffman, "We tell stories to give life meaning. We impose structure on chaos. We choose a beginning and an end; we elevate some details and discard others; we try to find lessons and useful information" (quoted in Becker 2017). Through narrative, we make sense of the world. We explain who we are and where we have been while providing direction for the future: we use narratives to tell the stories of our lives. The big "we," of course, extends into the lives of children, who spend their childhood weaving tales, stretching truths, and making meaning with stories, as they navigate the more playful and difficult times of their lives. As we get older, we tell different kinds of stories, often less interesting ones. Sometimes we remember those old stories, elaborating on them to make sense of things, retracing details of who we are and how we got here.

After all, one of the prominent cultural narratives of our time is that of childhood. Writes Adam Phillips (2014, 43),

Childhood was a story adults make up about themselves. It was to be the story that caught on. And psychoanalysis would catch on as a story about why stories about childhood matter. Freud was to make up a story about adult life out of a story about childhood; a story about development out of a story of assimilation. A story about civilization out of a story about immigration.

Today, a new paradigm, the social study of childhood, suggests we recognize that stories of children are not just about memories of what was or about what comes after. Rather, they are about complex lived experiences, in the here and now, and these stories can be told by children themselves (McNamee 2016; Corsaro 2015; Nybell, Shook, and Finn 2009; James, Jenks, and Prout 1998).

Every day, in all parts of the world, young people are crafting amazing stories. These are stories of children and teens who could not just go along to get along or accept the world's injustices as they are or were—of those who ignited the U.S. civil rights movement in the 1950s and who recently engaged in civil disobedience to protest congressional inaction to save the Deferred Action for Childhood Arrivals program. It is the story of high school students in Hong Kong in 2014, who endured tear gas in their struggle for democracy during a two-and-a-half-month occupation of the financial district, in defiance of the same Communist Party that had literally rolled tanks over protestors a quarter-century earlier (Sheehan 2014).

These stories capture the spirit of the U.S. high school students, such as Emma Gonzalez, who "called BS" on the National Rifle Association and the U.S. gun lobby, igniting a wave of students walkouts and civic engagement that left a former Supreme Court Judge contemplating the repeal of the Second Amendment of the U.S. Constitution (Stevens 2018). Or the persistence of Black Lives Matter youth organizers, who fight for the recognition of their humanity while their communities experience brutality at the hands of the state in the forms of racialized police violence, environmental neglect, and a myriad of other injustices. Or Greda Thunberg, 16, who started skipping school on Fridays to go to the Swedish parliament to condemn inaction and lobby it to do something about climate change; as we completed the edits for this book in March 2019, 1.4 million young people and a few grownups, including us, in 123 cities around the world, followed her lead and joined her act of civil disobedience. From Snapchats and videos, from tweets to podcasts, from punk to hip-hop, and from street art to direct action, young people channel the potency of stories as forces in social change, cultural resistance, and self-expression. These actions remind us that youth themselves are active agents in their own lives.

Agency, of course, is not always expressed through outward subversion or revolt, but also appears in the sensitive and ordinary ways in which children and youth negotiate the circumstances of their lives. We can see agency when youth reconstruct family through new peer relationships or with social workers when their biological ones are unavailable. We can see agency in the ways in which young people develop new identities by taking traditions from their homeland and integrating them with the new cultural norms of their adopted countries. Or through children's resilience as they cope and heal from trauma, becoming anew and full of possibilities. We can also see the boundaries of their agency tested by the social forces of poverty and inequality, exclusion, discrimination, and oppression. Consider the tragedy and trauma of family separations at the U.S. border or the staggering education inequality of U.S. public schools, which both widen the academic achievement gap for poor children of color and contribute to the school-to-prison pipeline.

Throughout this book, we consider such narratives, particularly stories and counter-stories, that challenge dominant ideas about childhood. Inasmuch as there are limits to a universal childhood, these stories explore the interplay of children in the environment and the structures that shape their lives. The telling of these childhood narratives itself is an inherently relational process, reflecting dialectic interactions between children and adults and, at times, expectations for their adulthood. We acknowledge that in scholarly spaces these stories are often told to or are witnessed by adults, and it is primarily through adult interpretation that we come to hear children's voices, even when children are part of the research process.

In this text, you will read stories constructed and co-constructed by adults who conduct research on or with children. Some stories are from adults who remember, contextualize, and tell of their own childhoods. Other stories are from those working with children through building helping relationships and who share their observations from practice. Embracing the relational process of telling stories about youth, authors make use of a variety of narrative approaches—such as life history, storytelling, ethnography, autoethnography, testimonios, counternarratives, narrative inquiry, case studies, and practice reflections—in the study of children's lives and commentary on their well-being. These approaches are also based on varied knowledge-building methods that range from more child-centered ones that include participatory action research, the use of poetry and art, ethnographies, in-depth interviews, and observations of childhood experiences to more adult interpretations: autoethnography, practice observations, reflections, and personal accounts. The latter methods sometimes reflect the real constraints in the process of research on and with children; for example, institutional review board (IRB) regulations may limit access to children and youth. These approaches also reflect the writing process itself, which can take narrators into different directions as they work to construct meaningful stories. Some authors found their chapters metamorphosing into autoethnographies and reflections as time went on. As Stanley Witkin (2014) confesses in *Narrating Social Work Through Autoethnography*, the process of writing ethnographies, particularly autoethnographies, can be vexing. Still, the authors of this book delivered story after story, and admittedly, the construction and reconstruction of stories have been the result of long labor for everyone involved in developing this book.

From the stories come multiple questions about the interactions and transactions that take place between children and youth and their environment. The stories ask how those working with young people might think about and respond to a changing landscape in practice. How do we define and construct childhood? How do poverty and inequality affect children's health and welfare? How is childhood lived at the intersection of race, class, and gender? How are globalization and neoliberalism shaping children's lives? How do children adapt and develop within a transnational, global, and technologically advanced environment? How do children negotiate changing social and cultural environments? How can practitioners engage children and adolescents in service through more culturally responsive and democratic processes?

But why the use of narrative approaches to answer these questions about children's lives? First, we believe that narrative approaches help contextualize and make sense of lived experiences by illustrating the interplay of the multiple forces acting on children that they have to negotiate. Thus, these approaches have a *goodness-of-fit* with both the ecological perspectives and emerging work in the study of childhood that emphasize the lived experiences of children. Second, narrative approaches open up spaces for voices that are often excluded from larger sociopolitical discourses (Moraga and Anzaldúa 1981). Finally, these narratives are potent and telling. Recall Ryan White, whose personal story of coping with HIV and its related social stigmas inspired the passage of the first federal AIDS legislation, the Ryan White Care Act. Over and over again, the telling of compelling stories engenders empathy in readers, opening spaces for messy truths in ways that traditional objectivist approaches cannot and serving as a call to action.

Throughout the rest of this introduction, we discuss commonly used theoretical frameworks in the study of children and youth and dive into how the narrative approaches align with emerging interdisciplinary approaches in the study of children and childhood. We reflect on the narrative and ethnographic turn in the social sciences, and we explore the meanings of these narratives, contextualizing our process for putting together this volume, its origins, and its stories. Finally, we provide an overview of the book's organization.

DIFFERENT WAYS OF SEEING CHILDHOOD

The first time I (Mery) worked with children was in a school setting. I was nineteen years old, barely out of childhood myself and volunteering as an aide to a school counselor in a public school. On my very first day at the school, within an hour of starting my new role and without much orientation, I was assigned to spend time with an eight-year-old boy. The counselor told me that Lucas could not remain in his classroom because he had been running around, distracting other children, and disrupting the teacher from instructing the other children. Before hurrying off, the counselor directed me to play some games with Lucas until he seemed ready to return to class. We were left in the tiny resource room, which was just big enough for the two of us, a table, and some disorganized bookshelves. I was a psychology major in my sophomore year at college, and I thought, somewhat presumptuously, that I was "great with kids." I started to open a Candy Land board game that had seen better days and asked Lucas if he had ever played it. He looked up at me for a brief moment, decidedly said "I'm outta here," and made a beeline for the door. As he disappeared out of my sight, I was taken aback and frozen with indecision. A few seconds later, I snapped out of it and ran after him. I would later share this story with friends, mostly making light of my predicament. I would ask "Why would he run?" and "Why would he run from *me*?" The answer to these questions would change over time, as my perception of children and understanding of childhood(s) did too.

Shifting Paradigms in the Study of Children

We are in the midst of a significant paradigm shift in how we think about children and childhood. The new social study of childhood, an interdisciplinary approach to theorizing and researching children and childhood, is concerned not only with the lived experiences of children but also has emerged to contest the notion of a universal childhood (McNamee 2016). In this framework, childhood is seen as a highly contextualized phenomenon and children as co-constructors of their world—one that is undergoing rapid social, technological, and economic global transformations—and as having collective interests and rights to participation. Scholars using this framework leave behind rigid disciplinary conceptualizations of childhood in favor of more integrative approaches. Still, so much of what we have assumed and continue to assume about children has been shaped by biopsychosocial theories, in particular, those developed in the field of developmental psychology (James et al. 1998). And these assumptions still drive much of the knowledge production about children and practice.

Early work in the developmental theories, was grounded in the natural sciences, in particular the evolutionary process. It was concerned with the deterministic nature, generality, and measurability of human behavior. Developmental theories posit that children move along neutral and biologically prescribed stages of development that naturally move from the inferior, "childhood" to the more complex "adulthood." Here, more emphasis is placed on the biological nature of childhood rather than on environmental influences. Therefore assumptions can be made about those children who do not move naturally from stage to stage or reach expected benchmarks about what is "normal" or "abnormal" and about what might happen later in adulthood (Taylor 2004).

As an undergraduate student I likely answered my questions about what happened with Lucas using a developmental lens through the framework I was then beginning to understand. I probably explained his inability to remain in the classroom or engage with me as "maladaptive behavior" and assumed it stemmed from a failure to adapt to his environment or master stages in the life course. Lucas himself was to bear the burden of being the "problem" at school.

Critiques of the development framework underscore its focus on deficits and its lack of attention to children's social context (James et al. 1998). This framework is also criticized for failing to properly acknowledge children's role in contributing to their developmental experiences; instead it still largely views children as subject to predetermined stages in the life course across time, culture, and place.

Similarly, albeit to a lesser extent, the field of sociology has contributed to how we have come to theorize about childhood (Corsaro 2005). Sociological research has broadly positioned children as "unknowing" passive recipients who internalize social scripts and norms. The social theory positioned subordinate position to adults within the structure of family and institutions, particularly schools. It is within these spaces that children, as learners, are regulated and guided toward a "competent" adulthood and becoming functioning members of society (Corsaro 2005; Wyness 2015).

Theorizing about children in these ways not only drove academic research but also served the aims of nation-building and the ability of schools, as institutions of the state, to be vehicles for developing future citizens (Wyness 2011, 2015). What children will become and how they can be shaped have been the purview of schools since the advent of compulsory attendance laws at the turn of the twentieth century. And it is through schools that "experts" are given access to children en masse—to be observed, studied, and treated within a framework of children as "becomings" (McNamee 2016).

Ecological Perspectives

During my graduate studies, I came to learn another way of seeing children. The ecological perspective, a framework derived from systems theory, is a major underpinning of current social work theory, research, and practice. Offering a lens for understanding the "person-in-environment," its focus is not just on individual adaptivity or the social forces that act on individuals but also on the reciprocity throughout the ecosystem. That is, it posits that development takes places within an ecosystem with which individuals interact. Through this lens, I could see Lucas, other children, and even myself not just as individuals with limitations or potential maladaptability but also as products of an environment that is either conducive or inhibiting to positive development.

It was Urie Bronfenbrenner (1979) who introduced ecological systems theory, a developmental framework, to explain the link between internal processes (the self) and systems in the environment: the family, the community, and the political and sociocultural environment. Germain and Gitterman (1996; see Germain 1980, 1991) furthered the ecological perspectives through their ground-breaking book titled *Life Course Model in Social Work Practice*. The life course model attends to the biopsychosocial development of individuals and their families within the context of history, culture, community, and society. But it perceives relationships as circular, in which transactions and influential "reciprocal exchanges" take place, instead of linear interactions. That is, the environment acts on us as we act on it.

Ecological perspectives underlie a great deal of work exploring children's risk and protective factors, and subsequently their resilience in the presence of adverse conditions (Fraser, Richman, and Galinsky 1999; Fraser 2004). Jens Qvortrup (1990) highlights, however, that ecological approaches often do not distinguish sufficiently between the child and the child's family, seeing both as a single system. When this occurs, children are positioned as dependent, and adult representations of children's interest are assumed to be fair and complete.

Still others critique the framework's lack of nuance. For example, in her discussion on risk and equity, Lee (2009) argues that, in the construction of risk, vulnerability is often viewed as pathological and indigenous to racial and ethnic minorities or the poor. In this manner, research both masks the vulnerabilities of the privileged and reinforces normativity in how resiliency should be expressed. Lee further notes that, historically, science has ignored that individuals have diverse resources and forms of navigating their environments: "the particular ways in which living under contemporary and historical conditions of oppression based on race, ethnicity, language, and class (including important intersections with gender) both structure risks, but also engender cultural repertoires of resilience" (p. 64). Therefore, despite the widespread use of the ecological framework in the study of child well-being, we must consider reshaping representations of children that reinforce expectations of what is "normal" and of normative ways to overcome adverse experiences.

A New Way of Seeing

As a clinical social worker, I worked with young clients who were often referred for multiple behavioral problems, mental health concerns, trauma, and family issues. They were primarily youth of color from low-income communities, many of whom were immigrants or children of immigrants; their backgrounds were similar to my own socioeconomic and cultural background. Their experiences revealed overarching inequality and a lack of resources in their communities. They also revealed exclusion, marginalization at the hands of institutions, and the realities of childhood at the turn of the twenty-first century. As they shared their stories with me, I learned of the many ways in which they negotiated challenges in their lives, in spite of a given diagnosis. Each of them shaped their identities and found ways to express their voice and worth, a sense of belonging, and a sense of control, sometimes with resourcefulness and other times with total defiance. In the counseling room I had space to explore their complex lives, but the interventions I was putting in place were much less flexible, largely structured to reflect the identification and treatment of individual pathology. There were no interventions to address the structures of oppression. The way we work with children who experience multiple barriers continues to be very much policy driven, prescribed, rigid, and quite hierarchical.

Notably, the advent of managed care restructured how we approached working with children and youth in health and mental health care settings. Managed care emphasized the coordinated, controlled, and efficient use of health and mental services, which reflected the neoliberal reforms sweeping across the health, social service, and education sectors since the 1970s (Moniz and Gorin 2006; Maskovsky 2000). It also meant having to justify the need for services. My role as a clinician reflected this: I met my young clients in in the office, if possible once a week, to assess and diagnose, intervene and reassess, and then end treatment. Clinicians had to ensure that treatment was evidence based, necessary, and delivered as efficiently as possible—even if that limited the cultural responsiveness of treatment and despite the complicated nature of our lives.

During this time an emerging movement, to be known as the sociology of childhood or the social study of childhood, began to contest deterministic and imperialistic models of research and practice with children, which prioritized the biopsychosocial nature of childhood and pushed for more contextualized ways of understanding their experiences. This paradigm shift considered childhood as historically, socially, politically, geographically, linguistically, and culturally constructed and as being significantly shaped by global economic factors was taking shape (Aries 1962; Corsaro 2005, 2015; James and Prout 1994; Holloway and Valentine 2000). A significant tenet of this framework, the *lived experiences of children*, is central to representations of diverse childhoods. So is the focus on children as collective beings in their own right, who are "knowing," who participate in the construction of their social world, and who negotiate social forces (Corsaro 2005). Because children are knowing social actors, locally and in society at large, their voice is essential to discourse, inquiry, and practice.

Historian Philippe Aries (1962) is widely considered to have sparked debate about the construction of childhood. He argued that childhood was a modern invention and that, throughout most of recorded history, children were not considered different from adults and childhood was not conceptualized as a unique stage in the life course. Aries based his claims on the examination of medieval art, noting that depictions of children were similar to those of adults. While there are certainly strong critiques of his methodology, he is considered a decisive scholar on these questions (Pollock 1983; Heywood 2001).

Chris Jenks, Allison James, and Alan Prout (1998; James and Prout 1990; Prout and James 1997) are credited as laying the groundwork for the new sociology of childhood. Their work emphasizes the lived experiences of children and youth as a central point of inquiry, in the here and now, instead of their potential *becoming*. As such, research within this paradigm is focused on children's agency and the inclusion of their voice and experiences at the intersections of race, gender, and class.

Outside of research, activist and policy makers have come to favor increased rights and participation for youth. The 1989 UN Convention on the Rights of the Child reflects tensions between views of "children as being in need of protection" and those that emphasize "children with rights to participation." These positions are preempted by, both, Western and paternalistic conceptions of children as a *special* and vulnerable group. Scholars and practitioners alike are grappling with such tensions in children's work, participation in research, citizenship rights, and body autonomy (Wells 2015; Mcnamee 2016).

Finally, globalization, shaped largely by neoliberalism, has had a major impact on both our conceptions of childhood and practice with children. Nybell et al. note, "The effects of globalization on children can be felt both directly, through policies that have reduced the social safety net or excluded certain young people from institutions of childhood, and indirectly, through changing ideas about the dangers and dangerousness of youth" (2009, 242). Economic shifts have changed the structure of the family, the expectations of children's participation in school, and their space in the labor market. The behavioral expectations of children to fit into these sociocultural structures have also generated varying degrees of institutional controls and regulation of children's lives. The over-surveillance and control of children limit their rights and autonomy and have served to exclude and marginalize some groups of children more than others. For these reasons, many are calling for a social justice orientation in research and practice with children.

Integrating Perspectives

As we examine the interplay between children and their environment over time, discipline-specific approaches can seem limited. Yet, each framework brings elements that are complementary to the study of children and childhood and that align with the aims of the new social study of childhood. Scholars, in looking at the complicated, messy, and multifaceted lives of children, argue for an integrated lens to help explore and make meaning of children's experiences (Taylor 2004; Uprichard 2008; Graham 2007b; Wells 2015). This lens would be one through which children can occupy both the state of "being" and of "becoming."

In research, this integration requires that we include children's perspective and voice. The use of life stories, testimonios, art, participatory action research, and narrative inquiry is vital in this process. Reframing and rethinking perspectives is also imperative. For example, ecological perspectives and resilience research must reject normative ideas about acceptable coping, be reoriented toward the strengths perspective, and include diverse and alternate ideas of resiliency. After all, children are social actors who negotiate their environment (Ungar 2004, 345). In practice, several social justice and restorative approaches have focused on including children, in constructing self-narratives, and meaning-making (Thorne 2003; Thomas and O'Kane 2000). Discourses of protection, dependency, and the "child in need" contrast with assumptions about the need for services and assistance, creating competing discourses of "needs" versus "rights" and competence (Thomas 2005).

We come to this text with the premise of the value of integrating perspectives, with particular attention to the ecological lens and the use of narrative approaches, in contextualizing children's experiences. Stories, which address questions about meaning, are a vehicle to understand complex experiences in the different spheres of children's lives and the relationships with which they are engaged (Weber 2002). The principles of the narrative support these aims because transactions can be examined through the relationship between thoughts and language. "Narrative inquiry, through its concern with stories that are located in social interaction, rather than existing as inherent characteristics within people, allows practitioners to think ecologically about their work" (Annan, Priestley, and Phillipson 2006, 26). After all, stories are told within social contexts (Cohler 1982; Plummer 1995). They serve as a means to explore children's agency and, whenever possible, include their voice.

SEARCHING FOR CLIFFORD AND FINDING BERT

We come to this project from different perspectives and experience in the field. We are both social workers. I (Shepard) never thought I would work with youth. The task always seemed too daunting. As a child, I suspected I would never have kids, even writing a manifesto on the topic in fifth grade.

Yet, the stories about children's lives kept me wondering what happened to children and why they end up as they do. Consider this excerpt from an interview I conducted with Stonewall veteran Bob Kohler; he recalled the youth who ignited the riot of June 1969 in New York City and considered the beginning of the modern Gay Liberation Movement:

By the end of the 1960s I said I was going to take two years off. After a career change I didn't know what to do and I was doing nothing. And I used to go in the park all the time and that's where the street kids were. I got very friendly with them and, even though I was older and represented a father figure to them, I wasn't old enough to be the dirty old man so they trusted me. And they'd confide in me. Their wigs, their stolen credit cards, anything—all their contraband I'd keep for them. They lived in the park. And those were the kids who rioted. And I'd gotten to know them and I kind of thought I had seen what happens to black people in Harlem; I had seen what happens to poor white people—I had seen all of that, but I had never seen this with gay teenagers. It was something I just didn't know about. Fourteen, fifteen-year-old kids with cigarette burns all over their bodies from a father who found out they were gay—or were permanently scarred, and certainly mentally scarred forever. And thrown out and living out of bags in Sheridan Square and washing in the little fountain. I did not know that. I had never understood that there were groups like that. So I got to know them very well. I got to know all of their problems, what they were doing, about their operations. You know they were all going to be huge stars when they got the operation. It got me very angry and the only thing I could do then was give them money and when I say money, I say quarters, not [bills]. And I would collect clothes for them. I was doing that for months and then Stonewall happened. (quoted from Shepard 2008)

Kohler would spend the next three and a half decades speaking for these youth, building friendships with them that lasted the same span of time. Narratives such as this one offer a thrilling means to consider children's lives.

But so do ethnography and autoethnography. "The power of autoethnography lies in its ability to deepen the author's understanding and respect for the self in context while doing the same for the other," writes David Harrison (2014, viii). He frames such interaction as an "analytic third" compelling the provider to observe the self, the other and culture. "When the text is very emotive or surprising, one's capacity for understanding the writer is enhanced, as is one's ability to seek fuller understanding of other people," he concludes (p. ix). Reading these words while preparing to write this introduction, I found myself thinking about my years as a service provider. Half of ethnography is confession, Clifford Geertz (1973) writes in *The Interpretation of Cultures*. Reading Stanley Witkin (2014) paraphrase these words in his *Narrating Social Work through Autoethnography*, I started feeling less guilty about my ambivalence about working with youth. "An autoethnography is an ethnography of one's self—usually focusing on a particular experience or life event—from a social and cultural perspective," notes Witkin (2014, 2).

For me, that particular life event happened in 1975 when my godfather, who had been my dad's best friend, put a gun to his head and pulled the trigger. In the years to come, the son he left behind took to setting fires. No one knew how to reach him, and we certainly could not bring his father back. None of us really knew why he left, and the wound lingered in most of our lives. Something was terribly wrong. Work was not right, life was not right, but the world kept moving. Everyone just moved forward, with few answers forthcoming. I never thought much about what any of these decade-old memories meant until I started thinking about this book and its methodological questions, autoethnography, and its lens into "ways of understanding people and their experience of life" (Harrison 2014, viii).

As a new social worker, everyone I knew in the field had his or her stories. For example, a woman who directed a child welfare agency confessed to playing with dolls to cope with the stress of a child welfare system with too many gaps and wounds. Over and over, the stories of providers and the troubled kids they worked with gripped me. I was drawn to their stories. "Autoethnographers use this form to explore the historically and culturally embedded social processes that help explain particular understandings and actions of the author/subject in relation to some significant experience, event, or understanding," writes Witkin (2014, 3).

When social work crossed the path of my life, I found myself working with people with HIV/AIDS years before there was treatment for it. Many of my clients were adolescents, living in single-room occupancy hotels, in and out of the streets, in a world of adults. Every day it seemed as if one of my clients died, and turnover in our housing program was constant. In between shifts at work, I bussed around town tape-recording the life stories of people with HIV/AIDS, trying to make sense of this experience, trying to capture the experience of a cohort of people living with AIDS before their time ran out. Two years into this project, I took a break to go to grad school. By then I had completed and transcribed some sixty life stories with people with AIDS, but I did not know what to do with my box of oral histories.

At graduate school at Chicago, I interned with the Chicago Area Project (CAP). This program worked with delinquent youth, hoping to divert them away from prison and institutions and back into the community. CAP provided mentors, creating programming for youth at the YMCA and with community organizations working with immigrants throughout Chicago. To guide CAP's efforts, the group's founder, Chicago sociologist Clifford Shaw, interviewed delinquents, tracking their experiences and aligning the programming with their perspectives. For Shaw, the life story was a social text with lessons for the larger social world; it was a part of the qualitative research tradition at the University of Chicago. Shaw noted that the "life-history record is a relatively new instrument for the study of human behavior (1930, ix)." Oral traditions, however, have been used for millennia to recount the shape and history of time, coalescing into worldviews of nations and cultures (Martin 1995, 4). Writing about Shaw's work, Howard Becker makes a case for the use of the life story for studying human interaction with the social environment: "The life story, if it is done well, will give us the details of that process whose character we would otherwise only be able to speculate about . . . It will describe those crucial interactive episodes in which new lines of individual and collective activity are forged, in which new aspects of the self are brought into being" (1996, xiv).

In graduate school I continued to grapple with various approaches to thinking about people's stories, client narratives, and community practice. William Borden, who taught my "Human Behavior in the Social Environment" course in 1995, would say that no story exists in a void. The life story offers a lens into community dynamics, changes, dislocations, and connections.

Over the next two years, I started collecting oral histories of those involved with the Chicago Area Project, many of whom had been involved with the group since the Great Depression six decades earlier. They all had stories to tell about working with Clifford Shaw, Jane Addams, and the delinquent youth the group was organizing. My challenge was how to justify my research approach in the increasingly conservative, positivist-steeped social work department. I wandered through the library, reading as much Chicago ethnography as I could, and perusing the stacks at the Seminary Co-Op bookstore, looking at course offerings.

One afternoon, I found myself looking at a pile of books assigned by Bertram Cohler for his oral history research seminar. Cohler, who had worked with Bruno Bettelheim and Heinz Kohut, was something of a legend at the university. He seemed to understand what I was trying to do with oral histories, or at least it looked like he did from his writings, which seemed to synthesize the psychology, philosophy, and sociology of life stories. Linking questions about meaning and coherence that Max Weber grappled with in *The Protestant Ethic and the Spirit of Capitalism*, Cohler argued that the life story account could provide insight into the depth of a social condition: "The human science is the most appropriate mode for understudying development and social change as forces impacting the study of lives over time" (1994, 171). Over and over again, he suggested that forces affecting lives also affect communities, so the life story had to be viewed as a community story. Life stories offer insight into needs and expectations, adaptation and development; they highlight areas of abundance and scarcity and demonstrate identity formation, growth, and, in some cases, metamorphosis. Thus, life stories serve as enormously useful data in the study of people's lives and resiliency. In the abstract to a 1991 paper titled "The Life Story and the Study of Resilience and Response to Adversity," Cohler summed up his thinking on the subject:

The concept of the life story is discussed as an important means for understanding continuity and change within lives over time, including means used to make sense of lived experience, particularly response to adversity. This perspective on the study of the life history is based on current approaches to the study of narrative within both the human sciences and the humanities, and views the life history as a story that is continually revised over time, and with age. The life story may be evaluated, both by its teller and by those listening or reading, in the same terms as any good or "followable" story within our own culture (Ricoeur 1977). Explanation of the origins, impact, and resolution of adversity appears essential both in the "good" story and the life history understood as a personal narrative or story, and is necessary to maintain [the] continuing experience of personal integrity or coherence across the course of life. (p. 169)

Cohler owned the classroom like few teachers I have ever known. He would just walk in, sit at a desk, not a lectern, and drop a question. "How was Weber? What problems did it pose?" Several students would respond, and the conversation was on. I was moved by the empathy Cohler showed for all the students in the room. My first day in class, he suggested we all read the diaries of Alice James, the sister of Henry and James, and talked about the context, challenges, and inequalities of writing about people's lives. He sympathized with the struggles of mothers and daughters, as well as the compromises we adapt to in order to make sense of our lives. He seemed to care what we all had to say, bringing out great things in all of us.

When we read John Bowlby's 1979 *The Making and Breaking of Affectional Bonds*, I made my first comment in the class, reflecting on the impact of my parents' divorce and the many other family dislocations of those in my cohort. Cohler acknowledged my sentiment, noting that children adapt. Pain is real, but people cope in countless ways. If people are knocked down, they tend to find ways to get back up. Resilience is like water in a creek, leading to a river. If it gets stuck, it moves in other directions, he continued, echoing a theme from his 1982 paper "Personal Narrative and the Life Course." When affectional bonds break, it is not always easy to repair them. But you can never count kids out, Bert elaborated. They can cope with a lot; nothing is determined. This is part of what is so important about studying people's lives.

Bert and I talked after that class and decided to continue our conversation over coffee. Cohler shared his experience as a student at the Sonia Shankman Orthogenic School, a residential treatment center and therapeutic school for emotionally disturbed youth run by Bruno Bettelheim, who became a mentor for Bert. Cohler lived in the Pirates Dorm. We all need essential others, he explained. They help us through. And sometimes we have to defend them. I shared my experience in San Francisco, looking at the stories of people with HIV and AIDS. Resilience was a theme that ran throughout our conversation. Both his work and mine addressed themes of stigma and adversity, as well as adaptation, looking to the life story to frame the dynamics of integrating changes, bringing these struggles to bear, integrating pain, and offering coherence. Still, there are broken stories, he explained.

At the next class session, Cohler invited me to a party at his house for queer students. He handed me the invitation in an envelope. I wondered why it all felt so clandestine. Yet Chicago was a homophobic space then. My experience in San Francisco had queered my experience, destabilizing what I thought life could be or should be. I was still queer in the streets, but straight in the sheets, as they say. But Bert was going through his own changes, which these larger conversations helped support. His wife had died in 1989, ushering in a new period in his life, which he embraced: it involved experimenting with public sexual culture and embracing homosexuality and its various meanings. As usual, Cohler put everything into his changed life, conducting ethnographies at the bathhouse he frequented, writing papers and books, expanding his encyclopedic mind into questions about homosexuality and the life course. He wrote a case study about one of his clients who refused to practice safe sex. He later taught such courses as "Sexual Identity and the Life Course of Gay and Lesbian Lives," exploring the social contexts of gays and lesbians from childhood to old age and adapting this research into his final books and papers (Harms 2012).

We continued our conversations even after I moved to New York in 1997. We would get coffee whenever I was in Chicago or he was in New York. He told me about his research on gay male life writing, and I told him about my research on public sexuality. He told me about his countertransference reactions to a gay client of his who was having "bareback" sex. Bert was always an advocate, offering free psychotherapy, even when he did not find resolution to the complicated stories of our lives (Harms 2012). The conversations would continue for the next fifteen years. We talked for hours, always circling back to questions about life writing and narrative, the way people tell stories and listen to others tell their stories. He helped me see how the oral narratives I was compiling and the assessments I was conducting as a social worker could function in much the same ways. During our get-togethers, we told stories about the clients we were seeing and the books we were reading, connecting psychoanalysis with questions about HIV risk, the vulnerability of youth, sexuality, and the use of narrative. Bert helped me connect lives in time with a philosophy of narrative, psychoanalysis, and increasingly with authoethnography as a method: he inspired me to explore. We talked about the blurry spaces between sexuality, identity, and a queer sensibility that could help us all feel a little more human and at home with ourselves.

The last time I saw him in 2005, we ate oysters at the Oyster Bar in Grand Central Station. "I just love oysters," Bert confessed over a beer. While waiting for Bert, I was reading Freud's case study of the *Wolfman*. Bert smiled when he saw what I was reading and he shared some other recommendations.

"Read *Wayward Youth* by Aichhorn from 1935," he counseled.

I jotted the title down on a page of my paperback. When I got home I looked it up. We talked about the lecture he gave at the William Allanson White Institute, where I was in training, and encouraged me to turn a paper I had written for him years earlier into a chapter or a book, which I ended up doing. There was no way to know that this would be the last time I would see him. Over the years, our correspondence tapered off. Bert was slowing down. Still, he supported and mentored me from afar, drafting letters of recommendation for my first academic job and supporting my contribution to his last book, *The Story of Sexual Identity: Narrative Perspectives on the Gay and Lesbian Life Course.*

When I was in Chicago in 2012, I called Bert. He said he was too tired to meet. Indeed he would only live a month longer. Over and over again, he demonstrated generativity—connecting, empathizing, and caring about others. My copy of the *Wolfman* case study still has those notes from that final engaged conversation. His view was that psychoanalysis should be for everyone, so he provided free long-term psychoanalysis to patients. He felt universities should be places where researchers teach, so he taught and taught, going beyond the call of duty. He believed that we have to empathize, as he learned from Heinz Kohut. He forgave his mentor Bettelheim's abuses. And he taught his students to think about the contradictions of peoples' stories. Writing about narrative, I think about the messy corners of our minds, our intentions, our dreams, and our stories. When I think about *Wayward Youth*, I think of Bert and his calls for us to understand identity and the life course via narratives.

THE CASE FOR NARRATIVES

Over the course of our working relationship, we discovered a shared interest in narrative approaches for practice, research, and pedagogy. In social work practice, these methods help clients reconstruct their life story to help them better cope with life's problems (see Cohler 1988, 1994; McLeod 1997; Miller 2006; Payne 2006). In research and writing, narrative approaches focus on human interaction and meaning construction, making the method ideal for the study of the life course (Froggett and Chamberlayne 2004; Poindexter 2002; Riessman 2002). Through "story" construction, the self emerges as a story capable of adapting to difficult circumstances, with subsequent developmental adaptations taking on a distinct narrative shape; these stories are told in historic time, quite often leading to increased coherence in the experience of telling or coauthoring stories (Cohler 1982; Schafer 1980; Schiff 2014). Through narrative, we explain who we are and where we have been, while providing direction for the future. And there are many types of narrative approaches.

Paul Ricoeur suggests that narratives "offer a phenomenology to existence," combining "two dimensions in various proportions, one chronological and one non-chronological. The first may be called the episodic dimension, which characterizes the story as made up of events. The second is the configural dimension, according to which the plot construes significant wholes out of scattered events" (Ricoeur 1980, 168, 174). Narratives help us connect the pieces of complicated, dispersed phenomena into a coherent whole.

Sociologist Charles Tilly argues that such stories help us grapple with social forces in three distinct ways (2002, ix–x):

1. They provide "evidence about social processes."
2. They explain social behavior.
3. They "borrow the conventions of storytelling."

These "stories play significant parts across a wide range of social life"; they help explain and "recast events after the fact in standard story form" (Tilly 2002, xi). Conversely, without narrative, we face a crisis of meaning (White 1980). Roy Schafer points out that there is no one objective reality or "no single definitive account of a life history" (1980, 26). Instead there are multiple points of view, constructions of images of reality, and, in the case of this project, childhoods (Nybell 2009).

Philosopher Richard Rorty (1979) demonstrates the ways in which questions of knowing in the second half of the twentieth century have shifted focus from notions of truth to those of significance and meaning. Neither science nor theology is outside of the influence of cultural bias or interpretation. No one has a monopoly on the truth. Instead, we have stories to help us interpret and create meaning within an increasingly complex social fabric (Jones 1996).

Yet, only some of these stories see the light of day. Outsider narratives—stories of the poor, the socially invisible, those organizing from the margins, or those struggling to obtain survival services—rarely find their way into public discourse, advocacy, or even program evaluation for social services. Throughout this book, we make the case for the inclusion of more stories from those for whom social services are created, calling for the use of ethnography, life stories, practice reflections, and case narrative in social services research and practice.

Consider the role of storytelling, where voices otherwise lost in objectivist approaches find expression and push for social change. Latina feminist pedagogy, in particularly testimonios, uses narrative as a tool to give voice to those on the margins (Anzaldúa 1990; Elenes 2000): "Testimonio is and continues to be an approach that incorporates political, social, historical, and cultural histories that accompany one's life experiences as a means to bring about change through consciousness-raising. In bridging individuals with collective histories of oppression, a story of marginalization is re-centered to elicit social change" (Bernal, Burciaga, and Carmona 2012, 364). The testimonio pushes through dominant discourses, challenging the grip of traditional hierarchical and elitist structures on the production of knowledge. It reclaims space for those who are so often unheard and screams out a call to action. In this spirit, narrative approaches engage and evoke, resisting the "neutral" voice of science; they enable readers to identify and develop empathy for others' experiences and for themselves: a key goal in social work education (Goldstein 1998; Craig 2007).

While much of the writing in practice-based fields is based on quantitative research, qualitative approaches have a long distinguished history in the field (Sherman and Reid 1994). Certainly, quantitative analysis is the currency of the realm, yet it often obscures from view questions about day-to-day program experience and meaning. Qualitative studies, in contrast, focus on questions about cultural experience, acknowledging divergent social standpoints of clients and providers alike (Hartsock, 1998) and opening up new ways of understanding the very nature of services (Sherman and Reid 1994).

From our point of view, narratives approaches help us highlight social meanings not found elsewhere in practice research. "Ethnography can help us fill the gaps in what we know about a community whose beliefs and behavior affect how federal programs operate," note the authors of a 2003 U.S General Accounting Office report on ways ethnography can help inform services. These studies help generate social knowledge about the hopes, barriers, and gaps in services. They also help those in need describe the meanings of their experience, the ways they cope, and how their efforts can be supported, not hindered. Through ethnography, we consider the "everyday meaning of formal social work/social services," notes Tracey Kathleen (2009–2010).

The case study is another way of doing social science research. It is best understood as an in-depth study that focuses on a person, incident, or community (Sherman and Reid 1994). This form of research is most appropriate for studies engaging questions of "how" or "why," when researchers have little control over the variables, and the focus is on contemporary real-life social contexts. At their essence, case studies contribute to our social knowledge of individual, group, social, organizational, and political phenomena. They help us grasp at big-picture meanings of life events and circumstances, life cycles, neighborhood changes, and organizational histories. There is a widespread misconception that case studies are merely exploratory in nature, without utility for description or hypothesis testing (Black 1993). Yet, some of the most famous case studies, including Whyte's *Street Corner Society*, have been both descriptive and explanatory in nature (Yin 1994, 2–3).

Runyan points out that the popularity of the study of individual lives has "waxed and waned" (1982, 9). From the early 1920s through World War II, the study of lives and life stories found widespread interest, particularly in the work of Clifford Shaw and the other Chicago social researchers. During the Depression, the Works Project Administration hired many unemployed workers to collect community-based oral histories, which are still widely read today. During the same era, advocates crafted case studies from the life stories of delinquents, highlighting meanings of their experience not found in quantitative accounts (Bennett 1988). Mary Richmond's *Social Diagnosis* is an early example of the case study method (Sherman and Reid 1994); Jane Addams's description of her years in Hull House in her case narrative *Forty Years in Hull House* is another. During the postwar period, there was increasing interest in more abstract theory, in social hypothesis testing, and in other forms of quantitative analysis. Yet, by the 1960s, interest in the study of lives and the life course grew again (Bennett 1988; Runyan 1982). By the 1990s, the social work journal *Reflections* began to publish personal and professional narratives of social work practice. In that venue, notable scholars like Richard Cloward and Frances Fox Piven published case studies of their efforts to register voters and defend the welfare state (Abels 2002; Cloward and Piven 1995).

The increased use of narratives can be seen as part of a "narrative turn" in social research, helping us consider life stories as narratives to be studied in terms of the ways they are created, heard, and understood. For children and adolescents in particular, narratives open a venue for their lived experiences and thus plays a role in shaping their lives. Even in a world governed by adults, children are active participants in their interpretation of their experiences. For professionals who work with this population and whose reflections often do not find space in objectivist approaches to knowledge building, the complicated stories of their experiences find opportunity for expression. With their emphasis on storytelling, narrative approaches are recognized as a powerful means for gaining in-depth understanding of these lived experiences.

ORGANIZATION OF THIS BOOK

Through stories, *Narrating Practice with Children and Adolescence* seeks to explore ways in which youth address core challenges to negotiating, coping, and adapting to the world. Will they find a sense of coherence in their lived experience and selves? Or will they find themselves living in a broken story, unable to "maintain" coherence (Cohler 1987, 400)? How do authors position the self in relation to their work with youth, and how do they promote agency of the child? Finally, and most poignantly, how do children's stories differ as a result of inequalities present in the social world (Wells 2015)? Through the study of their narratives we engage core questions about human development (Schiff 2014). The eighteen chapters in *Narrating Practice with Children and Adolescents* consider these and countless other issues in the lives of children and adolescents.

The contributors to this volume come from varied disciplines—social work, sociology, psychology, education, anthropology, nursing, law, and policy—to present contemporary issues in their work with children. Each author provides a rationale for the significance of the issue and for the use of narrative approaches in contributing to the discourse. Some chapters employ one narrative approach, and others employ multiple methods; some use ethnography and autoethnography, whereas others include practice reflections. The book is divided into three parts, based on the narrative approach used. In Part I, "Ethnographies, Narrative Inquiries, and Life Stories," Sharon Johnson, Sabrina Gonzalez, Stephen Ruszczyk, Margot Jackson and colleagues, Kristina Baines, Trevor Milton, and Yasemin Besen-Cassino present ethnographies and narrative inquiries. Bridging the gap between personal narratives and larger social forces, Mery Diaz, Sherri Rings, Benjamin Shepard, Elizabeth Paley, Jerry Otero, and Gretta Fernandes frame their efforts as forms of autoethnography, connecting life stories and storytelling in Part II, "Autoethnography and Storytelling." And finally, in Part III, "Practice Reflections and Case Narratives," Deborah Courtney, Margo Jackson, Erica Goldblatt-Hyatt, Susan MacDonald and Stephanie Wise, and Rebecca Judd and Benjamin May trace their practice reflections as case narratives.

All chapters weave through a brief review of the literature, identify a main thesis and a method to research the question, and provide a rich analysis and discussion. At the end of each are three questions for reflection and group discussion and a reference section. These narratives seek out the multiple stories of children's lives, of children and their brains, of struggles against oppressive systems, of child care policies and neoliberal controls, of engagement strategies and struggles over self-determination, of crossing borders and coping with poverty, and of efforts to reduce harms and support agency as youth take control of the stories of their lives. Each story points to the messy contradictions of the lived experiences of growing up. We hope the reader is engaged by these stories, and is encouraged to look at the lives of children and youth in all their meaningful complexities.

REFERENCES

Abels, Sonia L. 2002. "He Was Here: Remembering Cloward's Contribution to Reflections." *Reflections: Narratives of Professional Helping* 8, no. 1: 3–4.

Annan, Jean, Anna Priestley, and Roger Phillipson. 2006. "Narrative Psychology: A Tool for Ecological Practice." *Kairaranga* 7, no. 2: 20–27.

Anzaldúa, Gloria E. 1990. *Making Face, Making Soul/Haciendo Caras: Creative and Critical Perspectives of Feminists of Color.* San Francisco: Aunt Lute Books.

Aries, Philippe. 1962. *Centuries of Childhood: A Social History of Family Life*, trans. Robert Baldick. New York: Vintage Books.

Becker, Howard. 1966. Introduction to *The Jack Stroller*, by Clifford Shaw, v–xvii. Chicago: University of Chicago Press.

Becker, Robert. 2017. "Amy Hoffman: On the Importance of Storytelling." *Lambda Literary Review*. https://www.lambdaliterary.org/interviews/11/30/amy-hoffman /?utm_source=Lambda+Literary+Review+December+1st%2C+2017&utm_cam paign=Newsletters&utm_medium=email.

Bennett, James. 1998. *Oral History and Delinquency: The Rhetoric of Criminology*. Chicago, University of Chicago Press.

Bernal, Delores Delgado, Burciaga, Rebecca, and Carmona, Judith Flores. 2012. "Chicana/Latina Testimonios: Mapping the Methodological, Pedagogical, and Political." *Equity and Excellence in Education* 45, no. 3: 363–372.

Black, Thomas R. 1993. *Evaluating Social Science Research*. Thousand Oaks, CA: Sage.

Bronfenbrenner, Urie. 1979. *The Ecology of Human Development: Experiments by Nature and Design*. Cambridge, MA: Harvard University Press.

Cloward, Richard, and Frances Fox Piven. 1995. "The Declining Significance of Class? The Case of the National Voter Registration Act of 1993." *Reflections: Narratives of Professional Helping* 1, no. 1: 7–23.

Cohler, Bertram. 1982. "Personal Narrative and the Life Course." In *Life Span Development and Behavior*, ed. P. Baltes and O. G, Brim, vol. 4, 205–441. New York: Academic Press.

——. 1987. "Adversity, Resilience and the Study of Lives." In *The Invulnerable Child*, ed. E. J. Anthony and B. J. Cohler, 363–424. New York: Guilford Press.

——. 1991. "The Life Story and the Study of Resilience and Response to Adversity." *Journal of Narrative and Life History* 1, nos. 2–3: 169–200.

——. 1994. "The Human Sciences, the Life Story, and Clinical Research." In *Qualitative Research in Social Work*, ed. E. Sherman and W. Reid, 163–174. New York: Columbia University Press.

——. 1998. "The Human Studies and the Life Story: The Social Service Review Lecture, and Clinical Research." *Social Service Review* December: 552–575.

Corsaro, William A. 2005. *The Sociology of Childhood*, 2nd ed. Thousand Oaks, CA: Pine Forge Press.

——. 2015. *The Sociology of Childhood*, 4th ed. Thousand Oaks, CA: Pine Forge Press.

Craig, Rita Wilder. 2007. "A Day in the Life of a Hospital Worker." *Qualitative Social Work* 6, no. 4: 431–446.

Elenes, C. Alejandra. 2000. Chicana Feminist Narratives and the Politics of the Self. *Frontiers: A Journal of Women Studies*, 21, no. 3: 105–123.

Fraser, Mark W. 2004. "The Ecology of Childhood: A Multisystems Perspective." In *Risk and Resilience in Childhood*, 2nd ed., 1–12. Washington, DC: National Association of Social Workers.

Fraser, Mark W., Maeda J. Richman, and Jack M. Galinsky. 1999. "Risk, Protection and Resilience: Toward a Conceptual Framework for Social Work Practice." *Social Work Research* 23, no. 3: 131–143.

Froggett, Lynn, and Prue Chamberlayne. 2004. "Narratives for Social Enterprise." *Qualitative Social Work* 3, no. 1: 61–77.

Geertz, Clifford. 1973. *The Interpretation of Cultures*. New York: Basic Books.

Germain, Carel B. 1991. *Human Behavior in the Social Environment*. New York: Columbia University Press.

Germain, Carol. B., and Alex Gitterman. 1980. *The Life Model of Social Work Practice*. New York: Columbia University Press.

——. 1996. *The Life Model of Social Work Practice: Advances in Social Work Practices.* New York: Columbia University Press.

Goldstein, Howard. 1988. "Education for Ethical Dilemmas in Social Work Practice." *Families in Society* 79: 241–253.

Graham, Mekeda. 2007a. *Black Issues in Social Work and Social Care.* Bristol, UK: Policy Press.

——. 2007b. "Giving Voice to Black Children: An Analysis of Social Agency." *British Journal of Social Work* 37, no. 8: 1305–1317.

Harms, William. 2012. "Bertram Cohler, Psychologist and Esteemed Teacher, 1938–2012." *UChicagoNews,* May 14. https://news.uchicago.edu/article/2012/05/14/bertram-cohler-psychologist-and-esteemed-teacher-1938–2012.

Harrison, David. 2014. "Foreword." In *Narrating Social Work through Autoethnography,* ed. Stanley Witkin, vii–x. New York: Columbia University Press.

Hartsock, Nancy C. M. 1998. *The Feminist Standpoint Revised and Other Essays.* Boulder: Westview.

Heywood, Colin M. 2001. *A History of Childhood: Children and Childhood in the West from Medieval to Modern Times.* Cambridge, UK: Polity Press.

Holloway, Sarah L., and Gill Valentine, eds. 2000. *Children's Geographies.* London: Routledge. James, Allison, Chris Jenks, and Alan Prout. 1998. *Theorizing Childhood.* London: Polity Press.

James, Allison, and Alan Prout. 1990. *Constructing and Reconstructing Childhood: Contemporary Issues in the Sociology of Childhood.* London: Falmer Press.

Jones, Lois Mailou. 1996. "The Storytelling Animal." *Georgia Review* 50, no. 4: 649–669.

Lee, Carol, D. 2009. "Historical Evolution of Risk and Equity: Interdisciplinary Issues and Critiques Author(s)."*Review of Research in Education,* 33, no. 1: 63–100.

Martin, R. 1995. *Oral History: Research, Assessment and Intervention.* Thousand Oaks, CA: Sage.

Maskovsky, Jeff. 2000. "'Managing' the Poor: Neoliberalism, Medicaid HMOs and the Triumph of Consumerism among the Poor." *Medical Anthropology* 19, no. 2: 121–146.

McLeod, John. 1997. *Narrative and Psychotherapy.* London: Sage.

Mcnamee, Sally. 2016. *The Social Study of Childhood.* London: Palgrave.

Miller, Lisa. 2006. *Counselling Skills for Social Work.* London: Sage.

Moniz, Cynthia, and Stephen Gorin. 2006. *Health and Mental Health Care Policy: A Biopsychosocial Perspective.* 2nd ed. New York: Pearson Education, Inc.

Moraga, Cherríe, and Gloria Anzaldúa. 2015. *This Bridge Called My Back: Writings by Radical Women of Color,* 4th ed. Albany: SUNY Press.

Nybell, Lynn, Jeffrey Shook, and Janet Finn. W. 2009. "Introduction." In *Childhood, Youth, and Social Work in Transformation: Implications for Policy and Practice,* 1–31. New York. Columbia University Press.

Payne, Martin. 2006. *Narrative Therapy.* London: Sage.

Phillips, Adam. 2014. *Becoming Freud: The Making of a Psychoanalyst.* New Haven, CT: Yale University Press.

Plummer, Ken. 1995. *Telling Sexual Stories: Power, Change, and Social Worlds.* London: Routledge.

Poindexter, Cynthia Cannon. 2002. "Meaning from Methods." *Qualitative Social Work* 1, no. 1: 59–78.

Pollock, Linda. 1983. *Forgotten Children: Parent-Child Relations from 1500 to 1900*. Cambridge: Cambridge University Press.

Prout, Alan, and Allison James. 1997. *Constructing and Reconstructing Childhood: Contemporary Issues in the Sociological Study of Childhood*, 2nd ed. London: Falmer Press.

Qvortrup, Jens. 1990. "A Voice for Children in Statistical and Social Accounting? A Plea for Children's Rights to Be Heard." In *Constructing and Reconstructing Childhood: Contemporary Issues in the Sociological Study of Childhood*, ed. Allison James and Alan Prout, 85–103. London: Falmer Press.

Ricoeur, Paul. 1980. "Narrative Time." In *On Narrative,* ed. W. J. T. Mitchell, 165–86. Chicago: University of Chicago Press.

Riessman, Catherine Kohler. 2002. "Analysis of Personal Narratives." In *Handbook of Interview Research*, ed. J. F. Gubrium et al., 695–710. London: Sage.

Rorty, Richard. 1979. *Philosophy and the Mirror of Nature*. Princeton, NJ: Princeton University Press.

Runyan, William McKinley. 1982. *Life Histories and Psychobiography: Explanations in Theory and Method*. New York: Oxford University Press.

Schafer, Roy. 1980. "Narration in the Psychoanalytic Dialogue." In *On Narrative*, ed. W. J. T. Mitchell, 25–50. Chicago: University of Chicago Press.

Schiff, Brian. 2014. "Rereading Personal Narrative and the Life Course." *New Directions for Child and Adolescent Development* 145.

Shaw, Clifford. 1930. *The Jack Stroller: A Delinquent's Own Story*. Chicago: University of Chicago Press.

Sheehan, Matt. 2014. "Hong Kong's Summer of Love and the Umbrella Generation." *Huffington Post*. https://www.huffingtonpost.com/matt-sheehan/hong-kong-summer-of-love_b_6265190.html.

Shepard, Benjamin. 2008. "Bob Kohler Recalling: Collecting Oral Histories with a West Village Legend." https://inthemiddleofthewhirlwind.wordpress.com/bob-kohler-recalling/.

Sherman, Edmund, and William J. Reid. 1994. *Qualitative Research and Social Work*. New York: Columbia University Press.

Stevens, John Paul. 2018. "Repeal the Second Amendment." *New York Times*, March 27.

Taylor, Carolyn. 2004. "Underpinning Knowledge for Child Care Practice: Reconsidering Child Development Theory." *Child and Family Social Work* 9: 225–235.

Thomas, Nigel. 2005. *Social Work with Young People in Care: Looking After Children in Theory and Practice*. Palgrave Macmillan: Hampshire.

Thomas, Nigel, and Claire O'Kane. 2000. "Discovering What Children Think: Connections Between Research and Practice." *The British Journal of Social Work* 30, no. 6: 819–835

Thorne, Barrie. 2003. "The Crisis of Care," in N. Crouter and A. Booth, eds., *Work-Family Challenges for Low-Income Parents and Their Children*, 165–178. Hillsdale, NJ: Lawrence Erlbaum.

Tilly, Charles. 2002. *Stories, Identities, and Political Change*. New York: Rowman & Littlefield Publishers.

Ungar, Michael. 2004. "A Constructionist Discourse on Resilience: Multiple Contexts, Multiple Realities among At-Risk Children and Youth." *Youth and Society* 35, no. 3: 341–365.

Uprichard, Emma. 2008. "Children as 'Being and Becomings': Children, Childhood and Temporality." *Children & Society* 22, no. 4: 303–313.

U.S. General Accounting Office. 2003. US Federal Government General Accounting Office Federal Programs: Ethnographic studies can inform agencies' actions. Retrieved from https://www.gao.gov/products/GAO-03-455.

Weber, Max. 2002 *The Protestant Ethic and the Spirit of Capitalism*. New York: Penguin Books.

Wells, Karen. 2015. *Childhood: A Global Perspective*, 2nd ed. Malden, MA: Polity Press.

White, Hayden. 1980. "The Value of Narrativity in the Representation of Reality." In *On Narrative*. ed. W. J. T. Mitchell, 1–24. Chicago: University of Chicago Press.

Witkin, Stanley. 2014. *Narrating Social Work through Autoethnography*. New York: Columbia University Press.

Wyness, Michael. 2011. *Childhood and Society: An Introduction to the Study of Childhood*. London: Palgrave Macmillan.

——. 2015. *Childhood*. Cambridge, UK: Polity Press.

Yin, Robert K. 1994. Case Study Research Designs and Methods, 2nd ed. Thousand Oaks, CA: Sage.

PART I

Ethnographies, Narrative Inquiries,
and Life Stories

Chapter One

FROM DISEMPOWERMENT TO SELF-BELIEF

A Center of Hope for Vulnerable Youth in Cape Town

SHARON JOHNSON

In 2012, the courts sent two twelve-year-old boys, Bulelani and Liam, for protection to the last remaining education-managed youth care and education center (YCEC) in Cape Town, South Africa (SA). This chapter shares their stories of five years at the residential male state institution, where they both were enabled to heal dramatically from abusive and neglectful backgrounds. At the YCEC the boys developed self-belief—a trust in their own abilities—thanks to restorative care practices. One such practice is the "circle of courage" (Brendtro, Brokenleg, and Van Brokern 2002), which provides a behavioral support pathway toward belonging, mastery, independence, and generosity. These qualities were fostered by the boys' faith and effort, culminating in positive outcomes (Pickhardt 2013).

Restorative care practices are increasingly recognized for their effectiveness in building strength and self-confidence in children and adolescents, encouraging them to become motivated and to develop life goals. As an emerging approach, these practices focus on restoring and building relationships between individuals by encouraging the expression of feelings, as well as strengthening community social connections (International Institute for Restorative Practices 2016). The systemic use of informal restorative practices creates a positive milieu, an environment described by Wachtel (2013) as fostering responsibility, awareness, and empathy, rather than relying on punishment and sanctions. Initially focused on delinquents and at-risk adolescents, this practice area has broadened and developed scholarship, research, graduate education programs, and professional development courses for families and communities. Restorative justice, providing tertiary prevention after a harm has occurred, is related to this emerging modality.

The transition from adolescence to adulthood is a key period for the nurturing of a sense of self and an identity (Erikson 1980), and both Bulelani and Liam were at this sensitive developmental stage when they were helped to overcome violent and addictive elements in their lives. Growing up in a rural village, Bulelani described his new self-belief as "wak[ing] up my mind." Liam, who was from the violent gangland of the Cape Flats, also found a belief in himself: "God helps me and you must also help yourself." Along their paths, both boys encountered difficulties, but they experienced the benefits of care through personal connection, encouragement, love, and respect not only from staff and teachers but also from their peers. This care helped them overcome the distrust they had in their own abilities, which was fostered by the disempowering core beliefs of their traumatic childhoods. They learned to have faith in themselves, to remain committed, to persevere and try hard, and to focus on their futures.

Analysis of the narratives of adolescents is a process that not only reveals the past but also considers the future (Cohler 1982). In examining adolescents' life stories, professionals are challenged in conducting social research to go beyond the typical structure of a research paper: the problem statement, literature review, method, results, and discussion (Witkin 2000). They are encouraged to explore social and cultural contexts to describe the implications of meaningful life experiences and to present coherent outputs. And so I integrated the powerful experience of working with vulnerable youths, while collaboratively making sense of narratives within their specific contexts. In this collaborative process of meaning-making, I was caught up in a hermeneutic circle.[1] I listened to Bulelani and Liam interpret their lives, trying to make sense of their stories as a researcher, transforming them into a study received, applied, and interpreted by you, the reader. At times I added the voices of others to provide new perspectives; the exploration of the transformation of the boys' disempowering core beliefs, for example, was triangulated by interpretations of YCEC 's educational psychologist.

MY RESEARCH IN EDUCATIONAL INSTITUTIONS

My research in high-risk schools in the Cape Flats as I pursued my master's (Johnson 2010; Johnson and Naidoo 2013, 2017b) and doctoral degrees (Johnson 2013, 2015; Johnson and Naidoo 2017a) measured the efficacy of interventions to prevent teacher stress and burnout. Educators were struggling with violent, disruptive learner behaviors and children suffering from HIV/AIDS. During three years of participatory action research (PAR) with YCEC teachers and staff, a dated punitive discipline approach was replaced by contextually appropriate restorative care practices (see figure 1.1; Johnson 2019, in review).

I was both a consultant and participant researcher at the center. For the seventy to eighty boys (aged eleven to eighteen) housed in hostels there, I was a mother figure; for the forty teachers and staff (aged twenty to seventy), I was a peer. The YCEC, formerly classified as "colored," is now multiracial: a melting pot of cultures, traditions, religions, races, and ages. Conscious of power dynamics, I tried to model humility and compassion by recognizing the strengths and abilities of others, while being acutely aware that my whiteness reflected an abusive racist history.

FIGURE 1.1 Prison-like security at a Cape Flats School, Cape Town.

I came to know Bulelani and Liam as they turned eighteen and were about to leave their institutional home. Bulelani was a rural Xhosa from the Eastern Cape, a handsome, charismatic, well-built youth. Liam seemed more vulnerable; tall and slender, he was of Dutch and African descent, bilingual in English and Afrikaans, and came from the urban Cape Flats. Narrative perspectives give an intimate view of the participant's world, and perhaps the ideal setting for Bulelani's interview would have been sitting around a fire under the African stars, in the heart of a rural village. For Liam, it would have been the vibrant sprawling suburb of the District Six urban setting, where colored communities used to live in close proximity to the city center before being removed by harsh separate development legislation. This land is still largely unoccupied, a barren testament to inhumane past policies. Now, in postapartheid SA, both had found a safe space at YCEC.

After obtaining multilevel ethical approvals, I proceeded to conduct individual interviews with both young men. Each in turn settled confidently next to me on the lumpy, bizarrely bright orange and red couch in the therapeutic center's quiet counseling room. It was a darkened intimate space; there was only one small window covered by a flimsy curtain flapping in the breeze. Both were willingly engaged and reflective throughout, speaking fluently with little interruption.

The interview had three focus areas: The first was: "What brought you to the center?"; The second was: "What care have you received?"; and the third was: "What are your future goals?" Within these topics various questions were asked to encourage further insights or clarify points. They first solemnly described their difficult experiences before coming to YCEC, philosophically acknowledging their remarkable achievements at the center and reflecting on their mentors and surrogate parents, as well as difficult relationships and struggles. Finally, they contemplated life ahead as independent young adults. I met them several times, checking and rechecking their narratives, trying to ensure that the text accurately reflected their life stories. Knowledge is greatly shaped by changing sociocultural and historical factors (Schiff 2017): their narratives helped contextualize their experiences and gave shared meaning to the care practices that prepared them for independent living after adverse childhood experiences.

THE CONTEXT OF CHILDHOOD IN SOUTH AFRICA

South Africa is burdened by increasing violence and abuse against children (Optimus Study SA Technical 2016). Every year between 18,000 and 20,000 child sexual abuse cases are reported to the police; statistics from 2013/2014 reveal 18,524 cases: that is 51 incidents reported daily. One in three children have had some experience of sexual abuse, persistent over the lifetime and present in their daily lives. Boys and girls are equally vulnerable to sexual abuse. By the time they are fifteen years old, many children have suffered sexual, physical, or emotional abuse; neglect; and high levels of family and community violence.

The communities surrounding the YCEC have suffered a long history of colonial and racist exploitation that culminated in apartheid, a pernicious political system that entrenched white minority privilege. Sixty percent of all gang activity in the country occurs in Cape Flats, with its community members turning to crime and drug trafficking in the face of high unemployment and poverty (Plato 2012). An inhumane past and violent present provide a challenging context for children, who continue to suffer from the effects of intergenerational trauma and suffering.

In the 1970s, vulnerable children became heroes by marching for their human rights, demanding an equitable education. The June 16, 1976, uprising in Soweto—when students protested against the enforcement of the Bantu Education Act, which mandated learning Afrikaans in schools—changed the political landscape. The uprising's terrible toll was 69 children killed and 186 wounded, marking a turning point in apartheid resistance. This event is commemorated each year as a public holiday, Youth Day. Although SA has experienced more than two decades of democracy, racial tensions still run high: the black majority still suffers from historical injustices, with children being especially vulnerable.

Child care for abused and neglected children is currently provided in community foster homes, child and youth care centers, and temporary shelters; these children are also incarcerated in secure care centers alongside juvenile offenders (Bosman-Sadie and Corrie 2010). The phased-out YCEC model of care and education had its origins in colonial industrial schools and reform schools for juvenile offenders. As late as the mid-1990s, YCEC staff described discipline at the center as coming from the "dark ages" and being enforced by corporal punishment, with the children housed in detention cells and lockup facilities. The transformation of the care system began postapartheid around 1996, following the release from prison of more than one thousand children; many were transferred to unprepared places with inadequate facilities, exacerbating weaknesses in the residential care system and creating a national crisis. The system continued to improve, with the Children's Act of 2005 being implemented in 2010, when provision was made for alternate forms of care. Youth care facilities were transferred from the Western Cape Education Department (WCED) to the Department of Social Development (DSD) (Johnson, in press b), and the service delivery model changed to conform more to international best practices and regulations. As YCEC's educational psychologist explained, "In 2009 staff were trained in the 'circle of courage' to shift the mind, but I realized that we also needed to shift the heart."

INTERNATIONAL RIGHTS OF THE CHILD

Since 1994, all SA laws addressing child care have been governed by local and international conventions. Along with 196 other countries, but excluding the United States, SA ratified an international human rights treaty, the United Nations Convention on the Rights of the Child (UNCRC), that sets out the economic, social, health, civil, political, and cultural rights of children (United Nations Children's Fund 1989). Providing global ethical guidelines for child care, this convention considers developmental issues, but has been criticized for not including children's voices: it gives adults the responsibility to make child care decisions (McNamee 2016).

The South African Children's Act (Act No. 38 of 2005) consolidates and reforms the law on matters related to children. Although a Bill of Rights is enshrined in SA's Constitution, its implementation at the community level is often inadequate. For example, children in SA have the right to be raised by their own parents in their own culture and with a relationship to both parents, but this right was not available to Bulelani and Liam. In addition, although the law states that no child should be deprived of liberty unlawfully or arbitrarily, current lockup facilities in SA for behaviorally challenged vulnerable children may be in violation. In gradually moving from punishment to care since democracy in 1994, a new ethos of care began to emerge at YCEC, which can suggest a way forward for youth care throughout the country.

ETHOS OF CARE

The "circle of courage" ethos of care originated from research with Native Americans (Brendtro et al. 2002). This theoretical circle has four quadrants—belonging, mastery, independence, and generosity—which are part of a pathway to healing. These universal values are believed to develop resilience and self-worth. The YCEC manages violent and disruptive behavior through a focus on children as symptom carriers of family and community intergenerational trauma. A YCEC educational psychologist explained,

> Our youth need to feel close to someone. They need to feel proud of something, like school achievement, athletic skill, peer acceptance, and good behavior. They need adults to be present, attentive, attuned, and responsive in their interactions. In short, youth at the extreme end of behavioral breakdown have survived social ills and need a place to recover. Young people who find themselves at the end of suspension and expulsion, despite intensive proactive and preventative interventions, need specialized care to enable them to access a school curriculum responding to their needs. We propose a behavior support pathway of multiple practices.

This pathway to healing includes elements such as narrative meaning-making, outdoor activities, substance abuse education, animal therapy, and goal setting. Within the PAR self-care research program, teachers were assisted to normalize the boys' behaviors. They came to understand that these youths are survivors, which means that the boys, in fact, were adapting to their traumatic contexts with appropriate responses: anxiety, hyperalertness, emotional volatility, and physical agitation (Courtois 2009). Both Bulelani and Liam benefited from this pathway of support, which helped them recover from their traumatic childhoods.

BULELANI AND LIAM: EXPERIENCES OF ABUSE AND NEGLECT

Liam survived on the streets among drug merchants in a community that grew, as a result of apartheid-forced removals, on barren, sandy tracts of land far from the city. Gangsterism soon took root in his life. He shared,

I grew up in a gangster family. I traveled from place to place as my parents did not care about me. They let me sleep on the streets. My mother, Samantha, was two months pregnant with me [when] my father died—he was a "26" gang leader, shot in the back. . . . When I was about two years old, I was in an accident. That guy did pay the money out [but] my mother didn't tell me about it. I found out . . . six years afterwards how she was using my money for drugs—almost like a merchant—to make her own money. When I was three years old I stayed with my grandmother, Charmaine. . . . She was going out with Matthew, a Rasta guy, and so I had to stay with him [with] my sister. But he didn't treat us like he treated his own child. He was . . . a merchant selling marijuana. He forced us out at 12 at night, walking 10–20 km to buy marijuana because he wanted to sell it. We didn't want to go because it was too dangerous—we could get killed. He hit us every time. . . . So I ran away. . . . I went to stay with Sandra, [who was] like a grandmother to me. . . . One day my mother came to me and tell me I must stay with Charmaine. And I said: "Why must I stay with them? They treat me like a dog and never bring me food." If you give me money they take it off to buy drugs, to smuggle it to other people. Look at me. I am thin. I have to go from door-to-door to ask for food. Sometimes people say they don't have and I accept it.

While Liam's life of neglect and poverty reveals the breakdown of societal structures that should protect its most vulnerable members, Bulelani's village life was initially peaceful. He had a supportive mother, but was separated from her when she moved with his stepfather to Cape Town to seek employment. His grandmother then cared for him and his younger siblings. He had to travel long distances to school, and this created the circumstances that made it possible for tragedy to strike:

My mother and stepfather looked after us until I was six, when they left to work in Cape Town to support us better. . . . I went to a Xhosa/English school with two friends of seven and nine. Transport fetched us and brought us home. One day a guy called us. I thought it was our transport. They had a gun and wanted to shoot us. They kidnapped and raped two of us and afterwards we walked home. Every time they saw us they would threaten to shoot us, threatening us all the time: "Don't tell." I felt scared and wee'd [sic] in my bed, even during the day. I tried to protect myself and fought with anyone who was a big person; I had anger. The . . . threats happened for a year. My grandmother could see I was sick and asked why I was getting home so late, but I said I was cleaning the class. She got diabetes, and became blind and after that my aunty looked after me in East London, while my brother and sister moved to Cape Town to be with my mother. My aunty looked for a school for me. I was eight. The teacher saw that I was not working, would do my own drawings and I liked to fight a lot—I had quick anger.

Bulelani's aunt was a social worker and sought help for him. After staying in various institutions, including a lockup facility where his anger and violent behavior increased, he was sent to the YCEC. There he met Liam, and together they found an environment where they could begin to heal from abuse and neglect by developing faith in themselves.

Bulelani and Liam's narratives reveal the impact of abuse and neglect at interpersonal, familial, and societal levels in a country torn apart by colonial and apartheid policies. They were exposed to domestic and community violence, crime, substance abuse, unemployment, little to no family support, poverty, homelessness, and illiteracy.

GROWING FAITH: "I BELIEVE I CAN"

A belief in one's capacity is the foundation of self-confidence (Pickhardt 2013). In African psychology, faith in oneself is not only personal but also communal—*ubuntu*—and spiritual, drawing on a relationship with God. Ubuntu, an African Nguni word, focuses on the relational and inclusive nature of "being" (Nwoye 2006): "I am because we are" (Mbiti 1970). It calls on us to mirror our humanity for each other and to base our individual self-belief on a sense of ubuntu. Although originally cared for by neighbors, Liam found it hard to develop faith, being largely alienated from his family and surrounded by a violent community. Bulelani shared in the communal ubuntu spirit in the village, but his experiences of sexual abuse and violence shattered his faith in the community and in himself.

Both Liam and Bulelani bonded with peers and were cared for by teachers and staff in relational ubuntu at YCEC. Bulelani explained, "Here they don't *toyi-toyi* [a traditional dance for group cohesion], but they don't put you down. Also, Mr. M supports me. . . . I needed gym shoes—he bought them for me and supported me. I didn't ask; he just saw." One-on-one relationships with adults allowed the boys to develop personal and community faith, supported by relational bonds with peers. Ties with family members were strengthened at gatherings like sports and family days, which kept boys connected to their community structures. Ultimately, personal and communal faith strengthened their faith in God. Effort followed faith, as the boys were encouraged to find interests and hobbies.

EFFORT: "I WILL KEEP TRYING"

Adolescents need encouragement to keep trying, especially when their efforts do not yield immediate results (Pickhardt 2013). Encouragement, whose importance was first recognized by the humanist psychologist Alfred Adler (1956), is an act of interpersonal communication, a character strength, and an ecological group norm (Wong 2015). At YCEC, encouragement is reinforced both formally and informally. It is integrated into a variety of group activities, highlighted as a character strength in personal recognition and academic efforts, and is an integral part of interpersonal communication between boys and adults. While a few staff who continued with negative attitudes had an impact, Bulelani and Liam were mostly encouraged to confront and overcome disempowering beliefs that caused them to lack confidence in themselves. For example, Liam was told by a misguided teacher that he would amount to nothing; he would end up pushing a trolley in the garbage dump. He challenged this statement, questioning this belief and praying to God that this would not be the case.

At the center, Liam experienced the love and care of a family for the first time. Enjoying simple pleasures gave him a feeling of richness. He felt like he belonged, as he connected with the teachers, his counselor, and peers. He also developed an interest in cooking. With support, adversity made him stronger. He gained a generosity of spirit, reaching out to others, and resisting drugs. He explained,

> What I can tell you about this place is that it's wonderful. It's almost like, how can I say, you grow up in a rich family. You get everything you want. If you want to go to the beach, they take you to the beach, and on weekends you have a braai [barbeque], and [on] Sunday you have a decent plate [of food]. You go to school here. Sometimes the boys don't want to go into class, but the Sirs [teachers] encourage them to go in. Sometimes they go into class, but they don't want to write and Sir says, "Do your work; there is a benefit for you outside." Like

Nelson Mandela said, "Education is the most powerful weapon which you can use to change the world."

Liam also felt love and care:

The Sirs are like fathers and teachers like mothers. My mother has five children and lives with a Black man. He doesn't know about me. She has gone to jail for trying to sell drugs overseas. Sometimes the female teachers make you feel like they are your mother—it makes me tearful, but I don't want to talk about it. They show they love you. . . . I never had a father before. If people come into your life they will never be a father, but Mr. B. [his counselor] is like a real father. This is home.

However, it took time for Liam to build these relationships:

When I came to this school, I did not listen to the Sirs. They talked to me, talked to me: "You must change your life." One Sir cursed me: "You will become nothing, you will push a trolley and scratch in the bins, you will never succeed, you will never achieve these goals." It hurt my heart. Why do you say these things to me? You talk about my background; you say I will never succeed in life. Most of the people make me believe that you can become something in life. Get on your knees and pray that you will become something. Sometimes the people encourage me to do things in a positive way; then I do it. Others say: "No, don't do it, don't give [your] full cooperation." Some boys who smoke marijuana don't give their full cooperation. They run away.

The center also gave Bulelani a sense of worth, and he felt loved and cared for. He developed a special bond with the manager, Mr. M., who offered support during difficult times. They would sit for hours in comfortable chairs in his office, always with a bountiful bowl of fruit, seemingly limitless cups of fresh coffee, and a rescue cat curled up in the chair, giving a sense of safety and peace. Bulelani developed mastery in sports and karate, and woodworking gave him independent skills. His new confidence helped him excel and cope with challenges like controlling his anger outbursts. His generosity of spirit inspired newcomers as he became a role model:

I am an open person and talk to the other boys and I hear the teachers' stories. I start to help myself to listen and to work on issues. The stories make me feel proud of myself, not to feel down. I also have faith in God, who brought me here to the center to be right. First, I was the stupid boy. I brought myself down. Now I hear boys say if you say something, your tongue is powerful. I would tell myself I am stupid, but now I believe in myself and can work and have a family and a big house. . . . I speak a lot to Mr. M.—I told him everything; what I want to do. . . . He is like my father. . . . I must take things in two [both] hands; otherwise I am not right on top [pointing to his head]. A lot of things I have learnt for outside [are] what I have learnt here. They are my family. They took me as a child. I did not know them, and they did not know me; they took me in, helping me.

Even negative experiences encouraged Bulelani to try harder:

Not all teachers were positive; [some] put me down. I went to Mr. M. [He said] you need someone to push you down to learn. Outside it will be difficult. Be glad when you are told you will not come right; it will make me stronger and stronger. . . . I got a lot of support; they started to believe in me, although I did not believe in myself. [It] started to wake up my mind.

By excelling in sports, Bulelani was able to develop a positive identity. Learning karate, after focusing on kickboxing, taught him respect:

If I started to fight, I ran to the gym. . . . I punched and punched [the bags] and I helped myself, with the anger leaving my mind. [Last year] I joined karate . . . which has a lot of rules and respect and I started to see the difference. . . . I am proud of myself. . . . Karate teaches you to be calm.

While Bulelani benefited from his physical strength and talent, learning important qualities like respect, pride, and calmness, Liam found encouragement from the sense of family that he developed at the center. In the process, they were both able to develop skills to enable them to achieve positive outcomes in the future.

OUTCOME: "I WILL AFFIRM MY APPROACH DEPENDING ON RESULTS"

According to Pickhardt (2013), an adolescent's ability to cope with disappointment and failure depends on how well he or she is able to apply faith and effort. Faith is the foundation for self-confidence; effort in turn powers self-belief. Outcomes, unlike faith and effort, are not at a person's command and depend on trust (Pickhardt 2013). At the center, the ability to see the positive outcomes of negative experiences is a key factor in building self-belief. Liam, for example, struggled with overcoming substance abuse and addiction in order to realize his dream of becoming a chef:

I want to do something with my life. . . . This place is like the future. What you ask them for, they give to you. It was very slow, very hard for me to change my life. My friends would come, and it was like the devil was playing with my mind. I am finished with drugs—tik [methamphetamine] and mandrax [methaqualone] for a year and a half. [For] five months I have finished with dagga [marijuana], and two months ago I stopped sniffing glue [Steelbon/Genkem]. The Sirs talk to me and encourage me and say: "Don't do that, don't do that." I see boys smoking and I want to join them, but something is pulling me back.

Faith and effort can translate into many different beliefs, actions, and outcomes, as demonstrated by Bulelani's and Liam's responses to their experiences at the center. Both boys developed self-belief as they formed a positive identity and discovered their talents. Liam shared his thoughts: "God helps me and you must also help yourself. . . . I don't want to become a drug addict. My dream is to be a chef on a cruise ship." Bulelani also had dreams: "I am leaving next month . . . to live with my family. I would love to open my own karate dojo gym—I am a yellow belt. Karate places are very far [from community facilities]. [My family] told me they will support me."

LEARNING FROM LIAM AND BULELANI

These narratives give glimpses into the multiple ways that a restorative care ethos in state care can positively affect vulnerable youths. I was deeply touched by my encounters with Liam and Bulelani. They willingly shared the tragedies and triumphs of their lives, reflecting eloquently and insightfully on poignant experiences. We talked often about the meaning of their lives—the importance of God and the power of stories, sharing, connection, and freedom. Despite all their difficulties, they were aware of their triumphs and understood that they were not failures.

With children worldwide so often failed by inadequate institutional parenting and then leaving care (McNamee 2016), let us consider what makes the YCEC's powerful restorative care model so effective. It takes only one positive role model to turn the life of a child around (Goleman and Lantieri 2008; Ray 2007), and the teacher/carer is well placed to be this change agent (Van der Heijden et al. 2015). Similarly, it takes only one restorative care center to turn a youth's life around (Johnson 2019, in press a). This study suggests that institutional care—based on strengthening connections, encouragement, love, and respect along the behavioral support pathway—*can* indeed transform the disempowering core beliefs of adolescents such as Bulelani and Liam.

YCEC's institutional pathway of behavior support relies on restorative care. Staff and teachers enable this transformation in youths by forming caring attachments. This care can take many forms. It can be a coffee break in the manager's office when emotionally volatile boys are invited for a chat, or responding to a boy's needs—like providing a pair of shoes—without him having to ask. With the development of self-belief through restorative care,

FIGURE 1.2 Youth with peace certificates, standing outside the YCC's therapeutic hostel.

adolescents become active agents in their own social worlds, confidently building on elements of faith, effort, and positive outcomes and remaining flexible and open in the face of unexpected opportunities (figure 1.2).

Despite threatened closure and change from an education-managed WCED center to a DSD care facility, the YCEC remains a high-level support institution for behaviorally challenged children, including those who have suffered abuse and neglect. Liam has returned to his community to seek work in local restaurants; perhaps one day he will realize his dream of becoming a chef on a cruise ship. Although Bulelani was offered a free facility to start a karate center, he is training to be a chef with an international hotel group. Mr. M., the mentor and manager, was hit by a car and has recuperated from serious injuries. Everyone at the center prayed for his full recovery.

QUESTIONS FOR REFLECTION AND GROUP DISCUSSION

1. Describe the conditions that culminated in negative circumstances for Bulelani in his African village and for Liam in the Cape Flats.
2. Elaborate on some of the practices at the youth care center that helped both boys in change in different ways.
3. What were the processes that helped them move from disempowerment to self-belief?

NOTE

1. Brian Schiff (2017) suggests three aspects to the interpretive action, with movement going back and forth between who, where, and when in order to begin an argument for why. Text and context mutually produce one another, with psychological phenomena understood as personal and social processes.

REFERENCES

Adler, Alfred. 1956. *The Individual Psychology of Alfred Adler.* New York: Basic Books.
Bosman-Sadie, Hester, and Larry Corrie. 2010. *A Practical Approach to the Children's Act.* Cape Town: LexisNexis.
Brendtro, Larry, Martin Brokenleg, and S. Van Brokern. 2002. *Reclaiming Youth at Risk: Our Hope for the Future.* Bloomington, IN: Solution Tree Press.
Children's Act, Act No. 38. 2005. (2005). http://www.centreforchildlaw.co.za/images/files/childlaw/consolidated_childrens_act.pdf.

Cohler, Bertram. 1982. "Personal Narrative and the Life Course." In *Lifespan Development and Behaviour*, vol. 4, ed. P. Baltes and O. Brim, 205–241. New York: Academic Press.

Courtois, Christine. 2009. *Treating Complex Traumatic Stress Disorders*. New York: Guilford Press.

Erikson, Erik. 1980. *Identity and the Life Cycle*. New York: Norton.

Goleman, Daniel, and Linda Lantieri. 2008. *Building Emotional Intelligence*. Boulder, CO: SoundsTrue.

International Institute for Restorative Practices. 2016. "Defining Restorative." http://www.iirp.edu/imges/pdf/Defining-restorative_Nov-2016.pdf.

Johnson, Sharon. 2010. "Transpersonal Practices as Prevention Intervention for Burnout Amongst HIV/Aids Coordinator Teachers." Master's thesis, Stellenbosch University.

——. 2013. "Impact of Stress and Burnout Interventions on Educators on High-Risk Secondary Schools." PhD diss., Stellenbosch University.

——. 2015. "Reducing Teacher Stress and Burnout in High-Risk Secondary Schools with Transactional Analysis." *International Journal of Transactional Analysis Research* 6, no. 1: 70–85.

——. 2019 (in press a). "Psychobiography as an Effective Research Methodology for the Advocacy of Abused and Neglected Youth in South Africa." In *New Trends in Psychobiography*, ed. Claude-Helene Mayer and Kovary Zoltan. Cham, Switzerland: Springer.

——. 2019 (in press b). *"Lessons in Care: Triumph over Trauma and Tribulation at a State Centre for Vulnerable Youth in South Africa."* Cape Town: Amazon.

——. 2019 (in review). "Finding Safety in Trauma Recovery at a South African State Care Centre for Abused and Neglected Youth." In *New Ideas for New Times: A Handbook of Innovative Community and Clinical Psychologies*, ed. Carl Walker, Sally Zlotowitz, and Anna Zoli. London: Palgrave MacMillan.

Johnson, Sharon, and Anthony Naidoo. 2013. "Transpersonal Practices as Prevention Intervention for Burnout Among HIV/AIDS Coordinator Teachers." *South African Journal of Psychology* 43: 59–70.

——. 2017a. "Can Evolutionary Insights into the Brain's Response to Threat Suggest Different Interventions for Perceived Stress and Burnout for Teachers in High-Risk Schools?" *South African Journal of Psychology* 47: 401–415.

——. 2017b. "A Psychoeducational Approach for Prevention of Burnout Among Teachers Dealing with HIV/AIDS in South Africa." *AIDS Care* 29: 173–178.

Mbiti, John. 1970. *African Religions and Philosophy*. New York: Doubleday.

McNamee, Sally. 2016. *The Social Study of Childhood*. New York: Palgrave Macmillan.

Nwoye, Augustine. 2006. "Remapping the Fabric of the African Self: A Synoptic Theory." *Dialectical Anthropology* 30: 119–146.

Optimus Study SA Technical Report. 2016. *Sexual Victimisation of Children in South Africa*. Zurich, Switzerland: Optimus Foundation Study.

Pickhardt, Carl. 2013. *Surviving Your Child's Adolescence*. San Francisco: Jossey-Bass.

Plato, Don. 2012. *Gangsterism in South African Schools*. Public dialogue address by Minister for Community Safety, Western Cape. Cape Town: Centre for Conflict Resolution.

Ray, Dee. 2007. "Two Counselling Interventions to Reduce Teacher-Child Relationship Stress." *Professional School Counselling* 10, no. 4: 428–440.

Schiff, Brian. 2017. *A New Narrative for Psychology.* New York: Oxford University Press.

United Nations Children's Fund (UNICEF). 1989. *Convention on the Rights of the Child.* http://www.unicef.org (accessed July 15, 2017).

Van der Heijden, Monique, Jeannette Geldens, Douwe Beijaard, and Herman Popeijus. 2015. "Characteristics of Teachers as Change Agents." *Teachers and Teaching* 21, no. 6: 681–699.

Wachtel, Ted. 2013. *Dreaming of a New Reality: How Restorative Practices Reduce Crime and Violence, Improve Relationships and Strengthen Civil Society.* Bethlehem, PA: Piper's Press.

Witkin, Stanley. 2000. "Writing Social Work." *Social Work* 45, no. 5: 389–393.

Wong, Y. Joel. 2015. "The Psychology of Encouragement: Theory, Research and Application." *The Counselling Psychologist* 43, no. 2: 178–216.

Chapter Two

AGING OUT AND ON MY OWN

Stories of Youth Transitions Out of Foster Care

SABRINA GONZALEZ

As a former foster care youth, I am acutely aware of the challenges that "aging out" presents. I was discharged from the Philadelphia County Department of Human Services (DHS) in 1990 at the age of eighteen after being under the care of the child welfare system as a foster child for nine years. During my discharge period I encountered many obstacles, but eventually worked my way through them and made a "successful transition to adulthood," or "emancipation," as it is sometimes called. Unfortunately, my experience is not shared by all youth who age out of the foster care.

In this chapter, I explore factors associated with a successful transition to adulthood for former foster care youth, revealing how, in their own words, some were able to take constructive developmental steps into the world at large. These youth stories, constructed from intensive in-depth interviews with those who have moved out of foster care, outline the social, economic, and psychological barriers they faced while also charting the attitudes, behaviors, and experiences that allowed them to manage, to exit the foster care system in the best way that they could. The successes among this population are varied, hard-won, and tenuous. Ultimately, those youth who do manage to overcome multiple obstacles navigate transitions by tapping both internal strengths and external resources within their reach, including the ability to reconcile and move beyond disappointments, connect with others, and take advantage of available sources of support.

AGING OUT

In the United States, more than a half-million children are in foster care at any given time. The foster care population is disproportionately African American and Native American; three times higher than White children (Child Welfare Information Gateway, 2016; National Foster Care Awareness Project, 2000; English & Grasso, 2000). These youth in the care of the state become independent at an earlier age than those who are in the care of their families. Furthermore, those who leave the system between the ages of eighteen and twenty typically face poor outcomes. They encounter many challenges, including a lack of adult support, financial instability, poor educational/vocational opportunities and outcomes, and a lack of safe and affordable housing. They are more likely to experience unplanned pregnancy, unemployment, criminal justice involvement, and substance use. Many have an increased risk for behavioral and mental health difficulties after leaving foster care (Courtney et al., 2007; Stein, 2006; Freundlich & Avery, 2008).

For those youth that stay in care longer and exit the system at a later age, the transition is fraught with developmental and environmental upheavals and challenges. They carry the burden of a history of maltreatment, neglect, or abandonment, having faced the uncertainty and disruption of being moved from the family they know to a new and unfamiliar living situation, often among strangers. Faced with such upheaval, some may develop "troublesome" behavior, including delinquency and a variety of other behavioral and psychosocial difficulties. Tragically, a move meant to offer a lifeline or haven from the storm can instead result in yet another experience of isolation, injury, or defeat. After a childhood or adolescence that included difficult and uncertain circumstances associated with foster care or other out-of-home placements, it stands to reason that the successful transition to living independently is quite challenging (Silva, 2012; Syed & Mitchell, 2013; Arnett, 2004; Arnett, 2007 Bronfenbrenner, 1992).

While it is true that many individuals who age out of the foster care system face a number of difficulties and stressors, some, like me, have made the transition successfully and are able to lead satisfying, productive lives. My experience as a former member of the foster care population led me to explore the factors associated with making progress and achieving developmental milestones into early adulthood after foster care or out-of-home placement. Their experiences, what accounts for their personal triumphs, and what we can do to improve the odds of success for more foster care youth remain largely unexplored.

FROM FOSTER CARE TO RESEARCHER

As a researcher with life experiences similar to those of the youth whose stories I share in this chapter, I was acutely aware that self-reflection was critical and that I had to monitor my reactions as I listened to their stories. I have my own experiences in the care of the state, my own interpretations of the aging-out process, and my current experiences today. After my discharge from DHS custody in 1990 with my young son Troy (two years old at the time), I had to find a way to automatically become an adult. Over the years, many people have told me that they consider me "successful" based on where I am now. But it was and is a hard path on which to keep marching. It is filled with obstacles and the challenges of accepting my family of origin for who they are and accepting myself.

I faced economic challenges as well. Fortunately, I was always able to find work after I aged out of the system. I worked in the fast-food industry, then as a file clerk, and then as a secretary, along with multiple work-study jobs during college. I was organized and responsible in paying bills, but it was the burden of doing it alone that weighed on me the most. I lived with the constant fear of not being able to make each month's expenses and that if I took one day off from work or got sick everything would fall apart.

Most young people are able to ask their parents or family for money and support. I did not have that immediate support, and I felt that asking for help meant I had failed, so I tried very hard not to do so. Not having a family on my side often felt isolating; I felt empty and embarrassed, but I kept going. At school events I had no relatives there to celebrate my successes. While many young people feel alone for the first time when they go away to college, for me starting college just felt like I was on my own again, and again, and again.

My first semester as an undergraduate at Temple University was also the first year of school for my son and I needed help. My last foster mother, Binky, offered to help me take care of him. I really appreciated and needed her support. Later, when I did not have enough to pay for books I felt comfortable asking my child advocate social worker, Najma, for support. She had been with me since I was seven years old, when someone had called an abuse hotline, and she was sent from DHS to visit my home every week. Najma was my advocate throughout my childhood and into my adult years and did not hesitate to write me a check for $200 for books. More importantly, she was someone who cared about my well-being, and this really made a difference.

College also meant different kinds of obstacles. The academic and social expectations of attending college were difficult for me to meet. I had a hard time with remedial math and had to be tutored. I once cried during a tutoring session, but I did not leave it until I understood the math. I remember a geology teacher at Temple who yelled at me for having a new baseball hat, but not the lab workbook. I did not have enough money for the $35 lab workbook; I just happened to take really good care of my $7 hat.

My college experience was not all terrible. There were times I felt safe. There was peace in looking at all the possibilities for my future based on what I was working on in the present. Visualizing and thinking about all the foster care kids who came before me—"that poor kid," "that scholarship kid," "that immigrant kid"—was motivating. The best thing college gave me was the ability to define who I wanted to be and to find out what kind of person I was—to realize how caring I was and to be surprised at how smart I was. Getting to a good place took a long time, filled not only with letting go of the hurtful past but also being proud of it.

After college, Najma encouraged me to seek an MSW and later a DSW. I did not think I was smart enough at the time, but I applied to the MSW program just to make her happy. When I was accepted, I promised myself that I would do whatever it took to make it and achieve my goals. I am proud that I am one of those who made it out of foster care and was also the first in my family to go to college. I am the best and worst of my past, but I also consider myself a person with success in the present. I am motivated and have accomplishments that many people in my situation were unable to achieve. I continue to find abilities within myself, as well as the strength that comes from my life experiences. My past does not define me, but it is always with me.

I frequently wondered if there were others like me and if anything had changed for youth who age out. This research project gave me the chance to find out. It was another opportunity to challenge myself and continue to persevere and to grow. I share many things in common with the youth in this chapter, but there were also notable differences, and it was important for me to be able to see a full picture of our varied experiences, to analyze the facts with the feelings. I made sure to continue in counseling so that I could work through the many emotions that arose during my research. I wrote reflexivity notes for each interview to analyze my emotions and reactions and to process my memo writing based on the research questions and the data from each interview.

I was often taken by surprise when I was able to immediately connect so intensely with the youth I interviewed. Although they really had no reason to do so, they seemed to trust and appreciate my openness. This was a mutual experience. As their family story and emotions poured out easily and as they constructed their self-narratives, I felt connected to them—as if we were all part of this special club. When they talked about their pain, it felt like each person I interviewed was inside my head. "How did they feel the same emotions I did?" I asked myself. Each story was different, but the emotional responses to the experiences were similar, and I was often transported back in time to my own experiences and feelings as I was aging out. I heard heartbreaking reactions, verbally and physically aggressive responses, avoidant responses, and also vindictive ones. Their ability to adjust and think through events seemed to improve over time, but many expressed the precarious nature of their emotional stability. They only needed to be involved in one incident in which they lost the ability to emotionally regulate themselves, and the consequences could be ending up in jail or in a hospital.

I did not disclose that I too had been in foster care until late in the interview process. I was uncertain how to balance being this "good scientist" and being so connected to the young people I interviewed. Saying "I am just like you" at the end of each interview made it easier to focus and to say goodbye. But the light in their eyes and the comments they made to me, such as "Wow, you finished a lot of degrees and you were in foster care?" and "I hope I can go to college like you" made me feel like Superman. I had a hero or two, but could I be someone else's hero too? I had not thought about that, but I loved being able to give someone hope and motivation to keep going.

And the idea of hope was a two-way street. Toward the end of every interview, each young person also seemed to view his or her struggles and personal accomplishments as positive and hopeful. This gave me hope too. The outside world had always made me feel special, like I was the rare one to get out and make it in the world. But I am not the only one to do so. The young people I interviewed were all trying their best with the resources and circumstances at hand. I could see their determination, and it was just like mine. I was happy to know that others could find a way to success and happiness and that this "thing," the motivational drive, was just as strong in other youth leaving foster care. After leaving each interview, I felt like I had just visited my family, and I was proud of and hopeful for each person I interviewed.

Social workers wonder which kind of programs and services will make a difference in the lives of their clients and facilitate success. Is public assistance enough? Are medical coverage and Food Stamps enough? Are employment, education, and life-skill classes the keys to success? For the youth whose stories are shared in this chapter and for myself, the answer that emerges is that having a good relationship with a caring adult is essential. They knew how to survive, but their relationship with an adult who genuinely cared seemed to be key to their success. Having a relationship with someone who is consistent and dependable and uplifting is the best gift and "program."

TELLING TRANSFORMATIVE STORIES

Storytelling is a narrative approach that straddles the line between science and art. Through stories we aim to derive meaning and insight from the lived experiences of individuals. By sharing the voices of those who live on the margins, the life story can be a powerful tool for understanding the complexities of living through and aging out of foster care (Manteuffel et al., 2008; Riessman, 2002; Schiff, 2014). We know a lot about how many youth are in the foster care system at any given time, at what age they entered it, and when they age out, but we do not know a lot about what it means for them to experience aging out. In this chapter, I present the experiences of eight youth who shared with me what aging out felt like and what it meant for them: through reflecting on their lives before and during foster care, they identified life experiences that directly affected their current success in living on their own. All eight were African American: four identified as male and four as female. They all resided in Philadelphia.

The interviews took place in the spaces where the youth were studying or working. For those who were attending an alternative education program either to complete their high school education or learn a trade, the interviews took place around the time of those classes. Other interviews took place at their college or place of work. What struck me at the time was that each young person appeared to enjoy sharing his or her story, even when things were not going well. Their stories contained elements of strength, persistence, and the motivation to keep going, even to achieve simple goals. The obstacles they faced appeared to be a badge of honor, and all the youth felt that hardships made them stronger, wiser, and more prepared for the adult world.

Their stories unearthed transformative moments in their lives as they aged out of foster care. Through the telling of these accumulated experiences common themes emerged about how they perceived their connections, or lack thereof, with others during a vulnerable moment in their lives. Many told of their search for immediate and extended relatives and how, along the way, most were able to find supportive friends, relatives, or even professionals to help them in times of need and for guidance. Each young person created and used a network of social support to increase his or her ability to cope with stress and obstacles and to survive. Their experiences in the care of the state were embedded into their identity and used as an impetus for the future. They were also able to reconstruct the story they had lived so far into one of strength and healing as they transitioned out of state care and on their own.

THROUGH AN ECOLOGICAL LENS

While developmental models traditionally focus on the future, on what children become, and what outcomes they will experience, an ecological lens focuses on the here and now (Darling, 2007; Corcoran & Nichols-Casebolt, 2004; Pardeck, 1988). I use this framework to understand the experiences of the youth in this chapter because its focus is on how children and youth interact with the varied systems in their lives. Adults can be seen as those who have the potential to have a significant impact, whether supportive or destabilizing, and youth have to work to negotiate different dynamics in their relationships. Even when their relationships with adults were not ideal, some youth managed to find meaning and usefulness in them. Regardless of their history and reasons for entering foster care, each youth interviewed can clearly remember helpful adults who crossed their path and helped with one problem or multiple situations. These memories brought back smiles and a positive tone to their self-narratives; they were an indication that, with a little guidance, they were able to find their way through obstacles.

The ecological framework also takes account of the role of policies and institutions in the lives of foster care alumni. The youth in these stories all were involved with different institutions: school, nonprofits, juvenile justice, and the foster care system they exited. It is important to note that many policies are geared to specific age groups and so have shaped the lives of foster care children in different ways across different times. By the end of the twentieth century, numerous policies had been put in place to facilitate the aging-out process. These included extended medical coverage and welfare benefits, mandatory life-skill programs that started before the youth left care, educational programs, housing support, and independent living programs. In Philadelphia, a drop-in center, Achieving Independence Center, was created. Here former foster care youth up to age twenty-four can drop in for counseling and help in resume preparation. They also are given a practical handbook called "Knowing Your Rights," which provides information on how to obtain a Social Security card, birth certificate, welfare benefits, and driver's license; how to look for jobs; and how to obtain education loans and grants. Youth who aged out in my generation or earlier did not have access to all this information or services in one place and had to seek them on their own, one service by one service at a time. The ecological lens is useful for understanding how young people's interactions at different levels of their ecosystem contribute to or hinder their development of resilience.

MAKING YOUR OWN OPPORTUNITIES

Making your own opportunities is a recurrent theme in the stories shared by youth who were aging out. It reflects resiliency stemming not only from recognizing their limitations but also from having the confidence to move forward and make safe, healthy decisions given the resources at hand. Some of the youth I talked to were able to make their own opportunities because of their positive attitudes toward family, education, work, and the future. They were able to view life's difficulties as challenges and respond accordingly with constructive action, including the use of positive self-talk: reminding themselves of their strengths, abilities, and past experience overcoming hardships. However, not all reported doing well even as they strove to open doors for themselves. Many were struggling just to hold on, while working to achieve positive goals day after day.

Kanye's story stood out for me the most. He was honest and insightful about his attempts to manage hard and risky day-to-day decisions just to stay afloat and have a shot at something more in the future. He shared that he had returned to high school, but needed to sell drugs at night: his aunt had been happy to take him in for almost two years, but only as long as there was a check. Yet, there was little to no family interaction between the two, and when no money was coming in, Kanye's aunt would become distant and emotionally unsupportive. She would tell him, "You better find a way to take care of yourself; I don't have money to take care of you." Kanye seemingly understood the right path to take, but felt burdened by the limited help and choices available to him to do the "right things," like going to school and getting an education. He was risking his well-being by selling drugs, but felt this was the only way to provide for himself and give his aunt money. Kanye talked about "being a man" at age twenty and doing what he had to do to provide and make it in the world.

You gotta go out here and get it, you have to figure out a way to survive even if it is things you don't want to do, no one's gonna help you for free, no one cares that much. . . . I live with my aunt. . . . I don't think she likes me. . . . The money stopped and then she just stopped lookin' out for me. . . . I think things are going bad for me now. I am barely hanging in there; I just need to graduate so I can go in the army and leave all this behind and start new. . . . If I was smart, I would have stayed in care [longer]. . . . I am taking risks to survive, to make it.

Like Kanye, many others were barely holding on to school or a job and realized that at any moment things could get worse. The risk of homelessness and incarceration seemed to be always present, and they expressed more worry about these outcomes than peers who identified their transitions as more successful. Even though they hoped to keep going, finish school, get a better job, and find stable housing, the attitude was that they did not have much control over their situation and were on the verge of either sinking or swimming.

WEATHERING THE STORM

"Weathering the storm" is a theme or expression of resilience demonstrated by the ability to succeed and prosper in the face of setbacks and hardships. Several of the former foster care youth hardly had a childhood or at least a conventional one. Most did not have the foundation of typical family experiences that provide security, safety, and dependability nor tangible supports like having a stable place to live, food to eat, and someone to respond to their needs. Many of their parents and family were themselves struggling and did not have the capacity to care for themselves, let alone their children. So children watched the adults in their lives fail to protect them and were left wondering who would take on this role. Cognitively trying to process survival skills at an elementary school age can push a child to his or her limits when life becomes about choices: how to make it through each day with enough food, clothing, and safety and a place to live.

These young people's stories also describe their journey into foster care: a system that will feed you, clothe you, and make sure you get to school, but will not reach inside you to put the broken pieces together. Each foster care child has to figure out how to heal on his or her own. Along the way, a youth may ask for and accept help, but it is the consistent supportive relationships that teach them how to mend their broken hearts. Their relationships with other loving adults came up often in the youth stories. These adults taught foster care children and youth how to love and care and reciprocate; they taught the process of becoming and being a human. And through these relationships, both new ones and the ones that were restored, the young people were able to bounce back and keep moving forward, even under greater-than-average stressors.

When asked to examine all their many responsibilities—school, work, single parenting, peer relationship building, and creating new relationships with family—it was nearly impossible for any of the youth to identify the single most difficult obstacle they had overcome, because they faced so many challenges. However, a large part of their "weathering the storm" occurred within the context of relationships.

Gabe talked a great deal about his relationship with his mother and how much he loved her and wanted to protect her. He also talked about the many bad relationships with men she had had to maintain her drug habit. When he was fourteen years old, in foster care, and visiting his mother on a weekend home pass, he shot his mother's abusive boyfriend. He had no regrets about protecting his mother and acknowledged that the incident allowed him the only opportunity to ever meet his father, who happened to be in the same jail he was sent to after being convicted and sentenced. Gabe spent two years in prison.

After prison, he was working to heal his relationship with is mother:

I had to forgive my mother after both of us finished our drug program so I could build a relationship with her. So I love her the way she is, knowing there is some things she can do and help and not help with. I know it was the drug addiction that stopped my mom from being the best mom she could be.

All of the young people focused on healing their families' past and finding a way to be a part of their own families in the present. This was a necessary vision quest that often had sad results, but everyone "had to know" and find their place within their family, no matter how painful, before they could accept themselves. When connections failed with biological kin, they all searched for their immediate peer group or reached out to their former social workers, foster parents, and sometimes with the last agency that had provided services to them. This inner drive to be connected remained strong even when their attempts to repair old relationships did not succeed. Each had an ability to assess who in their lives was trying to help and who was unwilling to help. They could then hold on to whom they believed was in their corner. In addition to the expected adversity of living on their own for the first time, creating a safety net that should already exist was a journey on its own. Many shared their experiences in seeking positive relationships, but some relationships, including relationships with self, caused challenges along their way. Low self-esteem, constant worry and anxiety, low motivation, and low goal setting were persistent.

LIFE IS NOT A JOURNEY TRAVELED ALONE

In their attempts to repair and heal relationships with their biological family, the youth had to deal with the many disappointments associated with this process. Some believed that their families should have been waiting for this time to come and be eager to make up for lost time. And when that did not happen, it was heartbreaking. Each young adult described a moment when he or she woke up, realized that there was at least one other person who cared, and reached out to that one person and asked for help. It was at this starting point that efforts in building relationships became consistent and purposeful. Communication skills were developing, while they were practicing the skills of asking for aid and accepting the help offered. Learning how to work through conflict and disagreements was also added to their skill sets. All of these brave young adults created a new story about their past for their pain, for their rejection and loss. They seemed driven by and toward the person or people who had always been there, even if they were not related. They each accepted person(s) who would replace their parents. Such replacements included a social worker, a foster parent, a boyfriend, a stepparent, a newfound distant relative, and even a social service agency that employed caring people willing to help.

Nicole described couch surfing from one friend's house to another. She talked about needing to have a boyfriend just to have some place to stay, even if this meant having sex when she did not want to. "When I was stripping and making lots of money, it was scary being alone even if I could afford it. I still needed someone there next to me to feel safe." Nicole knew her biological family would provide little guidance to her; even though she stayed in contact with them and felt like they had a connection, she knew they were struggling as "old adults" and had the same problems they did when she was born, like using drugs and having no income. "I knew I couldn't ask them for help because they could not help themselves so I had no one else to ask but the social workers I knew, the nice ones would help me."

When Nicole wanted to go back to school, she just went to the social service agency and asked to speak to her old case manager, who was happy to help her make that happen. Now, Nicole goes to the school guidance counselor for help and support, talks to her teachers, and keeps in contact with her old social worker. Nicole is aware of key adult figures who will help her achieve her future goals and will be supportive: she accepts them as replacements for her parents, who are unable to provide her support.

Getting out of the foster care system, and stepping out into the world, was often described as quite a solitary journey. Each story described how the youth figured out ways to attain the next goal. Each story told different ways of getting through and around adverse events, no matter what. However, with every stop along the way, they were all able to describe interactions with at least one adult whom they perceived as helpful, who provided guidance, advice, finances, or a safe place to stay. Each young person had to decide how and when to ask for help and how and when to accept this help. It is important to note that these decision-making skills and problem-solving skills are developing during one of the most trying times of their lives; a real "trial by fire."

PROGRESS IS THE DISTANCE TRAVELED

Former foster care youth indicated that the lessons they learned while under the care of the state would carry over into the future and make it easier to negotiate upcoming obstacles. They believed their suffering was meant to be, that they were destined to suffer on the way to becoming stronger and to be able to face future pain and stress. The young people tended to see mistakes both as having created a shield of protection and as being a source of pride. They viewed their lived experiences—both good and bad—as an unavoidable part of becoming a young adult. With each mistake, they learned a new skill or new tool for their toolkit. This mental and physical toughness was the reason they were here and why they could handle anything in their future.

No one shared regrets, despite recounting difficult feelings of loneliness, emptiness, and missing connections with their family or other adult figures. None wished that they could have had a different experience or had more money or that they would be in a different place than where they are today. When others hear this, they often have difficulty believing these sentiments. Even I reacted this way, as I remembered how I constantly thought that, if I had parents who cared about me, my life and opportunities would be so different. I also imagined how my life would be different with capable parents, but that was a fantasy, something to increase my self-worth at the moment. I understood this viewpoint and remembered how deeply I believed it myself.

The youth felt both pride and a sense of accomplishment that they had triumphed over real-life difficult situations. They shared their belief that pain and struggle were necessary for growth and learning. They recognized that their continual adjustment to those circumstances, even while making mistakes, led up to this point in their lives where they are able to say, "Wow I am this amazing person, making progress even with my shitty past." Each alumni accepted his or her accomplishments, whether they were the result of learning from a mistake or making a good decision the first time around. This feeling of great satisfaction stemmed from accepting themselves—not just where they were from but also for whom they are now—which really meant loving themselves. The young people believed that they were currently where they needed to be in their lives: they were in the right place. They each wore their past as a badge of honor for having made it through. Their identity was directly connected to past events, lived experiences, and learning from mistakes. A sense of confidence, motivation, and positive self-worth all stemmed from having survived in spite of the emotional wounds they suffered as children. As a result, all of their life experiences, especially the negative ones, made them better people.

The youth were in the process of figuring out who they were by reaching out to their biological relatives who could fill in missing pieces of their childhoods and family histories: they were finding out where they came from, who cared about them, what their families were like, and other details of their family histories. Many also began defining themselves by characteristics they did not inherit or acquire from their families. This self-definition process seemed to be very important to them. They reported not wanting to make the same mistakes as their parents; they wanted to be better than their parents both emotionally and financially. There was pride in making it through their lives so far, and a stubborn insistence that they would not change any of their past behaviors.

Gabe went as far as saying that he was glad he had the experience of being in foster care:

I wouldn't do anything differently; honestly no—I love my life the way it is. Experience is the best teacher and that's how you learn from your mistakes. . . . I would do nothing differently—I would go into foster care. . . . I would shoot him again because I was protecting my mother and that was the only way to stop the abuse. . . . I would go to jail and I would have my daughter the same age because my daughter showed me that there was more to life. Before her, I was in to gangs and headed nowhere. . . . I wouldn't change any of the decisions–they were all important for me to learn from and mature and understand how life really works.

It is important to remember that children in foster care were forced to make decisions that adults should have been making for them or that adults should have been teaching them and preparing them to make. Under stress, they made the best decisions they could, given the circumstances and their developmental stage. As they got older and experienced the consequences of their actions, they were able to learn from them, to allow the obstacles to make them stronger, and to try not to make the same mistake twice. The bravery they displayed in searching for relationships and hoping to connect to family and others is truly amazing and appears to be related to the developmental fact that humans are social creatures and learn from relationships in their environment.

PATHWAYS TO ENSURE SUCCESS

Past "mistakes" served as experiences to learn from and try not to repeat. When I asked them what advice they would give to others, they talked of learning from their mistakes, but at the same time understanding that everyone needs to make his or her own path, which usually means making both good and bad choices along the way that would, they hoped, make them stronger people. All of the youth had the same pieces of advice, which they thought to be of equal importance: stick with and complete one's education, learn about earning and saving money, stay longer in the system to receive more services, ask for help and accept help when offered, find work before aging out of care, and spend more time on planning for the future. Each spoke with great confidence as if he or she were an expert in the field. The most importance advice given by all eight foster care alumni involved communication: find someone to talk to and speak up for oneself.

Shari's words were typical:

Definitely talk to your social worker as much as possible because if you don't have a good social worker, they will just wait until you're eighteen and you're just out the door. . . . Stay on top of the social worker. If you find out that the social worker is not getting back to your calls, find out who their supervisor is and always, always leave a message. . . . You find out where the office is and you go sit in the office.

Moreover, all foster care alumni advocated for having a strong plan and direction of where to go in life, keeping one's motivation and focus, and sticking to it in order to achieve success. Other recommendations included controlling emotions, anger, and frustration; learning how to talk and socialize appropriately; asking and learning about available programs and resources; staying in the system as long as possible until adequately prepared for independent living; and thinking first before impulsively leaving the system.

LOVING IN THE ABSENCE OF LOVE

This research was dear and personal to me. I went to great lengths to use it as an opportunity not only to heal but also to monitor my own pain and memories and to learn from young people about how they interpreted and negotiated their experiences in and out of foster care. As I "story" my own journey I am able to see the arc of my experiences from the time I entered the system, and much like the young people in this chapter, I too have struggled to come to terms with my past so that I could build a future.

I grew up in foster care from the age of nine until I emancipated myself at age seventeen and a half. I had my one and only son while in foster care. Currently I live in Florida with my wife. My now adult son also lives in Florida with his high school sweetheart, now wife, along with two of the best grandchildren in the world. There are no social workers. There is no Department of Human Service involvement. It took five generations before state interventions with my family ceased. It took five generations to break multiple cycles of poverty, lack of education, single parenting, absent parents, drug abuse, criminal involvement, and abuse. While it is a work in progress, it is a pleasure to help my grandchildren go through regular growing pains, not moments of trauma. I am confident my grandchildren will not know my pain and that, because I used my obstacles as strengths to move forward toward a positive life, I am leaving a healing legacy in my personal family as well as in my career.

I am currently a clinical family therapist providing counseling in the homes of teenagers. My recent clients have ranged in age from five to sixty-three years old. I chose my research project against all the advice of my dissertation committee members, who felt the topic was too emotional and would be "too hard" to complete. I chose it because I wanted to find out how those leaving foster care were doing. Had anything changed since my generation? Was this generation getting more help than I did? Were there better social workers or improved mentoring and connections with adults?

The answers to those questions were sometimes yes and sometimes no. But what did not change is knowing that those of us who make it out of the system struggle every day to figure out a way to do more than survive, to achieve, and to have dreams and hopes. Sometimes, these hopes include the desire that one's biological familial connections can improve: the past struggles are so important to one's journey. They drive the passion to break a cycle, and the struggles are re-storied to show that they were experienced for a reason: to make one stronger. I am so proud to work with such a population that can continue to love while not feeling loved, holding on to the hope that things can change, if only one person at a time.

QUESTIONS FOR REFLECTION AND GROUP DISCUSSION

1. The ecological approach enables a focus on the person's entire world. When one link is broken, such as the family unit, how do other immediate links and resources play into your life to keep you together and connected, as well as growing and learning?
2. Everyone creates a personal life story that tells of his or her struggles and achievements. This is part of the process that creates the human experience. What is your personal story of struggles and successes?
3. Can people heal through their story? Does your personal story heal you in some way?

REFERENCES

Arnett, J. (2004). *Emerging adulthood: The winding road from the late teens through the twenties.* New York: Springer.

——. (2007). *Adolescence and emerging adulthood: A cultural approach,* 3rd ed. Upper Saddle River, NJ: Pearson-Prentice Hall.

Bronfenbrenner, U. (1992). Ecological systems theory." In R. Vasta (Ed.), *Six theories of child development* (pp. 187–249). London: Kinsley.

Corcoran, J., & Nichols-Casebolt, A. N. (2004). Risk and resilience ecological framework for assessments and goal formation. *Child and Adolescent Social Work Journal* 21(3), 211–235.

Courtney, M., Keller, T. & Cusick, G. (2007). Approaching the transition to adulthood: Distinctive profiles of adolescents aging out of the child welfare system. *Social Service Review, 81*(3), 453–484.

Darling, N. (2007). Ecological systems theory: The person in the center of the circle. *Journal of Research and Human Development, 4*(3–4), 203–217.

Freundlich, M., & Avery, R. (2008). You're all grown up now: Termination of foster care support at age 18. *Journal of Adolescence, 32*(2), 247–257.

Manteuffel, B., Stephens, R. L., Sondheimer, D. L., & Fisher, S. K. (2008). Characteristics, service experiences, and outcomes of transition-aged youth in systems of care: Programmatic and policy implications. *Journal of Behavioral Health Services and Research 35*(4), 469–487.

National Foster Care Awareness Project (2000). Frequently asked questions about the foster care independence act, 1999. Retrieved from https://www.ilp.pitt.edu /files%5CdefaultPage%5CFacts%20about%20Chaffee%20Funds.pdf.

Pardeck, J. (1988). An ecological approach for social work practice. *Journal of Sociology and Social Welfare, 15*(2).

Riessman, C. K. (2002). Analysis of personal narratives. In J. F. Gubrium et al. (Eds.), *Handbook of interview research* (pp. 695–710). London, Sage.

Schiff, B. (2014). Rereading personal narrative and the life course. *New Directions for Child and Adolescent Development, 145*. Hoboken, NJ: Wiley.

Stein, M. (2006). Young people aging out of care: The poverty of theory. *Children and Youth Services Review, 28*(4), 422–434.

Silva, J. (2012). Constructing adulthood in an age of uncertainty. *American Sociological Association, 77*(4), 505–522.

Syed, M., & Mitchell, L. (2013). Race, ethnicity, and emerging adulthood: Retrospect and prospects. *Emerging Adulthood, 1*(2), 83–95.

Chapter Three

DREAMING DESPITE STATUS

Immigrant Youth in Contingent Migration Contexts

STEPHEN RUSZCZYK

What does migration mean in the lives of children who immigrate? In what ways do their social lives and their possibilities shift as they move from spaces in one country to those of another? Rooted in the narratives of four Mexican-origin migrants to New York City, this chapter argues that today's immigrant youth must navigate highly contingent paths as they remain active participants in the challenging processes of immigration and integration. Today, immigrant status, gendered expectations, and transnational possibilities bestow opportunities on, and test, immigrant youth.

The four biographical narratives in this chapter highlight the agency of immigrant/undocumented youths. They each aspire to achieve educationally, to fit in, and to give upward mobility their best shot. Luis, Leo, Aracelis, and Alma[1] actively strategize about how to take advantage of family resources, transnational resources, and (limited) work possibilities. Their undocumented status[2] shows the lengths that teenagers go through to become young adult women and men and follow their dreams. These four Mexican-born youths decide whether to return to Mexico for college or to stay and work to support families, negotiate how to become a man or a woman, and struggle with domestic abuse. Their situations are more extreme examples of issues that many immigrant youth face as they become adults, with their families divided by borders, unequal schooling contexts, and mixed legal statuses. Immigrant youth must play active roles—

managing tensions within the family, threats in the neighborhood, and uncertainties of the legal system—to enable them to continue working toward fulfilling their dreams despite the obstacles.

NARRATIVE METHOD

My path crossed with those of these four teenagers when I began teaching in a high school located in a working-class, predominantly Latino urban neighborhood. North Park, like many urban neighborhoods, had endured the detrimental effects of decades of white flight and disinvestment. The growth of the Puerto Rican, Dominican, and Mexican populations had steadied those downward dynamics and fed much of the student population in ABC High School. In 2005, Luis was a junior in my English class and an enthusiastic player on the soccer club I co-coached. I met his brother Leo when I first visited his parents' home in 2008. Aracelis was a reticent sophomore in my history class in 2006. Though I first met Alma after she had finished high school, her brother had been Aracelis's schoolmate.

I began conducting research with adolescents, both in and out of school, in 2008. The narratives of Luis, Leo, Aracelis, and Alma are crafted from spending time with them in class and in varied social spaces from the family breakfast table and church to time with friends in parks and parties, over a period extending from three years (Alma) to twelve years (Luis). I conducted multiple open-ended and grounded interviews with each of them, from which I draw material. In addition, I visited Luis's and Leo's families in Mexico three times. In 2008, Luis was considering moving back to Mexico to study, and his brother Leo had dropped out of high school to work. Their undocumented status shaped each of their decisions, although each brother exercised agency in very different ways. Managing family obligations and expectations strained these teenagers; their undocumented status meant that the assumption that academic success would bring later rewards weakened as each got closer to adulthood.

As teenagers move from adolescence to emerging adulthood, their self-narratives crystallize for the first time (MacAdams, 1993). My longitudinal ethnography—collecting data with youths over an extended period of time as they engaged with their family, in their schools, with peers, in church, and at work—overlapped with this coming-of-age process, facilitating the narrative inquiry. Narratives evolved from informants' experiences and through an iterative process of discussing events with them (Clandinin & Connelly, 2004). The four youths in these narratives reviewed them to add and confirm events, descriptions, and details. I used a biographical logic of analysis rooted in each youth's understanding of how his or her life unfolded to show each as a full person strategizing about how to best navigate choices that are constrained by lack of access to legal, social, and economic resources.

Sharing these stories puts them in a broader context. The rapid growth of federal immigration enforcement, anti-immigrant sentiment, and subsequent contestation from "sanctuary cities" like New York City surely has created a troubling context for these young people's coming of age. Negative public representations of undocumented people frame them as burdens or threats to the country (Chavez, 2008). Even representations that are more sympathetic often assume that undocumented youth live in the shadows and therefore do not act on their futures in important ways. The counterstories of these young people create voice for marginalized undocumented youth (Delgado, 1989). I invite you the reader to use empathy and suspend your received wisdoms about how undocumented youth should make the transition to adulthood (Knight et al., 2004; Massaro, 1989). In their narratives you can witness the sense of agency—and its limitations—that these youths experience as they grow into new understandings of their legal and social positions.

ADAPTING TO NEW CONTEXTS

Immigrant youth's agency is situated; that is, the paths that young people may trod depend on their social and geographical locations. Immigration scholars have distinguished, for example, between *first-generation* immigrants who migrate and their *second-generation* children who were born in the United States. More than one in four Americans is either a first- or second-generation immigrant, with the number split evenly between the generations (Zong & Batalova, 2017). Immigrants and their children make up a majority of residents in major U.S. cities such as New York City, Los Angeles, and Miami. Those who immigrated to the United States before adolescence are called the *1.5 generation*, because they have been socialized in American schools. For the children of immigrants, which includes both 1.5- and second-generation Americans, fitting in American society can take many forms. The segmented assimilation model (Portes & Rumbaut, 2001) highlights how family background and the local context of reception affect how the processes of immigration and integration unfold. Immigrants enter the country with different levels of education, financial resources, and legal statuses (e.g., as refugees, with an authorized or unauthorized status): these factors shape how immigrants integrate into their new society. Scholars also see different patterns of discrimination according to racial characteristics, the availability of jobs, and the strength of ethnic communities.

When Leo, Luis, Aracelis, and Alma immigrated from small towns in south central Mexico to the neighborhood where I was teaching, each strategically adapted to new family dynamics, new English-dominant schools, and a new neighborhood context. This neighborhood, North Park, has concentrations of Mexican co-ethnics, but interethnic, working-class tensions manifest for teenagers as gang issues there. Not only the broader society but also those in their neighborhood perceive them as racialized Mexicans. While the greater neighborhood is predominantly Latino, Puerto Ricans and Dominicans form the majority of this panethnic group. According to data from 2008–2012 from the American Community Survey, the population living in the youths' zip code is more than three-quarters Latino. Less than half of residents hold a high school diploma; most people do not speak English well, as nearly half are foreign-born. Although residents are employed at similar rates to other New Yorkers, their per capita income is about half the New York average, and a third live below the poverty level, as do nearly half of the children.

At the start of high school, the routines of undocumented children are in many ways indistinguishable from those of their classmates. All children have the right to attend elementary and secondary school. Their families, however, are likely to experience fear and stress because of the possibility of deportation and the financial pressure created by their exclusion from the social welfare system (Dreby, 2015). As teenagers begin to apply for jobs, get a driver's license, and apply for college financial aid, undocumented youth also realize they are excluded from many of the formal institutions in which most young adults participate (Gonzales, 2015). Despite their similar social and legal positions at the start of high school, by their mid-twenties Leo and Aracelis are working in low-wage jobs, Luis is studying and working in Mexico, and Alma has gained a green card.

TWO BROTHERS, TWO PATHS

The immigration stories of brothers Luis and Leo begin when they were six and five years old, respectively, and their father left a rural village in Puebla to come to New York in hopes of better work possibilities. While their father was away, their mother and grandparents cared for them. Many families undergo separation to meet family needs, but it is a challenge to family dynamics. Far away in New York, their father developed a relationship with another woman. In response, their mother left the family, leaving the two sons in their grandparents' care.

The first time Luis and Leo met their stepmother Theresa was when she stepped into the dusty *rancho* where they lived with his grandparents during the years their father was working in New York. Then pregnant, she had come to take ten-year-old Luis and his nine year-old brother to New York. A smuggler guided their crossing of the border and desert, which took a day and left them impressed with their hardy stepmother. When they arrived at their one-bedroom apartment in New York, Luis and Leo gave their smiling father a hug.

Each first attended bilingual schools, and it was at this point that the brothers began to trod different paths. Moving from a rural setting to an urban one made the older Luis nervous, and he spent much of the time indoors. His proclivity to stay inside, which kept him in a safe space where he could study, would reinforce Luis's drive to become a professional. A few years later, the family upgraded to a two-bedroom apartment only a few blocks away; his father had secured a better job at a pizzeria and occasionally earned extra money by singing in a band on weekends.

I first visited their new home in 2008. I noted the spare but tidy furnishings: plastic stacking chairs and aluminum chairs were placed around the plastic-covered dining table in the living room. Manuel, their father, sat in front of shelves that held their small TV/VCR and mini-stereo. Toys for Manuel and Theresa's new baby son were spread across the room's floor. Luis—who returned to Mexico, as you will learn—has not yet seen him in person. One of the two modest bedrooms was for Theresa and Manuel and their baby boy; a sister, Leo, and a second brother slept on the queen mattress in the second. Except for school, soccer practice, and work, Luis spent nearly all his high school years in this apartment.

When he was fifteen, his father helped Luis get a job at a nearby Mexican bakery. He began contributing to the family budget. Luis added, "It [also] gave me money to buy clothes and stuff for soccer." Other boys envied his trendy, masculine North Face jacket in the hallways of ABC High School. Likewise, he showed up to soccer practices fully dressed in an expensive Real Madrid uniform and proceeded to chide others, warning them he was going to shut them down.

Leo experienced a different transition to life in New York. As he moved from elementary school to Luis's junior high school, his marking period grades sunk to the 70s. While some boys admired his brother Luis for being athletic, Leo had to look for other ways to gain status. In seventh grade he smoked marijuana for the first time. Looking back he says, "I didn't really see it as bad but I wasn't with the good crowd." He was then assigned to a large neighborhood high school. Looking for inclusion, safety, and respect, he became involved with a "crew." After failing several classes, he was transferred to a large high school where he remained associated with the crew. "There was nobody keeping us there so we just cut a lot and hung out in [different boroughs] with the 23rd crew," Leo described. He never really developed college aspirations: "I was thinking, 'Where [is the crew] going tomorrow? Will it be dangerous for us to be there?'"

Leo's delinquency diminished his parents' hopes for him. Having given him the advantages of going to American schools, they had expected him to achieve more than they had. Immigrant within-family narratives are often based on immigrant parents' expectation that their children redeem the sacrifices they made in leaving their country of origin, mainly through educational success (Smith, 2005). Luis was making good on this "immigrant bargain." His father explained simply: "I work. Money is not a problem. . . . he just has to study." "[My father] sacrificed for me," Luis said poignantly and then qualified this statement by adding, the sacrifice was "mostly money." His stepmother (whom he just calls "Mom") saw Luis as "a good son, never in trouble."

For Leo, however, his move from school to the gang meant he was not fulfilling his side of the immigrant bargain. He was barely passing his classes and had inconsistent attendance. Luis saw him as a disgrace and stopped talking to him. "But I wasn't part of the bad stuff," Leo said, minimizing his gang involvement. His participation was more about masculine posturing and delinquency than about making money from drug sales or violent crime. Both Leo and his family wanted him to break free from it, which he eventually did. "Wanting [his] own money," Leo found a part-time job "moving boxes" after school for minimum wage. After a few months, "[my bosses] liked the kind of work I did and asked me to work full-time." He accepted the job and dropped out of high school a year short of graduation, working six days a week. His wages offered him status. But he came to feel more constrained as he became older and his salary did not increase much: "My way [to better wages] was to switch jobs."

By 2012, Leo's aspirations had shifted toward regaining a normal day-to-day routine. His father and stepmother had wanted him to finish high school—in acknowledgment of the immigrant bargain—but saw work as a positive step away from his gang association. The challenges of paying for college with undocumented status—no financial aid was available—and the improbability of finding a job commensurate with higher education made working the clear path forward. "I liked it. . . . I was an adult," Leo explained. Steady work took him away from his gang friends and lessened the financial burden on his parents. He began working six days a week for a religious school in New York, commuting by subway. His boss found him dependable.

His steady work pay enabled him to sustain a romantic relationship and emergent family life as he left adolescence. He met Mexican-born Rosa at a party when she was a junior in high school. She liked his adult life, and in 2013 they moved in together when she became pregnant. "I visit [my parents'] home more now that we have Samuel," he recounted. This distance and independence from his parents, which were enabled by his steady salary, improved his relationship with them.

His mobility outside of New York City is limited, however. As an undocumented resident, he is not eligible for a driver's license. He was pulled over for driving without a license in New Jersey, and he paid more than a thousand dollars in lawyer fees and court fines. While it is possible for qualifying undocumented youth to get a driver's license through Deferred Action for Childhood Arrivals (DACA), a program initiated in 2012 that offers temporary and renewable reprieves from deportation and work permits,[3] Leo did not apply. He hinted two years later that his reason for not doing so was that he was worried about being identified as a gang member, which could result in deportation. He explained to me in 2013 that he was focused on "just working for now and being with Rosa . . . getting ready for the baby." He has no plans to change jobs. Leo accepts the limitations of his social position and highlights his accomplishments: "I'm working, I got my family, we have an apartment. I'm alright."

Leo's narrative of family-based redemption through leaving school for work is one path of navigating a world of variegated opportunities. In contrast, Luis developed a different sensibility about growing up as a male undocumented teenager. His responsibilities as an older brother, sports-based masculine confidence, and professional vision pushed him toward college—and far from his family. Luis was a diligent, quiet student who would show up early for our 8:10 a.m. English class. Though in the hallways he mostly avoided the crowds, in the cafeteria he had a few friends with whom he would joke. His grades were mostly average, with no standout subject area. Luis used his brother's experiences as a sign of what not to become. He critiqued his younger brother's drug use and gang association as character weaknesses, contrasting his virtuous behavior with contempt for his brother's: "People I called friends [from my junior high school] tried to get me to smoke weed, but I refused. . . . I tried talking to him about [gangs] but he just wouldn't listen." Many times Luis tried to help Leo with schoolwork, but "he's just lazy." Luis came home after school to do homework and help watch his younger brother and sister.

Luis got his high school diploma on time in June 2007. Without disclosing his legal status to anyone (including me), he had already applied for admission to CUNY. "I always expected to go to college," Luis later told me in 2009, "I had to make it." "He wanted to go to college," his father told me. "We didn't know what it was about . . . how much it cost." He negotiated with his father to pay the annual tuition and fees, about $4,000. His father got an informal loan for the cost, for which they paid $500 in interest. In turn, Luis agreed to pay him every paycheck. When he began at LaGuardia Community College, four of his six classes were remedial classes. He did not do well, but he was driven to keep studying. A course in drawing and design piqued his interest, and he "wanted to work with big [construction] trucks." His professional hopes consolidated around becoming an architect. "When I decided to study architecture, I knew I couldn't stay there. It was so expensive. It was a waste of time and money."

Luis said his best option was studying in the city closest to his family's town in Mexico, which would allow him to make good on the immigrant bargain. Though he "didn't want to come back to Mexico the way [he] left," he transferred his dream of "making it" from getting a U.S. degree to getting a Mexican one: "I just really knew that I wanted to keep on studying until I had a degree." When Luis told his father he wanted to study in Mexico, he met some initial resistance; his father asked, "Why would you go back, after the efforts to bring you here?" But Luis stood his ground: "The cost will be less, I can see *abuelita* [grandma], I'll get my degree." His father realized Luis could stay with relatives forty minutes from the college, college costs would be very low compared to New York, and as a college graduate, he hoped to find a way to return. His father relented.

One year after high school graduation, Luis moved back to Mexico. Four months later, however, he did not pass the entrance exam for the public university. His stepmother fretted that he did not know Spanish as well as he thought. To his credit, Manuel paid for Luis to take private preparatory classes. I visited Luis during this first year, when he moved in with his uncle, who worked two jobs; his homemaker aunt; and their four children. Though the plumbing and interior painting of the home were unfinished, posters of Luis's favorite Mexican soccer club proudly adorned his bedroom's concrete walls. I expected him to show more frustration at not yet being in college, but instead he seemed to be experiencing a happy second childhood. His father sent him a laptop, and his seven year-old sister poignantly sent a school assignment in which she identified Luis as her favorite person. Two years after his high school graduation, Luis retook the university entrance exam and passed.

Transnational Context

Most immigrant youths' adolescence transpires in a transnational context, which is a source of social resources and future possibilities. Immigrants often measure success by criteria in both the country of origin and the country of arrival. Given this dual frame of reference (Ogbu, 1991), the poor, rural town Leo and Luis left when they were preteens remained an important reference point for them. Leo sees that his life is more steady than that enjoyed by many residents of his hometown. Luis moved back to a small city outside Puebla that had fewer than 300 college graduates out of more than 100,000 residents in 2010; he now lives in a Mexican town with 158 college graduates among the more than 30,000 residents (INEGI, 2014). Most residents work in cultivating agriculture and raising livestock. Luis, however, anticipated becoming a professional. "I always wanted to be more than what I am. You saw where I was born. I didn't want to come back as a nobody," Luis told me after he finished his first year of college.

COMPARING GENDERED NARRATIVES

Like Luis and Leo, the immigration stories of Aracelis and Alma begin when they were young children and their family members migrated to New York City. Each grew up in a poor household, Aracelis in a rural *rancho* in Oaxaca and Alma on the outskirts of a city in Puebla. Each would face a different set of difficult choices stemming from her lack of legal residence, yet one remained mired in marginality, and the other emerged to achieve mainstream success.

Gendered scripts offer teenagers a set of accepted behaviors to perform femininity and masculinity within their contexts (Eder, Evans, & Parker, 1995). Leo and Luis had done their best to fulfill expectations for a masculine young adult; indeed, those expectations had pushed their paths in different directions (Ovink, 2014). Each brother prided himself on fulfilling the male-breadwinner norm (Smith, 2008), and in some ways high school dropout Leo fulfills this better than his college graduate brother (who has not yet seen a quick economic return on his degree). Aracelis and Alma faced pressure to fulfill gendered roles as well, especially to be modest and do well in school (Eder et al., 1995; López, 2003). These performances in school align with teachers' behavioral expectations and are linked to greater educational attainment but also more relationships with in-school personnel (Suárez-Orozco, Suárez-Orozco, & Todorova, 2008). On the other hand, men physically dominated the space in which Alma and Aracelis, their mothers, and sisters lived. The family environment in which they grew up was marked by violent fathers, whose physical abuse was often related to heavy drinking. Teenage boyfriends also tried to enforce the girls' modesty. In Aracelis's and Alma's narratives, gender norms leave these two young women vulnerable to predation, but also offer them a means to legalization. Leo, in contrast, was excluded from DACA because of his teenage gang association.

Aracelis

When Aracelis crossed the border at age eleven using her American-born sister's passport, she had not seen her parents or brother or sisters in five years. Her grandmother had been raising her in what Aracelis described as a rural idyll with "trees all around, trees of mangoes, red and yellow, by the river where I used to swim . . . where you get to know everyone." Her mother had told her daughter the trip was for a vacation, so they could see each other after their years of separation. Aracelis arrived in New York, full of imposing buildings and "people you don't get to know." Once she realized she was staying for good, she "never wanted to move far from [the] neighborhood," because the new urban context was "uncomfortable."

Like for Leo and Luis, language shaped Aracelis's transition into this new urban space. Even in a middle school with a bilingual program, classmates teased those who only spoke Spanish. "I felt embarrassed about [speaking English] cause I saw this girl and [the other students] were making fun of her because of her English and I decided not to speak in front of the class." Then, "I felt stressed because [high school] was all in English." Nonetheless, Aracelis kept her grades in the 80s, and unlike many of her high school classmates, she consistently did her classwork and homework.

Academics took priority over social engagements, and she had few in-school friendships. After school, she went home to her family's converted two-bedroom apartment, which was nearby. In high school, Aracelis said, "My mother never lets me go outside, [hang out] with other people because they think I would do things I shouldn't do. By now [as a senior in high school] I'm used to staying in my room. Outside I'm nervous." She liked to think a lot, she said. Her two younger sisters called her boring.

As a high school junior, Aracelis set her sights on going to college in Mexico. A mix of factors—personal, professional, and legal status-related—guided her aspiration. Once she passed the entrance exam, she reasoned, she could accomplish her dream of becoming a pediatrician to help people in her native village. This was one way to make good on her grandmother's and mother's desire for her to "be something." She was also excited to see her grandmother and other family members again. And the cost would be significantly lower—because without financial aid, her family could not afford the upfront cost of tuition in an American college. Aracelis considered herself stronger in Spanish and would not be held back by the need to write in English in college, she reasoned.

Her family also valued education, but with their limited financial and educational resources their social support was more influential. They ate together and went to the park on weekends, but she sensed they favored her younger sisters, who had lived longer in the United States. Her stepfather hit her mother and her, and her mental health suffered. She was hospitalized after having a panic attack, and hospital administrators asked repeatedly for her American identification and health insurance, but she had neither. Her high school advisor[4] knew about her fragile mental health—she spoke Spanish, something Aracelis liked—but told her, "I don't get too personal." Her guidance counselor had learned that she was undocumented and told her she could not provide her much help about college. Her parents, neither of whom had graduated high school, nonetheless repeated that studying "was the only way to get ahead" and encouraged her to continue to achieve, even though they felt like they could not guide her. Despite these obstacles, Aracelis still graduated a semester early with an 85 average.

Her family and school educators were relieved when Aracelis decided to attend a Mexican university in Puebla: "I wanted to study [there] because they have more freedom [compared to Oaxaca].[5] My uncle studied there, he has experience about college there." Her limited social contacts, however, left her lonely. She did not qualify for her area of study in the entrance exam and was rejected. She began to drink alcohol for the first time, pressured by a new male friend who played in a band. Their relationship moved too fast for her, and her peers began spreading rumors that she had gone unhinged, having had sex and an abortion. She despaired and denied the rumors about the abortion. Her mother told her to come back to New York. Aracelis hoped that if she moved to the United States, she would get DACA status, which would make life more livable.

She crossed the border in 2013 in the same way as the first time. She applied for DACA and unexpectedly received it. She told me, DACA "gives you courage . . . it's like you're supposed to be here. They can't take you away." She excitedly asked me about the possibilities of going to college. But because DACA does not bestow any financial aid and she needed to work, college remained just an aspiration: "I can't go to school while I'm working, there's no time. But I dream of it." Instead, she endures the daily grind as a cashier six days a week, up to twelve hours a day, a job that her mother helped her get.

As when she was in high school, family and relationship dynamics both improved and worsened after her return. Her stepfather stopped hitting her mother, yet her relationship with her sisters was strained, and she moved out on her own. The Mexican community became more central in her life, because her legal status limited her mainstream engagements. Her coworkers are predominantly other undocumented Mexican young women.

Three things have kept her mentally afloat. First, she is introverted, and her inner world gives her control and an outlet for her creativity. Her troubles pushed her to write her own fantasy stories. She delved into manga and anime in high school and later into magic realism. She sees these outlets as a means to stay intellectually stimulated while she waits for some change in her legal status so she can attend college and "change my life." Seven years after graduating early from high school, she retains this sense that she will eventually get back on that college-bound track. Third, her sometimes turbulent four-year relationship with a boyfriend, also undocumented, gave her and her parents the sense that she was still accomplishing life goals. She took satisfaction in the simple pleasure of being able to spend her free day with someone.

Her long-term path changed when she and her boyfriend moved in together, with another couple whom they did not know. The male member of the couple violently attacked her. The experience was terrifying for Aracelis. Though she was initially too scared to call police, her neighbors drove her to the hospital. A social worker there put her in contact with a battered women's shelter, and a lawyer there realized Aracelis might qualify for a special visa for domestic abuse survivors. Meanwhile she renewed her DACA, dreaming of "when . . . if I get [a U-visa] I will get financial aid [for college] and I will quit my job. I'll get a part-time job." Three years later, however, she is waiting for her U-visa application to be approved. Despite her continuing college dreams, her contact with college-educated people and mainstream institutions has lessened since high school. When I worried that her academic readiness had also become rusty in those seven years, she showed me the Spanish-language copy of the Gabriel García Márquez book she was reading. For the time being, she was still dreaming beyond the present.

Alma

In contrast to Aracelis's journey, Alma's path has curved away from her humble, unstable childhood toward undergraduate success. It has also been a very contingent path, given the disadvantages of her social position in a family with an undocumented brother and parents in North Park. Her teachers' recognition of her abilities early in her U.S. schooling, her successful attempts to obtain help and mentors, the existence of free legal resources, and, of course, her hard work put her in an advantageous position.

Life for Alma's family in Puebla was a struggle for sustenance and was marred by her father's alcohol-inspired violence. Her grandparents had achieved relative stability by immigrating to New York, and her family followed a few years later. Alma was four years old when they moved, younger than Luis, Leo, and Aracelis when they migrated to the United States. The family moved into her uncle's Brooklyn two-bedroom apartment, already crowded with his family; they then moved to her grandparents' apartment in the same neighborhood.

Though she did not experience the same family separation as Aracelis, Alma's family dynamics were not easy to navigate. Her parents separated after her mother found a safer relationship with a coworker three years after they had immigrated. Alma remembers it as her mother protecting herself from being beaten by her father. Alma's brother, who had immigrated with her, stayed with his father. Her father got treatment for his alcoholism, and she saw him occasionally. But her stepfather, whom she saw more regularly, became a father figure. With time, however, he, too, faded from the picture, and her mother got a new boyfriend.

The stability in this phase of Alma's life was provided by her elementary school, where she had mastered English, loved her teachers, and received good grades. One elementary school teacher nominated her for a citywide award, and that nomination enabled her to enroll in a special program in a better middle school. This new context extended her intercultural exposure, as she moved from having black and Latino classmates to mostly Asian and European ones.

This boost was temporary, but its effects would be lasting; she entered an average high school as a particularly strong student and was placed directly into many tenth-grade classes. Her family dynamics and her legal status would hinder her advancement, however.

The uncertainty of her undocumented status left Alma in a precarious situation. Yet she felt that her status had unintended but positive consequences: she saw it as helping her develop into a better person. "Being undocumented, you don't get any help so you really have you be on your toes." This resourcefulness, combined with her feeling more comfortable telling adults about her status than her classmates, would help her later to find legal resources, get scholarships, and gain valuable internships. As she told me, her friends thought "I was an arrogant kid who thought highly of herself. I was like, you don't know what's going on [with my legal status], I might not go to college. So that's when it became like 'we didn't know, if we did, we might have been more sensitive, like sorry?'" She had not totally understood the implications of not being able to apply to FAFSA for financial aid; she had assumed her good grades would make her eligible for aid. Guidance counselors asked her how she was going to pay for college, because her undocumented status made it impossible to obtain financial aid, and available scholarships were few.

Around this time, she faced another type of risk, this time from within her household. Her mother's new, younger boyfriend—he was closer in age to Alma than her mother—developed a creepy habit of standing near the bunk bed she slept in. She woke up to find him there with his hand under the sheet. Her boyfriend and her brother advised her to tell someone if it happened again. "It happened to me like four or five times; the fifth time, he was like closer like by my thigh. . . . I was really scared, I was like what are you doing? He was like, 'I was looking for the phone' . . . my ex was really angry, like no one can touch you.'" She knew, however, that her mother, who was pregnant, depended on the boyfriend for rent. When Alma confronted her mother about it, her mother told her it would be best if she moved out. Later, Alma would not invite her mother to her high school graduation or thank her in her valedictorian speech.

The two obstacles blocking her dreams collided. Alma tearfully told a teacher about her problems, which led to two unusually helpful connections. Ms. Ascencion, who had a friend who worked in college financial aid, helped connect Alma to available resources, and she was offered a partial scholarship by a college in the CUNY system. Even more enduring would be the impact of connecting her with an organization that provides social and legal help to teens. She went through an intake interview with a lawyer, who helped her apply for special immigrant juvenile status (SIJS), based on the abuse from her father and her mother's boyfriend. A year later, they told her she was eligible for that status. Though she had finished her first year in college, she would need a guardian. A second teacher from her high school with whom she was close and who did not have children of her own, offered to serve in that role. Her teachers felt close to her and even cried over her predicament. She found their support incredible: "That's the thing I loved about [high school] like they really personalized your issue sometimes. Someone said if I couldn't cover the cost, they would cover it for the first year or first two years."

Alma received her green card two years later and was finally able to visit her family in Mexico, more than fifteen years after leaving. The normal travails of college seemed slight in comparison, and she graduated summa cum laude with a double major. Now in her first full-time job, Alma has found mentors to help her navigate her new professional world. Her ability to make good on her potential stands in stark contrast to that of Aracelis, or even Leo or Luis.

CONCLUSION

These cases provide a platform for richly contextualized discussion on how immigrant youth remain active participants in the challenging processes of immigration and integration. These immigrant youths' sense of space blends aspects of the hometown and New York society. These dual frames of reference motivate their mobility and creative use of transnational resources, helping them negotiate a highly contingent coming of age.

The first contingency comes from family separation, which disrupts family dynamics even when families try their hardest to be supportive and stay in touch. The family separation experienced during the process of immigration increases the importance of extended family, expanding the potential spaces of belonging and the possibilities of transnational life. Even after immigrating to New York, transnational life becomes a space for making good on one's dreams.

The uncertainties related to undocumented status compel these youths to continually strategize and restrategize about how to fulfill their dreams. Undocumented youth dream of gaining legal status in unclear, shifting political circumstances. Until they obtain legal status—and most cannot—low-wage work opportunities are more assured than upward educational opportunities.

Agency is also gendered. Expectations for being masculine push some, like Leo, to flirt with gang membership and later to work and support a family. Expectations for being feminine make educational achievement a sensible outlet for women, but also assert male prerogative, as experienced in the insecure domestic spaces of Aracelis and Alma. When male prerogative surpasses what is legally allowed, policy affords some protection for young victims. The counter-stories presented in this chapter highlight the resilience and personhood of these young people in the face of hostility from bureaucracy, law enforcement, and the public.

QUESTIONS FOR REFLECTION AND GROUP DISCUSSION

1. Describe the contexts in which native-born Americans become adults. How might the contexts in which immigrant youth integrate into society differ?
2. How did Luis, Leo, Aracelis, and Alma end up in such different spaces with such different lives?
3. How could social workers, teachers, or other adults intervene in these youths' lives?

NOTES

1. All names of people and places within the city are pseudonyms in accordance with IRB protocol.
2. Undocumented status concerns those who have overstayed a temporary visa or have entered the country without customs processing.
3. At the time of publication, the future of the DACA program looks bleak. The program was rescinded by President Trump, but three federal judges have issued stays to allow it to continue.
4. Advisors have a half-class period with students to cover nonacademic issues. Aracelis had this advisor for two years.
5. Oaxaca had several instances of government repression of teacher strikes and other demonstrations at that time. U.S. anarchist Brad Will was shot filming a strike there.

REFERENCES

Chavez, L. R. (2008). *The Latino threat: Constructing immigrants, citizens, and the nation*. Stanford, CA: Stanford University Press.

Clandinin, D. J., & Connelly, F. M. (2004). *Narrative inquiry: Experience and story in qualitative research*. San Francisco: Jossey-Bass.

Delgado, R. (1989). Storytelling for oppositionists and others: A plea for narrative. *Michigan Law Review, 87*(8), 2411–2441.

Dreby, J. (2015). *Everyday illegal: When policies undermine immigrant families*. Oakland: University of California Press.

Eder, D., Evans, C. C., & Parker, S. (1995). *School talk: Gender and adolescent culture*. New Brunswick, NJ: Rutgers University Press.

Gonzales, R. G. (2015). *Lives in limbo: Undocumented and coming of age in America*. Oakland: University of California Press.

Instituto Nacional Estadisticas y Geographia (INEGI). 2014. "México en cifras." Retrieved from http://www.inegi.org.mx/.

Knight, M. G., Norton, N. E. L., Bentley, C. C., & Dixon, I. R. (2004). The power of black and Latina/o counterstories: Urban families and college-going processes. *Anthropology & Education Quarterly, 35*(1), 99–120.

López, N. (2003). *Hopeful girls, troubled boys: race and gender disparity in urban education.* New York: Routledge.

MacAdams, D. P. (1997). *The stories we live by: Personal myths and the making of the self.* New York: Guilford Press.

Massaro, T. M. (1989). Empathy, legal storytelling, and the rule of law: New words, old wounds? *Michigan Law Review, 87*(8), 2099–2127.

Ogbu, J. U. (1993). Differences in cultural frames of reference. *International Journal of Behavioral Development, 16*(3), 483–506.

Ovink, S. M. (2014). "'They always call me an investment': Gendered familism and Latino/a college pathways." *Gender & Society, 28*(2), 265–288.

Portes, A., & Rumbaut, R. G. (2001). *Legacies: The story of the immigrant second generation.* Berkeley: University of California Press.

Smith, R. (2005). *Mexican New York: Transnational lives of new immigrants.* Berkeley: University of California Press.

Smith, R. C. (2008). Horatio Alger lives in Brooklyn: Extrafamily support, intrafamily dynamics, and socially neutral operating identities in exceptional mobility among children of Mexican immigrants. *Annals of the American Academy of Political and Social Science, 620*(1), 270–290.

Suárez-Orozco, C., Suárez-Orozco, M. M., & Todorova, I. (2008). *Learning a new land: Immigrant students in American society.* Cambridge, MA: Belknap Press.

Zong, J., & Batalova, J. (2017, March 8). Frequently requested statistics on immigrants and immigration in the United States. Retrieved from https://www.migrationpolicy.org/article/frequently-requested-statistics-immigrants-and-immigration-united-states.

Chapter Four

"HEAR ME"

Collaborating with Youth to Address Sexual Exploitation

MARGOT K. JACKSON, VERA CAINE, JANICE HUBER, AND
MUNEERAH AMIN VASTANI

BEGINNINGS

My days in the summer of 2013 had been filled with research and also clinical outreach through a student group called SHINE, when Ross's email arrived in my inbox. I often think about this initial request to engage in work alongside a community agency to address work with youth or young children who are at risk for sexual exploitation. In the initial email request Ross mentioned that the "purpose is to discuss possible collaboration [to create a] program, possibly involving research, to reduce sexual risk in female-bodied children and adolescents." Knowing where the agency was located, I called back memories of projects that had involved participants in the same neighborhood. It had been years ago that I had spent time providing nightly outreach programs to people working in the sex trade. I remember the busy nights driving along the street, stopping on occasions to chat or provide clean needles, knowing always that harm reduction was critical. It was around the same time that I worked with several indigenous women, including Tammy, Debra, and Deanna, inquiring into their experiences of living with HIV. Stories and experiences started to merge as I joined the conversation at the community agency. The voices of Tammy, Debra, and Deanna still echo in my heart and mind. Engaging in this new project meant revisiting what I had learned and reimagining how to work with difficult experiences.

As Vera recalls her initial experiences in the community agency, called North Central Children & Youth, we are reminded that we have been working within this project for more than four years at the time of writing. Soon after the initial request to assist the community agency in addressing the high risk for sexual exploitation of female children who attended their programs, Margot, Janice, and, two years later, Muneerah joined the project team. Members of the community agency were very much invested in their work and felt the need to implement interventions to address the issues they saw in their daily work—issues that were indicators of sexual exploitation. All of us were most interested in the voices of those most affected, the female children, and we knew that we could not address any form of intervention without them. As we sat down to write about our research project, Vera reminded us of how it began.

CALLING FORTH MEMORIES

I still remember my initial meetings with members of the community agencies in 2013. There was such a strong focus on finding interventions that could be applied within their own context. There were moments where I wish I could have pointed them to an easy and straightforward "fix." But I knew from living alongside Debra, Deanna, and Tammy that this did not exist, that there was no single program that could or did alter the trajectory of their lives. In thinking with Debra, Deanna, and Tammy's life experiences, it was evident that some of their most significant life changes were due to the long-term relationships they had formed with people in their lives. Sitting with Tammy at her kitchen table, I remember asking her about what interventions she thought would make a difference. Her response didn't come as a surprise: "Why don't you ask those kids?" Tammy continued along the same vein. "What I tell you and what I think is based on all the stuff that happened to me. I think it's different for the kids now. I don't know them enough to know what would work."

Tammy's insights shaped our subsequent collaboration. Vera became much more firm in her response to the community agency that we could not offer an intervention; what we could do instead was engage with youth as narrative inquirers to think through possibilities alongside them. In this way, the youth did not become the problem or the focus, but could become part of the solution in meaningful ways. While members of the community agency recognized that this would be a more engaged and participatory way to find solutions, there was, at least initially, also a reluctance to take this path. They raised questions about the process, how long it would take, and whether we could find an intervention that could be replicated. While these questions still sometimes surface, they have lessened in intensity. As with much of the research we have engaged in as narrative inquirers, we knew that, before we could do anything, we needed to become part of the lives of people who were seeking and providing services at the community agency. In this chapter we focus on the unfolding of the project over time and how we as researchers are positioned within the project. As narrative inquirers it is important to us to show who we are and are becoming as researchers and people in relation alongside the youth. As Vera continued to reflect on these beginnings, she turned back to her early memories of being at the community agency and fragments of moments she noted in some of her field notes.

FIRST ENCOUNTERS

It was another Thursday evening and I arrived at the community agency just before 5 p.m. I would come every week to be at the agency, to connect with youth, and to build relationships. The evenings unfolded almost always in similar ways. Youth were arriving at the agency after school had ended and before it was suppertime. The kitchen was always busy with supper preparations, and one or two of the staff worked with some of the youth in the meal preparation—home-cooked meals were an important part of each day. Between the time the youth arrived and supper, the focus was on helping everyone to complete their homework or to play sports. I loved playing sports most of all: it was easier to make connections, and it shifted the focus away from each person to play. We, the staff, youth and children, and on occasions people like me who were considered volunteers would eat supper all together—sometimes ten youth or children were present; at other times there were more than twenty-five around the table. After supper we would engage in activities again, and then slowly everyone would leave. It seemed like a simple rhythm that guided my engagement, and slowly, ever so slowly, did I get to know the side stories, cover stories, and hard stories that lived within each of the youth.

As we now think with these memories of Vera's and each of our first encounters, we are once again reminded of the significance of working alongside children, youth, staff, and one another. This work required a collaborative effort. We are reminded too that in trying to understand the life of others, this slow, gradual, and ongoing making of relationships lives at the heart of what we do as narrative inquirers. This focus on the relation sets our work apart from other narrative research in which the told stories are often the central focus of analysis. And there is reciprocity in these ongoing movements toward relationships: slowly, we metaphorically fall in love with participants. Just as we gradually came to know aspects of the everyday lives of many of the children, youth, and staff, they in turn came to know aspects of our everyday lives. Slowly, ever so slowly, we started to know one another as people in the midst of composing lives.

TAKING A TURN TOWARD THE RESEARCH

Vera, Janice, and Margot have all been engaged in multiple narrative inquiries with children, youth, families, and people who face multiple social vulnerabilities (Clandinin et al. 2016). In their work they draw on the work of Clandinin and Connelly, pioneers of narrative inquiry research. Narrative inquiry is described as both a methodology for studying experiences and a storied phenomenon (Clandinin and Connelly 2000; Clandinin, 2013). Our work is guided by the following definition of narrative inquiry: "People shape their daily lives by stories of who they and others are and as they interpret their past in terms of these stories. Story, in the current idiom, is a portal through which a person enters the world and by which their experience of the world is interpreted and made personally meaningful" (Connelly and Clandinin 2006, 375). Given the relational nature of narrative inquiry, relational ethics guides our work alongside participants and each other. Each narrative inquiry study is shaped by the three-dimensional narrative inquiry space of temporality, place, and sociality.

As our work unfolded, it become clear that this methodological approach would allow us to come alongside the youth in ways that opened up spaces of possibilities to hear their stories and to learn from their experiences. Drawing on pragmatist scholars, this focus on experience allows us to think *with* stories, rather than merely *about* stories. "As narrative inquirers, we do not try to get outside of stories. We linger in the complex layers of the intertwined and interwoven stories" (Clandinin et al. 2016, 20). This ontological commitment to thinking *with* stories and to finding ourselves part of the storied landscapes and experiences creates a particular vantage point into experiences. It is here that we begin to understand that lives are always in the making, are always still unfolding—that neither experiences nor lives can be fixed in time.

In the fall of 2016, feeling that our months of participation at North Central Children & Youth had supported us in developing strong relationships with several young women, we organized a meeting at a restaurant, with the help of Mary, the director, to talk with them about the possibility of moving into one-on-one conversations. In this chapter the focus is on our relationships with the youth and the agency as the work unfolded, rather than on the individual participants. Therefore, we provide only brief glimpses of each participant here.

By the end of the meeting we had decided who would meet with which girl, with the goal of holding six conversations with each young girl between then and spring 2017. By spring, Muneerah had joined the research team, and to introduce her and the youth to one another, as well as to meet with them as a whole group, we set up a meeting in late March. In her field notes Janice described this meeting:

Backpacks, coats, and three youth greeted me as I entered the upstairs room at North Central. As I set down the bags of food I inwardly noted the similarities between this scene and my similar in age daughter and her friends as Betsy, Brenda, Angelina, and Nicole were simultaneously on their phones, eating, and chatting. When Mary, the director, and Karen came up the stairs, Betsy and Nicole were just beginning to tell stories of having first met in kindergarten at a school in an east central neighborhood in the city, followed by memories of shaving their heads because of lice, of their clothing being made fun of by other children when they were new to a school, and of a teacher they found "creepy." Karen joined into the youths's conversation. Mary could not stay, and as she was leaving, Muneerah arrived. In between Mary's departure and Muneerah's arrival, the youth's storytelling had continued as they remembered other memories of going to the same school for a time, then not seeing one another for some months or a full school year when being in and out of foster care shifted their lives; stories of themselves as young youth, when they first started coming to North Central Children & Youth were also told. Karen had been coming to North Central Children & Youth the longest, and it was through her that Betsy and Nicole learned of North Central Children & Youth. Shared, too, were memories of times when Betsy and Nicole had not gotten along with one another, both in school and at North Central Children & Youth. For example, when Betsy remembered, "What I wanted to do to Nicole every single time she pissed me off, I'm like, 'Well, I need to calm myself.'" Nicole reflected, "Oh, yeah . . . we've gotten heated, . . . I think I've still got some messages online of you yelling at my mom."

While before this we had sometimes gathered as a whole group, those gatherings had often been organized with more of a focus on the participatory unfolding of our work together; for example, to collectively share and discuss the university research ethics forms and protocols and, at other times, checking in about how the one-on-one conversations were going. This March 2017 gathering was one of the first times when a number of the girls and some of us were able to engage in collective, relational sharing and in thinking with one another's stories as a whole group. We draw on some of Janice's field notes and the transcript of the conversation to give a sense of the tentative, co-constructed process that emerged during this gathering:

As a former teacher and now teacher educator, my heartbeat always quickens when memories of school are shared in research conversations. This started to happen early in the conversation when, as we were talking about ways that being in foster care influenced their lives, Nicole remembered that "in school . . . they'll explain something and then go, 'Well, I know none of you guys here have experienced it,' but there's the girl . . . going in her head, 'I have experienced it. Like, this has happened to me.'" Continuing, Nicole had commented that when a teacher made comments such as these, she would sometimes respond, "Yeah, well you're looking at someone that it happened to."

As this sharing and thinking with stories continued, Janice noted,

Soon, the markers and chart paper Muneerah and I had brought started to fill up as the youth took up our suggestion of recording aspects of their experiences they wanted to remember for our future collaborative curriculum design work. After deciding to name their list "Teamwork Ideas" a pattern emerged: as the youth, Muneerah, and I told and thought with one another's stories the youth stopped every few moments to decide what they wanted to add to the list:
-Teamwork Ideas

For example, early in the conversation, Nicole shared the following:

We were talking about this girl who was in a very serious court case about something that happened with a family member of hers. This was junior high, and
immediately the teacher thought like "None of you kids [have] ever been through
this," and I'm going, "I'm going through it right now, I'm dealing with a huge
court case because of something that happened to me and you are trying to
make it seem like nothing has happened to me, and I don't appreciate it." (Excerpt from transcript)

Carefully thinking with Nicole's story, the girls decided to add to their
list:

Ignorance is bliss

Although only a few moments earlier I had said I would be quiet, I could
not help share what Nicole's story was making me think of: *"That's a dangerous thing . . . when you think about teachers spending that amount of time
with you."* Already as I spoke these words, I was starting to feel inward tensions. Then came another of Nicole's stories that I have yet to stop thinking with:

I actually, I tried to tell one teacher what was happening and I started getting it out
and she was like "I don't want to know, I don't want to hear it, I don't want to hear
about this" and I was like, "You're my teacher and you are here to protect me and
you don't want to hear about what's happening to me?" Like she refused to listen
to what I had to say. I was like, "Like, I'm having some trouble, this is what happened to me." And she was, "I don't want to know, I don't want to be involved.

Again, the youth's list grew as they thought with this story:

Fairytale world (marked with a large X)

Nicole then continued:

Being an eleven-year-old girl and hearing from a teacher that she doesn't want to
know about what's happening, is—is especially hard when a teacher's job is to

protect her students. And . . . I want to be a teacher and if I heard that my student was going through something like this [sexual exploitation], I would immediately have done something. I would have said, "Ok, tell me everything that is happening. I am going to call the police or I am going to call child services; something is going to happen."

Again, the youth's list grew as they thought with this story:

Two faces (meaning to be aware of, awake to people who say one thing but live differently from what they say, especially when you depend on that person)

As the conversation continued, so did the list:

Self-awareness
Valuing self
Grandparents
Mental health
Inclusive, noncompetitive physical education & sports teams (playing for fun &
    health benefits)

And then:

Don't mind my language
But those groups
[GSA and Anti-Bullying]
Don't do shit . . .

[Our school]
Doesn't even have one . . .
Whenever you try and tell someone
That you're being bullied
They don't do shit . . .

When I . . . was getting bullied
I was the one
Getting in trouble
Not the bullies . . .

[Anti-bully clubs]
They don't exist
I have never heard of them
We have Anti-Bullying Day
Pink Shirt Day
Where all we get
Is popcorn
And compliments
What is that supposed to do? . . .

I've used the metaphor before
When I'm being bullied
And I'm trying to tell someone
It feels like I'm just standing there

Screaming at them
And they're just staring
Straight through me
Like I'm a ghost . . .

I'm standing there
Explaining what's happening
I'm yelling at them

And they're sitting there
Doing this [shows gesture for making a checkmark on a page]

   The final words added to the list were:

Hear me!

   As a team we talked often with each other about our experiences. It was important that we listened to each other, so that we could better hear the experiences the youth were sharing with us. It was in these ways, while we were immersed in the ordinary lives of the girls, that we also began to more closely frame our collective work on sexual exploitation.

BACKGROUND OF SEXUAL EXPLOITATION

Worldwide, children and youth are at a high risk of sexual predation and exploitation (Lalor and McElvaney 2010). The terms "sexual exploitation" and "sexual abuse" are used synonymously in law and literature to describe acts of sexual behavior toward underage children. Thomson et al. define sexual exploitation of children and adolescence as "a continuum of behaviors and circumstances: from youth who are sexually abused by a family member or friend, to those who are on the run without financial resources and forced to trade sex for food and shelter, to those who are victims of sexual assault or trafficking, and to those who are actively involved in prostitution" (2011, 1). Sexual exploitation can take various forms, including sex tourism, sexual abuse, child prostitution, child trafficking, and child pornography (Jaffer and Brazeau 2011; UNICEF 2006). Sexual abuse and exploitation are also referred to as child abuse because they constitute physical, emotional, and psychological abuse (Whitaker et al. 2008). Sexual exploitation, including trafficking, has generated many political and academic debates. Bernstein (2012, 233) calls us to have a greater "and more nuanced attention to the operations of gender and sexual politics within mainstream analyses of contemporary modes of punishment, as well as a careful consideration of the neoliberal carceral state within feminist discussions of gender, sexuality, and the law." This is an important call and requires the careful consideration of complex factors.

In Canada, little research and program development have been done with a focus on the implementation of programming seeking to prevent sexual exploitation at the community level, or on the recognition and enhancement of protective factors of the youth themselves. In British Columbia, Saewyc and colleagues (2008) conducted the largest study to date of Canadian street youth, finding that the common pathways for sexual exploitation included being a sexual minority, leaving home, coming from a home with domestic violence, being involved with government care, and using alcohol or marijuana. They found the average age for the first incident of sexual exploitation was between thirteen and fifteen years old, and these incidents involved indigenous youth disproportionately. In the same study, youth reported that the top three items exchanged for sex were money, drugs and shelter; although 50 percent of the sample acknowledged participating in these transactions, they did not see them as exploitation. Much of the research to date has been focused on children leaving commercial sexual exploitation situations or youth who are currently street-involved. Little research has examined those "at risk" for sexual exploitation due to their environment of limited choices (Homma, Nicholson, and Saewyc 2012; Melrose 2012; Pearce 2014). In addition, there have been few, if any, long-term multidisciplinary and participatory narrative inquiries exploring children at risk.

LOCAL REALITIES WITHIN

The communities that the North Central Children & Youth agency serves encompass families who represent Edmonton's lowest family incomes, have the highest proportion of rental dwellings and single-parent homes, and report the highest incidence of crime and family violence in the entire city (City of Edmonton 2011). A large majority of youth who attend the North Central Children & Youth are of First Nations status, non-status, urban-off reserve, visiting from reserve, or identify as Métis. While the status differs between these groups, all would identify as being Indigenous. Of the youth who attend programs, approximately 30 percent are in care of or are wards of Children's Services. These services are offered by the provincial Ministry. North Central also supports a small yet growing population of new immigrant and first-generation Canadian youth for whom English is an additional language.

Increasingly, North Central is called to meet the needs of ten- to sixteen-year-old female children, because they have often been victims of discrimination, neglect, and family violence and are exposed to sexual situations and abuse at an early age. As a result, they may use drugs and alcohol, engage in high-risk behaviors including unprotected sex, and cause themselves physical harm (e.g., cutting). This high-risk behavior leaves them vulnerable to exploitation by drug dealers, the sex trade, gang recruitment, and criminal involvement.

WHY DOES THIS WORK MATTER?

Early education and intervention are exceedingly important in preventing sexual exploitation and enhancing the existing protective factors of children and youth. Unfortunately, there are few services for younger teens, especially those who have not yet become entrenched on the streets (Saewyc and Edinburgh 2010). This missed opportunity for intervention at an earlier age has serious physical and mental health repercussions for children and youth. These include increased rates of sexually transmitted infection, pregnancy, physical and sexual abuse, and substance abuse, as well as of psychological disorders such as depression, self-harming behaviors, and trauma (Saewyc and Edinburgh 2010; Lokanc-Diluzo and Reilly 2010). Current service gaps include research and programming that are community led, enhance protective factors of children and youth, use peer leadership and mentoring, and are driven by the children and youth themselves. Youth who have been sexually exploited need interventions that are multifaceted, focused on both structural and individual factors, and participatory in nature (Feinstein and O'Kane 2008; Kingsley and Mark 2001). Honoring the voices, agency, and human right to be involved in planning interventions is essential to designing effective programs for youth sexual health (Feinstein and O'Kane 2008; Justice Institute of BC 2011; Kingsley and Mark 2001; MacDonald 2011; Villa-Torres and Svanemyr 2015).

TURNING TOWARD INDIVIDUAL YOUTH

Our sense of the importance of involving the youth in all stages of developing possible interventions that had meaning and relevance to the lives of the youth we worked with was affirmed on so many occasions. We knew our work needed to be slow. We wanted to be able to sustain our relationships with youth, the agency itself, and others who lived at the periphery of our work, including younger children, youth who chose not to participate, or youth who identified as male. Long before the meeting with the youth that Janice talked about, we focused on making relationships with the children and youth at North Central Children & Youth. This work was very slow and, as Margot recalled, opened up many questions:

MEETING THE TWINS

As I entered the gymnasium at the community agency I noticed two youths playing volleyball. They were both very similar in appearance with long brown hair, athletic builds and a strong presence in the large gym filled with children of various ages. I watched the youths as they finished up their game and went with them to have snacks in the main area of the agency. It was no surprise to me when I learned that the youths were sisters and senior members of their high school volleyball team. As the months came and went, we would often connect during visits at the agency; in time they agreed to become participants in the research study. This did not come without challenges! As the youths were so actively involved with sports, it became difficult to find times and dates to meet to share their experiences. This was a different experience for me as most of the youth with whom I had worked previously were not as engaged in extracurricular activities; these youths were different. They were extremely committed to sports and school, as well as their community church which did not leave a great deal of time to meet with me. Slowly I learned about their lives and how hard they had worked at finding meaning and belonging within a challenging world. For me, this opened so many questions: What motivated them to be so involved? What did sports and this church offer to them? Did their leadership skills and inner strengths evolve due to their involvement with these activities?

As our journey alongside the youth continued, we met many others and also continued our conversations with staff at the community agency. Over time we learned that the two girls who played volleyball together lived with their grandfather; they were and continue to be passionate about sports. Their lives were guided by their affiliation to a church. After joining our project Muneerah recalled the following:

MEETING KAREN

It was a splendid afternoon of May 2017 and I was sitting in the office learning about North Central Children & Youth's aims and ambitions, their success stories, and the impact they have for the youth and their families. Suddenly the door opened and a girl with a bright face and some serious expressions appeared right in the middle of the door, asking something about plans for the evening. After she left, Mary started talking about her; she was one of the children who joined North Central Children & Youth from a very young age. Mary mentioned to me that her journey from early childhood to adolescence was not easy. It was not long after when I met this amazing girl named Kira, and we talked at length about her life experiences. It was difficult initially, talking with Kira. But as time unfolded, so did our stories and we found the space and comfort to share our life experiences. As we were sharing our views about life Karen laughed and said, "It's hard, but, you know, what can you do?" This gave me a little sense of the hardship she went through in the early years of her life. She too talked about how important stability is to her now. I was very impressed with her courage. As Karen said, "My life has been really hard, I would say. But, I'm strong and I—that's what a lot of people tell me." I kept wondering where she gets such courage and who makes her strong? Who does she look up to? What's her source of hope and self-confidence? And where does this resilience come from? As time passed, Karen shared: "Well. I guess in Grade 8, was, like, when I was hanging out with, like, really bad people and I was 13 years old. . . . I remember I wouldn't go to school for, like, two months because I was just not really into the whole school thing when I was younger just because I was—I made up really bad excuses, like I was too tired. And I would, just hang out with people that, you know, did drugs . . . like tobacco, weed, yeah Marijuana, (they) smoked, and drank, and I obviously was a part of that."

"Thinking back, my teachers helped me a lot—a lot, in Grade 8." Apart from school, the organizations like North Central Children & Youth play a crucial role in bridging the gap between school and families. Karen recalls, "I grew up there (North Central Children & Youth), well, I think I was in Grade 2 when I went there (North Central Children & Youth) for the first time, and I'm in Grade 12 now. . . . actually, you know, it's always been a good place I can call home. And, everyone there's like—they're pretty awesome there. It's a good place to hang out, and stuff."

Muneerah came to know Karen as a brave and courageous fighter. She seemed to be able to tackle any situation. Her main focus was on helping others, and she was always sincere in her interactions.

BEGINNING TO LOOK ACROSS EXPERIENCES

After more than two years of building relationships with the youth and slowly engaging in numerous individual, pair, and small group conversations with them, we felt it was time to begin to think across their experiences to identify narrative threads that resonated across their lives. This way of looking across experience was important to us and the participants. Looking for resonant threads allows all of us to acknowledge the diversity and difference that existed within and across their experiences, which is different from other narrative research approaches. We began this process by sitting with one another, sharing and thinking together with the diverse experiences about which the youth shared stories. In this way we began to see four strongly resonant and interconnected narrative threads: families, systems/institutions, dreams/self-worth, and relationships. We then invited the youth to meet with us so that we could work together to further develop and deepen our exploration of these narrative threads. In her field notes of the first of these gatherings, Margot noted:

We arrived at the community agency on a Saturday to meet with the youth and discuss the next steps of the research project. At the time, I recalled being surprised that a group of teenage youth would give up four hours of their weekend to meet with a group of researchers. I was excited that they had come! Not only were the youth present, but they were very engaged in the process of sifting through transcripts of their previous conversations and identifying resonant threads within their experiences. Our idea was to build a "tree" of different colored paper on the wall of the upstairs room at North Central Child and Youth. Our collaboratively constructed tree would be part of our inquiry, consisting of main themes as the trunk, experiences and stories as the branches and leaves. It seemed a way to organize so many of our conversations—a pattern that we could all follow. The youth engaged in this process by reading each transcript, writing pieces of text on colored papers and pasting these to the wall through which a sprawling tree gradually took shape. The time flew as we worked side by side in a safe and trusting space, learning from each other as the research findings began to become more visible to each of us. I remember thinking on my way home, what a good day this had been. The youth and us as researchers had grown into a team.

On the way home we talked about each of the youth. We reminded each other how determined Betsy had always been and how wakeful she was to her possibilities. It was her quiet strength that stood out, as well as her strong relationship with her mom. As we turned to Nicole, we all smiled: we could see her love of the arts and of theater and the way she always performed, no matter where she was, or who accompanied her. Nicole always filled the room with her energy and presence. Nicole wants to be a kindergarten teacher one day, and we all could see that this was a real possibility and how lucky the children would be if she were their teacher. While Brenda was not there that day, we missed her outspokenness and feistiness. Brenda was rough around the edges, but she so firmly believes in what she knew. For us Brenda's personality always seemed bigger than the tiny girl we could see her as.

STAYING WITH COMPLEXITIES AND LAYERS

As we write this chapter we are in the midst of this relational process. Each of us, the youth, the agency, and we four are continuing to figure out our process as relationships continue to grow. As our chapter shows, engaging with the youth as narrative inquirers as we collaboratively attend to sexual exploitation has required our collective, ongoing attentiveness to the complexity and layeredness of lives. Staying in this process of relationally developing interventions that attend to the lives of children and youth at risk for sexual exploitation, and that situate their experiences as leading change, has been a slow, gradual unfolding. This unfolding has required attentiveness to each of our multiplicities and the tensions present in both the meeting of our lives with one another's lives and in the meeting of our lives with dominant social, cultural, and institutional narratives that may, instead, encourage us, as researchers, to look away from or to silence the many long-term personal and professional relational ethical responsibilities that these relationships and this inquiry continue to shape. Perhaps the most significant contribution of our work is that we made the youth themselves central to the efforts of developing early interventions within the context of sexual exploitation. "Hear me!" their voices continue to call us; their voices continue to work on us, on the youth, and our relationships with them.

QUESTIONS FOR REFLECTION AND GROUP DISCUSSION

1. What responsibilities do researches hold in relation to community organizations?
2. Relational ethics is at the heart of a narrative inquiry study. How does this shape the interactions with youth research participants?
3. What are some of the ways in which researchers and others recognize the strength of youth, rather than solely focus on the problems, issues, or what at times are termed deficits?

REFERENCES

Bernstein, Elizabeth. 2012. "Carceral Politics as Gender Justice? The 'Traffic in Women' and Neoliberal Circuits of Crime, Sex, and Rights." *Theory and Society* 41, no. 3. doi: 10.1007/s11186-012-9165-9

City of Edmonton. 2011. *Demographics and Profiles*. http://www.edmonton.ca/business _economy/demographics-and-profiles.aspx.

Clandinin, D. Jean. 2013. *Engaging in Narrative Inquiry*. Walnut Creek, CA: Left Coast Press.

Clandinin, D. Jean, Vera Caine, Sean Lessard, and Janice Huber. 2016. *Engaging in Narrative Inquiries with Children and Youth*. New York: Routledge.

Clandinin, D. Jean., and F. Michael Connelly. 2000. *Narrative Inquiry: Experience and Story in Qualitative Research*. San Francisco: Jossey-Bass.

Connelly, F. Michael, and D. Jean Clandinin. 2006. "Narrative Inquiry." In *Handbook of Complementary Methods in Education Research 3rd edition*, ed. J. L. Green, G. Camilli, and P. Elmore, 477–487. Mahwah, NJ: Ehrlbaum.

Feinstein, Clare, and Claire O'Kane. 2008. "Ethical Guidelines for Ethical, Meaningful and Inclusive Children's Participation Practice." *Save the Children*. http://childethics.com/wp-content/uploads/2013/09/Feinstein-OKane-2008.pdf.

Homma, Yuko, Dean. Nicholson, and Elizabeth Saewyc. 2012. "A Profile of High School Students in Rural Canada Who Exchange Sex for Substances." *Canadian Journal of Human Sexuality* 21, nos. 1–2: 41–52.

Jaffer, Mobina S. B., and Patrick Brazeau. 2011. *The Sexual Exploitation of Children in Canada: The Need for National Action*. Standing Senate Committee of Human Rights. http://www.parl.gc.ca/Content/SEN/Committee/411/ridr/rep/rep03nov11-e .pdf.

Justice Institute of British Columbia. 2011. *Commercial Sexual Exploitation: Innovative Ideas for Working with Children and Youth*. New Westminster, BC: Justice Institute of BC.

Kingsley, C., and M. Mark. 2001. *Sacred Lives: Canadian Aboriginal Children and Youth Speak out About Sexual Exploitation*. Vancouver, BC: Human Resources Development Canada.

Lalor, Kevin, and Rosaleen McElvaney. 2010. "Child Sexual Abuse, Link to Later Sexual Exploitation/High-Risk Sexual Behavior, and Prevention/Treatment Programs." *Trauma, Violence & Abuse* 11, no. 4: 159–177.

Lokanc-Diluzio, Wendy, and Sandra Reilly. 2010. "A Mixed Methods Study of Service Provider Capacity Development to Protect the Sexual and Reproductive Health of Street-Involved Youth." *ACCFCR Final Report*. https://policywise.com/wp-content /uploads/resources/2016/07/2014_05MAY_22__Scientific_Report.pdf.

MacDonald, Jo-Ann. 2011. "Asking to Listen: Towards a Youth Perspective on Sexual Health Education and Needs." *Sex Education: Sexuality, Society and Learning* 11, no. 4: 443–457.

Manion, Kathleen. 2006. "Voices of the Unheard: Perception of Success of Interventions with Commercially Sexually Exploited Girls in Three Countries." Unpublished PhD diss., University of East London.

Melrose, Margaret. 2012. "Young People and Sexual Exploitation: A Critical Discourse Analysis." In *Critical Perspectives on Child Sexual Exploitation and Related Traf-*

ficking, ed. Margaret Melrose and Jenny Pearce, 9–22. New York: Palgrave Macmillan.

Pearce, Jenny. 2014. "What's Going on to Safeguard Children and Young People from Sexual Exploitation: A Review of Local Safeguarding Children Boards' Work to Protect Children from Sexual Exploitation." *Child Abuse Review* 23, no. 3: 159–170.

Saewyc, Elizabeth M., and Laurel D. Edinburgh. 2010. "Restoring Healthy Development Trajectories for Sexually Exploited Young Runaway Girls: Fostering Protective Factors and Reducing Risk Behaviors." *Journal of Adolescent Health* 46, no. 2: 180–188.

Saewyc, Elizabeth M., Laura J. MacKay, Jayson Anderson, and Christopher Drozda. 2008. *It's Not What You Think: Sexually Exploited Youth in British Columbia.* Vancouver: University of British Columbia School of Nursing.

Thomson, Susan, David Hirshberg, Amy Corbett, Nikki Valila, and Denise Howley. 2011. "Residential Treatment for Sexually Exploited Adolescent Girls: Acknowledge, Commit, Transform (ACT)." *Children and Youth Services Review* 33, no. 11: 2290–2296. doi:10.1016/j.childyouth.2011.07.017

UNICEF. 2006. *Child Sexual Abuse and Commercial Exploitation of Children in the Pacific: A Regional Report.* http://www.unicef.org/eapro/Pacific_CSEC_report.pdf.

Villa-Torres, Laura, and Joar Svanemyr. 2015. "Ensuring Youth's Right to Participation and Promotion of Youth Leadership in the Development of Sexual and Reproductive Health Policies and Programs." *Journal of Adolescent Health* 56: 551–557.

Whitaker Daniel J., Brenda Le, R. Karl Hanson, Charlene K. Baker, Pam M. McMahon, Gail Ryan, Alisa Klein, and Deborah D. Rice. 2008. "Risk Factors for the Perpetration of Child Sexual Abuse: A Review and Meta-Analysis." *Child Abuse and Neglect* 32, no. 5: 529–548. doi: 10.1016/j.chiabu.2007.08.005.

Chapter Five

IN BETWEEN WORLDS

Narrating Ecological Heritage Practices for Teenage Wellness

KRISTINA BAINES

In a rural village in southern Belize, a young Maya woman sits on a low stool with a corncob in her hands. Deftly, she maneuvers the cob, spinning it so the dried kernels fall into the large plastic basket below. When it is bare, she tosses it into a pile and takes another to repeat the process. I follow along, copying her technique and eventually finding my own rhythm, and my own blister. While she shells the corn, she talks about her high school and about how she travels each day to the nearest town on the bus, and, as a result, leaves more work for her mother and siblings to do. She catches up with her responsibilities on weekends and in the evenings before she does her homework by candlelight, making tortillas for her family and helping out her grandparents on the other side of the village. On special occasions she brings them tamales or fruits gathered from the forest when they are in season. Balancing these two parts of her life seems challenging, but she does not complain and instead tells me more about her work for her family and the processing of the corn. She is hopeful she will be able to continue her high school education, but understands the burden on her family that attending school creates. Her grandfather worries that the students will lose their traditions and move away from their heritage, but she seems to live inside them easily, her body understanding what to do while she diverts her focus to talking to me and continuing to fill the basket with corn.

In an East Harlem apartment 3,500 miles away, another young woman sits at a small white table in her kitchen. She is holding a small bunch of a leafy herb in one hand and explaining to me what her mother uses it for, when her phone rings with a video call. She taps it to reveal a rural village in Mexico. Her grandparents and aunts are smiling for the camera as they sit outside their home shelling corn in much the same way as her counterpart in Belize. They laugh as she gets up to show them the snow falling outside the small window of the apartment. She shows them the herbs we were looking at, and they take the phone and show us the plants growing around their home in Mexico. They narrate their uses and then go back to shelling the corn. Soon, reluctantly, everyone says their goodbyes. After hanging up, the young woman begins to tell me about how she would love to visit her grandparents, but is unable to because of complications in the family's immigration status. While she is excelling in her college studies, she is aware of the price her family pays for her to be part of the formal education system in the United States, and feels that keeping connected through practicing her heritage traditions is important. She laughs when she talks of how her aunties are critical of her tortilla-making skills, saying that by her teenage years she should be better. While she agrees and tries to practice, there is so little time left after studying and working. Negotiating her worlds requires not only thought but also action and time: to sit and talk and listen. Telling her story at her table provides a space for that on this day.

Teenagers are often painted in the popular imagination as pushing back against the traditional practices of their elders. However, spending time with them as a participant observer as part of ethnographic practice reveals a deeper experience of engagement with heritage traditions. Through the "doing" part of ethnographic work, I came to understand that engaging with traditions requires not only knowledge of those traditions but also practicing them. The embodied ecological heritage (EEH) framework (Baines 2018; Baines 2016; Baines and Zarger 2016) highlights the importance of engaging with traditional ecological knowledge and practices through linking these practices to health and wellness, holistically defined to include their physical, mental, and social aspects. Definitions of traditional ecological knowledge (TEK) are plentiful and varied. For the purposes of this chapter, I follow the one provided by the Convention on Biological Diversity:

Traditional knowledge refers to the knowledge, innovations and practices of in-digenous and local communities around the world. Developed from experience gained over the centuries and adapted to the local culture and environment, tra-ditional knowledge is transmitted orally from generation to generation. It tends to be collectively owned and takes the form of stories, songs, folklore, proverbs, cultural values, beliefs, rituals, community laws, local language, and agricultural practices, including the development of plant species and animal breeds. Some-times it is referred to as an oral traditional for it is practiced, sung, danced, painted, carved, chanted and performed down through millennia.

Rather than considering tradition as simply ecological knowledge that can be passed down through families, this framework emphasizes the crit-ical nature of engaging with traditional practices.

This chapter uses the EEH framework in two ways: first, as in the cases just introduced, much of the narrative data were collected while engaging in heritage activities with the participants as part of a wider ethnographic study. Second, the narrative stories themselves are considered using the framework to identify linkages between heritage practices and health. I looked for ways that narrative storytellers talked more explicitly about how they felt, thereby not separating body and mind. This approach can be seen, in part, as responding to a failure of contemporary social work discourse to acknowledge that the body "not only encompasses specific, personal, cor-poreal experiences but also experiences that are socially and culturally constructed and reflective of larger social arrangement" (Tangenberg and Kemp 2002). By combining the phenomenological focus on capturing the lived experience of the body and the cognitive focus on the thoughtful structuring of the narrative in a way that highlights how ecological experi-ences and health are being thought and spoken about, I hope to illuminate the richness of the participants' experiences.

I argue that narrative practice, particularly in tandem with engaging with ecological heritage practices, provides a space and structure for teen-agers to begin to structure their experiences. Focusing particularly on how teens in rural Belize and those from immigrant families in New York City negotiate and make sense of their multiple "worlds" and responsibilities, I demonstrate how narrative in the context of a wider ethnographic experi-ence can lead to a deeper understanding of the nuanced way in which teen-agers engage with their heritage practices. The teenagers in the communities highlighted here are very explicitly navigating contrasting and conflicting experiences reflecting the changing norms around expectations for their age. The challenges around these contrasts—going to school or college or helping the family in traditional activities—are given a space to be articulated through narrative experiences. Narrative has been shown to significantly alter how an experience is perceived (Schneider 2004). This chapter suggests that the perceptions of heritage shift through the storytelling process. The chapter further shows how narrative can deepen the understanding of the ways in which traditional practices are linked to holistic health and wellness among the teenagers and, ultimately, create a rich picture of how they craft and experience a happy, healthy life.

NARRATING CHANGES: IDENTITY AND PRACTICE

Conveying a narrative is simultaneously a very personal, individualistic experience and an active social process. This tension between the experiences being relayed in the narrative and the bringing of a new partner, the listener, into the sense-making process related to those experiences is a fruitful space for inquiry (Murphy 2011, 245). This is both the space for the creation of the narrative identity—"an individual's internalized, evolving and integrative story of the self" (McAdams 2008, 242)—and the site of a deepening understanding of the researcher to become part of the story as it unfolds. If we accept that "the act of telling a story can be likened to a narrative journey of exploration and discovery" (Gunn 2009, 116), the researcher or listener can be conceived as both the guide and the follower, opening up a social space in which an individual story can be developed and its evolution can be witnessed. In this way, narrative construction is seen as an active process created within a social or ecological space.

As part of the ethnographic process, narrative as defined as social and active reveals "deep beliefs and assumptions that people often cannot tell in propositional or denotative form" (Mattingly 1991, 36). In this sense, it is a useful space for considering what people do and not just what they say. The movements and actions of storytellers reveal sensual and perceptional insights (Ingold 2000). The participant observation frequently employed by sociocultural anthropologists supports the value of building spaces of action for "going deep" and revealing deeply held rationales and identities. Incorporating the embodied ecological framework into this conceptualization of the narrative process capitalizes on these spaces of creation and revelation linking them to health and wellness. This is central to the EEH framework which defines heritage as not static, but as a fluid concept defined through practice in the present. The teenagers participating in the narratives discussed in this chapter define their heritage and the role of that heritage in their identities through active narrative co-creation. In this way, the production of the narrative, coupled with the embodied experience of actively relaying it, is linked to health and wellness.

Gibson's (1996) work supports the links among narrative, ecological heritage, and health, suggesting that people use narrative as a basic cognitive strategy for making sense of various aspects of the human experience, such as time and change. It seems useful to attempt to make sense of the changes that occur in the lives and worlds of the teenagers in the studies referenced in this chapter, in both explicit and implicit ways, through opening the narrative space. I argue that this process moves beyond cognition, however, to an incorporation of an embodied experience. As mentioned, the presence of narrative can significantly alter how an experience is perceived (Schneider 2004), but also the presence of the narrative space can alter that perception and the way it is manifested as a bodily experience. I, as the ethnographer and the "listener" of the narratives, form part of that space in ways highlighted in the following section.

AT THE INTERSECTION: TEENAGERS AND ECOLOGICAL HERITAGE

As a sociocultural anthropologist actively engaged in applied work, I often find myself in the midst of a flexible ethnographic data collection process. Both in rural Belize and in New York City, people lead busy lives, are not always easy to corral for a formal interview, and are often late for appointments. Teenagers in particular are often strapped for time, juggling multiple responsibilities of work and school, in addition to household chores and activities. This "difficulty to capture" is often balanced, however, by an openness and willingness to talk. My willingness to listen while the teens were engaged in other activities enabled the process of compiling the series of "embodied narratives" discussed here.

Narrative is a familiar part of the ethnographic process, both methodologically and in terms of conveying research results. Literally meaning "writing culture," ethnography is a multifaceted research process, which can include a wide range of tools and trajectories: participant observation; field notes; informal, semiformal, and formal interviews; mapping, both environmental and cognitive; free listing; pile sorting; surveys; and the collection of oral histories. Anthropologists often use narrative to capture the immersive dimension of the data as part of the process of "writing up" the research; it can be coupled with other qualitative analyses in addition to quantitative analyses. In this sense, it is a practical tool for both collecting and disseminating results. I often use it in my writing as a way to draw the reader into the community, to give them a sense of what it is like to be there, to live and work there. It makes the data more understandable and more accessible.

In the cases presented here, narrative proved to be a particularly useful method for collecting and disseminating the thoughts and behaviors of my teenage informants. The narratives were collected as part of larger research studies aiming to capture the relationship between participating in "traditional" or heritage ecological practices and health and wellness, both in Belize and New York City. The first study was conducted over three years in a Mopan Maya village in southern Belize. While engaged in the research, I was part of an interdisciplinary team: my role as part of that team was to co-pilot an environmental and cultural heritage workbook for integration into the Belizean primary schools (Baines and Zarger 2012; Baines 2016). In that role, I had a great deal of formal and informal interaction with the youth in the community and several surrounding communities. Gathering information from them in this context was not difficult: the data took the form of answers given to the pilot lessons, both in text and drawings, as well as on field trips and walks in the forest. The lessons and classes were offered only to primary school students (generally up to age twelve), and so they did not capture the perspectives of older youth. In many senses, the stories of these older youth were the most fascinating for my research, because they made up the group that was most actively engaged in decisions regarding ecological heritage practices, particularly around balancing their travel outside the village to attend high school and their contributions to their families in the community. They were moving between two worlds: that of higher education in a neighboring town that their parents did not have access to and what they described as a more traditional life in the primarily subsistence farming community of their home. As seen later, they skillfully negotiated these identities with thoughtfulness and grace.

After my fieldwork in Belize, I began teaching at an open-enrollment community college that was part of the City University of New York system. As my interest in the intersections of ecological heritage practices and health continued and I began preparing the opening narratives for the chapters of my book about a work in Belize, I began considering ways in which to continue my research path in New York. Soon after, I was awarded a small grant to conduct research in Latin American and Caribbean immigrant communities, testing the application of the embodied ecological framework in the context of those separated from the environments in which the practices were rooted. I wondered if people would still find themselves healthier if they engaged in practices that are separated from places. To gain introductions into those communities, I looked to my students. I asked if they had a family member who had started his or her life in a Latin American or Caribbean country and was still engaging in a traditional practice after moving to New York City. If they had family members who were interested in participating in the study, the students would often volunteer to assist me in setting up times for the interviews. This process, and my arrival at their homes to conduct these interviews, began the narrative process. While not the initial focus of the ethnographic interviews, the students—teenagers or in their very early twenties—became a fundamental part of my visits. Their critical role in volunteering to set up the interviews, and welcoming me into their homes, created a space in which they could openly speak to me, often at length about the negotiation of their identities. I began to realize that I was acting as a bridge between their worlds—of college and home, and of formal education and of the informal knowledge and practices of their parents and grandparents—which I was there to investigate.

In Belize and New York, as I participated in telling the stories of their worlds, narrative was both an easy part of the ethnographic process and an unintended way of creating a space for teenagers to share how their thoughts and identities were shaped by ecological heritage practices. During the preparation of this chapter, another space opened to consider the role of narrative in teenage lives. Students applied and were chosen to travel to Belize to participate in ethnographic research around environmental and cultural heritage as part of a global study course funded by a foundation at the college. These students wrote narrative accounts of their personal journeys in the course, documenting the evolution of their identities as students, researchers, and global citizens. Participating in the ecological heritage practices alongside their community counterparts in Belize gave them a space to consider their own ecologies, heritage, and identities. I include a discussion of these cases as a way of reinforcing and further considering the narrative process in this way.

IN THEIR WORDS AND IN THEIR WORLDS

Paola: A Seventeen-Year-Old Mopan Maya woman from a Rural Village, Population 450, in Southern Belize

As Paola appeared in the light of the doorway to the small thatch house, she saw me sitting in her father's hammock and smiled. He was across the room, perched on an upturned plastic bucket where he had been many times as I came by to talk about the role of traditional ecological practices in the well-being of the community. As she stepped into the home and I noticed her crisp gray and white school uniform, I heard the bus she had just come from rumble down the dirt and rock road. "Hello, Miss Kristina," she greeted me and quickly went to find her bucket of clothes and began to skill-fully change her clothes, modestly slipping on her Maya dress and quickly sliding her skirt out from under it. She carefully hung her uniform from the wooden beams of her home and slipped into the kitchen. Evening was approaching, and her father excused himself to go bathe in the river near their house, leaving the two of us. I wandered into the kitchen and sat on a small, low wooden stool that I would soon use to help bake tortillas for the family's dinner. I watched her and we exchanged smiles and giggled. "How are you, Paola?" I asked. "How was school today?" "Good, Miss Kristina." She was an excellent student, I knew. She was also the oldest of seven children, and I could see from her flurry of activity in the kitchen that she knew there was a lot to do since she had been away from her home and her responsibilities for the whole day. I watched her move around me, telling her I was feeling lazy, and we giggled more before she began to talk.

She was enjoying high school and excelling in her studies, although she was humble about her achievements. The choice to attend was hers, but it was clear that she realized schooling was a privilege and was financially feasible only because she received a scholarship. High school attendance is not mandatory, and most parents extended what I found to be a kind of autonomy to youth in decisions about school. If money could be found, most families were supportive of high school attendance, although students were certainly aware of how their choice to continue formal education affected their families, particularly in the short term through the absence of their labor during the school day. It was clear Paola understood this negotiation and spoke about high school as if it were a privilege that might become infeasible at any time. "I don't know" was her response when I asked if she was going to be starting her final year and would graduate next year. She expressed her deference to her family even while discussing how much she enjoyed her classes.

I followed her outside to pick a pepper to mash for the meal, and she glanced back down the road she had just traveled on. The journey to and from school was long, and it began at 5 a.m. She had homework to do by candlelight after dinner; yet she did not complain, even though it was obvious she was tired. She carefully walked up the grassy hill behind her home, jumping over a patch of mud and snatching a small, red pepper before coming back.

During our short walk, her mother and siblings had arrived home and were busy in the kitchen. They had been to the corn mill and in the center of the low table by the fire hearth sat a tower of freshly ground masa ready to be made into tortillas. Paola passed the pepper to her mother and sat on the stool closest to the fire hearth. I sat across from her, and we grabbed small handfuls of the moist dough and began making tortillas. She was quiet for a few minutes until her sisters began dropping subtle hints about a young gentleman who lived close by. She smiled as she looked down at her tortilla and shrugged her shoulders. Marriage was often delayed at least a few years when young women attended high school, but it was still critical to the social organization of the village. Shaping her tortilla, Paola quietly let me know that there was maybe a wedding in her future, but we both knew that I would have to glean how she felt about this from her glances across the cool mound of masa: in speaking at all about her relationship with this young man, she would have to tread a careful line between the norms of her community and those that were subtly communicated through her high school curriculum and not so subtly conveyed through the YouTube videos she could catch a glimpse of on the bus. She flipped the tortillas with a quick press and pinch of her fingers, as she had done thousands of times before, being careful not to burn herself. She told me that she would wait and see what would happen, and it was clear that she was hopeful and could see a way that she could have her education and her marriage too. As her world, values, hopes, and responsibilities came together at that low table that evening, she seemed to take comfort in the daily rhythm of working the masa for her family's meal. Her autonomy in that moment was nuanced as embodying the same practice as almost every other young woman in her community; she was actually shaping her identity as a Maya woman, a daughter, a student, and, eventually, a wife and mother.

Situated within the wider context of a multiyear ethnographic study, this narrative encounter created a space where Paola could be heard. I was able to hear her in conversation and through her practices, as I participated in them with her. Observing what she did—how her body moved carefully within the space of her family's thatch house—as she carefully spoke about her experiences at school, how she was feeling, and her expectations for the future added a layer to the narrative experiences. In situations in which words may be constrained, participating in everyday activities can provide a richness to the story.

Valeria: A Nineteen-Year-Old Mexican American Woman from East Harlem, New York City

I have to work hard, study hard for my mom. You know, give back and stuff. So like when I was in the jungle that helped me a lot to understand the stories. 'Cause it's one thing, you know, like being in class, hearing about the environment, how to make a difference and one thing like me having firsthand experience like farming, the whole thing. So I learned the significance and the importance of it.

I was sitting with Valeria at the kitchen table in the small apartment she shares with her mom and two uncles. I had arrived to help make tamales. This was my second visit; the first occurred one month earlier when I had come to interview her mother about the wild plants she collects in Central Park, and other ecological heritage practices she had learned in Mexico and brought with her to New York City. With no formal interview plans, we began spooning masa into corn husks and dripping in generous amounts of deep red mole. I asked her how her studies were going, and, in particular, about a study abroad trip she had taken to South America. Her explanation, which opened this section, led me to ask more about how she felt about visiting South America before Mexico, where her family is from. She responded,

I embrace both, although Mexico is like a folktale, you can say like a fairy tale. I know it's there, like I hear a lot about it and I imagine it, but I have not ex . . . out of my hand, like I don't know how to explain it, it a far reach thing. Like a dream, you know. So when I hear stories about my mom, it makes me want to go to Mexico and see these things and like learn their culture.

We began talking about culture and what she meant by it, and, because of the tamale construction at hand, the conversation quickly turned to food:

I told my mom before that I would learn the food, but for myself. Because I guess over there it's a big thing about marriage like you know. You have to know for marriage. And I'm like no, I have to learn for myself. . . . I always told her if I'm going to learn how to make it, it's for myself, not because I want to find a man. Cause, here in America I don't think food is a big thing in marriage.

I acknowledge that the ability to cook is sometimes important for marriage here and sometimes not. There are all sorts of expectations and desires in marriage. Valeria continued,

Like, when my grandma talks to me she tries to give me advice. It's hard for me because it's like, I'm used to the advice my mom gives me. Like she gives me more freedom, but my grandma, because she's like you know you have to do this, you're a young woman, it's important, and you know. And I think of like the gender norms that they put so I don't really follow the gender for, like if woman can do it, why can't men do it as well?

Throughout the process of building tamales, Valeria was building this narrative of negotiating between her worlds of higher education, particularly the study abroad opportunity, and the advice of her mother in New York City and her grandmother in Mexico. While engaging in the traditional ecological practice of making tamales, she shaped her personal and social identity through her understanding of the importance of culture in an abstract sense: "I'm going to learn how to make [the traditional foods]." However, she also clearly articulated this cultural importance through a lens of a successful, American college student: "I would learn the food for myself." Her values of independence and autonomy are clearly expressed in what she says, but also evident is her engagement in the family and the social processes solidified by us making food together. Her understanding of the importance of these processes reflects her understanding of their importance to her well-being. Her worlds are more distinct than those of Paola, but she has had a lifetime of negotiating them.

Jennifer: An Eighteen-Year Old Dominican American Woman from New York City, Traveling in Belize

The study abroad program in South America that Valeria participated in also sponsored a trip for students to travel to Belize. Before leaving New York, on each day while they were away, and on their return, students wrote narrative journal entries reflecting on their experiences. These written narratives show a similar, albeit more focused, negotiation of identity in the ecological space. Jennifer was asked to articulate this negotiation by discussing what she had learned while she was away:

The most important thing I learned about myself is that I love ethnography. I love learning about other people's culture and due to this, I can adapt to other environments with no problem. I learned that my body can adapt to places, but when it's raining season, and there's too many bugs, they will eat me alive. I learned that bugs love my blood type, so I have to find out what's my blood type. From the group, I was the main one that got bitten the most. As a person I learned that I love challenges. I loved when I hiked the reserved jungle to get to the Blue Pool, which is a river. I found the hike there very dangerous but it was a great adventure.

The only place that I disliked from the trip was Chris's farm. He lives in a forest— the farm mimics it. Since it's rainy season in Belize, it rains every single day, and because of this, there are many bugs. I disliked his farm because of the bugs. The first night that we slept there, I only slept for three hours or less because the bugs didn't let me sleep. Small bugs would get inside the net and bite me. I couldn't see them because they were too small. I tried sleeping in different rooms, and they were still biting me. I changed to long pants and to a long shirt, and they would still go through my clothes and bite me. Nothing would work, not even repellent. I felt so much anger that I felt like crying! I wanted to sleep but I couldn't. I was itching so much and even throughout the rest of the trip, I was still itching. That day, I couldn't wait for the day to start and thinking about how we were going to sleep there for one more day made me anxious. I didn't want to stay there for another day. Then, when I slept in Chris's living room, I felt better and I was able to deal with the situation. I learned from this that in some scenarios, there aren't solutions, but I have to learn to deal with it, especially with this opportunity. The whole experience in Belize overpasses that scenario with the bugs.

She extends how she feels about her body in the environment to how she feels about herself as a student and person in the world:

Before I traveled to Belize, I thought about having a career that involves traveling. However, I didn't know what I wanted to major in when I transfer to a four-year school. Now, that I traveled to Belize, I want to major in Anthropology in a four-year school. If I do not major in Anthropology, I want to major in something that has to do with international affairs. I want to be able to travel the world and feel like I made a difference in the world.

And, finally, she relates her personal choices to the wider ecological world:

One main thing I learned about in Belize was about the food. Food is one of the main resources for people to survive. In Belize, I learned the different ways of farming and what's one of the best methods. In the island that we visited, I learned how important the ocean is, not only for humans, but for animals as well. The act of fishing and throwing garbage in the ocean, especially the plastic garbage, is terrible for the ocean. Many species in the ocean are becoming extinct due to it. As we pollute the ocean, we are affecting the species and ourselves negatively. It is also affecting us because we are consuming those species that live in the water and we use the water that comes from the river to farm to grow our food. I connected with this personally because I started thinking about my health and how all this time I have been eating a lot of meat.

In this narrative, Jennifer relates how experiencing the ecology of Belize and conducting an ethnography of ecological and cultural heritage practices changed her. This narrative fits well into the discussion of the ways in which teenagers negotiate their world and articulate the intersections of identity and bodily practices in narrative format. It demonstrates how narrative provides a space to explicitly enhance or alter the way an experience is perceived (Schneider 2004). Without the narrative, Jennifer may not have perceived her experience in Belize to be transformative. She links the experience to personal growth and strength in addition to the solidification of career and life goals. An argument could be made that her experience may have created a false sense of possibilities and that basing her identity formation on a powerful but unique experience is problematic. Could the narrative space have created a false perception of possibilities? While this could be argued, I would posit that the narrative and its space for the articulation of identity formation also created a space for positive growth. The benefits for youth wellness are not lost even in the unique experience of being in another place. Yet, we must be cautious in overgeneralizing work with teenagers, who are in a fundamental space of change, and the global travel experience can emphasize this change.

CONCLUDING THOUGHTS

Teenage lives are lives at the intersections: of childhood and adulthood, most obviously, but also of the traditional and the modern, the family and the individual, and the cared for and the autonomous. Increasingly, as the world moves toward a development model that highlights formal education and individual economic independence, the dichotomies of the teenage experience become a space for the development of identities to engage with changing ecologies. This chapter has argued that the narrative process both provides this space and reveals these intersections and negotiations. The defining and redefining of the teenage self through the narration of, and engagement in ecological heritage practices demonstrate how the flexibility of identity can mirror the flexibility of heritage. The co-production of identity and heritage through narrative, viewed through the EEH frame, has a role in defining and living a healthy, happy life.

Paola, Valeria, and Jennifer provide us with a variety of methodological (recalled, recorded, written) and situational examples of how narrative can be particularly helpful in creating an open space for teenagers. The focus on ecological practices as part of the narrative experiences allows for connections to be made to health and wellness through the embodied ecological framework. Additionally, it anchors the narratives in action, adding a depth to the experience of their co-creation and perception of the researcher. For future work, it would be helpful to further explore the links to wellness created by this active space. What does it mean to promote wellness, and what can narrative add to our holistic view of health using the embodied ecological heritage frame?

QUESTIONS FOR REFLECTION AND GROUP DISCUSSION

1. How does the embodied ecological heritage (EEH) framework add to your understanding of the narratives presented?
2. Do you think that the three narratives presented here are more "in between worlds" than those of the "average" teenager? In what ways?
3. Explore the connections made between ecological practices and health. Do you think the narratives are helpful in making the argument for these connections?

REFERENCES

Baines, Kristina. 2016. *Embodying Ecological Heritage in a Maya Community: Health, Happiness and Identity*. Lanham, MD: Lexington Books.
——. 2018. "'But Are They Actually Healthier?': Challenging the Health/Wellness Divide through the Ethnography of Embodied Ecological Heritage." *Medicine Anthropology Theory* 5, no. 5: 5–29.
Baines, Kristina, and Rebecca Zarger. 2012. "Circles of Value: Integrating Maya Environmental Knowledge into Belizean Schools." In *The Anthropology of Environmental Education*, ed. H. Kopnina, 65–86. Hauppage, NY: Nova Science.
Gibson, Andrew. 1996. *Towards a Postmodern Theory of Narrative*. Edinburgh: Edinburgh University Press,
Gunn, Wendy, ed. 2009. *Fieldnotes and Sketchbooks. Challenging the Boundaries between Descriptions and Processes of Describing*. Berlin: Peter Lang.
Ingold, Tim. 2000. *The Perception of the Environment: Essays on Livelihood, Dwelling and Skill*. London: Routledge.
Mattingly, Cheryl. 1991. "Narrative Reflections on Practical Action: Two Learning Experiments in Reflective Storytelling." In *The Reflective Turn: Case Studies in and on Educational Practice*, ed. D. A. Schön, 235–257. New York: Teachers College Press.
McAdams, Dan P. 2008. "Personal Narratives and the Life Story." In *Handbook of Personality: Theory and research*, 3rd ed., ed. O. P. John, R. W. Robins, and L. A. Pervin, 242–262. New York: Guilford Press.
Murphy, Keith M. 2011. "Building Stories: The Embodied Narration of What Might Come to Pass." In *Embodied Interaction: Language and Body in the Material World*,

ed. J. Streeck, C. Goodwin, and C. LeBaron, 243–253. Cambridge: Cambridge University Press.

Schneider, Edward F. 2004. "Death with a Story." *Human Communication Research* 30, no. 3: 361–375.

Tangenberg, Kathleen M., and Susan Kemp. 2002. "Embodied Practice: Claiming the Body's Experience, Agency, and Knowledge for Social Work." *Social Work* 47, no. 1: 9–18.

Chapter Six

NEIGHBORHOOD SURVEILLANCE AND THE PRISON ASSEMBLY LINE

TREVOR B. MILTON

Before he was the executive director of Preparing Leaders of Tomorrow (P.L.O.T.), before he was an esteemed panelist on the president's Task Force on 21st-Century Policing, before he sold drugs and intimidated his neighbors on the streets of Crown Heights, Brooklyn, Jim was a wide-eyed ten-year-old boy from Haiti with a head full of dreams.

On his initial descent into New York City, Jim pressed his head against the airplane's tempered-glass window and marveled at the tall buildings, the endless urban landscape, and the nonstop hustle and bustle below. Innocent and cheerful, Jim was a typical small-town kid coming from the countryside of a Caribbean island and trying to settle into the density of Brooklyn. To him, the big city moved at a wild pace. People talked loud and seemed to end their conversations as quickly as they started. Cars barked, buses squealed, and ambulances roared past him. He was in awe of this concrete jungle that would become his new home.

Like many members of immigrant families escaping poverty, Jim's mother and grandmother hoped for a new start and a safe place for their child to grow. Jim dreamed of being a policeman or firefighter, while his mother preferred he become a doctor. But like numerous other preadolescent boys growing up in Brooklyn in the early 2000s, "wide-eyed-Jim" was thrown into the winds of a heavily policed/high-crime neighborhood where he would await his turn on the prison assembly line. Poverty and violence began to strip away at his innocence, only to be replaced by the hard reality of panoptic neighborhood supervision and preordained criminal justice involvement.

Jim is now years removed from his delinquent days. He described to me the adjustments he had to make as a teenager to survive in New York City:

> I went from being the kid with the accent. The skinny kid that everyone used to bully, to being the bully myself. When I was fifteen or sixteen, I would fight anybody. Anybody. Kids would come to me if they had beef with someone bigger than them, because I would always be down to fight.

Currently in the United States, more than 600,000 prisoners per year return to their home communities. Of that population, 80 percent of male (and 75 percent of female) ex-inmates will be arrested for a new crime within twelve months of their release from prison. This return to the criminal justice system (or return to criminal behavior) is known in criminology as *recidivism*. That precious and volatile time spent in the community after a prison sentence is known as *prisoner reentry*. Jeremy Travis—former president of John Jay College of Criminal Justice and current executive vice president of criminal justice at the Laura and John Arnold Foundation—defined prisoner reentry as "the process of leaving prison and returning to society" (2005, 4–5). Reentry is a concern for probation officers, corrections officers, the criminal justice system, criminologists, teachers, social workers, family members, and communities (whether marginalized or affluent) because of the stark contrasts between prison life and safe community living. It is also the focus of this chapter.

To explore this topic, this chapter uses the narrative approach. Narration is used to describe the experiences of youths who have tumbled onto the *neighborhood-to-prison assembly line*: a crime-control apparatus intended to increase public safety by removing delinquent youth from high-crime neighborhoods and forcing them into a cycle of continuous incarceration. Narration is a valuable tool for exploring the origins of carceral traps while highlighting the agency of at-risk youth. Dan McAdams once wrote that "stories are the best vehicle known to human beings for conveying how (and why) a human agent, endowed with consciousness and motivated by intention, enacts desires and strives for goals over time" (2008, 82). I used ethnography—the study of culture and people in their own environment—

to highlight the struggles and successes of three New York City youth: Jim, Phife, and Shanduke. Through hours of qualitative interviewing, my respondents shed light on the conditions in which they lived, the roadblocks that prevented their successful reintegration into society, and the role of personal responsibility in recidivism.

JIM

Though his family brought him to Brooklyn for a better life, Jim St. Germain began to engage in street fights, school truancy, and illegal drug use as he entered his teenage years. These behaviors eventually led to juvenile incarceration. By the age of seventeen, Jim had already served time in juvenile detention for assault, sale of controlled substances, and various other violent criminal charges. For one crime, he was imprisoned for two years "upstate" in one of New York State's Department of Corrections prison facilities. But with personal determination—and good legal guidance—Jim was able to turn his life around. Now in his twenties, Jim dresses sharp, talks politics, and has divorced himself from the negative aspects of street life. He has been a youth counselor in juvenile facilities, co-founded P.L.O.T., served on the Youth Advisory Council of New York State's Division of Criminal Justice Services, and is one of the leading voices in the movement to prevent adolescents from serving prison sentences in adult facilities.

Jim is one of the "lucky ones" who was able to make something out of nothing: he is a rare exception to the rule of prisoner reentry. Formerly incarcerated youth have a multitude of structural forces stacked against them as they try to initiate and maintain a crime-free lifestyle on their return: the stigma of a felony conviction, joblessness, the loss of legal rights, continued criminogenic neighborhood conditions, and cultural forces that push them back into crime. High-crime neighborhoods and the revolving door of recidivism have become so normalized in the American lexicon that many have lost hope of changing this cycle. Youth recidivism should be a major concern to all members of society, but because it is confined to a few select neighborhoods, very few people care.

Though Jim was considered by many to be a "good kid," he is also proof positive that all marginalized youth in disadvantaged neighborhoods can be pulled into the vortex of the neighborhood-to-prison assembly line. Jim's entrance into the criminal justice system was commonplace for a boy of his age and zip code. Many of New York City's youth have daily encounters with police officers, closed-circuit cameras, mobile surveillance units, school safety officers, temporary detention through "stop-and-question" police tactics, and other arms of the larger carceral system.

Neighborhood supervision is more intense in New York's most impoverished neighborhoods. Ninety percent of detainees in New York City jails—and close to 70 percent of prisoners in New York State prisons (Fagan, West, and Holland 2002, 170)—come from fifteen of New York City's fifty-nine community districts. Sixty-eight percent of youth who have had contact with New York's criminal justice system will eventually serve time in an adult prison facility ("Service and Treatment Programs" 2016). And eighty percent of those youth—who will reach adulthood while incarcerated—will return to their respective communities after prison and will be jailed again within three years. An important question for this chapter is how these high-surveillance/highly incarcerated neighborhoods came to be.

THE SEEDS OF THE PRISON ASSEMBLY LINE

In the late 1980s and early 1990s—as crime rates throughout the United States reached their peak—local and state police municipalities and city and state governments alike were all negotiating ways to bring down the crime rate. The illegal drug trade was burgeoning, producing somewhere between $300 billion and $700 billion in revenue worldwide. Violence against the ordinary residents was commonplace. In big cities like New York, Chicago, and Los Angeles, average citizens feared victimization on public transportation, empty parks, and nighttime sidewalks, even in well-lit places like Times Square.

The (then) unrecognized forces contributing to the crime peak were deindustrialization and major shifts in employment opportunities. Before the 1970s, factory work could be found in industrial cities, even by those without a formal education or language skills. Factories provided work with livable wages for all who were "able bodied." Throughout the first half of the twentieth century, those seeking job opportunities flocked to the cities from all over the world and from failing agrarian parts of the United States (particularly African Americans) to seek jobs that only required a day or two of training.

Crime and zones of "urban decay" can be understood as a byproduct of deindustrialization in the 1970s and 1980s. Factory zones became underused and working-class neighborhoods teemed with the formerly employed ,who for generations had not relied on education for advancement, but instead on "clocking in" and "clocking out" amid an abundance of manufacturing work. During the 1970s and 1980s, working-class neighborhoods (adjacent to factory zones) plunged into disarray, which is why crime was common in the "inner city" rather than on its outskirts.

In New York City, these former high-employed working-class neighborhoods included Bedford-Stuyvesant, Crown Heights, and Brownsville in Brooklyn; Woodside and Jackson Heights in Queens; and Mott Haven, Hunts Point, and Concourse in the Bronx. These neighborhoods predictably fell into a cycle of crime and heavy reliance on urban informal (illegal) activities. Crime accelerated in these neighborhoods and began to spread throughout the city. When the crime peak in New York City was reached in the early 1990s, the criminal justice system was only large enough to handle the most serious offenses. Then a major policy shift began.

With New York City taking the lead nationally under Mayor Rudolph Giuliani (1993–2001), "broken windows policing," which targeted *quality-of-life* crimes, became the backbone of the New York City Police Department. Mayor Giuliani and Police Commissioner William Bratton focused on "cleaning up the streets" by tripling the size of the police force, making police more visible, punishing property crimes and vandalism, and generally containing crime to a few "decaying" neighborhoods.

The neighborhoods with the highest crime rates in the 1970s and 1980s have stayed the same for more than three decades, creating a dynamic where they and the prison system have begun to mimic each other. Sociologist Loic Wacquant would go as far as to argue that "(the) ghetto and prison (are) kindred institutions of forced confinement" (2000, 377).

In fact, high-crime neighborhoods and prisons are indeed one and the same: they are equally dangerous and monitored intensively, and both keep the most undesirable away from society. French Philosopher Michel Foucault argued that prisons were fashioned after English "plague towns" of the fourteenth century. To prevent the spread of bubonic plague, towns were built with "meticulously sealed walls, uncrossable in either direction" (1997, 197). The prison repurposed the idea of the plague town to focus it on the criminal, as if crime were a contagion. Because decaying working-class neighborhoods no longer have a function in a postindustrial economy, this new era of policing has focused on isolating these neighborhoods (and their contagions) from larger society.

In the 2010s, the plague-town model has permeated the neighborhoods that feed the prison system. Because the cycle of crime, incarceration, re-entry, and recidivism (rinse and repeat) has been barricaded inside "bad neighborhoods," many outside those areas can watch in fascination without having to be concerned about its impact. This conveyer belt of "thugs" entering the prison system, then reentering the streets, and then recidivating has been confined to geographic bubbles—or prison assembly lines. The broader society does not need to worry about the contagion of crime and, subsequently, the "problem" of mass incarceration.

Certain neighborhoods act as a pipeline directly to jails and prisons. Wacquant calls these obsolete "hyperghettoes" that do "not have an economic function and (are) stripped of communal organizations, which have been replaced by the state institutions of social control" (2008, 381). Inside these neighborhoods, social workers, therapists, teachers, and school administrators have also become an arm of surveillance. In his book *The Real School Safety Problem,* Aaron Kupchik emphasizes that "the criminal justice system is now a real part of our educational system" (2016, 35). And in social spaces that have shifted "from sites of caring, where students' academic and social needs are met, to sites of law enforcement," (2016, 35) it is no wonder that even the most prosocial youth in these neighborhoods are still at risk of falling onto the assembly line.

Jim came of age in this new era of surveillance and labeling, and therefore he was familiar with its machinations. On the day I met with him, we sat in his office to discuss his past and his current mentoring and advocacy work. I asked him why residents outside the boundaries of the prison assembly line should care about the millions of people going to prison each year. Jim smiled and answered, "Dr. Milton, you have me smiling because you are asking me the question of my life!"

On a sheet of notebook paper, I began to draw a picture of a prison next to a neighborhood. I drew a large circle around both to encapsulate them in a bubble. I dotted the picture with my pen: "To outsiders it [crime] looks contained. How do you get people outside of the bubble to care?"

Jim folded his hands and stared at the picture, saying, "The problem is that there's not that human connection. Honestly, once you start mentioning

African American children, they stop listening. They stop caring. That's why when I do my advocacy, I don't mention race. I just talk about *children*."

Jim scoffs at the idea that juvenile recidivism is not systemic:

> The juvenile justice system is exactly a pipeline. The problem is that we apply the same rules for all kids. But every kid has a different set of circumstances. For example, "Johnny" [a made-up person] might come in—and Johnny is in the minority—Johnny has his mother, has his father. They're both working. They both have bachelor's degrees or associate's degrees . . . you know, they're alright. So, Johnny is going to be alright.
> But the majority of kids are not like Johnny. The majority of kids got no education. Daddy's not around. Daddy's locked up.

Jim began to mimic one of his clients: "I don't even know daddy. Smoking. Drinking. Heavily in the streets. The neighborhood they're from . . . it's probably a place where you wouldn't want to raise a kid."

Recognized in Jim's comments are the structural *and* cultural forces that influence young African American and Latino teens, who make up 90 percent of prison entrants in New York City, as they navigate peer pressure, sociometric rank, and structural deprivation. Young boys see the social rewards that come with acting like a thug: increased popularity, being feared by adults, and street credibility (Milton 2012, 42). The cultural forces—which tend to lend themselves to discussion about personal responsibility—are far outweighed by the structural forces that keep young men and women from breaking the cycle of the prison assembly line. The structural deficits weigh heavy on youth as they return to their neighborhoods from prison. I was able to witness this struggle through the experiences of one of my other respondents, Phife.

THE VIEW BELOW THE WATCHTOWER

I met with Phife in his home on Nostrand Avenue in Brooklyn. We met at his doorway, and he guided me to the second floor. The entranceway opened to his kitchen, revealing a floor with old white linoleum tiles, some of which were faded and dirtied. Other parts of the floor were torn up, exposing the plywood underneath. To my left, Phife's mother—dressed in a multipatterned nightgown and slippers—sat on a folding chair in a small pantry, intently reading the daily newspaper.

We passed through the small kitchen and went upstairs toward a single bedroom. Phife offered me a folding chair in the bedroom next to a fan. As I sat, Phife pointed the fan in my direction. It was a welcome escape from the outside heat that had made his room sweltering. Phife turned off a nearby television and sat on a bed where his girlfriend was seated in the corner closest to the far wall, diligently texting on her phone.

Phife was in his mid-thirties, but had the face of someone half his age. He was around five-and-a-half feet tall, but his arms were very muscular. Years of lifting weights in prison had sculpted his upper body into a shape only seen on covers of men's health magazines. He sat at attention, eagerly awaiting my questions.

Phife had recently come back to Brooklyn after serving twelve years and ten months in several of New York State Department of Corrections and Community Supervision's prison facilities. He completed 85 percent of his sentence for manslaughter, the result of a fistfight gone too far. I asked him about his experience with reentry into his old neighborhood.

Phife's smile disappeared, as he told me, "Going back to the neighborhood that I came from and seeing these towers that I just came from. On each corner. You know, NYPD, these towers." Phife came home amid New York Police Department's rapid increase in mobile surveillance units, CCTV surveillance cameras, and stationary observation towers, which use both police officers and cameras to watch for criminal activity. "When I came home I was like, this ain't right. I'm not supposed to be seeing stuff like this. It looked like jail to me."

Phife explained his anxiety: "I seen it. I mean, officers on each corner. To be honest, it scared me. Because it seemed like I just got released from my nightmare, and then I come home and I'm about to revisit it all over again. It was scary. Something I had to adjust to."

This anxious relationship between police officers and neighborhood residents has continued to worsen over the past few decades. Before the 1980s, officers were trained as community advocates and to be a calming voice of reason; they were given the option to intervene in neighborhood disputes without making an arrest. But under the control of Mayor Rudolph Giuliani and Police Commissioner William Bratton in the 1990s, NYPD moved more

toward enforcement and obligatory arrests and away from community relations (Krauss 1994).

The excessive use of surveillance on urban streets and urban schools has
also increased the likelihood of children entering the criminal justice system earlier then generations past, as Kupchik (2016, 3) emphasizes:

> We have already been fortifying schools for the past twenty years. We have added
> police officers, surveillance cameras, and locked gates. We now have drug-
> sniffing police dogs searching students' possessions. We follow zero-tolerance
> policies and suspend, expel, or arrest students for minor misbehavior that
> would only have led to a trip to the principal's office a generation ago.

For youth like Phife, the odds were clearly stacked against him. It is not
uncommon for any seventeen-year-old to engage in juvenile delinquency,
but the surveillance in his neighborhood fast-tracked him to the pipeline.
Once he entered, he, like many others, would have to either fight against or
succumb to the demands of prison culture.

ALL CALL-OUTS ARE MANDATORY

Around the time that I met with Phife, I sat down with an acquaintance of
his, one who was very familiar with the juvenile justice system in New York.
Shanduke McPhatter—founder of Gangstas Making Astronomical Community Changes Inc. (GMACC) and an advocate to end gun violence—had
a lengthy history of imprisonment. Shanduke began his teenage years as a
New York City "Blood" gang member and frequent flier in New York's
prison system. After fifteen years of continuously cycling between prison
and home, only to recidivate again, he learned to create a more legitimate
path for himself, but not without some hard adjustments.

The damaging effects of prisonization can be near permanent for many
in New York's ex-prisoner population. Most damaging are the habits acquired while serving time in prison. Violence, hypermasculinity, and a
survival-of-the-fittest mentality govern the actions of most prison inmates. Many of these values develop in the prison system and spill back
onto the streets. Prison can turn a pacifist into a fighter, a tolerant liberal
into a white supremacist, a child into a brutal killer—all in the name of
survival.

These habits are so damaging that most ex-inmates must relearn how to adjust to their respective communities. The three young men I interviewed all had tales of difficult social adjustment and reinvention of their personal identity. Shanduke sat across an office desk in his GMACC headquarters, wearing a red baseball cap and sunglasses. He always looked intense, serious, determined.

Shanduke lamented how prison is a "training ground" for criminals:

If I used to be a stick-up man [armed robbery], and I want to rob someone. I can keep robbing people. Or if I go to jail and I got my man's in there that sells weight [drugs]. And I want to sell the weight because the stick-up game is not making enough money for me. And that's pretty much all the conversation in there, is war stories. The majority don't look for change.

On the streets of deprived neighborhoods, impressionable youth view prison as a means of toughening up or earning street cred. Young boys hear the violent tales and assume that prison time is an efficient rite of passage to manhood. What they do not hear about are the permanent physical disabilities that result from the violence, the drug addiction that is rampant in prisons, and the sexual exploitation that occurs on a regular basis.

Even though they have been incarcerated for not following the laws of the state, prisoners do live by a strict code inside of prisons, enforced by other inmates. Young entrants to prison learn about this code and the consequences for violating it. Phife recalled that when he was nineteen years old, he was "street smart," but not wise to the code of prison culture. He told me, "You know, they've got a saying up north. They say, '*All call-outs is mandatory.*'"

"What does that mean?" I asked

Well, there's a [paper] slip on every gallery. On every tear [individual floor of a cell block]. It'll let you know if you have a call-out to go to a class or program. Or to go to the hospital to check on an illness. But then the prisoners take it to a whole other level, with certain things is just a "no-no" upstate. Like telling another man to "suck your dick." You can die for that.

Phife leaned forward and clapped his hands: "That's mandatory. Something *has* to be done. Somebody calls you out into a knife fight; fistfight. That's mandatory. All call-outs are mandatory. You have to respond."

Phife recalled the first time he was called out:

I was arguing with this dude, and I was like, "Yo, suck my dick!" And this dude's whole demeanor changed. He put on his shoes, and then waited until I went into my cell, and was like, "You know you're going to be upstate for a little while?" And I was like, "Why you questioning me?" He smiled and was like, "You got a foul mouth. And if you tell someone loosely to suck your dick, you might not make it home." And then he was just "boom, boom, boom" and started putting blows on me. And that was his way of telling me I disrespected him.

Phife smiled and raised his eyebrows, "And you know, he fixed me up."

Phife described another time in which he was stabbed without provocation: "I got stabbed with something. A sharp object. I was thinking that I could do what I'm used to doing in the streets in jail. And my brakes got pumped very quickly. And I didn't even feel it at first." Phife explained that the fight was unprovoked and unexpected, but his obligation to fight was mandatory: "When we began to tussle and then we parted ways, I started to feel this burn right here." He pulled down the top of his shirt to reveal a nickel-sized poorly healed scar on the top of his chest near his heart: "And when I got back to my cell I looked and was like, '*Oh shit.*'"

Warrior tales like these make the prison experience so fascinating to those watching from the outside, especially to young boys from deprived neighborhoods. Modern-day ex-prisoners have no need to conceal their prison stories, because adolescents (and preadolescents) look up to them like war heroes.

This worldview only accelerates the pace on the neighborhood-to-prison assembly line. Young boys and girls under the watchful eye of New York's police apparatus maintain a "cool pose" (Majors 1993, 5) through deviant and criminal activity. All adolescents engage in some form of deviance during their teenage years, but prison culture offers the *most* devious, *most* menacing, *most* fear-inducing path to manhood.

I asked Shanduke why neighborhood kids look up to ex-prisoners. He shook his head and said,

It's a rite of passage. When I first came home in '99, I did 3 years. My weight was up [he had put on muscle]. I came back and the community was like, "Wassup, man?" Dudes was ready to do whatever I wanted them to do. Just violence, anything. And I look at then and now, and it troubles me because it was easier for me to get people to do the violent/negative stuff than it is today to get them to do the positive stuff.

On his last reentry into society in 2008, after serving three years in prison, Shanduke understood that the temptation to return to street life would be too great if he returned to his neighborhood, so he chose to stay with his sister in Atlanta for one year: "If a prisoner is to reform he has to focus on his individual needs, but a big facility is not going to focus on his individual needs." All three of my respondents recognized that getting off the assembly line would be difficult. Sometimes the hardest part of all is going against what is expected of you.

CONCLUSIONS

When constructed in late eighteenth-century America, prisons were designed to punish individuals for crimes, rehabilitate them, and reintegrate them into society. As penologist Andrew Von Hirsch would argue, prisons were meant to be places where we "treat offenders as wrongdoers" and allowed them time to contemplate their wrongdoings (Von Hirsch and Ashworth 2005, 35). They were places where criminals learned to become "worthy citizens."

Today prisons have evolved into warehouses for the unwanted: those unable to find gainful employment, those who lack the education to compete in a postindustrial global economy, and, in particular, youth who refuse to comply with society's tightening prosocial standards. For youth in impoverished neighborhoods, the labeling and punishment of the criminal justice system are promised at a young age, because they are monitored from the moment they step outside of their homes to the time they spend roaming the halls of their neighborhood schools.

Currently, schools act as the gateway to prison life: whether by the rites of passage propagated by their peers or through social control agents strategically placed in educational settings. School success (or failure) can dictate a child's criminal justice involvement. According to the National Center for Juvenile Justice, high school "dropouts are more likely than educated peers to be institutionalized" (Sickmund and Puzlanchera 2015). They are sixty-three times more likely to be incarcerated than college graduates.

The neighborhood-to-prison assembly line disproportionately affects children of color and youth raised below the poverty line. According to the same report by the National Center for Juvenile Justice, "Minority youth accounted for 75 percent of juveniles held in custody for violent offenses in 2010" (Sickmund and Puzlanchera 2015, 196). Neoliberal polices have emboldened the wealthier classes and shrunk middle-class opportunities, all while neglecting deprived youth who seemingly have no place in the modern world. Social critic Noam Chomsky would argue that the United States is following the trend of past third world nations:

There is a sector of great wealth, enormous wealth, there are large numbers of people who live somewhere between suffering and misery, and then there is a sector who are just superfluous; they're of no use, that is, they don't contribute to profit. So you just have to get rid of them somehow. Every Third World society has the same structure, and that structure is now being imposed on the United States. (2003, 47–48)

This acceptance of a third world status quo is what makes the neighborhood-to-prison assembly line so effective. We believe there *must* be a bottom if a select few are to rise to the top. And what better system of categorization and labeling than the ready-made classifications of race, class, and youth?

The stories of Jim, Phife, and Shanduke demonstrate both the structural and cultural forces at play in impoverished neighborhoods that send youth onto the neighborhood-to-prison assembly line: from Jim's survival-of-the-fittest mentality, to Phife's exposure to NYPD's surveillance apparatus, to Shanduke's admission that prison culture only prepares youth for continued criminal activity. If they act in their neighborhoods on the impulse to survive by any means, youth can easily be hauled into prison by school officials and law enforcement agents. Young people's first encounter with the carceral system increases their likelihood of incarceration—where they will be schooled in the criminal trades—and then their return to their heavily policed neighborhoods to practice these newly acquired skills, only to return to incarceration and repeat this cycle.

Children are our most precious commodity. They must not pay for the deficits of neighborhoods, schooling, or overtly visionless politics. Structure, culture, and individual characteristics will all play a role in feeding the assembly line, but the race, class, and age disparities begin and end with the neighborhoods in which we are born. No matter where they are from, each youth deserves a chance to be successful. As Jim would say, "Just talk about [them as] *children.* And then all of a sudden, [we're] looking at human beings."

QUESTIONS FOR REFLECTION AND GROUP DISCUSSION

1. What were some of the economic conditions in the 1970s and 1980s that led to the rise in mass incarceration in the 1990s?
2. According to Phife, how does the phrase "all call-outs are mandatory" apply to how one survives prison culture?
3. What sort of choices could the three respondents have made to avoid imprisonment in the first place?

REFERENCES

Cannon, Ashley, and Stephanie Ueberall. 2015. "Priorities for Preventing Youth Crime." Citizens Crime Commission of New York City. Retrieved from http://www.nycrimecommission.org/pdfs/CCC-Preventing-Youth-Crime.pdf.

Chomksy, Noam. 2003. "Drug Policy as Social Control." In *Prison Nation: The Warehousing of America's Poor,* ed. Tara Herivel and Paul Wright, 47–48. New York: Routledge.

Fagan, Jeffrey, Valerie West, and Jan Holland. 2002. "Reciprocal Effects of Crime and Incarceration in New York City Neighborhoods." *Fordham Urban Law Journal* 30, no. 5.

Haken, Jeremey. 2011. "Transnational Crime in the Developing World." In *Global Financial Integrity,* 32. Washington, DC: Center for International Policy.

Foucault, Michel. 1977. *Discipline and Punish: The Birth of Prisons.* New York: Random House.

Krauss, Clifford. 1994. "Bratton Builds His Image as He Rebuilds the Police." *New York Times,* November 19. Retrieved from https://www.nytimes.com/1994/11/19/nyregion/bratton-builds-his-image-as-he-rebuilds-the-police.html.

Kupchik, Aaron. 2016. *The Real School Safety Problem: The Long-Term Consequences of Harsh School Punishment.* Oakland: University of California Press.

Majors, Richard. 1993. *Cool Pose: The Dilemmas of Black Manhood in America.* Lanham, MD: Lexington Books.

McAdams, Dan P. 2008. "Personal Narratives and the Life Story." In *The Handbook of Personality: Theory and Research,* ed. O. John, R. Robins, and L. A. Pervin, 82. New York: Guilford Press.

Milton, Trevor B. 2012. *Overcoming the Magnetism of Street Life: Crime-Engaged Youth and the Programs that Transform Them.* Lanham, MD: Lexington Books.

Office of Children and Family Services, New York State. 2016. "Service and Treatment Programs for Juveniles." Retrieved from http://ocfs.ny.gov/main/jj_reform/default .asp.

Sickmund, Melissa, and Charles Puzlanchera. 2015. *Juvenile Offenders and Victims: 2014 National Report*. National Center for Juvenile Justice. Retrieved from https://www .ojjdp.gov/ojstatbb/nr2014/.

Travis, Jeremy. 2005 *But They All Come Back: Facing the Challenges of Reentry*. Washington, DC: Urban Institute Press.

U.S. National Institute of Justice. 2014. "Recidivism." Retrieved from https://www.nij .gov/topics/corrections/recidivism/Pages/welcome.aspx.

Von Hirsch, Andrew, and Andrew Ashworth. 2005. *Proportionate Sentencing: Exploring the Principles*. Oxford: Oxford University Press.

Wacquant, Loic. 2000. "The New Peculiar Institution: On the Prison as Surrogate Ghetto." *Theoretical Criminology* 4: 377–389.

——. 2008. "Ghettos and Anti-Ghettos: An Anatomy of the New Urban Poverty." *Thesis Eleven* 94 (August): 113–118.

Chapter Seven

CONSIDERING INEQUALITIES

Experiences in Part-Time Youth Work

YASEMIN BESEN-CASSINO

KIARA'S STORY

On a busy shopping day, Kiara's car is parked in front of the popular sporting goods chain where she has been working for the past year. Her shift is about to start in mere minutes, and in her car, she is trying to change out of her frilly blouse, tailored pants and high heels to an athletic leisure look. In the past year, she has been juggling two jobs: she works both in the apparel section of the sporting goods store and as the receptionist at a physical therapy center for children. She is not happy with either position, but cannot quit because she needs the money. She would prefer working just one job, but neither employer is willing to give her enough hours. She is also on call and has to work some busy shifts, so on days like today, she does a full shift at the physical therapy center—hoping the last parents pay ahead of time—and drives miles to the sporting goods store. The physical therapy center wants her to dress professionally in dress shirts, jackets, and heels; the sporting goods salespeople have to sport an athletic/leisure look. It is not out of the ordinary for her to change her clothes in her car as she shuttles between jobs.

Kiara is a twenty-year-old African American college student who is an undergraduate at the nearby state university. She plans to go to graduate school and become a social worker. She is also a student-athlete running track and field. To help with school expenses, she has been working two jobs, which requires her to maintain two wardrobes and two distinct demeanors at work. Her experience with part-time jobs has been markedly different from that of her white peers.

In this chapter, I focus on the lived experience and everyday reality of part-time jobs from the perspective of the main actors, the young people themselves. When we talk about part-time jobs, we typically assume all of them are the same: they are often seen as minimum wage jobs, mostly in the service sector, and all the young people who take them are identical. Yet race plays a central role not only in access to part-time jobs but also in how they are experienced. Young people of color have a harder time finding jobs, and their experience in the same jobs vastly differ from that of white peers.

To better understand these part-time jobs, I conducted an extensive qualitative study of young workers. My qualitative data collection began in January 2016 as part of a larger, book-length project (Besen-Cassino 2018). In this chapter, I focus on the narratives of five participants that highlight the everyday, lived experience of work and inequality from the perspectives of the young workers. The use of these narratives and detailed stories is purposeful. While statistics can point to larger, broader trends of inequality based on race and gender among young workers, they cannot tell us about how these inequalities are experienced. In-depth interviews allow respondents to tell their stories and in their voice, which is essential for uncovering the daily mechanisms through which inequalities are created and reinforced in everyday life (see also Gubrium and Holstein 1998).

All five participants for the in-depth interviews and narrative analysis were from eighteen to twenty-one years old and were full-time college students who held part-time jobs. They were recruited through snowball sampling at one large state university and one private liberal arts college. Both institutions are located in affluent, predominantly white suburbs of a major metropolitan city. These locations offer ample opportunities for retail and service sector positions, as well as freelance jobs such as babysitting jobs. These narratives highlight the experience of finding and keeping jobs.

The stories provide insight into the racialized and genderized inequality these young people experienced in part-time work. On the surface, the jobs that young people take appear to be identical: they are retail or service sector jobs with similar pay. It is important, however, to acknowledge the individual differences of these workers and problematize workplaces as a site of inequality, both of which make the lived experience of part-time jobs vastly different. A qualitative approach is especially important because, more than unveiling inequalities, it can help us identify the mechanisms through which everyday experiences create and reinforce racial inequalities in the workplace for young people.

I met Kiara, whose story is central to this chapter, at the nearby college where she is a full-time student. I first interviewed her on campus, in between her classes, and focused on her work experience for my book *The Cost of Being a Girl* (2018). I had just finished a book, *Consuming Work: Youth Labor in America* (2014), for which I had interviewed mostly white, middle-class students about their work experiences in service and retail jobs in affluent suburbs. These suburban, middle-class youth gushed over their work experiences, describing the cool brands they got to associate with, the discounts they received for the products they already loved, and all the like-minded people whom they got to hang out with. Kiara's experience of the same type of part-time service and retail jobs was markedly different from these hundreds of work experiences I had heard from mostly suburban teenagers. Kiara then introduced me to others who worked in similar sectors and had similar experiences to her.

JUST A PART-TIME JOB?

Part-time work has come to be seen as an important component of young people's lives in the United States. The notion that it builds character, teaches a work ethic, shows the value of money, or just provides young people with some pocket change has ingrained part-time work as a quintessentially American phenomenon. It is contrasted with youth work and labor typically associated with developing countries and sweatshops, contexts that are often considered problematic and exploitive. Theories and studies of exploitive jobs for young people have focused on working youth in developing countries. Even the United Nations Convention on the Rights of the Child argues that children and youth benefit from light work, which is based on the part-time model of youth work in the United States. Perhaps because of these assumptions, the work conditions of youth in the United States have rarely been problematized, and we rarely think about the experience of young workers in the United States.

While young people have worked consistently, their labor force participation peaked around 80 percent during the 1980s, with higher labor force participation in the summers. However, with the recent economic recession and changes in service sector jobs, young people's labor force participation has dropped considerably. Many service and retail jobs have become exceedingly difficult to get. Chris Tilly and Francoise Carré (2011) have shown that previously these jobs could be obtained by simply passing the pulse test, by having a pulse, or the mirror test, by breathing and fogging up a mirror. Today, these jobs have become much more competitive, as young people vie for them alongside immigrants, older people, and many others. It is important to note, however, that not all youth have been affected equally by the decline in availability of jobs.

According to the Bureau of Labor Statistics, in 2016, the employment rate for youth between ages sixteen and twenty-four was 62.7 percent for white youth, 53.8 percent for African American youth, and 56.2 percent for Hispanic youth. In addition, African American youth have experienced a sharp 2.6-percentage point decline in employment rates since 2007. Similar racial and ethnic inequalities exist in unemployment rates. The unemployment rate is 11.5 percent for white youth between ages sixteen and twenty-four, in contrast to a staggering 20.6 percent for African American youth (Bureau of Labor Statistics 2016). Race thus plays a central role in access to part-time jobs. In this chapter, I explore the mechanisms through which that inequality is experienced from the perspectives of the actors: race also has an important effect on the way jobs are experienced.

AESTHETIC LABOR

In addition to the shrinking number of service and retail jobs, the hiring requirements for these jobs have been stricter in recent years. Since service and retail employees are the face of the business, employers are looking for workers who embody the look of the brand and who "sound right" (Grugulis and Bozkurt 2011; Gatta 2011). These "look" requirements can often be racially biased and disadvantage African American youth.

Because many companies want young and energetic people to represent them, young people have emerged as a natural pool of applicants for these jobs. Young women who possess the right look and the appropriate set of soft skills have become especially desirable in retail and service sector jobs, especially high-end clothing stores, designer boutiques, and artisanal shops. Lynne Pettinger's ethnographic study of London retail stores emphasizes the desirability of fashionable young women in high-end clothing boutiques: "Fashion orientation is one face of brand strategy and the ability to present a fashionable appearance is one of the skills needed by sales assistants in many stores" (Pettinger 2006, 468). Physical attractiveness and youth are important, as is self-presentation. David Wright's work shows that "physical attractiveness, particular style of dress, and types of physical comportment all contribute to the production of the retail space as meaningful and aesthetically pleasing to the customer" (2005, 305). After all, retail companies sell not simply the goods and services displayed but also a certain brand experience: the workers are not simply selling, but rather are mediating the relationship between the customer and the product, creating an interactive relationship between the products and the workers (Gatta 2011; see also Pettinger 2006).

Young workers, especially young women, have become central to the brand strategies of these companies. While this rich body of work focuses on the advantages that being young confers on these workers, the effects of race are left outside the discussion. The emotional and aesthetic requirements asked of an African American worker, like Kiara, are very different from those asked of the young white women in my sample. Even for young attractive people, race still matters and does so in unexpected ways.

GETTING THE JOB IS NOT EASY: RACE, GENDER, AND AESTHETIC LABOR

When I spoke with Shawn, a junior at a state university, he echoed many racial and gender biases. Born and raised in Newark, New Jersey, he is the first in his family to go to college. He is double majoring in sociology and political science; he is also an African American man, over six feet tall, with a large build. He told me that young women have it easy when it comes to finding jobs, but that because of his race and size, he does not meet the aesthetic labor requirements. Shawn was only able to find work as the Easter Bunny at the nearby mall, and he attributes his getting the job to the fact that he is completely in costume: "I dress as the Easter Bunny. They [the parents] would never let their kids sit on my lap if they knew what I really looked like." He applied for many retail and service jobs, but was turned down. "I didn't have the right look. . . . I never have the right look," he told me. "When I wait at the ATM, the line in front of me clears very quickly: they [the other customers] think I am going to rob the bank." In addition, many high-end boutiques in town or retail establishments at the nearby mall tossed his application aside when they saw his Newark address. Locally, Newark is seen as crime ridden. To avoid putting a Newark address on his applications, he now uses his campus address. "College girls," he said, "have an easier time getting jobs."

Indeed African American female students may have an easier time getting jobs than do their male counterparts, if they fit the aesthetic of the store to which they apply. Kiara recalled that when she applied for her job at a sporting goods store, her experience running track in college and high school helped her immensely. She said that, even though she could not afford the sporting goods sold at the store, she had an easy time getting the job because she fit the athletic aesthetic they were seeking. As Prue Huddleston observes, quoting the manager of a sporting goods store, the store sought employees who looked "like they do the sport themselves, for example, we've got people who are interested in skateboarding, cycling, climbing, that sort of thing; it's a lifestyle thing, and of course those are the sort of youngsters we get coming here looking for jobs" (2011, 115).

Kiara's case was similar: she had another athlete friend working for another department, who told her about the opening, and she was hired readily. Her athletic look, muscles, and sporty attire are what got her the job. Of course, this same aesthetic made it more difficult for her to get a job elsewhere, especially in the apparel industry. She got rejected from many clothing stores because she did not have the right look. She was told her athletic build and muscles did not really fit the "look" of those clothing stores: to them, she simply was not feminine enough. Another African American woman I spoke with, Janelle, was told that her hair was a "problem," that she had to control it, and that it did not look polished and professional. "Polished and professional hair" was described as straightened and nontextured: her natural hair was not considered appropriate for the brand. Of course, there are other ways in which aesthetic labor requirements can prevent young people from getting jobs: when Janice, an African American college student applied to a clothing store, she was told she would not fit into the clothes. Overall, the aesthetic requirements of many companies made it challenging for many participants I spoke to get jobs. Many were told their look did not fit the company's image. As a result they ended up settling for fast food jobs, or it took longer for them to find jobs.

Going into Credit Card Debt to Get the Look

As is well documented by a wide range of studies, many companies require or encourage their young part-time employees to use the products that they sell (see Besen-Cassino 2014; Misra and Walters 2016; Williams and Connell 2010). By using the products and wearing the clothes, the workers become the face of the corporation, thereby displaying the image of the store. Second, by doing so, workers show knowledge of the products and a commitment to them. Potentially, this knowledge and brand loyalty can make them more relatable and approachable to the customers. This constant requirement to display the look of the corporation forces many young people to acquire substantial amounts of debt. Applicants of color who have limited resources often go into credit card debt to get and keep the jobs they apply for.

Address Bias

Mason tells me one of the biggest obstacles to getting a job is his home address. He is from an a African American, low-income neighborhood in Newark. When Mason started looking for jobs, he wanted to find retail and service sector jobs close to his home. Unfortunately, few local outlets of franchises were nearby. He had to wait to find a job until he had a car and often had to travel long distances. The availability or lack thereof of jobs in lower-income areas has been well documented. John Bound and colleagues (1992) show that one of the causes of racial inequality in employment is the scarcity of jobs in areas where African American teenagers live. Jobs available to teenagers tend to be concentrated in predominantly white and more affluent locations. Such concerns are especially important to younger teenagers, for whom transportation can be a major limiting factor. Even after getting their driver's licenses, many may not have a car or reliable access to one. Because public transportation is often limited to less affluent areas, getting to and from jobs adds substantial time and cost to teenagers' job searches and work experience. Rosella Gardecki (2001) finds that residence constraints, lack of car ownership, long commutes, and high commuting costs often result in lower employment rates and limited job searches for minority youth.

These differences are not just confined to the early teen years: Gardecki finds that they persist even for workers between the ages of sixteen and twenty-four. While existing research documents the difficulties in access to jobs, they rarely explore the strategies young people use to find and keep them. Mason tells me because of the lack of retail outlets in his neighborhood, he has been applying to jobs at more affluent malls, which are far from his home. At the mall in Short Hills, which has high-paying jobs, he experienced "address discrimination." According to Mason, potential employers see his address in Newark and toss the application. Sometimes, businesses assume that his friends from Newark will come and hang out at the store. Others worry that his friends from the neighborhood will come to the store and ask him for free stuff. So just like Shawn, who as discussed earlier decided to put his campus address on applications, Mason uses his grandmother's address.

LIVED EXPERIENCE OF JOBS

For many youth of color, getting jobs is challenging, but inequality in access to jobs is only part of the picture: the lived experience of the job itself is markedly different for youth of color. Kiara tells me that the experience of the job and the job expectations are different for her than for her white peers. The sporting-goods store requires "a whole different level of mental preparation, especially if you're working the cash register." In addition to the mental switching she does before she comes into the store, she has to prepare herself for tasks that she knows will be unpleasant:

I talk to myself for a long time, [saying,] "You're going to be fine now," because I have gotten so many shoe boxes and other stuff thrown at me. . . . We don't take expired coupons or competitive coupons. [Customers] try to exchange Sports Authority merchandise, and they always compare us and shout at me. Like, "At Sports Authority, they don't do this." [I want to say,] "Well, then, go to Sports Authority. Then why are you here?" [But] if I said that, there would be a bigger argument. It's very aggressive with the customers. They are not friendly whatsoever; every once in a while you get a friendly one, but it's rare. You have to be friendly. We have a greeting; we have to greet every customer. . . . Because we do surveys, we get complaints, like, "You guys greet too much." [But] I don't know if someone greeted you in another department. They complain about too many greetings. . . . Sometimes they come in and ask for our managers specifically and complain like we weren't help[ful], but we ask a few of them [customers], "Where did we mess up?" They say we saw the customer or we didn't come and pick up the items—and, like, it is not our job to shop for you. They expect us to put [items] in their cart and walk with them. They expect to hand us a list and tell us what the[ir] child is doing, like activities, and [ask us], "Can you find all this stuff?" [They want us to say,] "Yeah, like, we'll shop for you."

Kiara felt the expectations of customer service for her were different than for her peers: there was extra pressure, and she felt that not all women her age were treated the same way at her work. Lisa, a white college student from an affluent suburb, for example, works at a yoga chain, and she said she has not experienced that type of customer behavior. She said her customers respond to her calm, quiet demeanor and overall Zen attitude. She rarely thinks about her work in terms of race and class, but her specific job placement within the yoga chain and the way she is treated by the customers are very different from Kiara's experience. Thus the race of the young worker has an important effect on what is expected of her in the workplace, especially in the emotional labor she has to perform and how customers approach her. On the surface, Kiara and Lisa might have similar retail jobs with similar pay, yet the lived experience of these jobs is markedly different because on their different race and class positions.

An important component of many service sector and retail jobs today is emotion work. In Arlie Russell Hochschild's (1979) study of flight attendants, she argues that women in the service sector embody not only interactive components but also middle-classness. Most flight attendants in her study were women from middle-class backgrounds, and in their work, they had to embody middle-class standards of appearance and attributes. They were assumed to have acquired middle-classness and middle-class interactive social skills while growing up and to be able to translate them into the workplace (Leidner 1993; Hochschild 1979; Otis 2011; Pierce 1995).

In addition to their class component, such expectations of self-presentation and emotion labor displays have a racial element: emotion labor, in addition to being gendered and classed, is also raced. Adia Harvey Wingfield (2009), for example, shows that the same emotions have different social meanings depending on the employee's gender and race. For example, the social meaning of anger and its expressions are different for African American men than for others. While African American men's expressions of anger and frustration are perceived as threatening and induce fear, white women's expressions of anger in the workplace are trivialized and not seen as real threats; they may even be interpreted as related to menstruation and not tied to work conditions. Because women's anger and frustration are seen as extensions of biology, they are more likely to be dismissed as irrational. Bodily self-presentations and expressions of emotions also rely heavily on gender stereotypes. Men and women are socialized to learn and internalize appropriate behaviors and expressions, and they come to be seen as natural (Butler 1993; West and Zimmerman 1987).

Kiara had limited options in terms of self-presentation. She was not allowed to be angry. She was supposed to be nice and serve customers with a smile. Yet when her white colleagues served with a smile, they were praised; she was not. Some customers even complained that she greeted them too much. Kiara said that when she is extremely nice, the customers shout at her even more. And when she failed to smile or greet someone, customers complained. Several times, when customers complained about expired coupons, they did so in very angry tones. Despite the fact that Kiara tries very hard to serve with a smile and mentally prepare herself before every shift to be nice and pleasant, her niceness is not met with the same customer reaction as that evoked by white workers. While the niceness of the white girls is seen as genuine, the niceness of an African American girl is viewed as a ploy and met with anger. A customer even complained because her smiles and concern did not seem genuine enough. In fact, she shared that she has been told that she was not genuinely nice, but was just pretending to be.

Yet, despite having shoe boxes thrown at her and being shouted at periodically, Kiara has had a very difficult time expressing anger and frustration. She would sit in her car to mentally prepare herself before her shift or would take breaks, but she rarely expressed her frustration in the workplace. She told me that arguing with the customers "would make it worse." When customers shout at her, she just takes it. When she complained about the customers to her supervisor or coworkers, she was met with little sympathy. While Wingfield's research suggests that anger and frustration are off-limits to African American professionals in the workplace, they are also expected to be pleasant. However, in the case of Kiara, attempts to be nice and pleasant were met with suspicion from the customers, and she was accused of not being genuine.

CONSEQUENCES

Young people's part-time jobs seem like a uniform category. However, not all jobs are the same and neither are all the youth. There are many layers of inequality among youth: race is a major source of inequality. Based on my in-depth interviews, I found that race plays a major role in access to jobs. Many African-American youth have a hard time finding jobs. With aesthetic labor requirements, many potential applicants are told they do not have the right look. These aesthetic requirements are harmful because they obscure the structural inequalities in hiring. In order to find jobs and keep jobs, many young people are acquiring serious credit card debt.

Being shut out of the workforce has important social and economic repercussions. The money earned by part-time works enables many young people to stay in school. Some need these funds to support their families and contribute to household expenses. In addition to economic benefits, part-time work also yields social benefits. My earlier work with a national coffee chain found that working fulfills a social function for many suburban teenagers by creating a common space and vocabulary to socialize (Besen-Cassino 2014); it provides an opportunity to meet new people and socialize with friends. Workplaces offer common spaces for young people to hang out free of the supervision of parents and the scrutiny of other adults.

CONCLUSION, POLICY IMPLICATIONS, AND FUTURE DIRECTIONS

Working part-time while still in school is a quintessentially American phenomenon. In their landmark study of youth employment, *When Teenagers Work* (1986), Greenberger and Steinberg assert that part-time work is so ingrained in our culture that we rarely think about its social significance. However, it is important to explore its social and economic implications for teenagers. More importantly, it is necessary to acknowledge, both methodologically and socially, inequality in access to jobs and in the lived experience of those jobs. Race and gender are key in understanding that inequality. African American teenagers find it much more difficult to get jobs for a variety of reasons, now that part-time work opportunities are not as widely available as in the past. The ones that are offered have aesthetic labor requirements: to look good and sound right to fit the brand. Such requirements result in bias against African American workers who are told they do not have the right look for the job. Geographic discrimination is another mechanism through which young African American workers experience bias in hiring. Young workers who live in traditionally African American towns and neighborhoods have reported that employers are reluctant to hire teens from lower-income neighborhoods. In addition, many African-American young workers have a different experience on the job than their white peers. The emotion labor expectations are more challenging for young African American workers to meet: they are expected to be happy and smile, but these expressions are not appreciated or seen as sincere and are not valued and rewarded as they are for white youth.

This chapter has explored the ways in which the access to jobs and the everyday lived experience of part-time jobs are highly racialized, with certain emotions not available to young workers of all races. The young people's narratives illustrate the challenges African American youth face in finding jobs and how, even when they get these jobs, their everyday experiences are markedly different from those of their white peers. They often face discrimination and abuse from customers, and their emotional expressions in the workplace are restricted.

These inequalities have both economic and social repercussions. Economically, many young people need part-time jobs to cover their own extra expenses, some contribute their salary to their families, and some depend on their earnings to stay in school. Socially, since many part-time jobs have social benefits, young people of color can also be deprived of these benefits if they are unable to find jobs. Even when they get these jobs, they face bias and abuse in the workplace, creating stress and anxiety.

It is important to understand these inequalities in part-time jobs. Methodologically, by focusing on narratives, we can uncover the mechanisms through which these inequalities are reinforced and experienced. Future studies should further explore young people's perspectives to determine if there are other forms of inequality for youth jobs. Theoretically, it is important to uncover structural inequalities and problematize the different experiences of young people, rather than seeing part-time work as a uniform category.

QUESTIONS FOR REFLECTION AND GROUP DISCUSSION

1. What policy changes can help young people of color in the job market?
2. What are the different ways in which race, gender, and class affect youth's experiences in getting work and at the workplace?
3. How do these narratives compare or contrast to your experiences with part-time work?

REFERENCES

Besen-Cassino, Yasemin. 2014. *Consuming Work: Youth Labor in America*. Philadelphia: Temple University Press.
———. 2018. *The Cost of Being a Girl: Working Teens and the Origins of the Gender Wage Gap*. Philadelphia: Temple University Press.
Bound, John, Richard B. Freeman, and Jeff Grogger. 1992. "Arrests, Persistent Youth Joblessness, and Black/White Employment Differentials." *Review of Economics and Statistics* 74, no. 1: 100–106.
Bureau of Labor Statistics 2016. *Employment and Unemployment Statistics*. August 17. https://www.bls.gov/news.release/youth.nro.htm
Butler, Judith. 1993. *Bodies that Matter: On the Discursive Limits of "Sex."* New York: Routledge.
Gardecki, Rosella M. 2001. "Racial Differences in Youth Employment." *Monthly Labor Review* 124, no. 8: 51–67.
Gatta, Mary. 2011. "In the Blink of an Eye: American High-End Small Retail Businesses and the Public Workforce System." In *Retail Work*, ed. Irena Grugulis and Ödül Bozkurt, 49–67. London: Palgrave Macmillan.
Greenberger, Ellen, and Laurence Steinberg. 1986. *When Teenagers Work: The Psychological and Social Costs of Adolescent Employment*. New York: Basic Books.
Grugulis, Irena, and Ödül Bozkurt. 2011. *Retail Work*. London: Palgrave Macmillan.
Gubrium, Jaber F., and James A. Holstein. 1998. "Narrative Practice and the Coherence of Personal Stories." *Sociological Quarterly* 39, no. 1: 163–187.
Hochschild, Arlie Russell. 1979. "Emotion Work, Feeling Rules, and Social Structure." *American Journal of Sociology* 85, no. 3: 551–575.
Huddleston, Prue. 2011. "It's Alright for Saturdays, but Not Forever: The Employment of Part-Time Student Staff within a Retail Sector." In *Retail Work*, ed. Irena Grugulis and Ödül Bozkurt, 109–127. London: Palgrave Macmillan.
Leidner, Robin. 1993. *Fast Food, Fast Talk: Service Work and the Routinization of Everyday Life*. Berkeley: University of California Press.
Misra, Joya, and Kyla Walters. 2016. "All Fun and Cool Clothes? Youth Workers' Consumer Identity in Clothing Retail." *Work and Occupations* 43, no. 3: 294–325.

Otis, Eileen. 2011. *Markets and Bodies: Women, Service Work, and the Making of Inequality in China*. Stanford, CA: Stanford University Press.

Pettinger, Lynne. 2006. "'On the Materiality of Service Work." *Sociological Review* 54, no. 1: 48–65.

Pierce, Jennifer. 1995. *Gender Trials: Emotional Lives in Contemporary Law Firms*. Berkeley: University of California Press.

Tilly, Chris, and Françoise Carré. 2011. "Endnote: Perceptions and Reality." In *Retail Work*, edited by Irene Grugulis and Ödül Bozkurt, 297–306. London: Palgrave Macmillan.

West, Candace, and Don H. Zimmerman. 1987. "Doing Gender." *Gender& Society* 1, no. 3: 125–151.

Williams, Christine, and Catherine Connell. 2010. "Looking Good and Sounding Right: Aesthetic Labor and Social Inequality in the Retail Industry." *Work and Occupations* 37: 349–377.

Wingfield, Adia Harvey. 2009. "Racializing the Glass Escalator: Reconsidering Men's Experiences with Women's Work." *Gender and Society* 23, no. 1: 5–26.

Wright, David. 2005. "Commodifying Respectability: Distinctions at Work in the Bookshop." *Journal of Consumer Culture* 5, no. 3: 294–314.

PART II

Autoethnography and Storytelling

Chapter Eight

FINDING JUSTICE

Transforming Schools with the Children We Serve

MERY F. DIAZ

A PRELUDE

There was not time to finish my morning coffee, already a sign of what the day had in store. Rushing to make the A train I dodged straphangers, but ran into a woman with my backpack when I jumped into the subway car. I exhaled the expected "Sorry!" and pushed my way in just before the doors closed—a small victory, because I would make my train connections to the South Bronx, just in time for the school's 8 a.m. morning meeting. It was the year 2012, and I had been commuting to various schools in the South Bronx; on this day I was headed to an elementary school. I worked for a nonprofit organization that partnered with high-need and underresourced urban public schools to develop integrated school-based mental health (SBMH) services. We addressed the academic and socioemotional needs of children by identifying at-risk students, improving counseling and referral to community services, and training teachers.

Over the past two decades, the implementation of SBMH programs has grown exponentially, not only because of their potential to improve academic performance but also because they fill a service gap when community resources are lacking. Federal mandates requiring the use of evidenced-based tiered approaches have also contributed to this growth. During my time working in Bronx schools, I learned that SBMH services, while critical to meeting student needs, can be challenging to effectively implement in underresourced public schools. The challenges to implementation are part of a broader context in which public schools are pressed for resources, where practice trends center on "fixing" children instead of systems and interventions fail to address the racialized and classed experiences of children in schools. For SBMH practices to be truly effective, they must also work to disrupt the reproduction of systemic inequality by eliminating exclusionary and oppressive policies that contribute to a revolving door of students in need.

I am a bilingual Latina social work educator who attended public schools. I came from a socioeconomic and cultural background similar to that of many of the children in the schools where I worked. Like most children who attend public schools, my school experiences were shaped by the educational policies, school practices, and socioeconomic circumstances of the time, which determined where I grew up and the schools I had access to. Social networks also played an important role in my educational experiences. While I personally never became involved with school mental health services, the intersection of poverty and exclusionary school practices certainly shaped my experiences. In my professional career I have borne witness to how these factors exacerbate already challenging socioemotional conditions for many children.

In this chapter, I offer a *testimonio*, a narrative construction of my varied experiences in New York City public schools as a student, a consultant, and a researcher into one cohesive account. The testimonio is a narrative method deeply rooted in critical Latina feminist pedagogical scholarship. Blackmer-Reyes and Curry Rodriguez (2012, 363) describe it as a "first-person oral or written account, drawing on experiential, self-conscious, narrative practice to articulate an urgent voicing of something to which one bears witness. The objective of the testimonio is to bring to light a wrong, a point of view, or an urgent call for action . . . the testimonio is intentional and political)." It does not intend to offer an unbiased perspective, but pursues social justice by countering dominant narratives through the act of storytelling. Bernal, Burciaga, and Carmona (2012, 527) write, "From these endeavors come documents, memories, and oral histories that can be used to recast and challenge pervasive theories, policies, and explanations about educational failure as a problem, not of individuals, but of systemic, institutionalized practices of oppression."

This testimonio explores how school practices and SBMH approaches fit within a neoliberal economic and educational context that limits public resources, disadvantages children, and especially marginalizes poor Black and Latin@[1] children. Neoliberal ideology posits that market-driven strategies are the key to innovation and improving the human condition. This set of ideas presumes that choice, competition, individualism, and the privatization of public goods facilitate motivation and efficiency. Arguably, neoliberalism has deepened inequality, weakened the welfare state, and increasingly relied on surveillance and the management of problems (Foucault, 1991; Piven, 2015). In education, this has meant reduced spending for public schools, increased competition for funding, harsh accountability measures, and rigid practices aiming to improve student outcomes (Ravitch, 2010, 2013). For SBMH practitioners, this has meant promoting child wellbeing in a context that narrowly focuses on risk identification, categorization, and management. For poor children of color, this has meant negotiating inequality and disempowerment in schools and being labeled as the problem. My hope is to continue to encourage a different way of thinking about children, contextualizing their overall experiences beyond labels and categorization. In so doing, I encourage movement away from placing the burden of change on the individual child toward changing the dominant structures that affect their lives.

I exited the subway, and as I crossed the street toward the school, a wintry mix of rain and snow forcefully hit my face. We know that more integrated schools fare better academically, but this school mirrored its surroundings (Rumberger & Palardy, 2005). The student body was almost entirely Black and Latin@ and was part of the most segregated school system in the country (American Community Survey, 2015). Racial segregation is not the only form of adversity that children in the Bronx face, however. More than 90 percent live in poverty. The Bronx also has some of the highest rates of infant mortality, children living in shelters, and food insecurity in the nation (Citizens Committee for Children, 2017).

We have also long understood that poverty negatively affects children's cognitive functioning, behavior, and socioemotional health (Jensen, 2009).

Socioeconomically disadvantaged Black and Latin@ youth are two to three times more likely to develop mental health conditions than other children, and the longer they live in poverty, the higher the risk (Reiss, 2013). As a former clinician, I was aware that connecting children to community services is crucially important, but incredibly challenging. Schools thus are an essential interface for the provision of mental health services, delivering up to 85 percent of the services that children do receive (Rosen, Nakash, & Alegría, 2014). Still, many children do not obtain much-needed support.

In New York State, for example, because schools are financed regressively, schools in low-income communities with a higher concentration of need do not receive adequate funding to support their students (Baker, Farrie, & Schiarra, 2018). This means they hire less qualified teachers and experience high teacher turnover, large class sizes, less space and equipment, and fewer student support personnel and training to meet their needs. Serving a staggering concentration of poor students, racial minorities, and English-language learners, Bronx schools are unsurprisingly the lowest performing in the city. Many low-income urban schools across the nation are also struggling with similar challenges. Acknowledging this lack of resources, there has been a surge of nonprofit organizational support for the development of varied types of SBMH programs (Picard Ray & Ahlem 2016; Weist et al., 2014).

When I finally made my way to the front steps of the school, I looked up at the aging gray and red brick building with gated windows. The schoolyard had been reduced to the size of an indoor gym to make space for the "temporary" trailers that housed the kindergarten classes. The trailers had already been there for five years while the city considered permanent expansion options.

Once inside the building, I signed in with the school resource police officer and flew up three flights of stairs. The weekly meetings to discuss at-risk or crisis cases took place in the principal's office. The other team members were already there. I sat down quickly at the conference table just as Wanda[2], the school social worker, was getting started, and said, "OK, good morning everyone. Let's begin. Today we have three cases. Two are follow-ups, and one is a new referral." I found myself thinking, "I hope this is working."

INSIDE AND OUTSIDE THE LABEL OF RISK

Lessons from my experiences as a student, juxtaposed with voices of youth from research on school experiences, reflect how an "at risk" framework in education can be a limiting and unjust paradigm for meeting the needs of children. Children's struggles in school are often perceived as intrinsic. Problems are seen as flaws of the individual child, who is then labeled "at risk," a term often predetermined by race, class, or gender, rather than linked to systemic inequality, the flow of capital, or a lack of opportunity and access to resources (Brown 2016; Pollack 2010; Wells 2015). The targets of intervention are the children who "cry out" for behavior and emotional help, and not the structural conditions that create barriers for all children.

My mother, an Ecuadorian immigrant, and my father, a Dominican immigrant, arrived separately in New York City during the late 1960s. Both skilled workers, they obtained visas at a time when manufacturing jobs still served as an economic engine in the United States. My brother and I were born in the city, but like many children with transnational immigrant lives, we lived in Ecuador with extended family during a rocky period in our parents' marriage. By the time we returned to the United States in 1984, still very young, my parents had separated. We lived with my mother who worked as a seamstress and struggled to obtain sufficient work in a rapidly disappearing garment industry. My older brother and I entered public school in Washington Heights, a northern Manhattan neighborhood then undergoing a rapid demographic transformation. During this time, the Irish and Jewish people were fleeing to the suburbs as Dominican immigrants flooded into the community. Broadway served as the border, dividing the remaining white middle-class residents on the west side from the newer and poorer Latin@ immigrants on the east side. Snyder (2014) writes that, during the 1980s and 1990s, Washington Heights was a neighborhood in the shadow of the Bronx. Economic and racial tensions, as endemic as in the neighboring borough, fiercely manifested in the schools:

Ninety percent of the students who crowded into District 6 were poor enough to qualify for free lunch. Eighty percent were Latinos, the majority of them Dominican making the difficult transition to a new language. . . . In 1984, only 35.2 percent of the students in District 6 were reading at or above their grade level, the lowest percentage of all of the city's districts. Citywide, the figure was 53.9 percent. (Snyder, 2014, 148)

The elementary school I attended tracked and grouped students by ability into classrooms, a practice shown to primarily benefit students in higher-ability groupings (Gamoran, 1992). Having just arrived from Ecuador, I was placed in a bilingual first-grade track. Bilingual education was originally intended to help immigrant children learn English, but has ultimately resulted in segregating them from their English-speaking peers; immigrant children typically remain in this setting for three years (Elizalde-Utnick & Guerrero, 2014).

I quickly came to understand that "bilingual" was perceived as "dumb" and had low status in the social order. *Mainstreamed* students often called out, "The bilingual kids are coming!" in jest as we entered the lunchroom, or they used the term pejoratively during fights. My Latin@ English-speaking peers, who predominantly spoke Spanish at home, had internalized that bilingualism brought little cultural capital in a space that demanded assimilation. In a cultural shift, today there is increasing interest in bilingualism through language-immersion education—a model where all students in a school are taught subject matter in two languages. Research demonstrates that students benefit cognitively and academically from mastering different languages (Nicolay & Poncelet, 2015), and some also laud bilingualism for its potential to increase an individual's marketability in a global economy. Activists, however, point to the lack of equal access to dual-immersion programs for poor children.

Throughout elementary school, my brother and I, "latchkey" kids, made our way home alone and waited for our mother to return from work. In those days, *las vecinas* (women neighbors) would check in on us while we watched afternoon cartoons. *Las vecinas* and my mother had met through the tenant's association that was formed to fight a landlord who refused to provide basic heat and hot water during the brutal winters.

Eventually the jobs in the garment industry dried out, and our mother lost her job; when unemployment benefits eventually ran out as well, our family had to rely on *"welfea"* (public assistance) and odd jobs for a while. We kept afloat, but the worry was constant. Worry about money. Worry about crime and drugs in the neighborhood. Worry about my brother's asthma. Worry about missing school due to hospital visits. Worry that people would judge our "situation." Worry about not causing more "worry" for our mother who was doing everything alone. I never saw a counselor or received support in school, however. I was not on their radar because I was not a "problem." I just managed like many of my peers going through similar experiences.

By third grade, I was already speaking English, but remained in the bilingual track. It was a *vecina* who prompted my mother to push the school to place me in an English-language classroom. This move set off a ripple effect in my academic trajectory. I did well in the new setting, and the next year I was promoted to the second-highest track class where I connected with my teacher. She was an older Black educator known for her strict classroom and high expectations, and she mentored me. Overall, I liked school. I was good at it, was "well behaved," and generally I felt teachers liked me— probably because I was not a "troubled child."

After elementary school I was zoned to attend an "underperforming" middle school. But with help from a local activist and family friend, I was able to negotiate a place in the competitive middle school, on the other side of the border, west of Broadway. My new school was more diverse, better resourced, and academically stronger. Through its art and music programs, advanced placement classes, afterschool supports, and activities, we were prepared to enter competitive high schools in the city. I loved drawing. An art teacher who noticed worked with me to prepare a portfolio for an audition for placement in a specialized arts high school. I made it in.

While in high school, which was well resourced and sociodemographically diverse, I was offered a rich curriculum and had the option to choose from many extracurricular activities. One afterschool program stands out as particularly influential. *Aspira* was a leadership program for Latin@ youth, where I was encouraged to develop a positive cultural identity and engage in civic action and activism. *Aspira* was an influential part of the process of figuring out who I was and understanding my Latina identity and my social position. I met role models who looked like me and understood my experiences. Challenging socioeconomic conditions, language barriers, and educational policies shaped my schooling experiences. I was able, however, to negotiate and overcome barriers with the support of positive social networks who saw value in me and programs that helped me build on my strengths. Not all children have these advantages.

Youth Voices from the Margins

Some children can overcome unequal and marginalizing school experiences. They might have access to social and cultural capital or to supportive individuals and programs in schools like I did. Many others, however, often excluded through socioeconomic circumstance, experience disengagement and isolation. These students, often labeled "at risk" or "troubled," might express agency through defiance and aggression, which can be self-defeating behaviors, to the degree that their schools are ill equipped to meet their needs. Explorations of youth interactions with their schools offer a window into how youth interpret and respond to their racialized, classed, and gendered school experiences.

In a South Bronx high school, Jonathan Kozol (1991), an educational reformer, talked with students about conditions in their schools. Alexander, a sixteen-year-old Jamaican boy, observed, "You understand things better when you go among the wealthy. You look around you at their school. . . . Then you come back home and see that these are things that you do not have." Janice, a student in the same school, shared, "I make it my business to know my fellow students. But it isn't easy when the classes are so large. I had 45 children in my fifth-grade class. The teacher sometimes didn't know you." Rosie, her peer, agreed: "The teacher asks me, 'Are you really in this class?' 'Yes, I've been here all semester.' But she doesn't know my name" (1991, 104–105). These youth reflect on how they perceived and negotiated the physical and human resources lacking in their schools.

In a study comparing Puerto Rican high school graduates (school kids) and those who dropped out (street kids), the latter shared themes of low self-esteem, behavior problems, bullying, disengagement, and exclusion (Flores-González, 2002). Manuel, a street kid, said, "I got kicked out of grammar school. Well, I have a temper, and I was real nervous, and for anything I got mad. So I grabbed the chair, and I threw it at her [teacher], and I broke her arm in three places. And they kicked me out . . . it was worse. All I used to do is fight. Just fight. I used to be a bad kid. . . . I had some cookies, and she took them away" (2002, 39). Another street kid, Angel, shared, "Grammar school was not that good. I had bullies [picking on me], and I was fighting all the time. . . . I had pretty much a hard time . . . insecure. . . . I was so quiet, and that attracted people to come mess with me" (37). In another study on the racialized and gendered ways in which Caribbean students experienced school, a student shares, "My junior high school was mostly Black people and Hispanic people. Being Dominican caused you to be in fights. It made you become a victim of maybe an African American or a Puerto Rican, so it was dangerous . . . it's different for girls: they are not tested in the same way" (Lopez, 2002, 51). Indeed, many of the girls in the study reported more positive relationships with teachers and were given more opportunities for advanced placement courses and honors activities than were the male students. Another young person stated, "The worst part about high school was teachers, and security guards had bad attitudes and things like that . . . some teachers spoke to you so low [condescending] like you're stupid" (2002, 52). Similarly, in the study by Luna and Revilla (2013, 29), a male student speaks grippingly about his experiences with discrimination in school:

With Latinos, everything is gang related. If three Latinos are hanging out, it's a gang. They'll [school police] stop you and pull up your shirt to check out your tattoos, then take pictures. I walked into one of my English classes and I just had a sweater and I just sat down and put my head down and the teacher actually, she called the school police thinking that I was going to shoot up the school only because I had my hoodie up and put my hands down.

These students' descriptions of their surroundings express their disillusionment. The disappointment and frustration about their interactions with adults remind me of many of the peers I went to school with and many of the children I saw through my work.

What Comes of Disinvestment, Segregation, and Exclusion

In a broad study of hundreds of metropolitan areas and school districts, Reardon, Kalogrides, and Shores (2017) found that the academic achievement gap was strongly linked to racial and ethnic differences in family income, level of education, and local racial/ethnic segregation, and affects educational opportunity and school segregation patterns. However, even after adjusting for racial socioeconomic inequality and segregation, the academic achievement gap between White students and students of color persisted in many districts, suggesting other factors. Similarly, Yosso (2006) argues that this inequality is often reproduced inside of schools through "deficit and subtractive practices" directed toward students of color: tracking into vocational and special education classes; segregation by race; overcrowded and poorly maintained schools; untrained teachers; little access to college preparation, advanced placement, and honors courses; increasing stakes based on biased standardized tests; and dismissive treatment. These structural conditions collide with the socioemotional needs of vulnerable students. Students in low-income, high-need urban schools exhibit higher rates of disruptive and externalizing behaviors, but the staff is often unprepared to deal with the range of issues. Consequently, Black and Latin@ children are three times as likely to be suspended, inappropriately referred to special education, or experience unwarranted emergency room referrals (Mickelson, 2003; Kohler & Lazarín, 2007). Notedly, for children who are in crisis or emotional distress, school police often become responders, setting off a ripple effect of inappropriate interventions and criminalization (Advocates for Children, 2017). In contrast, White middle-class children are more often "medicalized" to address their socioemotional and behavioral concerns (Ramey 2015). These outcomes, however, are not naturally predetermined, but are, by design, part of a system that is full of inequities. School mental health scholars and practitioners recognize these disparities and have pushed for increased SBMH services, but their effectiveness is limited when the racialized, classed, and gendered experiences of children go unaddressed.

THE PRACTICE OF SBMH IN A NEOLIBERAL CONTEXT

We are the beneficiaries of start-ups, ventures, and innovation in every other area of life, but we don't have that in education because it's a closed system, a closed industry, a closed market. It's a monopoly. It's a dead end.

BETSY DEVOS, 2015 SXSWEDU CONVENTION IN TEXAS

Not long ago, Betsy Devos, before being appointed the U.S. education secretary, delivered a speech that described the public education system as a "dead end" for innovation (Strauss, 2016). She is among many neoliberal education reformers seeking to privatize education. In her speech, she identified school choice and other market-driven strategies as the only options for saving "at risk" children from the grip of "failing" public schools. For many of us concerned with the well-being of children, these are familiar labels. They form part of a popular and neat narrative where a "broken" public education system threatens American competitiveness in the globalized world. Materialized into a moral panic, this narrative has seen billions of dollars poured into privatized attempts for solving the problem of schools. The proliferation of charter schools, nonprofit consultation services, increased testing, data collection, new technologies, and increased surveillance are occurring in tandem with the siphoning off of public school funding. But what are the implications of framing public schools as failing and children as needing to be fixed? What are the goals of a market-driven education system, and how does it drive school practices and SBMH services? And what does this mean for children?

Wanda began the meeting as she distributed the agenda. Crowded around the table were a second-grade teacher, the vice principal, the guidance counselor, two related service providers for special education students, a literacy master teacher, and the on-site mental health clinic social worker. Interdisciplinary teams are known for increasing collaboration and efficiency and are perceived positively by school staff (Bronstein, 2003; Diaz, 2015a; 2015b). When the school year began, the team had identified more than 50 children in a school of 1,200 who were academically and socioemotionally "at risk." This designation was based on their diminished academic performance, chronic absenteeism and lateness, history of suspension, and persistent behavioral issues. Students were prioritized from high to low risk and triaged. Student data and family histories were collected and presented. The team aimed to reduce behavioral problems through support services instead of reactionary and punitive discipline. An overarching goal was to improve student's standardized test scores and thereby eliminate the risk of school closure.

Earlier federal educational policies like No Child Left Behind, Race to the Top, and Common Core placed tremendous pressure on schools to improve children's academic performance (Ravitch, 2013). This pressure was palpable in every underfunded and underperforming school and among the teachers, staff, and students I worked with. When public schools fail to meet standards measured by standardized tests, they risk losing funds, teachers and administrative staff, and students; ultimately, they risk closure. To meet standards, many schools narrow the curriculum and focus on test prep. Schools have also increasingly adopted "zero tolerance" policies and punitive behavioral codes as ways to keep students on track (Brown, 2016). These practices are common, but are particularly found in "no excuses" urban schools that are not held to the same federal regulations as public schools: they place strong emphasis on standardized testing and have arguably deepened segregation for Black and Latin@ students by targeting low-income communities. Overall, schools are cutting back on curriculum and increasing the monitoring and policing of student behavior.

The second grade teacher attending the meeting went on to present the case of an individual student, identifying his problem behaviors that she had struggled to address. The child, new to the school, was having difficulty adjusting to the setting, sitting still, and transitioning, and he displayed aggression toward others. The child's mother spoke with the teacher early on about her unemployment and housing instability, but had not followed up with a meeting with the school social worker to complete a social history and intervention planning. The team asked the teacher clarifying questions about behaviors and triggers. They suggested strategies for helping the student become more self-aware and able to self-monitor behavior, as well as ways to restructure his day to reduce transition triggers. Wanda also suggested that one-on-one counseling begin when she had cleared space in her schedule.

As we talked, the assistant principal was suddenly called away to deal with a student incident and left the meeting. We needed his approval to restructure the student's schedule and wanted him to set up a parent meeting, but this would have to wait. The teacher also returned to her classroom. Focusing primarily on individual behavior, we did not discuss schoolwide approaches, nor did we identify support for parents.

We moved quickly to a follow-up case, conscious that we were short on time. That case involved bullying in a third-grade classroom where the guidance counselor had delivered a classroom conflict-management program. Students had been learning to diffuse conflict through the use of shared language and techniques to mediate problems as a collective. The counselor was enthusiastic about the decrease in classroom conflict. Bullying was a schoolwide concern, but with limited personnel to deliver classroom interventions, she could only reach three classrooms that year.

Ten minutes were left. Everyone started to shuffle papers in anticipation of their next task. The last case involved a student referred to the on-site school mental health clinic for withdrawn, depressed mood and inconsistent attendance. The student's family, recent immigrants who did not speak

English, had lived in three different places over the last two years. Her parents had been inconsistent with attending family counseling sessions, reporting issues with their work schedule. We recommended in-home intervention through our community mental health partner. The services offered both by the school clinic partnership and the community clinic partnership eliminated the wait time, but these much-needed resources relied heavily on external funding and coordination. The sustainability of the partnerships was uncertain.

After the meeting, Wanda and I met for our weekly consultation. We were interrupted often by staff and students looking for her for one reason or another, but we managed to discuss how things were going with her schedule. She told me, "Nothing is formal. The way time is in the school you have five minutes here, and you have fifteen minutes there. We get pulled in so many different directions. It's difficult when things pop up because your schedule does not allow for things to pop up!" With a dry sense of humor I appreciated, she added, "What's an appointment?"

"I do have one because you have to," Wanda continued as she discussed the challenges in keeping schedules and appointments. "So I have a schedule for when I go into the classrooms. I have a schedule of meetings and with my students for individual [counseling sessions]. Individual cases work better in the morning. Crisis for whatever reason seems to be less." Wanda had managed her schedule so that she could attend to individual students' crises and emergencies, which would increase as the school day progressed. She reminded me of another social worker working across ten schools struggling to manage her day, who shared, "I hardly have any time to actually use my education and training to help students with mental illness," and another who said, "One factor is time and availability on the part of teachers and myself. Teachers do not have enough time to sit and plan for children's needs in the classroom." Time is a precious resource.

We talked for a bit about her cases before I rushed to deliver a weekly professional development session with fourth-grade teachers. My team was building capacity by training all teachers over the span of three years on the sources of challenging behaviors, how to identify common triggers, and ways to implement classroom management techniques. We often talked about their feelings of ambivalence with the training. In these professional development sessions, teachers often expressed feeling unsupported by the school administration in their attempts to address student need, or they were frustrated by their inability to do so because they lacked the skill or the time, while facing pressure to increase student's test outcomes. They also felt parents were difficult to engage in addressing student needs and that some students were unmotivated. In turn I felt like I was placing one more responsibility on their shoulders.

It was easy to understand why school-wide mental health practices were last on the list. Even when there is ideological support for SBMH services, their effectiveness is hindered by a narrow focus on individual student change and the fact that resources are simply not there. Time and role constraints, heavy student caseloads, and limited funding pose barriers (Serpell, Clauss-Ehlers, & Weist, 2013). Lack of skills, training, and cultural responsiveness also pose obstacles, while the more intensive services are often limited to youth enrolled in special education, to those in crisis, or to those labeled as "at risk" (Kelly et al., 2016). Universal interventions— essential for changing the school climate, destigmatizing mental health services, and promoting positive student engagement—are the least-implemented aspects of SBMH. Recently, however, the Every Student Succeeds Act (2015) has shifted focus away from testing toward other aspects of school functions as measures of school quality. The act includes increased funding to address student's mental and behavioral needs. SBMH programs are positioned to help schools move away from harsh disciplinary responses in favor of increasing student supports; reflecting on how they fit into and potentially maintain the neoliberal status quo in schools is a critical step to moving toward more just, culturally responsive, and effective methods.

Risk, Surveillance, and Power

Foucault's (1991) concept of *governmentality*—the ways in which the state exercises control or governs its people—can be a useful framework for understanding the role of SBMH in the neoliberal education context. Neoliberal governmentality was of special interest to Foucault because of the ways in which it teaches people to govern themselves, shapes their conduct, and makes "the art of governing" an embodied experience. Furthermore, this framework highlights the structure and function of power in this process. School professionals, for example, have the power to categorize what is "normal" and "abnormal" student behavior and to develop techniques for "child saving" or rescuing, in order to help realize their potential as citizens within a neoliberal state. Children thus become discrete objects—individual "at risk students"—targeted with specific interventions that modify behavior.

Wells (2015) summarizes how governmentality works: "If the central reason of government is the production of problems, its central technique is the production of programs that aim to resolve the problems. Of central importance to how modern governments resolve problems is getting the people who are part of the problem to feel that they want to behave differently." Standard SBMH practices primarily operate in this manner, focusing on extensive and intrusive data collection regarding "at risk" children and targeted behavior interventions. Often SBMH programs come into schools through precarious relationships with nonprofit organizations, many of which are directed by corporate philanthropic boards that emphasize extensive data collection, assessment, and monitoring; targeted results; and the development of replicable models. The same market forces that exacerbate the need for student services through the economic destabilization of poor communities of color and through disinvestment in schools open new markets in the treatment of children, but do little to address the socioeconomic source of their problems.

TOWARD A SOCIAL JUSTICE APPROACH

> What are we doing in the name of interventions with kids and families? What do we believe about the sources of their troubles and why? Are interventions done in the "best interests" of other people's children ones that we would support for our own children?
>
> FINN (2009, 38)

As I ponder these questions and the kinds of school settings that I consider healthy, supportive, and inclusive, I think back to the early 2000s. During my last year as a master's-level social work student, I interned at a small alternative high school in lower Manhattan. The school occupied the corner sections of two floors within a larger traditional high school. The school social worker had taken on the supervision of three interns, in effect building a small counseling department. Nearly 200 students were enrolled in this alternative school. Serving primarily Black and Latin@ students, it was still slightly more integrated than the average school in the city at the time. Many students had transferred there due to academic, behavioral, or socioemotional concerns that were not adequately addressed in their prior setting. What struck me the most about this school was the relationships that teachers and students developed with one another. The environment was unlike any of my own school experiences or any I had seen by that time. It seemed as if everyone knew one another. Small groups of students attended a daily advisory session with a homeroom teacher. Every week, students and teachers met in a town hall meeting to discuss community concerns and make school governance decisions together. And students had a voice! They participated in *fairness committees* where they worked to resolve a variety of conflicts and disciplinary concerns. The counseling office was a one-stop shop for multiple arenas of student support: this setup served to destigmatize the counseling office because students could visit it for many reasons. As an intern, I met with students, ran socialization and interest groups, made referrals, and also helped with college and financial aid applications. I knew the school was a special place, but I did not yet know how or why it was special.

That school is Humanities Prep Academy (Prep). In her ethnographic study with students and faculty, Hantzopolous (2016) illustrates Prep's model for educating and building community and describes it as a human rights approach. It emphasizes participatory education, humanizing students' experiences, and democratizing school culture. Student are enabled to work through conflicts and ideological or political differences through the built-in structures designed to give them a voice and a safe space to question and contest, in sharp contrast to the trend of punitive disciplinary approaches in schools. Growing research in this area has led many schools across the nation to adopt various models or components of social justice and human rights school practices, acknowledging that positive school environments are critical for the emotional and behavioral well-being of children. Approaches that incorporate these elements go by many names, including restorative justice education practices, positive behavioral supports, pedagogical practices for border thinking, critical pedagogy, antioppression practices, just practice perspective, human rights education, and a culturally responsive model of recovery. The scope of this chapter does not allow me to go into an in-depth discussion of each approach, but this section highlights their shared elements that can serve to transform SBMH services.

At the core, social justice educational frameworks implement strength-based, culturally responsive, restorative, trauma-informed, and preventive practices for all students. Acknowledging and valuing students' layered identities and complex societal experiences are also essential to the process. A central goal is to engage student participation as active agents who can make decisions on issues that directly affect their lives, including conflict and behavior issues that arise in their school community. There is an effort to eliminate hierarchical structures and to disrupt the replication of power and inequality through building community and consensus. These practices also acknowledge inherent biases in traditional practices for addressing student need, and they work to reframe the ways adults think about, label, and interact with students. Another key focus is the creation of safe spaces for the most vulnerable students—those who are undocumented, homeless, or identify as LGTBQ—even when they are not on the school's radar. To reach these aims, it becomes critically important to hire sufficient, diverse, and inclusive staff—individuals in whom students can see themselves—to support students.

While not grounded in social justice, multitiered SBMH frameworks can be structured to integrate these concepts at the schoolwide level. As mentioned earlier, schools more often focus on individual and targeted group interventions. However, universal-level practices that involve students and families in decision making, strategizing, and developing responses to their needs can work to foster school connectedness. Other critical practices include creating interpersonal relationships between teachers and students and all members of the school community. This is done by serving together on committees; building shared norms, goals, and values; improving teaching and learning practices; building cultural identity as strengths; and dismantling organizational structures that serve to marginalize and disempower students. School connectedness is linked to improvements in student's emotional health, problem solving, well-being, self-regulation, academic outcomes, and school-related self-efficacy: it encourages positive development in young people (Clauss-Ehlers et al., 2013: Zullig et al., 2014). Finally, a critical social justice issue, and a highly contentious one, is that of integration. Research demonstrates that integrated schools are organized in ways that focus less on compliance and discipline, and more on development and achievement (Rumberger & Palardy, 2005). When schools have smaller concentrations of high-poverty students, educators can devote extra attention to their neediest pupils, significantly reducing gaps in achievement (Benner & Crosnoe, 2011). In short, embodying a social justice approach in school services contests and disrupts neoliberal and risk frameworks that reproduce inequality for children in schools.

SEEKING GOOD ENDS

Through the use of testimonio, a reflection of my personal and professional experiences in schools, and a review of the literature on school experiences, I explored ways in which neoliberal disinvestment and school practices marginalize and disempower children. Children, especially poor Black and Latin@ students, arrive in schools carrying the weight of social problems and inequality, but are expected to adjust to the demands of ill-resourced school environments. Those who struggle are labeled "at risk," and their needs are often met with punitive, unresponsive, or insufficient supports. Meanwhile the needs of those able to manage their settings are overlooked. While SBMH services help shift school practices from punitive approaches to ones that support students, effective implementation can be difficult in underresourced and segregated schools. Funding, time, resources, skills, and cultural responsiveness are often insufficient. The ways in which schools think about children and the sources of their problems also present challenges. If SBMH services are to effectively address the needs of poor Black and Latin@ students they must adopt a social justice perspective. This means acknowledging the socioeconomic and environmental factors contributing to their needs, dismantling exclusionary and demoralizing school practices, and resisting placing the burden of change on children alone. Corrigan et al. (2005, 365) observe that a social justice perspective

would target institutions that traditionally may not be considered worthy goals for change because they seek good ends (such as healthcare providers or police officers), but do so in ways that marginalize, exploit, or, in the worst case, victimize people with mental illness. A social justice perspective would scrutinize the means and the unintended effects of how institutions and larger political arrangements do not enable or empower people with mental illness.

Schools, in seeking good ends, must work to center the experiences and dignity of children, especially those who are most vulnerable. They must transform how they perceive, talk about, interact with children and how to democratize power: including children and youth in decision making is an integral element of school mental health practice.

QUESTIONS FOR REFLECTION AND GROUP DISCUSSION

1. How can factors outside of school affect children's academic and socioemotional outcomes?
2. What is neoliberal ideology, and how does it shape school practices and services?
3. What social justice interventions have you experienced in your schooling, if any?

NOTES

1. The use of Black with a capital B is used by scholars and activists to represent an empowered identity and to acknowledge the collective culture, ethnicity, and historical experience of Blacks in America. Black references the people of the African diaspora, understanding colonialism and slavery as central to the experience of American Blacks. Similarly, the use of Latin@ (latino/latina) represents a collective political identity, and the symbol @ is used by activists to promote gender inclusivity while rejecting patriarchal notions of the gender binary. It is important to note that all racial and ethnic categories are capitalized in the U.S. Census.
2. Wanda is a pseudonym, and her story represents the experiences of social workers I worked with in schools and those I interviewed for research.

REFERENCES

Advocates for Children. (2017). *Children in crisis: Police response to students in emotional distress.* Retrieved from http://www.advocatesforchildren.org/sites/default/files /library/children_in_crisis.pdf?pt=1.
American Community Survey. (2015). Press release. Retrieved from https://www.census .gov/programs-surveys/acs/news/data-releases/2015/release.html.
Baker, B., Farrie, D., & Schiarra, D. G. (2018). *Is school funding fair? A national report card* (6th edition). Newark Education Law Center. Retrieved from www.school fundingfariness.org.
Benner, A. D., & Crosnoe, R. (2011).The racial/ethnic composition of elementary schools and young children's academic and socioemotional functioning. *American Education tion Research Journal, 48*(3), 621–646.

Bernal, D. D, R. Burciaga, & J. Carmona. (2012). Chicana/Latina *Testimonios*: Mapping the methodological, pedagogical, and political. *Equity and Excellence in Education*, 45(3), 363–372.

Blackmer-Reyes, K., & Curry Rodríguez, J. E. (2012). *Testimonio*: Origins, terms, and resources. *Equity & Excellence in Education*, 45(3), 525–538.

Bronstein, L. R. (2003). A model for interdisciplinary collaboration. *Social Work*, 48(3), 297–306.

Brown, K. D. (2016). *After the "at-risk" label: Reorienting educational policy and practice*. Disability, Culture, and Equity Series. New York: Teachers College Press.

Citizens Committee for Children. (2017). *Keeping track of family homelessness*. Retrieved from https://www.cccnewyork.org/data-and-reports/publications/keeping-track-of -family-homelessness-in-new-york-city/.

Clauss-Ehlers, C. S., Serpell, Z., & Weist, M. D. (2013). *Handbook of culturally responsive school mental health: Advancing research, training, practice, and policy*. New York: Springer.

Corrigan, P. W., Watson, A. C., Byrne, P., and Davis, K. E. (2005). Mental illness stigma: Problem of public health or social justice? *Social Work*, 50(4), 363–368.

Diaz, M. (2015a). Facilitating urban school social worker collaboration with teachers in addressing ADHD: A mixed-methods assessment of urban school social worker knowledge. *School Social Work Journal*, 39(2), 63–78.

——. (2015b). Tales and trails from consultation: Improving interdisciplinary teams and collaborative practices for school social workers and teachers. *Reflections: Narrative of Professional Helping* [Special issue on Interprofessional Collaborative Education and Practice], 19(4), 41–50.

Elizalde-Utnick, G., & Guerrero, C. (2014). Best practices in school-based services for immigrant children and families. In P. L. Harrison & A. Thomas (Eds.), *Best practices in school psychology: Foundations* (pp. 99–111). Bethesda, MD: National Association of School Psychologists.

Finn, J. L. (2009). Making trouble: Representations of social work, youth and pathology. In L. Nybell, J. Shook, & J. Finn (Eds.), *Childhood, youth, and social work in transformation: Implications for policy and practice* (pp. 37–66). New York: Columbia University Press.

Flores-González, N. (2002). *School kids/street kids: Identity development in Latino students*. New York: Teachers College Press.

Foucault, M. (1991). Governmentality. In G. Burchell, C. Gordon, and P. Miller (Eds.). *The Foucault effect: Studies in governmentality* (pp. 87–104). Chicago: University of Chicago Press.

Gamoran, A. (1992). The variable effects of high school tracking. *American Sociological Review*, 57(6), 812–828.

Jensen, E. (2009). *Teaching with poverty in mind: What being poor does to kids' brains and what schools can do about it*. Alexandria, VA: ASCD.

Kelly, M. S., Frey, A., Thompson, A., Klemp, H., Alvarez, M., & Cosner, S. B. (2016). Assessing the National School Social Work Practice Model: Findings from the Second National School Social Work Survey. *Social Work*, 61(1), 17–28.

Kohler, A., & Lazarín, M. (2007). Hispanic Education in the United States. *Statistical Brief* (National Council of La Raza) 8, 1–15.

Kozol, J. (1991). *Savage inequalities: Children in America's schools.* New York: Crown

Lopez, N. (2002). *Hopeful girls, troubled boys: Race and gender disparity in urban education.* New York: Routledge Press.

Luna, N., & Tijerina Revilla, A. (2013). Understanding Latina/o school pushout: Experiences of students who left school before graduating. *Journal of Latinos and Education, 12* (1), 23–37.

Mickelson, R. A.(2003). The academic consequences of desegregation and segregation: Evidence from the Charlotte-Mecklenburg schools. *North Carolina Law Review, 81,* 1513.

Nicolay, A. C., & Poncelet, M. (2015). Cognitive benefits in children enrolled in an early bilingual immersion school: A follow-up study. *Bilingualism: Language and Cognition, 18*(4), 789–795.

Picard Ray, K. & Ahlman, C. (2016). Mental health services in the schools: Collaboration in a multi-tiered system. In L. V. Sosa, M. Alvarez and T. Cox (Eds.), *School social work: National perspectives on practice in schools* (165–176). New York: Oxford University Press.

Piven, F. F. (2015). Neoliberalism and the welfare state. *Journal of International and Comparative Social Policy, 31*(1), 2–9.

Pollack, S. (2010). Labelling clients "risky": Social work in the neo-liberal welfare state. *British Journal of Social Work, 40*(4), 1263–1278.

Ramey, D. M. (2015). The social structure of criminalized and medicalized school discipline. *Sociology of Education, 88*(3), 181–201.

Ravitch, D. (2010). *The death and life of the great American school system: How testing and choice are undermining education.* New York: Basic Books.

——. (2013). *Reign of error: The hoax of the privatization movement and the danger to America's public schools.* New York: Alfred A. Knopf.

Reardon, S. F., Kalogrides, D., & Shores, K. (2017). The *geography of racial/ethnic test score gaps* (CEPA Working Paper No.16-10). Stanford Center for Education Policy Analysis. Retrieved from http://cepa.stanford.edu/wp16-10.

Reiss, F. (2013). Socioeconomic inequalities and mental health problems in children and adolescents: A systematic review. *Social Science & Medicine, 90,* 24–31.

Rosen, D. C., Nakash, O., and, Alegría, M. (2014). Disproportionality and disparities in the mental health system. In R. Fong, A. Dettlaff, J. James, & C. Rodriguez (Eds.), *Addressing racial disproportionality and disparities in human services: Multisystemic approaches.* New York: Columbia University Press.

Rumberger, R. W., & Palardy, G. J. (2005). Does segregation still matter? The impact of student composition on academic achievement in high school. *Teachers College Record, 107*(9), 1999–2000.

Serpell, Z. N., S., Clauss-Ehlers, C. S., & Weist, M. D. (2013). Next steps: Advancing culturally competent school mental health. In C. S. Clauss-Ehlers et al. (Eds.), *Handbook of culturally responsive school mental health: Advancing research, training, practice, and policy* (pp. 251–260). New York: Springer.

Snyder, R. W. (2014). *Crossing Broadway: Washington Heights and the promise of New York City.* Ithaca, NY: Cornell University Press.

Strauss, V. (2016). The telling speech Betsy DeVos gave about education—full text. *Washington Post,* December 21. Retrieved from https://www.washingtonpost.com

/news/answer-sheet/wp/2016/12/21/the-telling-speech-betsy-devos-gave-about
-education-full-text/?noredirect=on&utm_term=.a99953732df6.

Weist, M. D., Lever, N. A., Bradshaw, C. P., and Owens, J. S. (2014). Further advancing
the field of school mental health. In M. D. Weist et al. (Eds.), *Handbook of school
mental health: Research training, practice, and policy.* New York: Springer.

Wells, K. (2015). *Childhood in global perspective* (2nd ed.). London: Wiley.

Yosso, T. J. (2006). *Critical race counterstories along the Chicana/Chicano educational
pipeline.* New York: Routledge.

Zullig K. J., R. Collins, N. Ghani, J. M. Patton, E. Scott Huebner, & J. Ajamie. (2014).
Psychometric support of the school climate measure in a large, diverse sample of
adolescents: A replication and extension. *Journal of School Health, 84*(2), 82–90.

Chapter Nine

FITTING IN, LETTING GO, AND OTHER COMMON CONCERNS FOR CHILDREN WITH DISABILITIES

SHERRI L. RINGS

I am a licensed clinical psychologist and tenured associate professor at a large, East Coast urban college. I also count myself among the approximately 15 percent of the world's population (more than one billion people) who lives with a disability (World Health Organization 2011). I have cerebral palsy. This disability can present itself in different ways. It can affect body movement, posture, balance, and reflexes, as well as muscle control, movement, and coordination. Speech, hearing, or visual impairments, as well as learning disabilities, intellectual disabilities, and epilepsy, can affect individuals with cerebral palsy (Cerebral Palsy Alliance 2018). Cerebral palsy can occur during or shortly after birth. In my case, I was born five weeks prematurely, and the umbilical cord was wrapped around my neck several times, cutting off oxygen to my brain. The main symptom I experience is muscle tightness (spasticity) in my legs, which affects the way I walk and sometimes my balance. For example, I cannot walk up a flight of stairs without holding onto a railing, and I have to be very careful walking on icy sidewalks.

As a psychologist and professor, I have read a lot of research and literature about what life was supposed to be like for me and other children with disabilities. I say "supposed to be" because, while it can be helpful to know the symptoms of a particular disability, how the symptoms might progress over time, and challenges that children with disabilities (and their parents) might encounter, I have found that the research does not adequately capture my childhood experiences with or my feelings about having a disability. The generalizations drawn from research samples often do not reflect my unique experience, especially during childhood, or the experiences of many others with disabilities whom I have counseled or known in other contexts. Therefore, while I cite statistics and other information here and use research to inform what I write, this chapter is an autoethnography. I reflect on how I experienced my disability, how my parents co-experienced and adjusted to my disability, my school experiences, my relationships with parents and peers, perspectives and policies that have shaped those experiences, and life lessons I have learned. By taking an ecological perspective in this exploration, I contextualize my experiences and those of other children with disabilities within a broader cultural and sociopolitical environment and disability discourse. The ecological perspective is a good fit for exploring disability experiences because it takes into account the "complex interplay of psychological, social, economic, political, and physical forces" in shaping an individual's experiences (Pardeck 1988, 134).

I was born in 1970, the same year that Congress enacted the Education of the Handicapped Act (P.L. 91–230). The purpose of this law was to encourage states to develop educational programs for individuals with disabilities. However, it preceded the Rehabilitation Act of 1973, the Individuals with Disabilities Education Act (IDEA), and the Americans with Disabilities Act of 1990 (ADA). Although each of these disability laws was designed to improve the lives of those with disabilities, people with disabilities generally experience greater poverty, poorer health, lower educational attainment, and fewer employment opportunities than those without disabilities (World Health Organization 2011). The experiences of children with disabilities are heterogeneous and intersectional. Their ability to negotiate societal perceptions of their "difference" and their status as protected or marginalized and excluded are highly contextual. I have come to realize that growing up in a white middle-class family; having a support system that accepted me and my disability; and having parents who were employed, had medical insurance, and were able to advocate for me and navigate the red tape of the medical and educational systems played a large part in the person I have become today.

ADJUSTING TO DISABILITY

I begin this ethnography by reflecting on what we understand about parental adjustment to their children's disability. I start here because so much of what children experience is shaped by how adults and caretakers view them and their capacities and vulnerabilities. Most new parents are excited about the birth of their child or children. For months or even years, they may have imagined what it would be like to have a child whom they can love, teach, and shape. They have likely imagined their child's future—what career their child should pursue, the friends he or she will have, the sports their child will play or other hobbies he or she might have, and how their child will grow up to be an independent adult. But what happens if parents find out their child has a disability? How might their ideas, plans, and feelings change?

Kathleen Kotel, whose daughter Talia was born with a heart condition and Down syndrome, has described how she felt after Talia's birth (2013, 208):

The days that followed were filled with confusion, fear, and anxiety. My life suddenly turned into a world of experts, doctors, and lists of things to do to attempt to make my daughter as normal as possible. Our family and friends were extremely supportive in their own way. . . . They were trying to be encouraging. I wish we all knew then what we know today. Her life, just like that of any other child's, is to be celebrated. Not to be grieved, feared, or a reason to make us hero parents.

Kotel's experience is not uncommon. With parenthood comes a rush of different emotions and expectations, some of them societally determined. Learning about and adjusting to a child's disability can seem overwhelming at times, and parents may need to imagine a different future for themselves and their child. Much has been said about grieving the loss associated with finding out you or someone you love has a disability. While the process of grief has sometimes been described as a series of stages, it is not universal. However, common emotions associated with the grief process include denial, anxiety, fear, guilt, depression, and anger (Moses 2004). Moses points out that, although each of these emotions can be viewed negatively in our society, they also serve a purpose. For example, denial "buys the time needed to blunt the initial impact of the shattered dream, to discover the inner strengths needed to confront what has really happened, and to find the people and resources needed to deal with a crisis for which one could not be prepared" (2004, 3). Similarly, while too much anxiety can lead to inaction, having some anxiety can also mobilize us to act—to seek more information, put necessary resources in place, and the like. Furthermore, guilt can result when individuals begin to question why their child has a disability. Did they do something wrong? Is God angry with them? Seeing an innocent child with a disability, for example, may violate our belief that good things happen to good people and bad things happen to bad people. However, experiencing guilt also helps redefine cause and responsibility as it relates to loss.

When my parents realized I was not hitting developmental milestones, they took me to the doctor to find out what was wrong. I know my parents experienced many of the emotions mentioned earlier. Mom experienced guilt and wondered what she might have done wrong to cause my disability. Both of my parents experienced anxiety about what activities I could and could not do and what my future might hold. As a child, I was not always consciously aware of my parents' guilt, anxiety, or other negative emotions. With the benefit of hindsight, however, I wish they would not have worried so much. Although my parents and I could never have predicted the course my life would take, I am very happy with my life so far. Adjustment to my disability will be a lifelong process, but I am grateful that my parents were extremely committed to getting me whatever services or other help I needed to be able to function as well as possible.

Because my disability was visible, interventions were available to improve my functioning, and my parents had medical insurance to help cover the cost of services: the benefits of being diagnosed with a disability were very clear. However, in my experience as both a person with a disability and as a psychologist who has worked with many children and adolescents with disabilities (and their parents), I have found that making the decision to seek a diagnosis, undergoing the process of being diagnosed, and finding and paying for the services needed can be a very fragmented and challenging process. The decision can be particularly difficult when a child's disability is not physical and is more "hidden," such as a potential learning disability, attention deficit disorder, or a psychiatric disability. No matter how enlightened and accepting we may think we are as a society, there still is a stigma attached to these diagnoses: people seem to be more fearful of things they cannot see and do not understand. However, a label is often needed for a child to qualify for services and for insurance to pay for those services. Moreover, although we recognize that many disabilities can have a biological basis, in our society we still often tend to blame the parent for their child's behavior. Blum explains,

Mothers of varied class and race location share the paradoxical experience of both relief and dread in obtaining a medicalized diagnosis for a troubled child. Such labels frequently (but not always) offer access to school services and to health insurance coverage. Just as important, they offer recognition and a name, allowing mothers to begin making sense of distressing, largely hidden family experiences. (2015, 123)

CARE AND PROTECTION

When I was two years and eight months old, I was referred by my pediatrician for an educational evaluation. After the five-day evaluation, it was determined that I was functioning at my age level with regard to cognitive, speech, and language development; however, I could benefit from physical therapy, occupational therapy, gross motor programs, and interactions with peers. Therefore, the evaluation team recommended that I be enrolled in an orthopedic classroom at the Preschool Physically Handicapped Program. In their written evaluation, I was described as an "attractive child" who was "alert and very verbal," but also a "somewhat demanding child who did not wish to be separated from her mother."

I think this description in the written evaluation seems appropriate. For the first few years of my life (until my younger brother was born), I was an only child and seemingly the center of my parents' universe. They were also the center of mine. Unlike most children my age, I did not walk. I have no doubt that I was demanding at times, and I was very attached to and dependent on both of them. I know that my mom especially worried about me not getting what I needed, getting physically or psychologically hurt, or otherwise ending up in harm's way. Both of my parents were very protective, even into my teens and early twenties.

Many times, my parents put aside their own needs to focus on mine. I have seen this dynamic with other parents of children with disabilities: making many sacrifices so their children's needs are met is a priority for these parents, but this can be exhausting. Parents of children with developmental disabilities may experience greater levels of stress than parents of typically developing children because of the unique challenges of having a child with a developmental disability (Howe 2006). Some parents may feel like they are the only ones who can truly understand their disabled child's needs and provide the best care; therefore, it can be difficult for them to enlist the help of others. This may be particularly true if their child has a severe disability or other complex medical needs. While parents of typically developing children can hire a babysitter or leave their child with extended family for a night out or a much-needed break, this might not be as easy for parents of children with disabilities, which can put additional strain on marital relationships or the relationship with their children. Research also finds that parents respond to their children's vulnerability by increasing their level of care and that children with disabilities are often distressed about having little privacy or being in the constant presence of a caregiver (Priestly 1998).

It is also not uncommon for all children to pick up on their parents' anxiety, fear, exhaustion, or other emotions and to react accordingly, perhaps even feeling responsible for their parents' emotions. As a young child, I sometimes knew my parents were afraid or concerned for me, but they also tried to shield me from "adult conversations" about their concerns. Understandably, parents want to protect their vulnerable children from harm as much as possible. Being firstborn and a girl might also have contributed to my parents' desire to protect me. Sometimes it seemed like they were more protective of me than my younger brother.

One of my closest friends from childhood, who has a young daughter with cerebral palsy, has said to me, "I used to think your mom was overprotective; now I totally understand." My response to her and other parents has been, "I get how you feel, but try not to let your anxiety become your child's."

My friend explained, "But it's hard when you're not there, you don't know what's happening, and your daughter can't necessarily tell you if something goes wrong." She also reminded me that during school was not the only time when I felt "different." She remembered vividly a time in our early teens when our families were on vacation together at a beachfront cottage during the summer, and instead of allowing me to go off with my friends, my mom wanted me to wait for her. She was afraid I might get hurt crossing the street with them! I know she meant well and was just trying to keep me safe, but try to imagine the frustration I felt: I was old enough to have a crush on a boy, but she did not even want me to cross the street alone! However, you cannot protect children from everything. Furthermore, parents need time to relax and de-stress, and children need to learn to trust, develop autonomy, and interact with others outside their immediate family who have their best interests at heart.

As I child I was largely unaware of all the effort that went into coordinating the services and care I needed, but at times this must have seemed like a full-time job for my young parents. They had to sift through a lot of information to decide the best course of action for my future. They took time off from work to accompany me to doctors' appointments, physical therapy, and hospital stays and to help me recuperate from surgeries. As I mentioned before, I came from a middle-class family. My parents were married, and one or both of them were employed throughout my childhood and adolescent years. We were fortunate to have a fairly large support system of family and friends who could help with child care and other responsibilities when necessary. I know some very dedicated parents who have been forced to make difficult choices: they risk losing their job if they take time off from work to care for their child, face possible bankruptcy because of high medical costs, and accept what they are told about their child's prognosis and the services covered by insurance or fight for the services their child needs. Accessing and coordinating needed services can be a difficult process even for those who are economically well off: higher-income families may not qualify for any public assistance to cover medical costs, and they may fear a loss of social status if their child is diagnosed with a disability that makes him or her seem "different" from other kids.

FROM SPECIAL TO MAINSTREAM AND EVERYTHING IN BETWEEN

In first grade I was mainstreamed into the local elementary school. That year I used crutches to help me walk, but eventually I was able to stop using them. When I was mainstreamed, physical therapy and other disability-related services were no longer integrated into my school day; my whole day was spent in the same classroom with nondisabled peers. Mainstreaming is now common practice in educational settings. However, even as some children experience overall inclusion (as I did), receiving support services inadvertently serves to separate some children from their mainstream peers, and place them into small groups based on needs or abilities (Holt 2004). I went from being one of many students with a disability in preschool and kindergarten to being the only kid in my first-grade class who had a visible disability. However difficult it was, I still think being mainstreamed was the best thing for me.

It took several surgeries, leg braces, and physical therapy as a child to enable me to walk. Later in elementary school, I also had surgery on my eyes to uncross them. Do I resent my parents for having me go through multiple surgeries and physical therapy? At the time I disliked medical appointments and hospital stays and having to endure sometimes painful and exhausting physical therapy to stretch my tight muscles. I still have vivid childhood memories of appointments in which I was asked to walk barefoot, without pants, down hallways with cold tile floors, while one or more medical professionals watched and assessed my gait. Sometimes I felt so awkward and embarrassed! When I was older and expressed my displeasure at having to walk around in my underwear, one doctor suggested I wear a swimsuit under my clothes. After multiple medical appointments in which adults (basically strangers to me) moved and stretched my limbs, assessing and gawking at me and sometimes talking about me as if I were not even there, I felt more like an object, an oddity, or a diagnosis than a carefree little kid. Children with disabilities often experience a great deal of medical monitoring and interventions (Priestley 1998). These days, my appointments are much less frequent and more humane—and I get to walk down the hallway fully clothed!

My nondisabled parents had always known the benefits of being perceived as "able bodied," and they wanted me to experience as many of those benefits as possible. Yet, because my disability has always been part of my identity, grief has not always been a conscious process for me. I do not remember ever feeling a definitive sense of loss myself. In contrast to a previously nondisabled child who becomes disabled due to an accident, for example, and must cope with loss, my childhood was more about physical gains than losses. I think my "grief" about and adjustment to my disability were more momentary and situation specific. For example, the dreaded medical appointments and surgeries were always a reminder that I was different; they highlighted my physical limitations and meant spending time away from school and my peers. Similarly, I felt upset and sad when being teased repeatedly by two boys on the playground in first grade (until I confided in my teacher and she intervened) or when singled out when I could not participate in some activities in gym class like the balance beam. Incidents like these reminded me that I did not always fit in.

Ironically, however, I usually enjoyed gym class. One of my favorite memories of first grade was being able to ditch my orthopedic shoes once a week in gym class, where I got to wear sneakers like every other kid in the class! Instead of choosing from a limited selection of orthopedic shoes, most of which looked like they had been designed for babies or elderly people, my parents let me choose which gym shoes to buy from a whole array of colorful, kid-friendly sneakers. Hooray! I remember picking a multicolored pair and being so excited to wear them. If wearing orthopedic shoes and walking differently did not make me stick out enough, for a while in elementary school, my orthopedic shoes actually had metal "scuff guards" that made noise (like tap shoes) with every step. Whenever I walked, people knew I was coming! (Several years into elementary school, my doctor said I could ditch my orthopedic shoes forever, another incredibly happy moment.) Regardless of the shoes I wore, though, most of the time other kids accepted me as part of the group, and I had several close childhood friends. Looking back, I think a lot of the anxiety I felt about being different was already internalized and was not always due to the way other kids treated me.

Now that I am an adult and a psychologist, I am very cognizant of the extent to which children learn how to react to unfamiliar circumstances by watching and listening to how peers, parents, or other adults react. For example, even now it is not uncommon for me to be walking down the street and hear a young child ask, "Mommy, why is she walking like that?" Some children have even tried to imitate the way I walk. As a child I felt conspicuous, embarrassed, and upset if another child "mocked" the way I walk, although I often kept these feelings to myself. Now, although I might still feel self-conscious, I realize that the child is not making a value judgment about me; he or she is just curious about why I walk differently. When a child asks about me, the parents' reaction is very important. Sometimes parents explain, "She has a disability," or "She has an injury." Other times parents become annoyed that their child would say something out loud that embarrasses them. They then shush the child and quickly whisk them away.

At times, when I felt the need to comfort the child or educate the parent, I acknowledged that I do walk differently and explained that I was born this way (with a disability).

As this example illustrates, although my disability is often visible to others (e.g., when I am walking around), I am not always conscious of it. This is probably because, unless I happen to pass by a mirror, I do not often see myself walking. However, I am reminded of my disability by the way others treat me or the presence of physical barriers in the environment that sometimes make it more difficult for me to get around. Conversely, sometimes I have to tell others that I am disabled because they see me sitting in the front seats designated for people with disabilities on public transportation and mistakenly assume that I am an insensitive, nondisabled woman taking the seat of a disabled person who needs it.

AN INDIVIDUAL DEFECT: ABLEISM AND THE MEDICAL MODEL OF DISABILITY

Like many parents, my parents first turned to medical professionals to try to understand why I was not meeting developmental milestones. Consistent with the medical model, I was given a deficit-based diagnosis to explain what was "wrong" with me. The goal then became to correct my deficits so I could lead as "normal" a life as possible. The medical interventions did lessen the impact of my disability, enable me to walk, and allow me to function more independently. For those things I am very grateful. However, the medical model's limited focus on individual deficits perpetuates ableism and the idea that individual differences are wrong. According to Thomas Hehir,

Applied to schooling and child development, ableist preferences become particularly apparent. From an ableist perspective, the devaluation of disability results in societal attitudes that uncritically assert that it is better for a child to walk than roll, speak than sign, read print than read Braille, spell independently than use a spell-check, and hang out with nondisabled kids as opposed to other disabled kids, etc. (2002, 3)

Rather than celebrating differences, ableism is based on the idea that doing things the typical way is most beneficial, and therefore children with disabilities need to be "fixed" in order to participate fully in society. The medical model also may perpetuate the stereotypical view that children with disabilities are weak or incapable and can marginalize them. I did not realize it at the time, but as a kid who wanted so desperately to pass—to be like my nondisabled peers—I had internalized ableism! I would internalize people's rude comments and make every effort to blend in or appear "normal." I did not want to be different, ask for help, or be singled out. I wanted to be just like every other kid my age.

We also can exhibit ableism in the words we use, how we communicate with others, or how we think about disability. For example, the words "retarded," "idiot," and "moron," which used to be diagnostic labels to indicate intellectual disability, are now used to insult and demean others (Liebowitz 2015). Using the words "crazy" and "insane" to describe those with psychiatric disabilities could be considered ableist language as well. Furthermore, Liebowitz (2015) points out that talking *about* people with a disability when they are in the room, rather than talking directly *to* them (similar to my childhood experience at the doctor's office), can be a form of ableism. Parents may be more accurate reporters of a child's medical history, but medical professionals should not treat the child like he or she is invisible! The misconception that students with learning disabilities should not need academic accommodations if they are already getting passing grades is also a form of ableism. When advocating for students, I sometimes have had to explain that disability accommodations are not designed to give disabled students an "unfair advantage," but rather to level the playing field and allow them to show what they are truly capable of without the impact of their disability.

THE MINORITY MODEL OF DISABILITY: ENVIRONMENT AND ATTITUDES MATTER!

As a child, I was focused on what made me physically different. As an adult, I am better able to understand the impact of individual, social, political, and other factors on my experience as someone with a disability. The minority model (also known as the sociopolitical model) emerged in the 1960s and takes these factors into account. This model, which is consistent with the ecological perspective, views disability "as a social construction shaped by environmental factors, including physical characteristics built into the environment, cultural attitudes and social behaviors, and the institution-alized rules, procedures, and practices of private entities and public organizations" (Scotch 2000, 214). Furthermore, because people with disabilities are stigmatized, the minority model recognizes that they have experiences similar to other stigmatized groups, including racial and ethnic minorities.

Joy Weeber (1999), who has lived with the effects of polio since infancy, articulates some of the parallels between racism and ableism. She describes being denied entrance to public facilities or having to use a back service entrance because the main one is inaccessible, not being able to visit classmates' homes, enduring painful procedures to make her appearance more acceptable, being viewed as less intelligent, eliciting low expectations from others, and other difficulties she and other disabled children and adults have faced. She explains, "My disabled brothers and sisters and I experience such acts of discrimination on a daily basis. And the pain that these encounters cause is the same pain that racism causes people of color. It is the pain caused by the unconscious beliefs of a society that assumes everyone is, or should be, 'normal' (i.e., White and very able-bodied)" (1999, 21).

I can relate to Weeber's experiences. Her words made me realize how societal attitudes and expectations have created a conundrum for children and adults with disabilities: to avoid being viewed as incapable, weak, or too dependent, we overcompensate, work as hard as we can, and try to overcome our "flaws" (or hope that others will not notice them). Furthermore, Michael Rembis (2013, 112–113) asserts that "passing need not always involve the act of concealing one's impairment, but rather depends upon how well one can approximate the gendered, white, heterosexual, nondisabled norm for conduct, competition, appearance, and performance." Although Rembis was discussing passing among disabled athletes, this quote also describes the pressure I sometimes felt to fit in, particularly during childhood and adolescence.

As an indication of how successful I have been at passing, others have told me they did not notice my disability or do not consider me disabled. Growing up I considered this a compliment, a sign that I was accepted. Now, statements like that make me realize how prevalent negative stereotypes are about people with disabilities and those in other minority groups. Although I might not fit people's stereotypes, I do have a noticeable disability, and I am also a capable human being.

Consistent with the minority model, civil rights laws like IDEA (which is supposed to guarantee that children with disabilities get a free and appropriate education tailored to their needs) and the ADA (which is supposed to guard against discrimination in employment, public accommodations, public transportation, and telecommunications and reduce barriers for people with disabilities) are a step in the right direction. However, we still have a long way to go before all services, buildings, websites, transportation, and other areas are fully accessible to people with disabilities. Moreover, ableism and discrimination against children with disabilities are often more subtle than inaccessible buildings or services, but can be just as damaging. Low expectations can become a self-fulfilling prophecy. As a society, we need to do more than merely comply with the letter of disability laws and instead act in accordance with the spirit of them. Ideally we would not just tolerate and grudgingly accommodate children with disabilities, but genuinely accept and value their individual differences.

LESSONS LEARNED: ADVOCACY, ACCEPTANCE, AND SOCIAL CHANGE

Given my experiences, I believe it is important for children and adolescents with disabilities to develop a sense of agency and self-advocacy skills. My parents were excellent role models when advocating for me; they taught me by example how to advocate for myself. However, because I was so protected as a child, I experienced a steep learning curve as I grew up and separated from them. Even crossing the street without them was a big deal! (My parents were afraid I might fall and get hurt.) I had to learn that people I did not know and experiences outside of my routine were not necessarily as dangerous or scary as I had originally thought. Without my parents around to fight my battles, I had to stand up for myself. I also found that the strangers I had been wary of as a young child were often well intentioned and willing to help me if necessary. As I successfully navigated day-to-day challenges, my parents became more comfortable letting go. With time, they saw that I could go out with friends, cross a busy street, have fun, and come home unharmed. And if I fell, I learned to quickly get back up again (literally and figuratively). Consequently, I developed more self-confidence and my anxiety lessened. I was able to relax and "be myself" without worrying so much about what others thought. I developed an identity independent of my parents, focused more on what I had in common with my peers, and worried less about being different. I knew I was not alone. I realized most of my peers were also wanting more independence from their parents and also experienced angst about what the future might hold. Would we pass our next test? Get a date for prom? Go to college? Get married? As I became more comfortable with myself, I was able to embrace my differences and view my disability not as a deficit, but as a valuable part of me that has shaped my career path and the person I have become.

My support system, the skills I have learned, and the services available to me have played a pivotal role in my life. In today's political climate, however, I fear that our society is becoming more individualistic. Services for children in need and the right to affordable health care for everyone (including those with preexisting conditions) seem to be under attack. The government might help nominally, but beyond that each of us is on our own. Instead of creating a sense of collective responsibility for the well-being of all members of society, it seems to be every family for itself. It also seems more acceptable to discriminate against those who are different (e.g., disabled, gay, nonwhite, member of a religious minority, etc.).

Given support, access to necessary resources, and acceptance, children with disabilities can grow up and reach their full potential. However, there is a tendency in our seemingly ableist, youth-obsessed, individualistic culture to resist thinking about others and planning for the future. It is ironic that, if we live long enough, we will all grow old and face a decline in our physical, intellectual, and cognitive functioning. If we were more accepting of the changes that come with age, perhaps we would be more compassionate toward others who may function differently than we do. We would also realize that many of the accommodations designed to help people with disabilities, such as large print, curb cuts, and flexible schedules, can also be beneficial for nondisabled people.

As I reflect on my experiences so far living with a disability, I have learned three other important lessons:

- *I do not want society to pretend my disability does not exist.* Instead, let us work together to reduce disability's adverse impact (from attitudes, physical barriers, policies, and the like), so those of us with disabilities can lead a full life and make the most of our skills and abilities. Earlier, I highlighted some similarities between racism and ableism. Just as not acknowledging the importance of race in one's identity can be disempowering and detrimental, so too can ignoring one's disability.

- *Do not believe everything you see or hear.* Today we are besieged with information—on TV, the internet, the radio, in magazines and newspapers, in books, and from medical professionals. It can be hard to separate fact from fiction and broad generalizations (based on groups of people) from specifics. I have learned that my disability experience may be very different from someone else's, even if our diagnostic label is the same. Similarly, nobody can definitively predict a child's future. Technological advances, individual and societal attitudes, and the political climate may be very different twenty years from now, which also can change a child's disability experience.

- *Change can be a long, slow process sometimes, but progress can be made.* It has been more than twenty-five years since the Americans with Disabilities Act was signed into law. Change has occurred, but we still have a long way to go. Consistent with the ecological perspective, change can occur psychologically, socially, economically, politically, and physically (to the individual and/or the environment). Sometimes change is abrupt (e.g., hearing or reading something that immediately changes one's perspective), but often change is an excruciatingly slow, laborious process (e.g., challenging long-held beliefs, policies, or ways of doing things). For me, adapting to my disability and advocating for social change will be an ongoing process. However, I know that I have a responsibility to make the world a better place for myself and others from minority groups. In the current sociopolitical climate, with income disparities increasing and difference seemingly being something to fear, fighting for positive change is more important than ever.

Throughout this chapter, I have shared my experiences growing up with a disability, along with experiences of my parents, friends, and others. Clearly, adjustment to disability is not a universal, predetermined process. The experiences of children with disabilities do not occur in a vacuum; they are shaped by individual characteristics, socioeconomic status, and social support, as well as societal beliefs and policies. Parents and others can play a pivotal role in helping children with disabilities access needed services and adjust to their disability. Helping children develop a sense of agency and the ability to advocate for themselves also is important. As a society, we must be willing to examine and change those beliefs and actions that hinder individuals with disabilities from living up to their full potential. Each of us, disabled or not, has a role to play in making our society more inclusive for people with disabilities.

QUESTIONS FOR REFLECTION AND GROUP DISCUSSION

1. If you were in charge, how might you improve the way educational needs are determined and services delivered to children and adolescents with disabilities?
2. How are society's attitudes toward people with disabilities similar to and different from their attitudes toward other minority groups? How might one's awareness that he or she can become disabled at any point in life affect those attitudes, either positively or negatively?
3. What else can be done to change society's attitudes toward people with disabilities and to make society more inclusive?

REFERENCES

Blum, Linda M. 2015. *Raising Generation Rx: Mothering Kids with Disabilities in an Age of Inequality.* New York: New York University Press.

Cerebral Palsy Alliance. 2018. "What is Cerebral Palsy?" https://www.cerebralpalsy.org.au/what-is-cerebral-palsy/.

Hehir, Thomas. 2002. "Eliminating Ableism in Education." *Harvard Educational Review* 72:1–32.

Holt, Louise. 2004. "Childhood Disability and Ability: (Dis)abelist Geographies of Mainstream Primary Schools." *Disability Studies Quarterly* 24. http://www.dsq-sds.org/article/view/506/683.

Howe, David. 2006. "Disabled Children, Parent-Child Interaction and Attachment." *Child &Family Social Work* 11: 95–106.

Kotel, Kathleen A. 2013. "That's Okay. They Are Beautiful Children." In *Both Sides of the Table: Autoethnographies of Educators Learning and Teaching with/in [Dis]ability,* ed. Phil Smith, 199–211. New York: Peter Lang.

Liebowitz, Cara. 2015. "Everyday Ableism and How We Can Avoid It." https://thebodyisnotanapology.com/magazine/everyday-ableism-and-how-we-can-avoid-it/.

Moses, Ken. 2004. "The Impact of Childhood Disability: The Parent's Struggle." http://www.pent.ca.gov/beh/dis/parentstruggle_DK.pdf.

Pardeck, John T. 1988. "An Ecological Approach for Social Work Practice." *Journal of Sociology & Social Welfare* 15: 133–142.

Priestly, Mark. 1998. "Constructions and Creations: Idealism, Materialism, and Disability Theory." *Disability and Society* 13: 75–94.

Rembis, Michael A. 2013. "Athlete First: A Note on Passing, Disability, and Sport." In *Disability and Passing: Blurring the Lines of Identity*, ed. Jeffrey A. Brune and Daniel J. Wilson, 111–141. Philadelphia: Temple University Press.

Scotch, Richard K. 2000. "Models of Disability and the Americans with Disabilities Act." *Berkeley Journal of Employment & Labor Law* 21: 213–222.

Weeber, Joy E. 1999. "What Could I Know of Racism?" *Journal of Counseling and Development* 77: 20–23.

World Health Organization. 2011. *World Report on Disability*. http://www.who.int/disabilities/world_report/2011/en/.

Chapter Ten

BETWEEN LIFE STORIES AND THE STRUGGLE FOR HOMELESS YOUTH

BENJAMIN HEIM SHEPARD

Over and over during my dozen-plus years as a social worker providing AIDS services in New York and San Francisco from 1993–2005, I heard stories about homeless youth who put themselves at risk for HIV in order to qualify for benefits. Many reported there was no other way to qualify for housing. It was a tragic narrative and one that continued to be repeated again and again, even until today.

Several speakers echoed that point during a press conference held on a cold, snowy day at City Hall in New York City in February 2015. We were there to support City Council member Corey Johnson's introduction of proposed city legislation to change the medical eligibility criteria of the HIV-AIDS Services Administration (HASA) to include asymptomatic HIV. Known as "HASA for All" this proposed legislation would expand HASA benefits to all low-income, HIV+ New York City residents. Advocates, such as myself, were there to demonstrate community support.

"It's really inhumane that people have to wait to get sick" to receive housing, noted Kate Barnhart, the director of New Alternatives for LGBT Youth and a long-term ACT UP member, who was once homeless herself. Through her work, she connects her history of AIDS activism with larger questions about the need for services, as well as concerns related to race and poverty among runaway and homeless youth (RHY). The underlying issue—homelessness among youth—has deep roots in New York City. For as long

FIGURE 10.1 The corner of Christopher and Weehawken Streets in the West Village of New York City, where many LGBT youth hang out and work. Photo by Benjamin Shepard

as most current residents can remember, youth, many the offspring of immigrants or runaways, have filled the streets of New York City (Sheehan 1993), facing difficult challenges (figure 10.1).

At an August 2017 rally in East Flatbush, a neighborhood in Brooklyn, Kate Barnhart carried a sign with a photo of David Felix and the caption, "Murdered by the NYPD" (figure 10.2). The rally was held in front of the home of Dwayne Juene, a mentally ill man who himself had been killed by the New York Police Department on July 30, 2017. David Felix, a "24 year-old polyglot, aspiring fashion student," was a homeless young man killed by the NYPD when the police sought to force their way into his room at a shelter in the Lower East Side and he attempted to run away (Ram and Conner 2015). A young black immigrant and former foster youth, David struggled to survive in the city, as he coped with mental illness. He was traumatized by his experiences with policing institutions; reportedly some of his last words as he ran from the cops were that he was not willing to go back to jail. David was well known to homeless youth providers (Ram and

FIGURE 10.2 Kate Barnhart holding an image of Felix.

Conner 2015). His story connects narratives about race, immigration, the treatment of the poor and mentally ill, and the lack of resources for RHY. His death had a significant impact on many providers, advocates, and social workers who work with homeless youth. There is a room dedicated to him at the Urban Justice Center, where he worked with the Peter Cicchino Youth Project.

Race plays an integral role in the experiences of RHY in New York City. But their experiences are shaped by many other factors: sexuality, class, immigration status, homophobia, violence, police harassment, brutality, abuse, poverty, HIV, barriers to accessible care, and exposure to the elements in New York City. At the press conference at City Hall described earlier, Carl Siciliano of the Ali Forney Center, a services center for homeless LGBT youth, noted that he was going to be brief because the youth with him already spent too much time outside in the cold. He referred to a new study by the Urban Institute on "survival sex" among homeless LGBTQ youth. Queer[1] youth have been out in the streets for far too long—escaping abusive homes and hoping to find something better only to encounter more closed doors, limited services, and gaps in the services that are available for them (Dank et al. 2015). Even when they obtain services, many are simply told where to find the best couches or to sleep on the trains (figure 10.3; Shepard 2013).

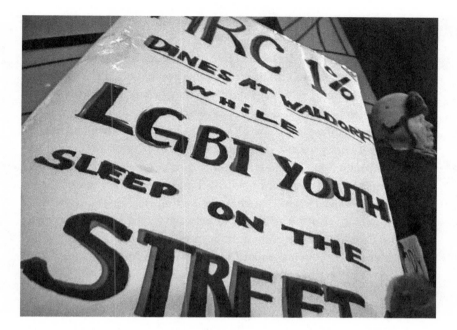

FIGURE 10.3 The Human Rights Campaign dines at the Waldorf-Astoria while LGBT youth sleep in the street. Photo by Benjamin Shepard

The story of homeless youth in New York City cannot be separated from the issues connected with gentrification and subsequent displacement, which put housing prices beyond the reach of low- and middle-income New Yorkers and decimated the stock of single-room-occupancy units (SROs) that many on the margins historically relied on. From the 1970s through the present, New York City's local geography shifted radically as the poor were priced out of neighborhoods throughout the city (Fitch 1999; Gibson 2011; McNamara 1995; Tracy 2014; Wallace 1999). City government actively sought corporate-centered redevelopment and rebranded itself to attract a wealthier population in the wake of the 1970s fiscal crisis. RHY services developed in that context.

"There's no time at which the City has matched resources to estimates of the RHY population," notes Craig Hughes, a long-term provider for homeless folks. The fundamental reality of RHY in New York is they are overwhelmingly people of color, says Hughes. Adds Barnhart, "About 25 percent of our youth are [HIV] positive."

This chapter presents narratives of homeless youth in New York City obtained using the ethnographic and life story methods described in this book's introduction (Cohler 1994; Harrison 2014; McAdams 2008; Witkin 2014) to highlight the needs of this vulnerable population. It traces the personal stories of three service providers who themselves coped with institutionalization and chemical dependency as adolescents before they joined these service organizations: New Alternatives for LGBT Youth and the Icarus and Streetwork projects. These life stories provide us with insights unavailable through other methods, detailing themes of adaptation, resilience and coping (Martin 1995; Shaw 1930). Such narratives open spaces for social action, personal agency, change, and meaning creation (Polletta 2006). These are narratives of survival, traced between public and private selves, contending with both who one might be or dream of being and an unforgiving external world of judgments, punishment, and homophobia, which leaves many in the streets or locked up. As McAdams writes,

The stories people fashion to make meaning out of their lives serve to situate them within the complex social ecology of the modern world .... [They] are fundamentally about our struggle to reconcile who we imagine we were, are, or might be in our heads and bodies with who we were, are, and might be in the social contexts of the family, community, the workplace, ethnicity, religion, gender, social class, and culture writ large. (2008, 242)

WAYWARD YOUTH

In New York, young people continue to arrive at the Port Authority bus terminal every day and make their way into the city. In the late 1960s and into the 1970s, many of these travelers were part of and were attracted to the counterculture movements (see, for example, the origins of Covenant House; Wosh 2004). After arriving some go to Times Square, others walk west to 12th Ave. or the waterfront. Most reject foster care, where assault and abuse run rampant, in favor of fending for themselves (Sheehan 1993).

However, that narrative of homeless youth being drawn to New York City clashes with another fundamental fact: most RHY have roots in the city. Contemporary youth homelessness in New York City stems from local dynamics, which view these youth, who are predominantly young people of color, as increasingly disposable and thus deserving of fewer resources. In addition, about 40 percent of the homeless youth in New York City are LGBT/queer.

Randy Wicker, one of the early members of the Mattachine Society, told me about some of the struggles he and others experienced on these streets:

> It's just universal discrimination. Discrimination against trans people, who cannot find other work. You run away from home and come to New York and find there are 12 beds for runaway LGBT youth. No jobs, no bed, literally forced into the streets. Then you do a background check years later and the arrest [that happened years prior] is still there. In today's digital world, it lasts forever.

Wicker's rebel friends Sylvia Rivera and Marsha P. Johnson, both of whom embodied a post-Stonewall queer sensibility, coped with these challenges for years as they fought for supports for homeless youth (Shepard 2015). Their struggles inspired a wave of service providers to offer care to LGBT homeless youth (Shepard 2013). For example, the Streetwork Project, when it started in 1984, was funded with federal money targeting "juvenile prostitutes" in Times Square. Prostitution was rampant then in Times Square, and Streetwork's founders quickly found that these young people were often engaged in heavy substance use as well ("A 'Simple' Notion" 1987).

Also located in the Times Square were Safe Space, Covenant House, and the Ali Forney Center (AFC), founded by Carl Siciliano and named in memory of a queer youth of color who was murdered. As Mayor Giuliani sought to clean up Times Square, RHY were essentially chased out, and programs had to go elsewhere to appropriately serve them: AFC and Streetwork's drop-ins centers are now located on 125th Street, and one Streetwork site is on the Lower East Side (Gibson 2011). Similarly, the gentrification of Greenwich Village, fueled by economic development and neighborhood-supported policing efforts, has increasingly caused the dispersion of RHY from the piers along the Hudson River (Gibson 2011). Those in need of services have been left to scramble for themselves. In response, organization such as New Alternatives for LGBT Youth and Streetwork offered services and support for these lost youth.

FROM SYLVIA'S TO NEW ALTERNATIVES

Kate Barnhart is a tireless advocate for RHY. She grew up in New York City, going to the Little Red Schoolhouse where Pete Seeger used to come play for the students; she attended ACT UP meetings as a teenager (figure 10.4). Barnhart went to Hampshire College after being institutionalized for a time, spending a summer in high school in a group home run by the Brooklyn Society for the Prevention of Cruelty to Children. She ran away from the facility several times during this period, only to be sent back by her mother who suffered from mental illness. Her empathy for those with nowhere to go stems from that experience. She can never forget the memory of being stripped and having every mark on her body photographed or seeing the other youth in the home become subject to the demands of the sex trade while living there. "The men in that neighborhood treated that place like all the girls were up for sale," she told me.

At the time, there were no LGBT shelters; there was only Covenant House, and queer youth did not go there. When Kate tried to go home, her

FIGURE 10.4 Kate Barnhart as a young activist in ACT UP.

mother sent her back to the group home. She made it through the summer, and fortunately a mentor helped her out of her situation. Kate recalls, "I was a fucked-up young person who had gone crazy at that point. I had been in a group home. The principal of Stuyvesant actually called the financial aid people [at Hampshire College] and talked [to] them. And so I went to Hampshire. Of course I still don't have a high school diploma. They didn't care."

Kate was planning to go to medical school after college. Then around the time she graduated college in 1996, the first viable treatments for HIV came out. The landscape changed: there was effective medication, but it was rarely accessible for the neediest, and many were being left without services—and her mother got sick. So instead of going to medical school Barnhart started working with teens: "Doing that, I realized that healing is not just physical but there's a lot to be done on a mental level. . . . Some people might see it as like absorbing a lot of pain, but to me it's more like taking the pain and transforming it."

Kate told me about her work with New Alternatives, the agency she started with her friends after serving as director of a shelter called Sylvia's Place:

> I was unhappy with some of the mandates that were coming down from above, from the church administration, and I also saw some big gaps in the services available to LBGT homeless youth. In particular, I saw a lack of high-quality, long-term case management. A lot of places still tie their case management services to their housing services, which means that if you're somewhere for thirty days, you start case management there, and then you hop to another program and then you start case management there. And so you're starting over constantly. Housing, in particular in New York City, is a very long-term process. I mean, years, and so you need somebody who's gonna stick it out with you. But the other thing is if you look at the clients. They've almost all been traumatized pretty severely, and the only way you can start to establish a real level of trust in the setting of trauma is through time.

For Barnhart, relationship building takes places through a low-threshold model of engagement described as harm reduction, a pragmatic, highly humanistic approach to service provision that acknowledges drug use and self-injuring behavior as parts of life that need to be recognized and reduced, not stopped:

It's through really spending time and gaining trust and working together on things, and it's only once you have that that you can start to address some of the deeper issues, especially around mental health and substance use. I don't think just meeting someone and being like "Hey, you're a junkie. You should go to treatment. I won't work with you till you go, until you sober up [will work]." All you do is make the client shut down. And so I feel like it's really important to start to actually heal some of that stuff.

This healing takes place gradually through the provision of direct services and trust building, one step at a time.

Barnhart described to me the needs of those who walk into the doors at New Alternatives:

Our clients have a tremendous range of needs. You have the relationship with a client where you can. If you need to take them in, you can take them in. Where, you can trust them if they say no I'm not gonna hurt myself, you can really trust that your relationship is strong enough. And you can intervene. On the other hand, they have to know that they can say to you what they're thinking without being fucked over.

There has to be some degree of honesty to make these relationships work. Much of her work is organized around notions of social action, which bridges the divide between direct action and direct services:

Well to me, they go hand in hand. We're specifically doing activism to clear a way. I see all these barriers in my daily life. Today, this client, a trans woman with AIDS, was talking about how she'd spent the last week on the street. I know she has HASA so I said, "Well, why didn't HASA place you?" She said, "I don't know; they just they told me this, that, and the other." And I said, "Well, that's illegal. HASA has to place you the same day." She was kinda like, "I don't know about that." And I told her, "No. I know about that because I was one of the people who fought for the creation of the agency that's now called HASA."

Barnhart then described her past housing advocacy actions: "I remember I went over to the hotel [where one of her clients was illegally denied a place to stay], and tried to talk to them and find out what was going on and then we all went back and we basically occupied [the welfare office] and wouldn't let them close." Barnhart and her fellow activists told the staff at the welfare department: "We are not leaving your office here until there's housing for these people and they finally put them at the McBurney Y." The activists worked for months to make sure the city followed its own Local Law 49, a law passed in 1997 that guarantees shelter to people with HIV/AIDS shelter the day they ask for it. Barnhart continued, "I see clients who are being fucked by the system. It's good to be able to dig in and fight back and try to improve the things that are affecting my clients' lives."

Barnhart specifically looks to stories as a form for advocacy. "Just coming and telling their stories" can be effective: "I'll say to them all right, so when somebody screws you, you want to get their name and, keep notes of every crazy interaction you have with this agency . . . If the cop's fucking with you, get the badge number, if you can, discreetly." Getting this information enables people to counter the official story. "I always find it interesting how many different storylines, how many different stories people are trying to live. It's just complicated because sometimes they're so burdensome that they can't live it. They've got this idea and a dream of a life they're gonna live. With the young people there are still these dreams and this hope and, you know, so it's about okay, let's start clearing away the obstacles."

Barnhart recalls one client, a young trans man, who "had grown up in small-town Florida, as a girl, came to New York City to go to the School of Visual Arts, which his family was paying for." And then things got complicated:

He was living in the dorm; he starts feeling comfortable, starts transitioning. So then he tells his family, "Guess what guys? I'm a man," and they freak, and they cut off all his support and so he can't stay in the dorm; he can't go back home, and so then he's homeless. Not only homeless but also just despondent, because he felt that he couldn't finish school and that was gonna ruin his life. He was depressed and so he came to us. First things first, we got him into Trinity, which is an LGBT shelter. So he had some safe place to live, and then we did a lot of basically counseling, like trying to get him to see that no, his life is not over and eventually got him to the idea that he could go back to school as an independent student. And so he applied to a bunch of places and got in and wound up picking Hampshire, where I went. And so, being a family, we drove him up there and moved him in. And then his last year there, he was studying sculptures so he calls me up; he says, "I need ninety pounds of polymer clay for my thesis show." So I called Brownie who orders it and has it shipped there. We went back for his graduation and he lives in Boston. He has a job. He has a partner and an apartment and a dog and is thinking about grad school.

Many of the clients develop powerful loyalties to Barnhart. Trust is the cornerstone of this process.

She recalls the story of another former client, JD:

JD was maybe sixteen when I met him at the Neutral Zone [a drop-in center for LGBTQ homeless and at-risk youth]. And he was at that time identified as a lesbian and had been kicked out by his super Christian aunt and had been sleeping in a park in the Bronx under the bleachers. And he was really angry. and he kept getting himself in situations because he was so angry. He was in danger of being kicked out of the program because he had put a hole in the wall. I said, "You know, better the wall than a person." I got some nonhardening clay and I said to him, "All right, when you're angry come in my little office and you're gonna just throw this at the wall." And he used to do that. He would just come in and go wham, over and over, but he didn't hit anything. So that was good. And then, he got involved doing activism.

JD worked with FIERCE (Fabulous Independent Radicals for Community Empowerment), an advocacy group of LGBTQ youth of color, organizing rallies and acts of civil disobedience. But the challenges continued. He was arrested for smoking pot in the Bronx. Barnhart went to court and got them to release JD. She took JD out for a bite afterward:

So we're sitting there. JD always, you could feel his intelligence. And so I just said to him, "You know, have you thought about going to college?" And he was really shocked cause nobody had ever really seen that in him before. That was a turning point for him because, well first of all, having me actually show up to get him out of jail, that was the trust moment, and then he was able to hear what I said about college and take it in. So then he went to Hampshire. Which is the story: this is a pattern, right.

After he graduated, "JD became a peer leader at the Neutral Zone and then I hired him to work overnights at Sylvia's and then when I went to New Alternatives he worked at New Alternatives." For Barnhart, her relationship with JD is a story of friends, family, relationship building, sharing a little social capital, harm reduction, and advocacy.

Barnhart's proudest moment was starting New Alternatives, an organization providing meals, groups, case-management, testing, and prevention services:

> I literally just gathered up the best people, like volunteers and staff from Sylvia's and we rented a room at the Center and we sat down and we said, "All right, what are we doing?" and we started in October of 2008. I worked for New Alternatives for the first year without taking any pay cause we didn't have anything. We started with nothing and we made it through the years. And we keep making it.

LOST IN THE MIND: ICARUS PROJECT

While Kate Barnhart works with youth trying to find a home, other providers help those who grapple with feelings of being lost not only on the streets but also in the mind (figure 10.5). Today, many organizations have

FIGURE 10.5 Sascha Altman DuBrul, cofounder of the Icarus Project. Photo by Chris Boarts Larson.

come to look at mental illness and reality in new ways. Rather than rely on medications, which fill the coffers of pharmaceutical companies, these programs, such as the Icarus Project, trace alternative narratives for those labeled with psychiatric disabilities. Looking beyond deficits-based psychiatric approaches, the Icarus Project, which was founded in 2003, seeks "new space and freedom for extreme states of consciousness." Its mission, as stated on its website (https://www.icarusproject.net), is to create

a new culture and language that resonates with our actual experiences of 'mental illness' rather than trying to fit our lives into a conventional framework. . . . We believe these experiences are mad gifts needing cultivation and care, rather than diseases or disorders. By joining together as individuals and as a community, the intertwined threads of madness, creativity, and collaboration can inspire hope and transformation in an oppressive and damaged world. Participation in the Icarus Project helps us overcome alienation and tap into the true potential that lies between brilliance and madness [http://theicarusproject.net].

Instead of psychic prisons, the group "call[s] for more options in understanding and treating emotional distress."

The organization's cofounder, Sascha Altman DuBrul (2017), writes, "As someone who was told as an 18 year old that I had a biological brain disease and that my visions and behavior meant I needed to be held down and shot up with antipsychotic drugs for months in a locked mental hospital, I take very personally how our current psychiatric system treats young people who've been diagnosed with psychotic disorders."

DuBrul works to redefine the language and culture of mental health and illness by sharing his life history. For Sascha, storytelling is a key tool in the process in changing perceptions about mental illness. He told me his story as we sat together across the street from Tompkins Square Park in the East Village.

He began, "My political consciousness started right here in Tompkins Square Park with the punks, meeting at the Anarchist Switchboard at 9th street and Avenue A" (figure 10.6). He traced the Icarus Project's roots to the do-it-yourself (DIY) punk ethos of the Lower East Side of Manhattan, where there is a history of youth forming alternate cultures, supporting community gardens, squatting, and quite often living on the streets. Hanging

FIGURE 10.6 Photo of Sascha DuBrul holding the sign to the right, on Memorial Day, as protesters in Tompkins Square Park prepare to confront the police on Avenue A, on May 27, 1991. Photo by Q Sakamaki

out in the neighborhood, he became friends with both the punk kids and squatters, such as Jerry the Peddler. He found

people there, coming out of foster care, coming from the middle of the country where there was abuse at home, coming out of the military families. Kids coming out of abusive homes, kids who had grown up real fast, doing drugs. This was a community where there were kids coming from a lot of backgrounds, trying to figure out these identities. I was a kid coming from a more privileged background than a lot of the other kids on the street, but I wasn't the only one. And what we all had in common was we were really alienated from the larger society around us and we were all hanging out together. . . . I had my own problems at home and for the first time in my life, I found a group of people who accepted me even though I didn't fit in at school. There were kids making their own music, art, playing in abandoned buildings. It was the most amazing thing I had ever seen in my life. . . . I came of age in a community where we all understood that society was crazy. We took that as a given. If you were normal according to society's standards, that meant there was something wrong with you. The identity was about being oppressed and an outsider. By the time I got locked up in a psych hospital, I had this whole other worldview that protected me from thinking I was mentally ill. I didn't take them seriously when they told me I had a biological brain disease.

His experiences there left him wondering what home could look like:

I remember getting out of the psych ward in a couple different situations. In one of them, I was living back with my mom and I was working at Barnes & Noble and trying to figure out what the hell I was doing. I was taking a couple college classes, and I came back down to this neighborhood after being gone for a long time and ran straight into my friends. The people in the park embraced me. And that was so important. . . . It made me feel connected to something larger than myself and I really needed that. . . . There was all this vibrant art and music and people being wild, really being themselves and not caring what society thought.

He paused and reflected on the stories he found in the neighborhood: "I still think it's powerful to think about creating your own world, your own story, to look at the people around you and realize it's possible to create incredible things out of nothing. . . . We were making our own music; we were making our own culture."

This experience laid the groundwork for Sascha's DIY challenge to deficits-based categorizations of mental health:

I started playing in a band with kids from down the street. As a young person trying to find my identity, it was so important to have a project to work on with other people. I just left behind the sense that I was mentally ill. That idea just didn't fit into the cultural context I was inhabiting. And in some ways, maybe I even felt more legit than I did when I was younger, because I had been through some really rough times and that was respected by the people around me.

Over time, he found a new kind of autonomy, riding freight trains and letting go of caring what other people thought. Having these experiences became more important than fulfilling other people's expectations, so he dropped out of high school.

I think subconsciously I was scared. But mostly, my strategy was just to fuckin'
shine. I just burned really bright. . . . I was getting arrested regularly in NY
for stupid shit, mouthing off to cops, hopping the turnstiles; my mom really
wanted to get me out of the city for the summer. My friend Joe had gotten a
scholarship to University of California Berkeley (UCB) and he told amazing
stories of the punk scene and Telegraph Ave. I had old communist step-
grandparents in Santa Cruz. I convinced my mom to let me take classes at
UCB for the summer. The week before I left there were riots in Tompkins over
the eviction of the tent city. [At UCB] they placed me in a dorm overlooking
People's Park. I was 16. I fall in love for the first time, moving out of the dorms
and into a punk house, got arrested with my girlfriend running down Ban-
croft Avenue smashing windows, and ended up in Oakland juvie. That trip
changed my life, never the same. I spent six years traveling and living and
working all over the place, and then when I was twenty-four I crashed really
hard.

Sascha described feelings of being lost in his own life.

I came back to New York and I crashed right into my childhood . . . all of those
feelings, all of the teenage stuff that I had of like feeling like I wasn't legit, that
I wasn't as hardcore as all my friends who had had rougher lives, that I wasn't
like a real person—all of that stuff hit me so hard. I basically created a whole
narrative for myself as a freight train riding person without a past. And I
wanted to die. I remember I would walk through Tompkins Square Park, and
I was so suicidal that all I could think about was hanging from all the blos-
soming trees.

That was during the late 1990s when social, political, and cultural movements were arising all over, many growing out of his neighborhood. Inspired by the cross-currents between community gardens and critiques of
neoliberalism, Sascha went to Seattle for the World Trade Organization pro-
tests in 1999: He was on the road a lot.

The final straw for me was the month I spent in LA Country jail in the psychiatric
wings, being held down and being shot up with antipsychotic drugs. When I
recovered from that experience, and put my life back together, I realized that
even though society was crazy, I was more sensitive than other people and I really

needed to take care of myself. I was still part of the anarchist punk community, and I had a column in magazine that a lot of people read. And I started writing about mental health.

The Icarus Project grew out of those writings. "Punk rock heroic narratives are just one way to tell a story . . . I want to create space so that all of our stories can explode the whole system and create a thousand new ways to be free," he said. "Icarus was creating and challenging ways of looking at things." Over time, the group outlined a new model of mutual aid, producing the book *Friends Make the Best Medicine: A Guide to Creating Community Mental Health Support Networks,* which argues that the best medicine is community, not meds. And Sascha completed his master's degree in social work.

Since 2016, Sascha has been working as a peer specialist at the New York State Psychiatric Institute, providing care for young people who have undergone their first psychotic episodes. In this role he aims both to complement standard psychiatric treatment and subvert traditional models of the clinician–patient relationship, so that patient narratives are viewed as resources and sources of strength, rather than sources of pathology. Through such efforts, he continues a tradition of advocates dedicated to rethinking categories of mental health, connecting free minds with social movements aimed at a "more human organization" of communal life (Robinson 1969, 4). He hopes to help rewrite the way we think about mental health, democratizing knowledge while dismantling imbalances in power between doctor and patient (Waterman 2017).

Much of the process begins with asking people to learn from the stories of lost youth and to see the possibilities of those struggling with psychosis, rather than their deficits. "In order to create a mental health system that works for people, we need to be able to shift our perspectives and truly adopt narratives of liberation rather than narratives of sickness," he explains. "What if we saw psychological crisis [as] an opportunity for growth and potentially transformational, not a disease with no cure?"

"There is so obviously a battle for control of the psychosis narrative right now," he concludes. And there are still too few services for the wayward youth of the city.

STREETWORK PROJECT

One of the few organizations in the city to provide services for many elements of the RHY population—the local homeless, itinerant homeless, and those lost to services—is Safe Horizon's Streetwork Project (https://www .safehorizon.org/streetwork). According to its website, this is a program for youth who have endured trauma, "family abuse, violence, rejection, and instability," whose "families had already been broken down by intergenerational poverty and family homelessness as well as punitive criminal justice and child welfare policies coming out of the drug war." At their drop-in centers, youth "can socialize in a safe, non-judgmental place" and "can get help with: Daily necessities such as meals, showers, clothing, as well as wellness activities, medical care, legal assistance, mental health services, sexual health help including HIV prevention, syringe exchange and low threshold drug treatment, obtaining public benefits, linkages to emergency shelter, and housing advocacy." In addition to basic harm reduction services, Streetwork provides street outreach services, going to places where youth hang out and providing snacks, overdose reversal training, and survival supplies such as toiletries, as well as other services and referrals.

I spoke with several counselors who had been involved with the group's Harlem and Lower East Side centers. John Welch is a clinical social worker and therapist, with a long history in the Lower East Side harm-reduction world. "I was originally drawn to the Lower East Side by the music scene—especially noise music of the 80s—and to the free and open feeling of the area," he told me at the beginning of our interview. Welch was immediately drawn into the milieu of the squatters who were occupying abandoned buildings. He began dating an anarchist and started to question the liberal politics with which he grew up. "Eventually, I applied to live in Umbrella House, a squat."

In the early 1990s, he became a part of a small self-help HIV buddy program started by a friend: "I had a buddy for several years. He refused to take his meds even after anti-retrovirals came out. . . . He would periodically get hospitalized and then call me to help get him out against medical advice. . . . It was a horrible ethical problem." Observing his buddy's health deteriorate, Welch found himself thinking about "thorny issues of self-determination and care." He followed his friend's wishes until he died. "He could have lived," lamented Welsh. Client self-determination versus the worker's responsibility to give ethical care was an issue that came up again and again in his work over the years.

"I was afraid of [working with] youth at first. I hated high school and never thought I would want to be around teenagers again. I had a friend at Streetwork and learned about needle exchange and youth work from her." He would spend the better part of the next two decades working at Streetwork Project, beginning in 1992 (figure 10.7). Gradually, Welsh became familiar with the philosophy of harm reduction:

My father died early, and I was raised by a mother struggling with addiction and mental illness. Many of my friends were dealing with addiction, as heroin and crack were everywhere in the Lower East Side at that time, and some died. Plus, I had my own experiences with drugs, so the ideas of harm reduction were totally relevant to my everyday life and that of my community.

People needed to talk about the complicated experiences of their lives, the drugs they took, and ways they handled pain. Harm reduction offered a safe way to engage around these issues.

His first job with Streetwork was as a cleaner. "I did the kids' laundry, and just fell in love with the young people there." After a stint at graduate school studying literature, he felt drawn back: "Streetwork was incredible and very strengthening. A lot of that felt very personal. . . . Meeting people I wouldn't have known otherwise, as a white middle-class person, made me think about race and class differently and question my own received perspective."

The staff at Streetwork worked, painfully, for years, to deal with racism and to understand how it affected the lives of their clients. Welch learned to meet everyone who walked in the door where they were at, respecting and trying to make sense of their ways of looking at the world:

In harm reduction agencies, staff members are going through a lot of their own stuff. And a lot of their problems come out in the work, and are exacerbated by the work, so I have always felt that you need to have flexibility, but to stay very aware of boundaries. Many have been physically and/or sexually abused and have not experienced much safety in families or institutions, so Streetwork's job is to offer a more comprehensive, more flexible, more healthy family structure for clients . . . because they haven't had that.

FIGURE 10.7 John Welch doing a syringe exchange training for a new staff member.

To this end, Streetwork's harm reduction emphasizes flexibility. One cannot "expect people to be attracted to traditional services that don't offer the basics that they need in a voluntary and open way where the participants get to decide how they want to participate," said Welch. He reflected on the nature of his work:

The work was very intense. It was also very warm in a lot of ways. It was challenging to look at yourself and figure out what you could use of yourself to connect with this other person. Some people are different from you, or really difficult for you, or being very challenging, even sometimes on purpose, to test the relationship. Or, they may be hurting other people, or hurting themselves in a really serious way.

Welch told me about his Streetwork clients:

All of them were homeless. Most were not "runaways," because there was no stable home or family to run away from. Most were New York youth of color who had circulated through foster care, the family shelter system, and youth incarceration or youth mental health placements before winding up street homeless. Many worked informally or were in the sex or drug trades. A fair amount were transgender. There was also another set of people who wouldn't use any services besides Streetwork Lower East Side who were mostly white, transient young people coming from other parts of the country—"travelers" deeply involved with alcohol and heroin who got to New York via freight train.

Many were the people Sascha knew in Tompkins Square Park, the crusty punks who lived in the street, lost. "For most of those kids, addiction was primary and overdose a constant threat. Most of them were essentially working-class from very unstable families where addiction and incarceration are part of the picture," Welch told me. One example he shared was of a young woman who had been living with her grandmother after her father went to jail. When her grandmother died, she had no option but to move in with her meth-addicted older sister. At age eleven, she then had to care for her nieces and nephews, because her sister's life was too chaotic. Welch told me, "These youth are often seen as just experimenting with a hippie or punk lifestyle, but those subcultural affiliations, and the traveling, are ways out of impossible, painful situations for them. Sexual and physical abuse was so common for them."

Welch worked with his clients to try to "make sense of drug use and trauma." To do so, he started by building a working relationship and alliance based on confidentiality, care, and respect:

There was both a very practical harm reduction approach based on a detailed understanding of how each person uses drugs and where harm could be reduced, and a more clinical approach where you offer, with your presence and responsiveness, a safe container in which a person can explore their feelings, their present circumstances and the way past experiences and interpretations of the world shape current behavior and worldview. This process is led by the client, in their way, at their pace. . . . The relationship was a special safe space that was quality checked by close clinical supervision of staff based on support to handle the difficult emotional issues that come up when you are deeply engaged with people in pain.

The primary needs of his Streetwork clients were housing, food, and income, explained Welch. But more than that, he suggested they needed connection:

A relationship you can count on is really essential for anybody, having a community where there is some sense of a boundary, but the community is still free and develops in an organic way. . . . The best harm reduction comes from the people who are taking the risks, understanding the ways they practice harm reduction and building on those strengths. This is where harm reduction programs can help people frame what they do as self-care and amplify it. It is not all dependent on a program. . . . You create a therapeutic communal environment imbued with the spirit of harm reduction where good things happen and can be built upon by how you are involved with and interact in the space. I encouraged staff and participants to recognize their influence on the space and how a sense of safety and freedom in a stable space grows a community and spreads values of care and self-care within it. . . . I am proud that we were able to carry Streetwork on as a relatively stable place despite so many challenges for so many years. Streetwork has existed since 1984. It was really exciting to still be there when someone would show up from 10 years ago and the place was still there, and you are still there, it still has the same meaning and it has the same philosophy, and you managed to transmit the philosophy to generation after generation of young people.

In his years at Streetwork, Welch had to say goodbye to many clients who left this world too early. "I recently had two die who were both long-term people and my own clients for many years until they died. Those moments really fucked me up." He told me about one client, whom he described as "a shining star" and knew for twelve years. This client had contracted HIV very early in his life and often refused to take his medication. Welch said,

He died of straight-up internalized homophobia, a social toxin, is my belief. I would visit him in the hospital where he was sick. He used to tell me how he felt like dying because he couldn't accept himself, and now he actually was dying and realized he was he was too young to die, and I could see he felt a new self-empathy that I wish he had more of before.

Concluded Welch, "Young people need to be respected and understood. To feel that they are part of a community, are loved, and are not patronized."

CONCLUSION

In "Personal Narratives and the Life Story," McAdams posits that six principles can be traced through the personal narratives of peoples' lives: (1) that "the self is storied," (2) "stories integrate lives," (3) "stories are told in social relationships," (4) "stories change over time," (5) "stories are cultural texts," and (6) "some stories are better than others" (2008, 242). In this chapter, I shared the narratives of three service providers reflecting on their own lives. Each involves elements of the "narrating suffering, growth and transformation" that McAdams describes. These are stories of adaptation and coping; of widely diverging experiences based on race, gender, and class; and of struggles in relationships to institutions. Barnhart recalls her efforts to provide services and create relationships with homeless LGBT youth. Sascha Altman DuBrul traces a narrative of his own struggles over his life story and the contested meanings of childhood mental illness. And John Welch shares some of the lessons of eighteen years of working with homeless youth, navigating the space between homelessness, foster care, and the streets.

In 1900, Sigmund Freud suggested that the stories of our lives offer count-less insights (Freud 1900/1953). One can certainly see a few in the life sto-ries traced throughout this chapter. Each points to a nagging problem ab-sent a larger solution. It is clear that more has to be done to engage youth lost to services. And while personal narratives are thought to elicit support from social actors (Polletta 2006), the question remains if these narratives can transform public indifference into social action for those in need. Too few providers are doing enough to respond to the complex realities of RHY or, for that matter, to respect their choices and challenges. As a result, far too many wayward youth find themselves at arm's length from services, spending their nights on subway trains, doubled up on couches, locked up in psych institutions, or trembling in the cold.

QUESTIONS FOR REFLECTION AND GROUP DISCUSSION

1. Why do kids become homeless and what lessons do you learn from the narra-tives traced here?
2. What is harm reduction and why is it important?
3. What would it look like if we could see young people struggling with psychosis as having something to teach us? Instead of looking for limitations, what are the strengths of RHY and those struggling with psychosis?

NOTE

1. By "queer" I refer to the term as both an abbreviation for Lesbian, Gay, Bisexual and Transgender people, as well as to Warner's (1991) point that queer is an outsider status. "Every person who comes to a queer self-understanding knows in one way or another that her stigmatization is intricated with gender, with the family, with notions of individual freedom, the state, public speech, consumption and desire, nature and culture, maturation, reproductive politics, racial and national fantasy, class identity, truth and trust, censorship, intimate life and social display, terror and violence, health care, and deep cultural norms about the bearing of the body. Be-ing queer means fighting about these issues all the time, locally and piecemeal but always with consequences. It means being able, more or less articulately, to chal-lenge the common understanding of what gender difference means, or what the state is for, or what 'health' entails, or what would define fairness, or what a good rela-tion to the planet's environment would be. Queers do a kind of practical social re-flection just in finding ways of being queer" (6). In this respect, Warner suggests, "The preference for 'queer' represents, among other things, an aggressive impulse of generalization; it rejects a minoritizing logic of toleration or simple political

interest–representation in favor of a more thorough resistance to regimes of the normal. The universalizing utopianism of queer theory does not entirely replace more minority-based versions of lesbian and gay theory—nor could it" (16).

REFERENCES

Becker, Howard S. 1966. "Introduction." In Clifford Shaw, *The Jack Stroller: A Delinquent Boy's Own Story*, v–xvii. Chicago: University of Chicago Press.

Cohler, Bertram. 1994. "The Human Sciences, the Life Story, and Clinical Research." In *Qualitative Research in Social Work*, ed. E. Sherman and W. Reid, 163–175. New York. Columbia University Press.

Dank, Meredith, Jennifer Yahner, Kuniko Madden, Isela Bañuelos, Lilly Yu, Andrea Ritchie, Mitchyll Mora, and Brendan Conner. 2015. *Surviving the Streets of New York: Experiences of LGBTQ Youth, YMSM, and YWSW Engaged in Survival Sex*. https://www.urban.org/research/publication/surviving-streets-new-york-experiences-lgbtq-youth-ymsm-and-ywsw-engaged-survival-sex.

DuBrul, Sascha Altman. 2017. "Crazywise—Revisioning Narratives of Psychosis." May 15. http://www.mapstotheotherside.net/crazywise-revisioning-narratives-of-psychosis/.

Elliot, Andrea, and Rebecca. Ruiz. 2014. "New York Is Removing over 400 Children from 2 Homeless Shelters." *New York Times*, February 21.

Fitch, Robert. 1999. *The Assassination of New York*. New York. Verso.

Freud, Sigmund. 1900/1953. "The Interpretation of Dreams." In *The Standard Edition of the Complete Psychological Works of Sigmund Freud*, ed. Strachecy, vols. 4 and 5. London Hogarth Press.

Gibson. Kristina E. 2011. *Street Kids: Homeless Youth, Outreach, and Policing New York's Streets*. New York: New York University Press.

Harrison, David. 2014. "Foreword." In *Narrating Social Work through Autoethnography*, ed. Stanley Witkin, vii–x. New York: Columbia University Press.

Martin, Ruth R. 1995. *Oral History: Research, Assessment and Intervention*. Thousand Oaks, CA: Sage.

McAdams, Dan. 2008. "Personal Narratives and the Life Story." In *Handbook of Personality: Theory and Research*, ed. O. John, R. Robins, and L. A. Pervin, 241–261. New York: Guilford Press.

McNamara, Robert. 1995. *Sex, Scams, and Street Life: The Sociology of New York City's Times Square*. Greenwood, CT: Praeger.

Polletta, Francesca. 2006. *It Was Like a Fever: Storytelling in Protest and Politics*. Chicago: University of Chicago Press.

Ram, Marissa, and Conner, Brendan M. 2015. "David Felix: Jailed by an Unjust System, Failed by City Services, Killed by the Police." *The Guardian*. June 10.. http://www.theguardian.com/commentisfree/2015/jun/10/david-felix-immigration-mental-illness-killed-by-police?CMP=share_btn_fb.

Robinson, Paul A. 1969. *The Freudian Left*. New York: Harper.

Shaw, Clifford. 1930. *The Jack Stroller: A Delinquent's Own Story*. Chicago: University of Chicago Press.

Sheehan, Susan. 1993. *Life for Me Ain't Been No Crystal Stair*. New York: Vintage Books.

Shepard, Benjamin. 2013. "From Community Organization to Direct Services: The Street Trans Action Revolutionaries to Sylvia Rivera Law Project." *Journal of Social Service Research* 39, no. 1: 95–115.

——. 2015. *Rebel Friendships: "Outsider" Networks and Social Movements*. New York: Palgrave Macmillan.

"A 'Simple Notion' Offers Hope for Street Youths." 1987. *New York Times,* September 27.

Tracy, James. 2014. *Dispatches from Displacement*. Oakland, CA: AK Press.

Wallace, Deborah. 1999. *A Plague on Your Houses*. New York: Verso.

Warner, Michael. 1991. "Introduction: Fear of a Queer Planet." *Social Text*, no. 29: 3–17.

Waterman, Wanda. 2017. "Punk Rock "Wounded Healer" Helps Co-Design a New Model of Psychiatric Care." *Design Is Political*. une 15. = http://designispolitical.com /third-sector/punk-rock-wounded-healer-helps-co-design-a-new-model-of -psychiatric-care//

Witkin, Stanley. 2014. *Narrating Social Work Through Autoethnography*. New York: Columbia University Press.

Wosh, Peter J. 2004. *Covenant House: Journey of a Faith Based Charity*. Philadelphia: University of Pennsylvania Press.

Chapter Eleven

CHILDHOOD AND THE POLITICS OF CARE

ELIZABETH PALLEY

As I sit down to write this chapter, I realize that writing an autoethnography is a challenge. Although I am a qualitative researcher, I have been trained positivistically. Much of my research has been exploratory and focused on finding *truth*. Autoethnography requires me to find a moment in time or a story that provides a critical moment to describe my experience with child care. My interest in child care came before I had my own children, but peaked soon after my first child's birth. A couple of days after my daughter was born, I received a call from the dean's secretary asking if I was going to take *unpaid leave*. I was taken aback because I was expecting to be paid during that time and thought I had worked everything out before going on maternity leave. I was in tears over the phone as I wondered how we could possibly afford child care without my salary. My initial impulse was to call back and say, "I quit," but even in my state of hysteria I knew that was not a solution. I needed to earn money with a new child to support and the impending cost of day care. I had also worked hard for my career and, for the most part, enjoyed it.

Concerns about the cost of child care and what to do with young babies when parents work are hardly unique to me. There is no systematic strategy in the United States to address this problem, leaving most parents to struggle with or be unable to access quality, affordable care for their children. As it turned out, I was placed on disability for the remainder of the semester as a result of health issues related to my labor and delivery, and fortunately, my university had a fully paid disability policy.

I recognize that I was and am privileged. I am married, have parents who could help me pay for child care, and have a professional job that provides me with a lot of flexibility. Though the average American child resides with two parents (69 percent), many others do not (U.S. Census Bureau, 2016a). Further, the median U.S. household income was $56,000 in 2015 (U.S. Census Bureau, 2016b). My husband's and my combined income was considerably more than that. Still, I struggled to manage many obstacles related to child care. I wanted what most parents want—to ensure a safe environment in which my daughter could thrive—and the moment I received that phone call I felt overwhelmed. For many American families with fewer resources, the challenges of child care can be staggering.

In this chapter, I chose the methodology of autoethnography because of my overlapping personal and professional connection with the fields of child care and child care policy: it allowed me to raise issues from both my own experience and the literature. In so doing, I examine what drew me to this topic, and I share both my research in the area and the implications of existing policies related to early education and care, or the lack thereof, for children. Autoethnography suggests that in research "the personal is political." As noted by others "research is a political, socially-just and socially-conscious act," and it is not value free. (Ellis, Adams & Bochner, 2010, para 1). Witkin further notes that autoethnography is hard to categorize. It is both a narrative and a dialogue with the reader and has "a focus on enriching understanding," as opposed to "discovering truth" (2014, p. 15). Research suggests that high-quality care is important for early brain development, so why is child care such a problem in the United States? Why is it politicized and not perceived as a universal need/good? This chapter draws both on my personal narrative and relevant literature on child care policy to address these questions.

CHILD CARE POLICY

My interest in early education and care policy began when I was pursuing my PhD in social welfare policy at the Heller School at Brandeis University in Waltham, Massachusetts. The more I studied social problems, the more convinced I became that many of them could be reduced or eliminated with appropriate early education and care. Before attending the Heller School, I had practiced as a lawyer specializing in special education; in that work I found that some, though certainly not all, of the problems children had for which they needed special education services could be minimized with high-quality early intervention. The young brain, as research has shown, is amazingly malleable, and early experiences affect the ways in which it develops. The early learning environment is crucially important for the later development of cognitive skills and emotional regulation abilities (National Scientific Council on the Developing Brain, 2007).

After finishing my dissertation, I moved to New York to begin work as an academic. A couple years later, I met my husband. About eight years after moving to New York, I began to focus my research on early education and care. . In October 2007, we had our first child, a daughter named Amelia. At the time I had been working as a professor for about five years. When Amelia was born, I was unprepared for the challenges I would face both personally and professionally while trying to figure out care for her. And four years later, my daughter Charlotte was born, making the work–life balance even more complicated. As I noted earlier, I am privileged in many ways. I had my first child in my late thirties at a time when my career and finances were relatively stable. I was in a loving relationship with a partner who equally contributed to my family's finances and provided both child care and emotional support. My parents were also in a financial situation to help me with the cost of care. As I, who was so fortunate, struggled to manage child care, costs, and work, I wondered, how single parents, low-income parents, and less resourced parents dealt with child care in the United States.

My pediatrician recommended caring for Amelia at home and waiting to place her in a formal child care setting until she was two. This recommendation was based on the vulnerability of young infants to frequent illnesses. However, I was hesitant to have someone work in my home for a number of reasons. I was not comfortable with the idea of a stranger staying with my new baby without any additional oversight. What if I misjudged the person I hired and she was not kind to my child? Who would see her potentially mistreating my daughter? Jocelyn Burke (2015), who wrote *The Nanny Time Bomb: Navigating the Crisis in Child Care*, talks about middle-class moms who do not know how to be employers because they did not grow up with household help. Although I had been cared for by a nanny as a very young child (until I was school age), I felt that I fit into this mold too, and I was not eager to learn how to be an employer. I also understood the vulnerability of in-home employees and, as a result, was uncomfortable putting someone in that situation. Employed caretakers are vulnerable to exploitation. Employers can choose not to pay them a fair wage or may pay them for fewer hours than they worked, and caretakers often have little recourse. Undocumented caregivers are even more vulnerable and are less likely to complain about unfair conditions for fear of retaliation.

I was also uncomfortable with the power dynamics that are present between upper-middle-class white women and the working-class brown women they employ as caregivers. This relationship highlights differences in economic and employment opportunities. While upper- middle-class and rich women are able to progress professionally because they have the support of caregivers, the caregivers did not benefit in a comparable way.

Child care workers are predominantly women, and many are women of color. Child care is one of the lowest paid professions in the country—whether one is a professional provider who works in a day care center, someone who provides care in her own home for children, or a nanny (Whitebrook, Phillips, & Howes, 2014). In her book, Burke (2015) noted the existence of a hierarchy among New York nannies, with white and European nannies being the most highly paid and immigrant women of color generally being the most poorly paid. I did not want to have to worry about the structural inequalities that exist in our society when dealing with care in my own home. I simply wanted to be able to raise my own child while at home. I also wanted to be able to keep my job.

Shortly after my daughter was born, I began to look for a child care opportunity in my neighborhood that would take a three-month-old child. The day care setting I was interested in had a waitlist and was extremely costly. I could find no other conventional center-based options for children under two. However, I wanted to ensure that my daughter would be placed in high-quality care, which is typically expensive. According to Child Care Aware (2017), which collects the most comprehensive data on child care costs in the United States, the average annual cost of center- based infant care in 2014 in New York State was $14,200 and $17,160 in New York City (Eisenstadt, 2014). Considering that the median household income before taxes in New York City from 2011–2015 was $53,000, this represented more than one-third of most families' incomes (U.S. Census Bureau, 2016c). At the time, center-based child care did not feel like a feasible option for my family.

I began to look for someone to come to my house. I wanted to provide a living wage, contribute to the caregiver's Social Security, and pay for health benefits. I hoped to find someone to share a nanny with me to make this affordable: I was not sure how my husband and I could afford to pay for this care on our own without a *nanny share*.

When my daughter was about four months old and I returned to work, we hired Sarah, who herself had an eighteen-month-old child, to care for my daughter for about ten hours a week. Sarah was a social worker who had left work when her child was born. She received health insurance through her husband. She became and is still a close personal friend. This arrangement worked for about six months until we needed additional help.

When Amelia was nine or ten months old, I placed an ad on a neighborhood Listserv for a caretaker. My husband and I interviewed many people. The majority were not legal U.S. residents, including the woman we thought was the best match for our family. Although she had many years of experience and was the only applicant who made us feel comfortable, I was faced with a dilemma: I wanted to hire someone who had legal documents, but I also did not want to discriminate against someone who seemed the most qualified to care for my child.

Although it is difficult to get data on the undocumented workforce, it is estimated that immigrants make up 18 percent of the child care and early education workforce. Whereas only 29 percent of native-born U.S. citizens who are child care providers work in home-based care (either their own or their employers), 50 percent of immigrant workers are home care providers (Park, McHugh, Zong, & Batalova, 2015). This type of work is inherently more vulnerable because employers usually terminate the caregiver's employment when they no longer need child care. In an agency, presumably there are new children every year.

To make the child care arrangement more affordable, we hired Hilda part-time while she remained in her preexisting job working for another family several days a week. Even though both my husband and I were tenured professors, we could not afford to pay a living wage for full-time care. My parents were, fortunately, in a position to help us. How could lower-income parents work and find affordable child care? The whole system or lack thereof that we have in this country did not make sense to me. Many parts of the industrialized world have both state- mandated paid maternity leave and free child care (International Labour Organization, 2014). Why were these not priorities for our country?

We hired Hilda when Amelia was almost one, and she became a temporary part of our family. When my daughter was just shy of two years old, we placed her in a licensed home care center in the neighborhood where we saved on costs and received many more hours of care. This setting also gave our daughter the chance to interact with a group of children her age, and she loved it. Yet I realized that part of my responsibility as an employer was to help Hilda find another job, or she would be left without the salary we were paying her. We gave Hilda several months' notice and agreed she would leave should a job opportunity come up before we were really ready to let her go. Because my husband and I are academics, we had a lot of flexibility over the summer and could have lived without child care if necessary. Though the process was stressful, everything worked out, and we have remained friendly with Hilda as well.

We were lucky. Our first home-based care providers were both excellent. They read to our daughter, and Hilda even read in both English and Spanish. Both took her to the playground and made friends with other nannies in the neighborhood. Hilda had a granddaughter a year older than Amelia who sometimes came to play with her, and Sarah brought her daughter as well. Amelia was well cared for and loved by both women. The home care center that we chose was run by two women who had early education degrees and who had worked in the neighborhood for more than twenty years; the center is still thriving. All of the families for whom they provide care paid market rate for it. My daughter attended for a year until she entered a more formal preschool.

When my second daughter was born, theoretically we could have put ourselves on a list to get her into a child care center at three months. However, we needed someone who could occasionally care for both of our children, so a day care center no longer made sense. Our initial efforts to find a home-based caretaker were unsuccessful. After two or three weeks of interviewing, we contacted Hilda to ask if she had any friends to recommend. She referred a friend of hers, whom we ultimately hired. Her friend was an American who wanted to return to paid work after raising four children. After two years, we placed our second daughter in the same care center that Amelia had attended.

We again had a generally good experience with the child care center. I recall one incident, however, that left me frustrated. One morning when I went to drop off my younger daughter Charlotte, I was met at the door by a provider who whispered to me, "You cannot come in because the regulators are here. Can you come back in a half-hour?" I was a little frustrated because I had intended to go to work then. Fortunately, however, I did not have to go to work right away so Charlotte and I played in the park around the corner. They called me about twenty or so minutes later and told me that the aide would watch my daughter at the park. When I picked Charlotte up that afternoon, the center directors explained what had happened. They told me that they had done a favor for a mom whose child was scheduled to be in care only two days a week: they let the child come a third day so that her mother could go to an appointment. By allowing an additional child, they had violated the regulations on the number of children that they were allowed to watch. As luck would have it, on that very day, the inspector had come. I was irritated because I had been inconvenienced, and I was also concerned that they were not properly following the regulations. Ultimately, I did nothing and decided to keep trusting that my daughter was in a good child care situation.

At the same time that I was struggling with my own child care situation, I began to write a book on child care policy titled *In Our Hands: The Struggle for U.S. Child Care Policy* (Palley & Shdaimah, 2014). The book included some of the research on early care and education that follows. As noted already, I was surprised by how difficult it was to navigate child care and early education in New York. I had friends in other cities who seemed to be experiencing similar struggles, even if their children's care was not quite as expensive as care in New York. My mother had returned to work shortly after I had been born thirty-seven years earlier, and most of my friends' mothers had worked. Why was it still so difficult to balance work and young families? Why was there no systematic way to address the care needs of young children in the United States? This was not a new issue. My friend and colleague, Corey Shdaimah, who collaborated with me on the book project, and I were both well aware that many other countries had better leave policies and better supports for families raising children, including national child care systems.

CROSS-NATIONAL COMPARISONS

When I was about seven months pregnant with Amelia and traveling by train to Canada, I met a woman from Montreal who was also about seven months pregnant. She told me that she had been harshly questioned on her arrival into the United States for fear that she was traveling there just to have her child born in the United States. She explained why she was laughing about this treatment she received by saying something to this effect:

> I am a chef. In Montreal, I have full health benefits and will receive eighteen months of paid maternity leave. If I stayed in the U.S., I would be forced to pay thousands of dollars for the labor and delivery and then, I'd have no paid leave. Then, when I am ready to put my child in care, I'll be able to send him or her to state supported child care which would not be available for me in the U.S. Why would I or anyone chose that over being a Canadian? I certainly wouldn't want to do that to my child.

Maternity leave, particularly paid leave, is relevant for child care because if women (or parents in the case of parental leave) can afford to be home with their young children after birth, it is not necessary to find replacement care. In 2000, the International Labour Organization (ILO) of the United Nations created standards for maternity leave that included fourteen weeks of paid leave of at least two-thirds of the woman's salary. This recommendation was later increased to eighteen weeks. The ILO specified that women should receive medical insurance throughout this time, and if benefits were not available through their employer, they should be provided by government social assistance funds. By 2014, all Western European countries exceeded the proposed standards. In some countries, such as Norway, women receive between thirty-six to forty-five weeks of paid leave. The United States in 2014 was one of only 2 of 185 countries to provide no cash replacement during maternity leave and provided less legally allowable leave than more than half of the countries in the UN (International Labour Organization, 2014).

State-supported child care is more broadly available in much of the rest of industrialized world. In Mexico, children are required to attend state-funded preschool at age three. France provides one of the most comprehensive systems of universal child care: children are eligible for state-subsidized, high-quality child care at day care centers from three months until thirty months or until they are three years old and begin preschool. Three-quarters of the people working in a child care center are required to have a degree in early education and care. The centers are open for eleven hours a day for eleven months of the year. From the time that children begin preschool until age six when they begin elementary school, they are eligible for eight hours a day of free early education and care in public programs, and half of the staff of these programs are required to have appropriate degrees. The state subsidizes on average 75 percent of the cost of care for children who attend a child care center, with parents paying sliding-scale fees based on income (OECD, 2006). If European countries and even Mexico, can provide state-subsidized early education and care, why is the United States not doing so? Why are we as a nation not talking about the struggles women and families face regarding the cost of care, the availability of care, and the quality of care? Politicians spend a lot of time debating abortion and the rights of fetuses, but still do little to provide material support to children.

BACKGROUND RESEARCH ON CHILD CARE

There has been a tremendous amount of research conducted on child care and early education, ranging from the socioemotional importance to the economic benefits of quality child care. In other words, the verdict on whether or not children are harmed in care has largely been resolved: as long as children receive quality care, they will not be harmed. In fact, many will benefit from it (Zigler & Hall, 2000; Heckman, 2008; Vandell, Belsky, Burchinal, Steinberg, et al., 2010). High-quality care helps children develop the social and emotional skills that are necessary for them to be successful in kindergarten and throughout elementary school (Boyd et.al., 2005; National Scientific Council on the Developing Child, 2007). The problem is that many children in the United States who are in child care are not receiving high-quality care: they are getting custodial rather than developmental care (Melmed, 2008; U.S. Department of Education; 2015). Custodial care refers to care that is basically babysitting, as opposed to developmental care, which is designed to address children's social, physical, and emotional needs (Zigler, Marsland, & Lord, 2009). While custodial care alone may keep children safe, if they are not sufficiently engaged or are neglected during critical periods of early development, they can face long-term developmental problems. As noted by the National Scientific Council on the Developing Child, "impoverished early experience can have severe and long-lasting detrimental effects on later brain capabilities" (NSCDC, 2007, 6).

Some of the key elements of high-quality developmental care include low provider–student ratios, extensive instructor training and development, good physical spaces, and positive caregiver interactions. Positive caregiver interactions are more likely to occur with low caregiver–child ratios (Bowman, Donovan & Burns, 2000; Vandell, Henderson, & Wilson, 1988). Another important aspect of quality child care is the opportunity for children to engage in pretend play, which enables them to develop both cognitive problem-solving skills and linguistic interactive skills (Bergen & Mauer, 2000). These opportunities allow children to learn to exercise agency and develop emotional regulation skills that are important life skills.

Perhaps the most-referenced research on child care comes from the Perry High Scopes research that was conducted in Ypsilanti, Michigan. In this study, children were provided with high-quality day care and then tracked until young adulthood (Belfield, Nores, Barnett, & Schweinhart, 2006). The Nobel Prize-winning economist, James Heckman, calculated the effects of this quality care, finding that every dollar invested in high-quality care yielded an $8.60 benefit in lower incarceration rates, a greater likelihood that children would be tax-paying contributing members of society, and reduced rates of public social welfare program dependence (Heckman, Grunwald, & Reynolds, 2006).

Yet, despite this research on child brain development and the importance of high-quality early education and care, there has been little or no effort in the United States to develop a national system of care since the 1970s. In 1971 President Nixon vetoed a bipartisan national child care bill that was designed to ensure universal access to early education and care that would be federally subsidized, for which payment would be on a sliding scale based on parental income. In his veto, he noted that he did not want children raised in institutions, fearing the effect of "Sovietizing" child care. No universal child care bill has since been proposed in the United States (Palley & Shdaimah, 2014).

Though public opinion polling suggests that most parents believe that parental care is better than center-based care, the data are not conclusive

(Bostrom, 2002; Robison, 2002; Sylvester, 2001). In any event, there seems to be some public recognition that, even if families may prefer mothers to be the primary care providers for young children, many are not doing so. In 2013, Hart Research and Public Opinion Strategies and the First Five Years Fund conducted surveys whose samples included both Democrats and Republicans and found broad-based support for the federal government to help states and localities make child care more affordable.

Though the Obama administrations did draft some legislation to increase the availability of high-quality child care, bills that would have significantly expanded funding did not pass. In the Trump administration, there has been less focus on quality care and more on tax benefits to help parents pay for whatever care they can afford (Palley, 2016).

MY RESEARCH ON CHILD CARE POLICY

Two years after Amelia was born, Corey Shdaimah and I began our research together by interviewing child care advocates and researchers and asking them why they felt that we had not been able to develop better child care policies in the United States. We interviewed twenty-six women, many of whom had spent long careers advocating for improved child care policy and funding. We also researched the history of U.S. child care policy in our political system and the factors influencing U.S. policy development to try to understand what had happened. We made an effort to interview conservative policy advocates, but none were willing to speak with us about why they did not support government funding of child care.

To find out more about the views of conservative policy advocates, we looked at the websites of their organizations. We found that, unsurprisingly, there are many reasons that we do not have a universal child care policy in this country. One reason is that, as noted earlier, though there was a bipartisan movement to establish such a policy, Nixon vetoed the bill to make it possible in 1971. We also looked at the role of campaign financing in strengthening the conservative movement. The need for national child care increased at the same time that the anti-tax movement blossomed. Though this movement takes no direct position on child care, it suggests that reduced government spending is in the public's best interest. Creating new publicly supported programs for children would increase government spending, and the neoliberal environment, with a focus on lowering taxes and the deficit, worked for many years against increasing federal government involvement in any service program, let alone child care. During the Obama administration, the focus on increased government intervention targeted health care, arguably a commodity that affects everyone directly, as opposed to child care, which does not affect everyone directly—and even if one can make an argument that quality child care is important for the broader society, many of its effects are less direct. Further, child care has been funded by a patchwork of policies. This has created many separate interests and, at times, has limited the efforts of advocates because they are all trying to keep the resources that they had, and existing programs were vying for the same pot of money. Policy feedback is a political science term that has been used to explain the limitation of policy options because of existing policies (Palley & Shdaimah, 2014).

After completing our initial project, we developed an online survey for parents to gauge their support for universal child care. If there was such a huge need, we wondered why there was no mass movement to expand access to child care. Our survey sample was biased, leaning to the left politically and involving primarily parents from two-parent family households. As expected, the vast majority supported some government role in subsidizing child care, but we were surprised by some of the concerns that were raised. More parents were supportive of subsidizing care for low-income parents than providing universal access. Many were concerned by the lack of available care options where they lived. Furthermore, several people who took the survey responded that they wanted control over the type of care they chose for their children, and some expressed concern about being taxed for programs from which they themselves might not be able to benefit (Shdaimah & Palley, 2016).

The final piece of our research on child care involves understanding provider perspectives (Shdaimah, Palley & Miller, 2018). Child care providers are poorly paid; on average, they earn approximately $20,000 a year. As a result, more than half of all child care workers are eligible for public benefits (Bureau of Labor Statistics, 2015; Whitebrook et al., 2014). Child care workers are also disproportionately women of color (Gould, 2015). To ensure high-quality care for children, we, as a nation, must ensure that their providers are economically and emotionally stable and have appropriate child care and early education skills (Whitaker, Dearth-Wesley, & Gooze, 2015). Efforts to improve care for children by regulating the behaviors of providers are intended to keep children safe. Our research was designed to explore just how these policies affect child care providers in their day to day provision of care (Shdaimah, Palley & Miller, 2018).

We conducted interviews and focus groups with both licensed home-based providers and center-based program directors (many of whom had been providers or were currently providers as well) throughout New York State and are seeking funding to conduct this research in other states. The goal of this study was to learn about the challenges that providers face. How do they perceive the state regulations? Do they feel that they are being supported by the state in their efforts to care for children? Our findings indicate that child care providers are struggling financially, feel there is a disconnect between the goal of the regulations—to protect children—and the day-to-day provision of care, and perceive that state licensors implement the regulations inconsistently. One example of a regulatory disconnect that home-based providers raised was that policies designed for center-based care, such as never having children out of your sight, are being implemented in homes with one provider (e.g., "How can I ever go to the bathroom with this policy in place?"). Both home- and center-based providers raised concerns that focusing on complex check-in sheets (often multiple forms are required for different state-funded programs) often meant that providers and parents could not attend to the transitional needs of the children adequately. Overall, our findings indicated that child care workers face regulatory, financial, and practical impediments that prevent them from providing optimal care. Regulatory schemes often have unforeseen, inefficient, and sometimes harmful results, and staff are left out of the process of deciding what is important to improve the quality of care for the children they serve (Shdaimah, Palley & Miller, 2018).

CONCLUSION

Though my professional interest in child care preceded my having children, the experience and challenges I myself faced when I had children and the struggles I experienced as I worked to provide them with substitute care while I was working shaped my perspective on the importance of child care and the need for more broader-based advocacy around child care policy. Yes, with all of my privilege, I survived my children's early years, but my experiences gave me a greater understanding of the struggles faced by all parents, especially low-income single parents. Child care should not be seen through the lens of individual challenges, but rather as a more systemic problem. When my children were in others' care, I wanted to be confident that they were learning important skills that were necessary for them to develop into cognitively, socially, and emotionally healthy children and, ultimately, adults. My experience led me to believe that other parents of young children felt the same way. Who would not want that for their child? I also became interested in the struggles of the providers. What supports could and should we be giving to providers to ensure that they too are able to get their needs met and that they have the skills to provide good-quality care for all children? It seems clear to me, as perhaps it was at the beginning of my research, that we need to invest more money in child care as a nation at the federal, state, and local levels. There is no reason that this should not be a bipartisan issue. Both Republicans and Democrats have children and struggle to provide for their care when they are young. It is also clear to me that any advocacy movement needs to include both providers and parents. The current tax proposals to offset the cost of care for higher-income Americans, and hypothetically for low-income Americans if they are able to save money on their meager incomes, will do nothing to address the needs of providers. Ultimately, we need to invest in the education of providers and provide income supports for qualified providers if we are going to ensure quality care for all children and not just the few upper-middle-class and rich parents, like me, who can better afford it.

QUESTIONS FOR REFLECTION AND GROUP DISCUSSION

1. What struggles did the author face finding quality care for her children?
2. How was her experience similar or different from the struggles faced by "average' Americans?
3. Why, as one of the richest industrialized countries in the world, do so many families struggle to find quality, affordable care for their children? And why is the need for child care not seen as a bipartisan issue?

REFERENCES

Belfield, C., Nores, M., Barnett, W., & Schweinhart, L. (2006). The High Scopes/ Perry Preschool Program: Cost benefit analysis using data from age 40 follow-up. *Journal of Human Resources, 41*(1), 162–190.

Bergen, D., & Mauer, D. (2000). Symbolic play, phonological awareness, and literacy skills at three age levels. In K. A. Roskos & J. F. Christie (Eds.), *Play and literacy in early childhood: Research from multiple perspectives* (pp. 45–62). New York: Erlbaum.

Bostrom, M. (2002). *The whole child—Parents and policy: A meta-analysis of opinion data concerning school readiness, early childhood and related issues.* Frameworks Institute. Retrieved from http://www.frameworksinstitute.org/assets/files/ECD/the _whole_child.pdf.

Bowman, B., Donovan, M., & Burns, M. (Eds.). (2000). *Eager to learn: Educating our preschoolers.* Washington, DC: National Academies Press.

Boyd, J., Barnett, W., Bodrov, E., Leong, D., Gomby, D., Robin, K., & Hustedt, J. (2005). *Promoting children's social and emotional development through preschool.* New Brunswick, NJ: National Institute for Early Education Research. Retrieved from http://nieer.org/resourcespolicyreports/report7.pdf.

Bureau of Labor Statistics (2015). Occupational employment statistics, child care workers. Retrieved from https://www.bls.gov/oes/current/oes399011.htm.

Burke, J. S. (2015). *The nanny time bomb: Navigating the crisis in child care.* Santa Barbara, CA: Greenwood.

Child Care Aware. (2017). Parents and the high cost of child care. Retrieved from http:// www.usa.childcareaware.org/wp-content/uploads/2017/01/CCA_High_Cost _Report_01-17-17_final.pdf.

Eisenstadt, M. (2014). How much does your child care cost you: New York child care costs by county. Retrieved from http://www.syracuse.com/news/index.ssf/2014/03 /child_care_costs_in_onondaga_county_among_the_highest_in_the_state .html.

Ellis, C., Adams, T., & Bochner, A. (2010). Autoethnography: An overview. *Forum Qualitative Sozialforschung / Forum: Qualitative Social Research, 12*(1). Retrieved from http://www.qualitative-research.net/index.php/fqs/article/view/1589/3095.

First Five Years Fund (2013). *Take action now.* Retrieved from http://growamericastronger .org/wp-content/uploads/2013/07/Poll-Fact-Sheet.pdf.

Gould, E. (2015). *Child care workers are being paid enough to make ends meet.* Issue Brief 405. Economic Policy Institute. Retrieved from http://www.epi.org/files/2015/child -care-workers-final.pdf.

Hart Public Opinion Strategies (2013). Bipartisan phone survey. July 8–11.

Heckman, J. J. (2008). Schools, skills and synapses. *Economic Inquiry, 46*(3), 289–324.

Heckman, J. J., Grunwald, R., & Reynolds, A. (2006). The dollars and cents of investing early: Cost-benefit analysis in early care and education. *Zero to Three, 26*(6), 10–17.

International Labour Organization. (2014). Maternity and paternity at work: law and practice across the world. Retrieved from http://www.ilo.org/wcmsp5/groups/public /—dgreports/—dcomm/—publ/documents/publication/wcms_242615.pdf.

Melmed, M. (2008). *Statement of Matthew Melmed, executive director of Zero to Three to the Committee on Education and Labor, U.S. House of Representatives*. Retrieved from http://zerotothree.org/site/Doc-Server/1-23/2008_Investing_in_Early_Education_Testimony.pdf?docID4841.

National Scientific Council on the Developing Child. (2007). *The timing and quality of early experiences combine to shape brain architecture*. Working Paper #5. Retrieved from http://www.developingchild.net

Organisation for Economic Cooperation and Development (2006). Start Strong II: Early education and care. Retrieved from https://www.unicef.org/lac/spbarbados/Implementation/ECD/StartingStrongII_OECD_2006.pdf

Palley, E. (2016, Sept. 14). Trump's child care plan is a good start but it is still not enough. *Foxnews.com*. Retrieved from http://www.foxnews.com/opinion/2016/09/14/trump-s-child-care-plan-is-good-start-but-it-s-still-not-enough.html.

Palley, E., & Shdaimah, C. (2014). *In our hands: The struggle with U.S. child care policy*. New York: New York University Press.

Park, M., McHugh, M., Zong, J. & Batalova, J. (2015). *Immigrant and refugee workers in the early childhood field: Taking a closer look*. Washington, DC: Migration Policy Institute.

Robison, J. (2002). *Should mothers work?* Princeton, NJ: Gallup.

Shdaimah, C., & Palley, E. (2016). Elusive support for US child care policy. *Community Work & Family*, Retrieved from http://www.tandfonline.com/doi/full/10.1080/13668803.2016.1230841.

Shdaimah, C., Palley, E. & Miller, A. (2018). "I'm not a babysitter": Child care providers' perspectives on professional respect and societal support for quality child care. *Social Work and Society, 12*(4), 1–18. Retrieved from http://rdcu.be/GSZs.

Sylvester, K. (2001). Caring for our youngest: Public attitudes in the United States. *Future of Children, 11*(1), 52–61.

U.S. Census Bureau (2016a). The majority of children live with two parents. *Census Bureau Reports*. Retrieved from https://www.census.gov/newsroom/press-releases/2016/cb16-192.html.

U.S. Census Bureau (2016b). Income and poverty in the United States: 2015. Retrieved from https://www.census.gov/uat/facets-publications/2016/demo/p60-256.html.

U.S. Census Bureau (2016c). Quick facts: New York City, NY. Retrieved from https://www.census.gov/quickfacts/fact/table/newyorkcitynewyork/HSD410215#viewtop.

U.S. Department of Education (2015). *A matter of equity: Preschool in America*. Retrieved from https://www2.ed.gov/documents/early-learning/matter-equity-preschool-america.pdf.

Vandell, D., Belsky, J., Burchinal, M., Steinberg, L., Vandergrift, N., & NICHD Early Care and Research Network. (2010). Do effects of early care and education extend to age 15 years? Results from NICHD study of early child care and youth development. *Child Development, 81*(3), 737–756.

Vandell, D. Henderson, V., & Wilson, K. (1988). A longitudinal study of children with varying quality day care experiences. *Child Development, 59*, 1286–1292.

Whitaker, R.C., Dearth-Wesley, T., & Gooze, R. A. (2015). Workplace stress and the quality of teacher–children relationships in Head Start. *Early Childhood Research Quarterly, 30*, 57–69.

Whitebrook, M., Phillips, D., & Howes, C. (2014). *Worthy work, STILL unlivable wages: The early childhood workforce 25 years after the National Child Care Staffing Study.* Berkeley, CA: Center for the Study of Child Care Employment. Retrieved from http://www.irle.berkeley.edu/cscce/2014/report-worthy-work-still-unlivable-wages/.

Witkin, S. (2014). *Narrating social work through autoethnography.* New York: Columbia University Press.

Zigler, E., & Hall, N. W. (2000). *Child development and social policy: Theory and applications.* New York: McGraw-Hill.

Zigler, E., Marsland, K., & Lord, H. (2009). *The tragedy of childcare in America.* New Haven, CT: Yale University Press.

Chapter Twelve

LIVING ON THE FRONTLINE

Reality-Based Drug Education in the Era of Black Lives Matter

JERRY OTERO

Spanning 55,000 square feet and soaring eight stories above the downtown Brooklyn intersection of Smith and Pacific Streets stands "Sign Language," a colossal eye-popping mural of a teenage boy, defiantly rising above the neighborhood for a grab at the abandoned bicycle tire dangling on the street sign overhead (figure 12.1).

"Sign Language" (Cre8tive 2012) is an adaptation of a 1978 photograph by preeminent street culture and art documentarian, Martha Cooper (1980). Then a staff photographer for the daily *New York Post*, Copper used her left-over frames of film to photograph the scrappy kids she encountered on the street during her end-of-day walks back to the newspaper's headquarters. While recounting the backstory of her first encounters with this band of local kids, Cooper recalled how they prowled the city streets, looking for bicycle parts to build their own stylized two-wheeled creations. "Sign Language" is critically acclaimed as an enduring example of contemporary urban street art, yet its genesis as a 2012 high school drug education project is easily overlooked. Under the tutelage of veteran teaching artists Chris Stain and Billy Mode, thirteen apprentices of color (ages fifteen to twenty-two) worked in teams and were involved in every aspect of this large-scale public art project's design, production, and installation.

"Sign Language" is the sixth volume in Cre8tive YouTH*ink's, the Art School Without Walls (ASWW) program, a New York City-based antiracist

FIGURE 12.1 "Sign Language." Cre8tive
YouTH*ink 2014. Commissioned by the Quinlan
Development Group and Lonicera Partners, 237
Pacific Street, Brooklyn, NY. Photo by Mista Oh.

creative arts youth development program that revives the spirit of appren-
ticeship in the arts by pairing aspiring youth of color with top arts professionals to create significant works of art. The cornerstone of Cre8tive
YouTH*ink's mission is the idea that a creative, ethical, critically thinking,
and socially engaged urban youth constituency can be cultivated through
an engagement with the arts (Cre8tive 2012)

In this chapter I describe Cre8tive YouTH*ink's multidisciplinary model
of drug education that combines art making with a "each one, teach one"
harm reduction (HR) approach, undergirded by elements of developmental psychology, attachment theory, social justice youth development, and
community service. The program has a twofold focus: to foster both the
conscious development of its youth members and their positive relationships with adults.

DRUG EDUCATION IN THE UNITED STATES

From the nineteenth-century temperance movement to Nancy Reagan's
"Just Say No" (Godfrey 2016) campaign and beyond, Americans have des-

perately fought teenage drug use with hysterical racist claims and scare tactics (Beck 1998) Yet, Rosenbaum (2014) has noted "despite our admonitions to abstain or delay trying drugs, most students will try alcohol or other drugs by the time they graduate high school." Instead of threatening or shaming kids into abstinence an HR framework shifts the focus from punitive restrictions or zero tolerance of risky behaviors to keeping young people safe from their potential associated harms. For youth of color (YOC) these strategies must necessarily include keeping them safe from the harms inflicted by drug prohibition.

The U.S. war on drugs has our children squarely in its crosshairs. Drug prohibition, supposedly enforced to protect youth, actually threatens them twice. First, it blocks the honest discussions that would reduce riskier forms of drug use, improve health, and save lives. Second, it makes youth—above all, YOC—targets for law enforcement and our vast prison-industrial complex. In 2015, an astonishing 75 percent of people arrested nationally for marijuana offenses were YOC under the age of twenty-nine (FBI 2015).

Social services workers often lament the difficulties of engaging "hard-to-reach" YOC, who typically come to their attention with oppositional and other behavioral problems, academic failures, or deficits in coping skills, anger management, and impulse control.

Hijacked by a psychology of white adolescence, conventional youth programs are unable or unwilling to examine the complex social, economic, and political forces that impinge on YOC's lives. The unintended consequences are that many YOC never enroll in programs aimed at serving them, or enroll, but are unable to adjust to program demands. Many drop out and do not participate long enough to earn education credentials, improve their work readiness and life management skills, or achieve any other real benefit (Jessor 1993).

It is vital to our work with YOC to recognize that America's prohibition of drugs is a far more pernicious monument to racism than any statue of a Confederate general. It has been driven by decades of charged rhetoric depicting YOC as dangerous—a menace to be feared and controlled. This nihilistic worldview simply channels the crushing reality of the odds against them. YOC from communities like Brooklyn face serious issues of identity development, racism, sexism, police brutality, poverty, and other social issues every day (Million Dollar Blocks 2016). has led to an overemphasis on criminal justice solutions to social problems and an underemphasis on solutions related on health, education, and other human services (Ginwright and Cammarota 2002).

"We care more about how we can punish YOC than we do about their life outcomes," said Deborah Small, founder of Break the Chains. In this kind of social climate, it is the rare program that intentionally seeks to create healing attachment experiences with "hard-to-reach" youth. Dominant social work narratives promote a risk-factor paradigm that views young people as problems, deficits, and pathologies (Robinson 2016; Saleeby 1996). Case and Haines (2015) support the view that traditional approaches are too managerial and reductionist, oversimplifying children's lives and failing to account for the complex and trauma-inducing social, economic, and political factors that affect YOC (Bottrell 2007; Bottrell and Armstrong 2007).

A century of enforcement of prohibitionist policies has resulted in YOC living in a highly militarized war zone, in which selective enforcement and extrajudicial murder are greater threats to their well-being than drugs like marijuana ever were ("Race and Criminal Justice" 2017; Alexander 2011). In the era of Black Lives Matter (BLM), real concern for YOC's safety has become the cornerstone of a relationship-building process that is rooted within the positive social youth development movement (Hawkins, Catalano, and Miller 1992; Lerner et al. 2015), but goes beyond convention to provide opportunities for the development of the self within a postcolonial matrix (Ginwright and Cammarota 2002)

This chapter highlights my story as a harm reductionist using an approach specifically designed to trigger attachment, positive bonding, and supportive relationships, especially with "hard to reach" YOC. On a personal note, I could not have predicted that my life would be so profoundly affected by the students I have come to know. Harm reduction is all about relationship building. By listening, they taught me much that I needed to know to support them. Responding authentically to their needs has made me a better man.

In the counselor's spirit of talking less than I listen, I will keep my own story short.

I was born in the Bronx and grew up as a fairly unenlightened, multicultural cis male. My father was Jewish and a "real gangster," a money man for the Mob. My Puerto Rican mother was a barmaid at a Times Square after-hours bar. My family was the first to be relocated in the federal witness protection program. I was in foster care between the ages of three and ten. Moving around throughout my teens, I soon dropped out of high school and ran away from home at age seventeen to work for the county fair and carnival as a photographer. I later survived heroin addiction and the trauma of a harsh confrontational treatment system. Driven by these experiences, I obtained a general equivalency diploma, attended a BA/MA program at The City College of New York, later earning a masters' degree in clinical psychology from Adelphi University's Derner Institute. During the last fifteen years, I've became a youth mentor, drug educator, and a drug policy and social justice reform activist—a troublemaker. All this unfolded in New York, California, and Puerto Rico.

My clinical career followed a similarly circuitous path through multiple service systems, in which I mostly played the role of a renegade, gaming the system for the public good. I worked in child welfare, homeless services, mental health, and drug treatment. At every turn, I saw the devastation the war on drugs has inflicted on communities of color, and I had become interested in working with people earlier in life. So, in 2006, I made the fateful decision to transition from my position as clinical co-director of a men's shelter on the pre-gentrified Bowery to managing a drug prevention and intervention program for the New York City Department of Education.

That is how I came to a failing public high school in Brooklyn. It was Day Three since I had hung a shingle outside of my tiny basement office. I had already developed that sinking feeling of waiting in vain for party guests to arrive. Suddenly, I was shaken out of my reverie by a sing-song voice at my door: "Yo! Can we hang out in here?"

"Sure!" I said.

The girl at the door yelled down the hall to her friends: "Toshanna! Tineal! Come here, bitches! This teacher says we can hang out in his office!" Then, turning to me, she asked, "Are you a teacher? What's your name? Can I charge my phone?" That was my introduction to Monique and her friends. They came to the door and peeped in, unsure whether to enter. They asked, "Can we really come in?"

"That's exactly why I'm here," I replied. "I've been waiting for you."

"You dead-ass?"

Without missing a colloquial beat, I replied. "Yes, I'm dead-ass."

I was delighted when they arrived and then quickly dismayed as they ignored me, talking among themselves for the next hour. Monique huffed at me once. Her telephone battery had died, but she had no charger with her to recharge it. She acted like she was going to die. The bell rang, they got up to leave, and out of the earshot of the others, she asks, "Yah gonna be here tomorrow?"

I could easily have entertained cynical notions about Monique's apparent lack of engagement with me, but she gave me just enough to respond to. I made a mental note to bring iPhone chargers with me the following day and felt gratified that she was curious enough about me to know what tomorrow might bring.

One often-dismissed but important perspective is Donald Winnicott's (1971) theory of the emotional development of children and their relationship to the challenges and resulting traumas of the holding environment. Harm reduction is all about relationship building (Shepard 2007). In Monique's case, I bent the environment around her, rather than the other way around. By bringing iPhone chargers for the girls to use or otherwise fulfilling some dependency need without fanfare or discussion, these seemingly small gestures serve to create a "holding environment" centered on and working in the service of the child that gives rise to feeling moments of "magical omnipotence." These powerful developmental experiences help build durable self-esteem and the strengths needed for good social, school, and other forms of functioning. Boom!

Within a few days, the girls brought other friends with them. The boys soon followed, impeccably dressed in their colorful "hipster-hop" style, with skinny jeans and flats, sneakers and hats. They sat three high on each other's laps. They chattered away; I could not shut them up. The stories abounded.

Over the next few years, Monique and her friends returned almost every day to "recharge their batteries." They had a vague sense that prohibition targets young people and that drug arrests disproportionately affect them, but they knew less about the history of this policy. So, their drug education started with my unpacking drug prohibition's backstory. I explained that this country was built on the backs of slaves to sell addiction for profit: tobacco, sugar, alcohol. I stressed that racism was not a natural phenomenon—it was invented—and it could be dismantled. They were curious. Engaged. Open. Their previously expressed lack of interest in society just vanished.

One of Monique's friends, Chris, who is twenty-five at the time of writing, joined Cre8tive YouTH*ink in high school. Describing the program to a newer younger member, he told her:

> I wasn't going to graduate on time. Nothing, especially my art, was going my way. I smoked a little weed and everyone was on my case as if that were the problem. One day, I pulled-up to Mista Oh's [Jerry Otero's] office. At first, I thought he was full of shit. But I fucked with him because he kept his word about little things and was curious about me and what I wanted do. I began to trust him. . . . I didn't even know he was a psychologist till a year after I met him. He never told me stop smoking, but instead helped me to weigh out my options. I learned that I had work to do—that championships were won in the off-season. To be true to myself. That I was needed. That I didn't even like weed that much. We made a plan with manageable goals that made sense to me, and I did graduate.

Chris's and my interactions were marked by acceptance, fun, and, most of all, safety. My attention to him—and my intention for us to work together on his plan—provided the basis for personalized attunement between us (Beebe and Lachmann 2014). Chris is now a parkour instructor and the lead singer in a death metal dubstep band. Looking up at "Sign Language," the mural he helped create, he said, "That's me. I've left my mark on a city that can seem so hard on me. I'll never forget that."

"Rigid" therapeutic techniques often fail because of their emphasis on verbal interpretation (Balint 1969). Rather than being directive, I focus on building relationships with a nonjudgmental stance and having faith in youth competence. When this competence emerges, nested within secure relationships, it gives young people a powerful sense of mastery. This fosters their abilities to calmly focus on goals and effectively deal with the multitude of daily microtraumatic reenactments they experience.

Rarely can you look ahead and see how the dots connect. Only now do I realize how, in that basement office twelve years ago, I began assembling the elements of Cre8tive YouTH*ink. One early clinical choice was to borrow a page from the Motivational Interviewing playbook. The simplest guideline for engagement is the 70 percent listening, 30 percent talking rule that I had learned as a drug treatment counselor. It was designed to open space for the client to reflect and emote, and I duly found that the more I listened, the more they spoke.

In my office with Monique and friends, I never lectured them about the dangers of drugs, yet they soon started to come to me when they had questions. They also came to tell me about feeling misunderstood, lost, and unappreciated. They described their cynicism and lack of faith in significant adults in their lives. They shared their feelings about immigration and diasporic dynamics, as well as their hope and determination to change the world. Despite this growing awareness, they were still children. They could be infuriating, acting out much of the time. They continued to frequently ignore me. But they were also comforted by knowing I was listening, and they let me know that. It was our secret language.

Since we first met, Monique has directed a professionally produced autobiographical film that premiered at the Brooklyn Museum of Art, earned a four-year degree, and interned at *ARTnews* magazine and the Studio Museum of Harlem. I have watched her grow into a competent, forward-thinking young woman. She has matured in a way that any parent should be proud of. I certainly am.

Recently, Monique told me of her disappointment in a job she had taken with high hopes: "I get so angry. I feel everyone looks down at me. I feel like I'm from another planet." She felt that her colleagues were condescending, yet she blamed herself. Each day at the office was becoming more and more of a drag. However, she was locked in place by her ambivalence, telling herself, "I know I could do better if I tried harder."

I reminded Monique that working hard has never been a problem for her. For example, as a young filmmaker, Monique started with neither a camera nor a computer, but she saved her earnings from working in retail for eighteen months to buy them. She then revealed that the real problem was that she always felt inadequate at work: "No one even helps me. I never got a job description!"

"Why is it so important for you to return to a place where you feel so terrible all the time?" I asked her. My intention was to neutralize the toxicity of her shame and increase the likelihood of self-reflection and accountability.

She thought deeply for a moment and responded, "I ain't got time for nobody's shit! I've worked too hard to let anyone treat me like that."

A few days later, she called to tell me that she had found her employee manual: "Now I really feel like an idiot. I don't remember receiving it."

"Are you kidding me? I don't think I've ever read one of those things."

"Mista Oh, I really appreciate that, but I should have been paying attention. A lot was at stake."

I relented. "Yes, you fucked up, but it seems they could have assigned you a point-person to onboard you."

Applying the 70/30 rule, I then kept my mouth shut and waited for Monique to respond.

"All the information was in my binder. And someone did check in with me, but I didn't believe that she really wanted to help and I never followed up. And I've been drinking too much."

Having smelled alcohol on her breath the last time we met, I simply responded, "I know. Do I need to be worried about you?"

She started crying. "I am always so afraid, feel like I'm in the wrong place, alone, angry." After a while, I said, "Me too, Monique. If I started telling you how many things I've screwed up, I'd be crying right there with you and we'd really be in trouble." We laughed together for a while, and that was that.

Two weeks later she gave notice at her job and was back to feeling herself. I no longer smelled alcohol on her breath: there was no need to remind her to behave or to teach her a lesson. Instead, supported with empathy and kindness, she had, through her own process, been reflective and accountable and had gained a valuable and enduring piece of self-awareness.

Few metrics exist to measure the degree to which Monique is now readier to face life. Having found a new job she likes, she is back to worrying about more appropriate things. Congratulations, Monique—job well done!

Similar relationships have played themselves out many times in my work. I do find much of what I hear about young people's day-to-day lives upsetting: the places they went to, the people they went with, and what happened there.

These relationships take time to build. Some years ago, I was walking home from an art opening with Eric, the young man who would later tell the Lippman Commission in 2017, which was tasked with recommending whether to close the prison at Rikers Island, that it was easier in his neighborhood to get a gun than a job. At that point we had known each other for three years. To my surprise, he confided that when he was a teen, he was going to join the gang that "repped" the public housing development where he grew up.

"Wow, Eric!" I said. Slowing the conversation down a beat, I asked, "How'd that work out?"

He replied, "A few days before my gang initiation, I tagged along on another initiation. I didn't like what I saw. I changed my mind. After that I enrolled in college. When I met you, I changed my major to Illustration."

"Have ever you ever told anyone about that?"

"Like who?"

"Parents? Another adult? Your friends?"

"They wouldn't understand. They'd probably be upset that I had considered it."

I waited another beat and then said, "Thank you for sharing that with me. That sounds like a serious life decision. I am proud of you."

We have never spoken about it again. Taking a deep breath, I remind myself that the model I use is a powerful tool in establishing the working alliances that can transform lives.

ADULT ALLIES SHARING A COMMON VISION OF SOCIAL JUSTICE AND PUBLIC ART

Harms are everywhere growing up. This is part of the appeal of the HR approach to engagement (Marlatt 1996; Shepard 2007). The term "harm reduction" covers a lot, but at its essence, it is about alleviating pain. It describes a core value and a widely applicable philosophy and a model of education. It designates a broad coalition movement of policy wonks, street activists, and clinicians. In addition to practical provisions for people who use drugs, it also describes a comprehensive, coordinated policy approach to drug use, one that attempts to balance public order and public health to create a safer, healthier, more equitable community. Sometimes known as the "four pillars" approach—harm reduction, prevention, treatment, and enforcement—it was first implemented in Europe in the 1990s (Pugh et al. 2013).

The case for programming focused on nurturing adult attachments with youth from historically oppressed communities could not be clearer. A hallmark of Cre8tive YouTH*ink's relational model is working alongside teens as adult allies. By sharing a common commitment to social justice and public art, Cre8tive YouTH*ink works with YOC to build a more equitable society through the engagement of a critically conscious youth constituency.

At a 2017 Lippman Commission town hall meeting, twenty-five-year-old Trevonne stood, stood mic in hand, addressing the panel. "What kind of policy can fix the city's 13-to-one spending ratio between incarceration and my brother's high school education?" (Lippman Commission 2017). Twenty-six-year-old Eric spoke next: "In my neighborhood, it's easier to get a gun than a job."

Both young men have recently earned bachelor's degrees in the arts. Both continue as peer mentors using art to engage youth in the community. Eric was recently overheard saying, "We worked together on a mural commissioned by The Bronx Museum of Art and I immediately joined the group and changed my major to illustration. But it was the #CLOSErikers campaign that really opened my eyes. I felt like I could actually make a difference."

WHAT DOES DRUG EDUCATION LOOK LIKE IN A PLACE LIKE THIS?

What we are doing is not working now and has not for decades (Rosenbaum 2014). There is no way to inoculate children against trying drugs. The large majority will do so without disaster—but they still deserve all the protection we can give them. To reach clients, harm reductionists connect, create trust, and build relationships with those in need. In this way, the work is very consistent with the relational school of psychoanalysis.

Steven A. Mitchell (1988) helped initiate this framework as a supervising and training analyst at the William A. White Institute in Manhattan. Founded by Clara Thompson and Eric Fromm with Harry Stack Sullivan, the White Institute emphasized the interplay between individuals and their social environment. It combined Fromm's view of psychoanalysis as a means to relieve basic human suffering and Sullivan's emphasis on active collaboration between therapist and patient. Mitchell's (1988) central thesis was that personal relationships and human interaction help determine the nature of human health and functioning. Much of the sidewalk psychotherapy of harm reduction grounds the practice in relationship building (Marlatt 1996; Shepard 2007).

Harm reduction is a pragmatic approach that has an emphasis on flexibility and acknowledges diverse approaches to practice. It is a lens through which to see, not a thing to do. The patient is considered an expert on his or her own story. Such a view involves an implicit rejection of paternalist motives in which practitioners all too often seek to alter the lives of the poor by improving their moral worth and behavior. The point of a dialogue is that it requires a breakdown in social hierarchies to enable both parties to actively work together.

In this way, power is shared in a collaborative dialogue. The utility of this approach is it brings honesty into the nexus of the clinical relationship, which allows for healing, personal development, and growth (Mitchell 1988). Rather than "the big lie" in which providers and clients each share half-truths about drug use and other less socially controversial yet common behaviors, harm reductionists emphasize the frank acknowledgment of desire, which helps move the relationship and the treatment forward. Such a model emphasizes client strengths, rather than viewing people as difficulties or the totalities of their problems (Saleeby 1996). The relationship is key (Shepard 2007). Given the social isolation, stigma, and shame experienced by individuals using drugs, it is essential that those engaging in harm reduction build trust with this community to support and promote use of the services offered at HR programs such as Cre8tive YouTH*ink.

CONCLUSION

Before our current lens and language enabled us to articulate simple truths, hidden by conventional thinking, about the sufferings of marginalized people—encompassing intersections of race, gender, sexuality, geography, and class—harm reduction gave us the frame to work on their behalf, within our most optimistic understanding of what it means to be human (figure 12.2).

In professional practice, harm reduction is not a practice, but rather a way to be that stresses the importance of the relational to human existence. Marlatt (1996) has laid out a pragmatic public health alternative to the conventional models of drug use, addiction, advocacy, and therapeutic work. Denning and Little (2017) and Tatarsky (2002) have proposed working clin-

FIGURE 12.2 Cre8tive YouTH*ink members ready to take on leadership roles in their communities. Photo by Mista Oh.

ical models of HR interventions that are gaining wider acceptance in clinical practice.

Amid the realities of a post-prohibitionist world, progressive approaches to drug education and prevention have emerged. Some are sensible, and their emphases range from cognitive training to social-influence models, environmental, youth-led, public health approaches, and more. Such approaches begin with reasonable assumptions about the roots of drug use and problematic behaviors and the best strategies to address them. But, in practice drug education is rarely based on what works, but instead on stakeholder agendas, which are determined by funders, staffers, or politicians—anyone, in fact, but the kids themselves ("Youth Illicit Drug Prevention" 2003; NREPP, Conflict of Interest; "This is Your Brain on Drugs" 2016). In this context, even well-meaning youth programs, like drug or violence "prevention" efforts, can be cynical, reductionist, or victim blaming—denying YOC agency and taking as real that their natural trajectory is toward trouble.

Harm reduction represents a continually evolving macro- and micro-level set of humane, pragmatic, idealistic, and health-improving ideas. The political implications of a HR mindset also lead to a post-prohibition world with a regulatory system for all currently illegal drugs. Ideally, such a system would empower responsible adults to protect young people from potential dangers.

"The biggest barrier to harm reduction approaches with teens and young people is fear," said Sheila Vakharia, who works at the Drug Policy Alliance. "Fear that if we give teens age-appropriate factual information, we couldn't trust them to make healthy choices for themselves. So instead we give them nothing—or worse, myths—and hope for the best" (Vakharia and Little 2016).

The following are some pragmatic HR tips for young people:

- Test before you ingest. (DanceSafe 2019)
- Know the dose.
- Start low. Go slow. Take half now, half later.
- One person should stay sober in case shit gets funky.
- Friends tell friends what they plan on taking. Take responsibility.
- Know what to do in an emergency.
- Know about Good Samaritan laws where you live.
- Drugs—any drug—can be dangerous.
- Just Say Know.

QUESTIONS FOR REFLECTION AND GROUP DISCUSSION

1. How could you apply the principles of harm reduction to your own work outside of the context of drug use?
2. How should your own background and identity affect your approach to working with your clients?
3. Why is harm reduction about relationship building?

REFERENCES

Alexander, Michelle. 2011. "The Failed Drug War Has Created a Human Rights Nightmare—How Can This Happen in Our Country and Go Virtually Undiscussed?" *Alternet*, April 28. http://www.alternet.org/story/150785/the_failed_drug _war_has_created_a_human_rights_nightmare_—_how_can_this_happen_in _our_country_and_go_virtually_undiscussed/.
Balint, Michael. 1969. *The Basic Fault: Therapeutic Aspects of Regression*. Evanston, IL: Northwestern University Press.

Beck, Jerome. 1998. "100 Years of 'Just Say No' Versus 'Just Say Know': Reevaluating Drug Education Goals for the Coming Century." *Evaluation Review* 22, no. 1: 15–45. https://doi.org/10.1177/0193841X9802200102

Beebe, Beatrice, and Frank M. Lachmann. 2014. *The Origins of Attachment: Infant Research and Adult Treatment.* Relational Perspectives Book Series. New York: Routledge.

Bottrell, Dorothy. 2007. "Resistance, Resilience and Social Identities: Reframing 'Problem Youth' and the Problem of Schooling." *Journal of Youth Studies,* 10, no. 5: 597–616.

Bottrell, Dorothy, and Derrick Armstrong. 2007. "Changes and Exchanges in Marginal Youth Transitions." *Journal of Youth Studies* 10, no. 3: 353–371.

Case, Stephen, and Kevin Haines. 2015. "Children First, Offenders Second Positive Promotion: Reframing the Prevention Debate." *Youth Justice* 15, no. 3: 226–39.

Cre8tive YouTH*ink. 2012. "About Us." https://cre8tiveyouthink.org/about-us/

——. 2013. Vol. 6. https://cre8tiveyouthink.org/art-school-without-walls/art-school-without-walls-volume-6/.

Cooper, Martha. 1980. "City Play: Martha Cooper's New York." Museum of the City of New York. https://www.mcny.org/st.ory/city-play-martha-coopers-new-york

Dancesafe. 2019. Standard Set Of 4 Testing Kits https://dancesafe.org/product/complete-adulterant-screening-kit/

Denning, Patt, and Jeannie Little. 2017. *Over the Influence: The Harm Reduction Guide to Controlling Your Drug and Alcohol Use.* New York: Guilford Press.

Federal Bureau of Investigation. 2015. "Crime in the US, 2015." https://ucr.fbi.gov/crime-in-the-u.s/2015/crime-in-the-u.s.-2015. Ginwright, Shawn, and Julio Cammarota. 2002. "New Terrain in Youth Development: The Promise of a Social Justice Approach." *Social Justice* 29, no. 4: 82–95.

Godfrey, Will. 2016. "Nancy Reagan's 'Just Say No' Campaign Was a Disaster: How to End It for Good?" *The Influence.* https://www.rawstory.com/2016/03/nancy-reagans-just-say-no-campaign-was-an-absolute-disaster-how-to-end-it-for-good/.

Hawkins, J. David, Richard F. Catalano, and Janet Y. Miller. 1992. "Risk and Protective Factors for Alcohol and Other Drug Problems in Adolescence and Early Adulthood: Implications for Substance Abuse Prevention." *Psychological Bulletin* 112, no. 1: 64–105.

Jessor, Richard. 1993. "Successful Adolescent Development among Youth in High-Risk Settings." *American Psychologist* 48, no. 2: 117–126.

Lerner, Richard M., Jacqueline V. Lerner, Jennifer Brown Urban, and Jon Zaff. 2015. "Evaluating Programs Aimed at Promoting Positive Youth Development: A Relational Development Systems-based View." *Applied Developmental Science* 20, no. 3: 175–187.

Lippman Commission. 2017. *A More Just New York City.* New York: Independent Commission on New York City Criminal Justice and Incarceration Reform.

Marlatt, G. Alan. 1996. "Harm Reduction: Come as You Are." *Addictive Behaviors* 21, no. 6: 779–788.

"Million Dollar Blocks." 2016. Million Dollar Blocks | Spatial Information Design Lab. http://spatialinformationdesignlab.org/projects.php%3Fid%3D16.

Mitchell, Stephen A.. 1988. *Relational Concepts in Psychoanalysis: An Integration.* Cambridge, MA: Harvard University Press.

Pugh, Tracy, Julie Netherland, Ruth Finkelstein, Kassandra Frederique, Simone-Marie Meeks, and Gabriel Sayegh. 2013. *Blueprint for a Public Health and Safety Approach to Drug Policy. Report*. New York: New York Academy of Medicine. 2013. "Race and Criminal Justice." 2017. American Civil Liberties Union., 2017. https://www.aclu.org /issues/racial-justice/race-and-criminal-justice.

Robinson, Anne. 2016. "The Resilience Motif: Implications for Youth Justice." *Youth Justice*, 16, no. 1: 18–33.

Saleeby, D., ed. 1996. *The Strengths Perspective in Social Work Practice*. New York: Longman.

Rosenbaum, Marsha. 2014. "Safety First: A Reality-Based Approach to Teens and Drugs." Drug Policy Alliance. http://www.drugpolicy.org/resource/safety-first -reality-based-approach-teens-and-drugs

Shepard, Benjamin. 2007. "Harm Reduction Outreach Services and Engagement of Chemically Dependent Homeless People Living with HIV/AIDS: An Analysis of Service Utilization Data to Evaluate Program Theory." *Albert Einstein Journal of Biology and Medicine* 23, no. 1.

"Sign Language.' 2012. The Art School Without Walls, vol. six. https://cre8tiveyouthink .org/portfolio/vol-6-sign-language-w-chris-stain-and-billy-mode/.

Tatarsky, Andrew, ed. 2002. *Harm Reduction Psychotherapy: A New Treatment for Drug and Alcohol Problems*. Lanham, MD: Jason Aronson.

"This Is Your Brain on Drugs." 2016. *The Influence*. http://theinfluence.org/this-is-your -brain-on-drugs-2016-new-ad-campaign-resurrects-silly-propaganda/.

Vakharia, Sheila P., and Jeannie Little. "Starting Where the Client Is: Harm Reduction Guidelines for Clinical Social Work Practice." *Clinical Social Work Journal* 45, no. 1: 65–76.

Winnicott, Donald. 1971. *Playing and Reality*. New York: Routledge.

"Youth Illicit Drug Use Prevention: DARE Long-Term Evaluations and Federal Efforts to Identify Effective Programs." 2003. Memo from Marjorie E. Kanof to Richard J. Durbin, January 15.

Chapter Thirteen

POOR MOTHERS, POOR CHILDREN

The Feminization of Poverty in Rural India

GRETTA M. FERNANDES

I was a community organizer for nearly five years during the early years of the twenty-first century in the rural villages in Pune in western India. After completing a master's degree in social work, my first job in the field was with a nonprofit organization based in Pune, Maharashtra. I worked with other social workers to develop women's empowerment programs with the aim of improving economic conditions for both women and their children: these women and children were poor, and most belonged to the lower castes. The work initially involved the creation of self-help financial groups (SHGs). SHGs have been instrumental in changing women's socioeconomic circumstances and choices (Sen, 1999, 2000). At a later stage in our work we also developed youth leadership groups. It was through this work that I observed the connections between maternal and child poverty.

In this chapter, I share accounts from my five years in the field. I explore how the experiences of poor children are inextricably tied to the feminization of poverty and the construction of caste in rural India, factors that can ultimately serve to diminish their health, education, socioemotional outcomes, and safety. Alternatively, it is through economic independence that women are empowered to make decisions about their children's well-being. The development of youth leadership offers a younger generation opportunities for change both in the here and now and in the future.

STORIES FROM THE FIELD

Churchill and Churchill (1982) argue that storytelling is a compelling method for illustrating a narrator's interpretation of events by connecting the past, the present, and a future. Bruner (1984) deconstructs the development of stories (narratives) and identifies four parts: *life as lived*, what really happened; *life as experienced*, what we believe and feel happened; *life as told*. the story as it is comes out and as it is heard, all determined by context; and finally, *life as retold*, the knowledge and meaning that is drawn from the story. I use storytelling as a narrative tool, in particular autoethnography, to re-create instances from my work in Pune. These moments would otherwise be lost with the passage of time.

Autoethnography requires me to conjure memories of critical moments and to craft these memories into a cohesive narrative that is contextualized through historical elements, policy and theoretical discourse, and data on poverty (Witkin, 2014). In this chapter I share reflections from the field that illustrate the complexities of childhood poverty in rural India. Because very young children depend so extensively on adults, their experiences must be viewed not only discretely, but also as intertwined with those who are charged with their care, be it the family or state. Traditionally and historically, mothers have taken on the role of caretakers for children, especially during the early years. As caretakers, they provide access to the lives of children, and it is through the mother–child relationship that I primarily witnessed the context of their lives in rural poverty, as shaped by gender and caste through the generations.

CHILDREN'S LIVES IN POVERTY

Childhood poverty is a globally endemic phenomenon. While not specific to the developing world it can look entirely different in rural parts of the Global South than in other parts of the world. The World Bank Report (2016) indicates that the global poor are predominantly rural, young, poorly educated, and working in the agricultural sector. The situation in India mirrors that in the Global South. Eighty percent of India's poor live in rural areas. Moreover, rural poverty can take on even more distinctive qualities, which vary from community to community, by region, and by social strata. Children living in poverty experience a range of stressors that have a long-lasting impact on their well-being, academic achievement, and psychosocial and physical health. Poverty is highly correlated with negative outcomes in each of these domains. Childhood poverty is increasing, and the impact accumulates the longer the child continues to live in poverty (Downs et al., 2000). A significant amount of quantitative research on child poverty exists, but by comparison, much less qualitative inquiry is available. However, more and more qualitative research exploring how children interpret and subsequently negotiate their lives in poverty is emerging.

Yet, quantitative and qualitative research in this area can often appear at odds (Corsaro. 2015; Wells, 2015). On one side of the field, sociological studies of children position children within the structure of their families. On the other side, there is a justified focus on centering children as actors and agents in their own right. And yet still another position considers that children's experiences are inherently relational to adults, whom they are dependent on and who make decisions on their behalf. It is in the spirit of this relational framework that I share stories from my work with mothers, through whom I met their children and witnessed the circumstances of their lives in poverty. And it is through stories about this work that I consider the role of historical, political, economic, cultural, and sociostructural elements in childhood poverty.

UNTOUCHABLE LIVES

During the early stages of my work in Pune, I did extensive outreach. I visited the villages day after day and many times stayed overnight with families because our late evening meetings often went past midnight. I learned to speak Marathi so that I could better communicate with locals, some of whom also spoke some Hindi. Although our primary work was self-help group development, we also offered leadership training for women and youth, helped them attain income-generating skills, and facilitated discussions on gender equality and women's empowerment at the individual, community, and local government level. This work primarily focused on those living below the poverty line, most of whom also belonged to a lower caste according to Hinduism.

The caste system has a long, complicated, and ever-changing history in India. It is both a structural and cultural phenomenon that takes on different qualities in rural areas. At one point, the caste system was based on occupation and a division of labor, but it has become increasingly more complex over time (Ghuman, 2015). The caste system divides society into four Varnas (classes): Brahmins, who perform priestly rituals; Kshatriyas, rulers of the kingdom; Vaishyas, businesspeople; and Shudras, the serving class. The communities who are outside of these four Varnas are considered untouchables; they are the ones who do menial physical labor. Despite claims of eradication, the caste system persists, and the so-called untouchables are still at the bottom of the hierarchy of Indian society (Singh, 2005). The stratification that results from caste is embedded in the division of labor, gender scripts, marriage, property ownership, the economy of a village, education, and other social structures.

As someone outside of the Hindu caste system, I was mainly an observer of the interactions among those living in the village. These interactions or lack of them were quite apparent during meetings we held in the community center or near the temple area. Women from different castes did not interact with one another. Initially, untouchables sat separately or outside of the meeting walls. Over the five-year period of our work in the village, however, this arrangement changed. Women and children from different castes began to sit together and eat meals together. Eventually, they also traveled together to meetings in solidarity with the common aim of improving their life circumstances.

CHILDHOOD IN MANJARI

According to the 2011 Indian census, the Manjari Block (a cluster of villages) in Puna has a population of 36,816 people, of whom 19, 244 are male and 17,572 are females. A block is a group of villages in the district. I remember the area well from my time working there. In each village, a cluster of houses was separated from the vast expanses of farming land. To approach each village, we had to travel through mud and dirt roads. There was little public transportation in the area, which meant that the villagers, especially women and children, had little to no access to the city. This, in turn, meant the absence of opportunities. Children had little to no chance of obtaining a higher education or a job with a livable wage and economic benefits.

The rich or well-to-do, those belonging to a higher caste, lived on the other side of the village and in concrete houses. The homes of poor people were smaller—many were just one small room—and built of lightweight and inadequate materials, with tiled or thatched roofs. Everyday life in the village was structured around divisions of labor. During the day, only older people remained in the village, as most adults went to work in nearby farms, fields, and factories. Some had small businesses, like grocery stores, tea shops, and laundry services.

Some children were able to attend a primary school in the village. Children who wanted to attend middle school or high school had to walk on foot to the closest town that was five miles away. It was not the distance alone that was problematic, but for girls there was an added concern about their safety: young women risked abuse or assault when traveling by foot. Boys, in contrast, did not have the same concerns and were encouraged to have bicycles to use for commuting to another town. A consequence of this real and perceived danger for girls is that they are less likely to complete high school than their male peers of the same age. The lack of educational attainment further entrenches poverty among girls and women and is likely to continue into the next generation. In response, we helped set up a local government program that provided bicycles for girls, and we encouraged families to allow them to use the bikes. Soon after, girls also began to ride bicycles to school.

By the time they reach secondary school age, children from lower-income families tend to work both at home and on farms (Galab et al., 2011). In the village, children as young as six years old help their mothers with household chores or care for younger siblings. It is girls who primarily helped their mothers fetch water, clean the house or the yard, and assisted in the kitchen. In essence, girls are trained in housework from a young age. Nieuwenhuys' (1994) ethnographic work in Kerala points to this experience as being specific for girls. The girls, however, do not describe the work as such, but rather as helping out. By comparison, boys begin work at a later age, sometimes because their tasks require more physical strength and stamina. However, when they engage in the same work as girls, they expect and receive compensation. Overall, for both boys and girls, house labor takes priority over other areas in the life of children in the villages, such as play time or education.

I remember a young girl named Ratna who was then about eight years old; she was responsible for fetching water, cooking rice, and cutting the vegetables for her family. School work came secondary, and she was able to do homework only after her responsibilities were completed. This meant completing assignments at night by the light of a kerosene lamp, because most poor households did not have electricity.

Rural poverty poses multiple barriers for children, and these barriers are often felt more strongly by girls. Their lives are prescribed by gender scripts from a very early age. Even as some girls might want other options or see an educational future for themselves, economic constraints, geographic limitations, and threats to their safety quickly dash their hopes.

HELPING MOTHERS, HELPING CHILDREN

Similar to as children are, rural women in India are forced to conform to gender roles and scripts (Desai & Andrist, 2010). They are often socially and economically marginalized, and their role is considered subordinate to men (Kandiyoti, 1988). They are segregated from men in the workplace and other societal functions, and they are likely to marry at a young age and have lower educational attainment (Maertens, 2013). Their overall autonomy is limited, because they cannot make decisions on finances, the household, when and how many children to have, and how to care for them. These gender structures are repeated generation after generation.

For this reason, the initial part of our work in the villages involved building trust and rapport with the women and introducing the concept of self-help groups. This process took at least six months. SHGs first developed in Bangladesh as microfinancial services or village banking. The SHGs are mostly formed by nongovernmental organizations (NGOs), with each consisting of up to twenty members. The SHG members meet regularly and make regular savings contributions to a group savings account in a local bank. By opening and maintaining a group savings account, individuals are able to borrow loans to develop mainly income-generation activities; each group has an internal borrowing system, with the interest rate it fixes. Davidson and Sanyal (2017) point out that SHGs can provide numerous benefits for women, such as developing social capital, enhancing socioeconomic mobility, and, above all, improving their quality of their life. Most of the women had been earning less than a dollar a day, and many times their daily wages were forcefully taken from them by their husbands for gambling or alcohol. They and their children often went to bed hungry.

Patel and colleagues (2006) highlight the multiple health and social risks that poor rural women face. Lack of access to a toilet and limited power in negotiating sexual relationships are significant risk factors for infection. We found that most poor families did not have a toilet and that there were no public toilets in the village. Open areas such as fields and grazing grounds were used for defecating. Women and girls, who would go out into these open spaces only in the dark, were especially burdened during menstruation. We worked to increase awareness about the benefits of private toilets and to secure subsidies from the local government for those families who came forward to build their toilets.

The physical safety of women and girls in the village was also precarious. Our organization would receive frequent phone calls about acts of violence against women, both in and outside the home. On one occasion, a woman was hit by a motor vehicle while returning from her farm work. On another, a woman was physically attacked by a man from another caste. There were no hospitals or doctors in the villages, and transporting someone to the hospital outside the area, often late in the evening, was only possible through the mercy of a rich person who owned a motor vehicle in the village. So many times, the injured person would spend the night at home and go to a public health care facility the next morning.

There was a prevalent culture of violence against women who belonged to the lower caste; it took many forms. Moreover, their children often witnessed the violent crimes against their mothers, many times perpetrated by upper-caste men who saw no value among women from the lower caste. The authorities were often reluctant to register the First Information Report (FIR) when women reported these attacks, especially if they involved men of a higher caste. The police also discouraged social workers from taking up the cases of domestic violence against women, suggesting that they were family matters into which outsiders should not interfere.

Yet, when a thirteen-year-old girl from a poor family was found to be three months pregnant, the villagers were very concerned. The girl was raped, but no one knew who had committed the crime and where, and she did not tell anyone about it. I was called by the women members of the SHGs, who informed me of the incident and asked me to come immediately to the village. Along with one of my colleagues, I reached the village to find that most of the village elders had gathered in different pockets of the village to discuss this issue. After meeting with the girl and her family, I was in tears for their pain. Their helplessness was unbearable. The little girl was afraid. Rape and unwed pregnancy carried deep stigmas for the victim and family.

A group of nearly twelve women from SHGs was ready to help the family. Together we went to the local police station, where we waited for hours before we were told to go to the neighboring police station to register the FIR. When we arrived at the neighboring police station, police were already aware of the incident and made us wait for another hour before we could register the report. The women felt the discrimination and poor treatment they received was because they belonged to lower castes. They banded together and supported the family throughout the entire process, accompanying them to the hospital to meet with the doctors and ensuring that the girl received the necessary health services.

The Breakthrough

It took us a long time to develop a trusting working relationship with the women and families in the village. We would attempt to engage the older folks sitting around the temple or in the plaza area. We would go into farms/fields to find the villagers, especially the women, who were working as day laborers; however, we could only talk with them during their lunch hour. The village women responded in a lukewarm way to our initial attempts. When we would greet them, they would not respond to us, or when they did greet us back, they would quickly turn around and continue their work. Most villagers avoided interacting with us or doubted our intentions. At the time there were substantial rumors of body organ trafficking occurring in many rural parts of India.

We had to be patient as we talked to the women about the issues affecting their daily life. We continued our visits to different parts of the villages, especially during noontime when most farm workers had their lunch breaks. It took three to four months before we saw an openness and willingness to meet with us and to discuss what mattered most in their lives.

Moneylenders, landlords, upper-caste people, local government members, and men in general were particularly suspicious of us. They would speculate about our motives for visiting the villagers, especially the women. Moneylenders were especially threatened by the formation of self-help groups. They charged interest rates that were two or three times the amount that local banks levied. Since self-help groups were already functioning in the neighboring districts, moneylenders were aware of the threat they posed. The SHGs were also known to encourage women to aspire to local community and government leadership. When some of the women came to learn that, in the neighboring villages, the SHGs were successful and women were benefiting through economic rewards, personal bank accounts, income-generation activities, and literacy classes, they too came forward and asked us to assist them in the formation of self-help groups in their village.

The breakthrough came when the village women asked us to come and meet with all the villagers about our plans. Our first community meeting took place in the evening, and everyone was invited to attend. It was mostly men and village elders who attended, and we started a dialogue. They were aware of the self-help groups in the neighboring district, and when they heard from us that we could work with them to form similar groups in their village, they seemed to like the idea and were happy that we could assist their women as well. From then on, the meetings took place late in the evenings: most women did not leave the farms/fields until 6:00 to 7:00 p.m. and then had to go home to prepare food for their families and put their children to bed. Only after that were they free and relaxed and able to sit around in groups and share their stories.

Once the women accepted us social workers as genuine and wanting to work with them, there was a willingness to have the meetings late in the evening. Some of the women also brought along their small babies. At times children came with their mothers as well. Children listened as their mothers narrated stories of their struggles at home or work; sometimes, they would fall asleep, and moms would carry them home after the meetings. Most children were aware of caste discrimination and violence against women.

Most women signed their name by using a thumbprint because they did not know how to write their names. Six months into the rapport-building process, we offered literacy classes. Initially, they were apprehensive about taking them and kept saying that it would be hard for them to learn to read and write. They laughed often during the first couple of sessions.

The only time they were free to learn was after 8:00 p.m. But soon they were proud of being able to sign their names. Once the SHGs began, they each had a bank account and a passbook with their photo. They also began taking a day off from their weekly farm work, as a day of rest, though they would use it to do their weekly shopping, visiting, or doing the laundry. It is very typical of rural women to never get to rest: because of their culturally defined roles, rural women always have work to do.

Women mostly shared common concerns affecting poor women and not so much about their personal needs or those of their family. Eventually, the attitudes of women toward their daughters and other women began to change. They encouraged their daughters to go further in their studies and prompted and supported women to run for local government positions. Women began to take an active part in civic engagement and cleanliness efforts in the local village.

Soon after we began to form a youth group. We expected that it would attract few participants, but the women encouraged their teenage children to become involved. One of the social workers led monthly youth meetings that were focused on building self-awareness, self-esteem, and leadership through experiential activities. Local community case managers/animators also animated the meetings. The animators were primarily from the villages and visited the SHG members on a weekly basis and guided or counseled the women if needed. When they were not able to assist the women, animators would contact the social workers for further assistance. The youth participated in role plays, developed skits, engaged in group discussions, and formulated games to communicate and encourage youth participation in the local community.

The goal in forming SHGs was to empower women not just financially but also socially. This process of empowerment was slow, but the positive changes in women and children were immense. Women gained self-confidence, self-esteem, and self-respect. They changed their attitudes toward their children, and their children's ideas about women and possibilities changed too. They each began to see a place for themselves, a space for participation in local government that helped improve not only the lives of individual women but also the overall quality of life for the entire village.

THE FEMINIZATION OF CHILD POVERTY

Various factors contribute to the problem of poverty among women, mothers, families, and children in rural India. Gender- and caste-based discrimination contribute to the realities of entrenched poverty for many women and children. The Department for International Development (2005) defines caste discrimination as a social exclusion process whereby specific categories of people are systematically discriminated against due to race, age, gender, religion, or where someone might live. Specific people and groups are excluded from resources and participation, and there are adverse effects on quality of life based on these constructs (Levitas et al., 2007). The consequences of these exclusions can be seen in the high rates of illiteracy, low wages, violence against women, and the little to no access to opportunities for higher education and jobs for women and their children.

The term "feminization of poverty" was first developed in the 1970s by the United Nations Development Fund to indicate that maternal poverty affects children because poverty disproportionately affects women and mothers. Downs and colleagues (2000) point out that poverty has negative effects on children that can range from obvious to the subtle. Children in poverty lack opportunities in school, experience hunger, and live in over-crowded homes (Oswald et al., 1999). Their families themselves may not be in a position to help their children.

The Indian Planning Commission in its 2014 report estimated that up to 29.5 percent (363 million) of the total population was living below the poverty line in 2011–2012. One of the initiatives of the Indian government's to reduce poverty and bring Below Poverty Line families out of poverty is Swarnjayanthi Gram Swarozgar Yojana (SGSY). This rural development program is based on the tenets of social capital theory, using bonds, bridges, and linkages to link people to resources so that they can move up the social ladder; Hanifan (1916) coined the term "social capital" to indicate that social relationships and membership in various groups or communities can provide individuals with resources.

Operating from a strengths perspective, we looked to empower women and their families through the development of self-help groups. These groups offer valuable opportunities for women to develop social capital through social contacts and networking (Davidson & Sanyal, 2017). Women participating in SHGs create a new type of social solidarity and connections. They are encouraged to take advantage of government credit/subsidies and bank loans to start income-generating programs, ranging from goat rearing to dairy farming. For most SHG women it would be the first time they held a bank checkbook in their hands. Once women started to earn more money through income-generating activities, they no longer needed to borrow money from moneylenders. Women gained respect in their families from their husbands and in-laws and were able to take part in decision making concerning household purchases and their children's education. Children and teenagers who attended SHG meetings became familiar with finances of the group and knew the benefits their mothers were receiving as members. These young people witnessed their mothers move from subservient lives to becoming independent thinkers and contributing members of their local community. They also learned about local politics as they saw their mothers becoming actively involved in the local government.

The most significant benefit women gained was economic independence, which has also affected how children, especially girls, were viewed in the poor families. SHG women critically analyzed the socialization of gender and began to question the preference for boys over girls. They began to actively advocate for their daughters to obtain equal opportunities in society. Women created income-generating programs/projects, such as goat rearing, dairy farming, doing laundry, preparing lunch boxes, running food carts, and selling and making jewelry. This earned them respect, and their husbands and in-laws came to consider them as essential stakeholders in the family and business decision-making process. Youth groups undertook various initiatives in the village to promote cleanliness village, celebrate International Women's Day, and participate in other community events.

CONCLUSION

In this chapter, I use storytelling to explore the ways maternal poverty and caste discrimination can affect children in rural India. When mothers live in poverty, their children experience limited educational opportunities and face safety and physical health concerns. Despite the ongoing challenges the women and their children faced as a result of living in poverty, their resilience and strength were remarkable. Policy and collective action provided an avenue for overcoming structural barriers. Through my experiences working in Puna, I learned invaluable life lessons: how to remain strong in the face of hardships and how solidarity helps people overcome adversity and break down barriers. I continually felt proud and in awe of the women and children I worked with. There is a famous African saying that goes, "When you educate a woman, you educate an entire village or a nation or a race." I dream that we will live in a world where all women, regardless of caste or race, receive equal access to education and the support necessary to escape the chains of poverty. Then they will be able to provide the life they want for their children and improve their children's outcomes in all areas of life.

QUESTIONS FOR REFLECTION AND GROUP DISCUSSION

1. How does the concept "feminization of poverty" help us understand the reality of child poverty?
2. How are the experiences of children living in poverty in rural India similar to poor children living in the United States?
3. What elements in the self-help groups empowered women and children?

REFERENCES

Bruner, E. M. (1984). Introduction: The opening up of anthropology, In S. Plattner & E. M. Bruner (Eds.), *Text, play and story: The construction and reconstruction of self and society* (pp. 1–16). Washington, DC: American Ethnological Society.

Churchill, L. R., & Churchill, S. W. (1982). Storytelling in medical arenas: The art of self-determination. *Literature and Medicine, 1,* 73–79.

Corsaro, W. A. (2015). *The sociology of childhood* (4th ed.). Thousand Oaks, CA: Pine Forge Press.

Davidson, T., & Sanyal, P. (2017). Association participation and network expansion: Microcredit self-help groups and poor women's social ties in rural India. *Social Forces, 95,* 1695–1724.

Desai, S., & Andrist, L. (2010). Gender scripts and age at marriage in India. *Demography, 47*(3), 667–687.

Department for International Development. (2005). *Reducing poverty by tackling social exclusion: A DFID policy paper.* London: DFID.

Downs, S. W., Moore, E., McFadden, E. J., & Costin, L. B. (2000). *Child welfare and family services: Policies and practices* (6th ed.). Boston: Allyn & Bacon.

Galab, S., Vijay, K. S., Prudvikar, R. P., Singh, R., & Vennam, U. (2011). *The impact of growth on childhood poverty in Andhra Pradesh.* Oxford: Young Lives.

Hanifan, L. J. (1916). The rural school community centre. *Annals of the American Academy of Political and Social Sciences, 67,* 130–138.

Kandiyoti, D. (1988). Bargaining with patriarchy. *Gender and Society, 2*(3), 274–290.

Levitas, R., Pantazis, C., Fahmy, E., Gordon, D., Lloyd, E., & Patsios, D. (2007). *The multi-dimensional analysis of social exclusion.* London: Department for Communities and Local Government.

Maertens, A. (2013). Social norms and aspirations: Age of marriage and education in rural India. *World Development, 47,* 1–15.

Nieuwenhuys, O. 1994. *Children's lifeworlds: Gender, welfare, and labor in the developing world*. London: Routledge.

Oswald, D. P., Coutinho, M. J., Best, A. N., & Singh, N. N. (1999). Ethnic representation in special education: The influence of school-related economic and demographic variables." *Journal of Special Education, 32*, 194–206.

Patel, V., Flisher, A., Cohen, A. (2006). Social and cultural determinants of mental health. In R. Murray et al. (Eds.), *Essentials of psychiatry* (2nd ed.) Cambridge: Cambridge University Press.

Sen, A. (1999). *Development as freedom*. Oxford: Oxford University Press.

——. (2000). *Social exclusion: Concept, application, and scrutiny*. Mandaluyong, the Philippines: Asian Development Bank.

Singh, J. P. (2005). Caste system. In H.S. Verma (Ed.), *The OBC and the ruling classes in India*. New Delhi: Penguin.

World Bank Report (2016). Retrieved from http://documents.worldbank.org/curated/en/187011475416542282/pdf/WPS7844.pdf.

Wells, K. (2015). *Childhood in global perspective* (2nd ed.). London: Wiley.

Witkin, S. L. (2014). *Narrating social work through autoethnography*. New York: Columbia University Press.

PART III

Practice Reflections and Case Narratives

Chapter Fourteen

UNDERSTAND THE BRAIN, UNDERSTAND OUR CHILDREN

DEBORAH COURTNEY

PHOTOS THAT CRY

I look into your eyes,
And I see innocence.
I look at your smile,
And I see happiness.
Then I just look at you,
And I see defenseless.
I cry just thinking,
How you were let down,
So many times,
From your loved ones.
I wish I would've been there for you.
To wipe your tears,
And fight your fears.
Your pure kind heart
Was stomped on
Spit on
So many times.
But that never changed you.
Never did it make you bitter

Nor hate the world,
Just stronger and wiser.
I don't know when I'll start feeling,
More proud than sorry for you,
Knowing that you are me.
(WRITTEN BY KIM IN 2016)

A brave and wise young woman wrote this poem after looking back at her childhood photo album and simultaneously feeling nostalgic and deeply sad. It was the fall of 2009 when I met her for the first time at the ever-so-confusing age of fourteen. Her name is Kim, and her black nail polish and funky outfits completed with either Converse sneakers or Doc Martins had a way of completely brightening up my small, windowless office in the mental health clinic where I was working at the time. She was new to psychotherapy, and I was two years postgraduate school. Kim and I have worked together weekly and intermittently for almost ten years since then. Our work together is the focus of this chapter.

LEARNING FROM STORIES

How does understanding the impact of trauma on children's brains help us better understand their mental and emotional well-being and, ultimately, more effectively serve them as human service professionals? To answer this question, I alternate between two stories, Kim's and my own, dancing between an autoethnographic exploration of my practice with her and developing a narrative case study of her experiences. The case study explores Kim's story and healing process, while grappling with my role in Kim's healing and deciding which appropriate therapeutic theory to use are the focus of the autoethnographic piece.

I use this approach to answer the question I posed earlier for several reasons. First, trauma and the brain have been studied and expressed quantitatively at length. This chapter complements quantitative understandings by offering new insights through real-life, relatable experience (Reiss, 2009). Narrating stories can make the complexity of treating trauma in children more accessible by adding meaning to their experiences and enabling a more holistic view of how children and youth interact with their world. Narratives also align with an ecological perspective for understanding these interactions, a framework critical to social work practice (Annan, Priestley, & Phillipson, 2006). While the generalizability of narratives is limited, it can be argued that the general stems from the particular and that knowledge derived from these explorations can help improve practice and program development (Reis, 2009). Readers can vicariously learn from the image of Kim's story as I develop her case. They can then determine what applies to their work and reconstruct it to improve their practice (Erickson, 1986; Stake, 2005). Kim's narrative and our extensive work together can facilitate the readers' exploration of the impact of trauma on the brain through the shared experiences, reactions, and emotions in our therapeutic relationship. Kim's story also highlights how this knowledge changes the course of case formulation and treatment. Similarly, the autoethnographic approach is vital because it allows me to intimately connect with readers by drawing on my private experiences as a human service practitioner (Méndez, 2013). This personal expression helped me reflect on my role with clients and emphasized the need for continued self-discovery and practice wisdom in my practice. Overall, this chapter weaves my account of learning about trauma's impact on children's brains with Kim's courageous story to help paint a comprehensive and hopeful picture of trauma-informed treatment for both young survivors of trauma and the workers who walk beside them.

BEGINNINGS

In our first meeting, Kim made it clear that she was not there by choice and was not excited about "talking about feelings." She was a spunky, twelve-year-old Latina girl who had recently disclosed to her pediatrician that her brother, who was five years her senior, had been sexually abusing her for years. In return for this disclosure, she received a mandate to attend therapy. It was a confusing time for her, because she had wanted to tell someone what had been happening for a long time, yet immediately after doing so was questioning if she had made the right choice. Her disclosure had serious repercussions. Her brother moved out, and as much as she hated him for what he had done to her, she equally loved him. She was under pressure to continually retell the story to the prosecutor, an experience that she described as "torture." Her once joyful mother was devastated by this news and stressed by the new involvement with both Child Protection Services and the legal system. In the midst of this emotional confusion, Kim landed reluctantly in my office.

After our first couple of meetings, I recall feeling a myriad of emotions as well. That nagging, new clinician anxiety of "I need to fix it!" and "How can I help her?" regularly made itself known in a helpless sensation in my stomach. My patient, wise supervisor had to continually remind me that it was not my job to take Kim's pain away or fix the family's struggle. Instead, the goal was to create a safe space for her to heal, in which she could feel seen and heard with compassion and empathy. As I reflect on those lessons from my supervisor and write about them here, I chuckle to myself because I now share similar wisdom with my students.

WHY SAFETY FIRST?

Kim's fidgeting and nail-biting were hard to miss during the first few sessions. These anxious behaviors reminded me of the importance of creating a safe space for our work. Developing a sense of safety with a client is essential to a successful therapeutic relationship and outcome (Herman, 1992; SAMSHA, 2014). I used play techniques during the first few sessions since Kim was new to therapy and not yet on board with the process. I wanted to take some of the pressure off of her being new to therapy and to meet at her developmental level. I pulled out the deck of playing cards, drawing paper, or the Jenga game and we played. And as we played, we got to know each other. I learned about her passions for music, art, and poetry writing, which in turn enabled me to highlight her strengths, such as her artistic ability, independence, and wisdom. I also was mindful of my own body language and facial expressions, careful to make sure that I demonstrated openness, caring, and nonjudgmental qualities to exhibit empathy. I asked Kim for permission to share some information about trauma with her, while also emphasizing that she was the expert on her life experience (Casement, 2013). The research I shared found that one in four children are sexually abused as children, most commonly by someone they know, and later, survivors often experience anxiety or depression as a result (Gagnon and Hersen, 2000). Kim listened quietly with her eyes fixated on me and expressed powerful, short responses such as "So, it's not just me?!" and "I'm not crazy then." The psychoeducation strategy helped her feel less isolated and to realize that her responses and behaviors were "normal."

Developments in brain and trauma research are useful in understanding Kim's experiences. As a result of the many years of sexual trauma, Kim's sympathetic nervous system—the division of the autonomic nervous system responsible for the fight, flight, or freeze (FFF) response—had been turned on high alert, causing a perpetual protective response. "Flight" was apparent as Kim anxiously fidgeted in her seat during our initial sessions; "fight" presented itself in the stories she shared of telling friends often to "fuck off" when they frustrate her or get too close; and "freeze" made itself known by the stunned gaze that turned on when the session material got too intense and we talked about her brother. FFF is the typical reaction of the mind and body to protect the self from the threat of abuse (Cannon, 1932). It includes hormone surges of norepinephrine, epinephrine, estrogen, testosterone, cortisol, dopamine, and serotonin (Jansen et al. 1995) and bodily changes: increased heart rate and respiration and shaking. Typically, when a threatening event is over, the parasympathetic nervous system, which allows the body to "rest and digest," takes over and returns the body to a state of homeostasis (Padgett & Glasser, 2003). Since the threat of abuse continued throughout Kim's childhood, the "rest and digest" mode did not have an opportunity to operate regularly.

For Kim, the perpetual FFF response manifested as panic attacks, difficulty regulating emotions, and angry outbursts, followed by depressive exhaustion. These neurobiological-induced behavioral responses affected all aspects of Kim's life: school, family relationships, friendship, and dating. She often had intense arguments with her boyfriend, close friends, and her mother. These arguments would ensue typically when Kim felt misunderstood or "smothered" by those in her life. These bouts of anger at those around her resulted in feelings of isolation. She would tell me, "No one gets me or cares about me." These behavioral and emotional consequences of the FFF response indicated that helping Kim develop a sense of safety was paramount.

Empowerment, a multidimensional process that helps clients take control of their lives, is a critical component in developing an internal sense of safety (Page & Czuba, 1999). Personal empowerment can occur in the psychotherapeutic process as clients gain knowledge, skills, and more adaptive attitudes. During one of our sessions, I used a psychoeducational strategy to help explain the FFF response to Kim:

> Imagine you are driving in a car and almost rear-ended the car in front of you. At that moment, you may feel your breath stop, your heart race, your stomach drop, etc. You experience those sensations because your brain has become overwhelmed by the threat of the potential car accident, which signaled the sympathetic nervous system to turn on, activating your FFF response. That is your body's automatic reaction to the threat. It is likely that shortly after that your brain will understand that the near-dangerous event is over, that everyone is safe and then the parasympathetic nervous system will take over. The FFF response will turn off, and your body will return to its moderate level of functioning. However, if a threat is ongoing, the brain continues to signal the nervous system that there is a danger, maintaining the FFF response.

This continued preparation for survival leads to the development of physical and emotional discomfort (Rothschild, 2000), which can feel like uncomfortable body sensations, sadness, exhaustion, and worry. Kim stared at me, wide-eyed, as she often did when I shared information about the trauma response. As I inquired, "What are you thinking about right now?" she calmly replied, "It makes sense. Lots of things make sense now."

Through the use of breathing and mindfulness techniques, individuals can quickly calm the nervous system. Learning skills to turn off the FFF response helped Kim feel more in control of her emotions. We often engaged in deep breathing, progressive muscle relaxation, and guided imagery techniques. At first, these suggestions were met with some pushback. "This is stupid" was followed by huffs and puffs. Although this response caused me to feel some hesitation about continuing with the skill development, I carried on because I had witnessed powerful effects with other clients. With patient consistency and time, Kim embraced these skills. A meaningful guided imagery exercise that Kim used was the creation of a safe place. Visualizing a safe place gave her a sense of calm and relaxation as she closed her eyes and imagined herself on a calm and beautiful beach. She then practiced using this skill at home and school when she started feeling emotionally dysregulated.

The first month of treatment both honored Kim's lack of enthusiasm for starting treatment while examining my feelings about her resistance. I was continually holding a space for Kim's pain while she shared her narrative. I often felt powerless because I knew I could not go back in time and take her painful experiences away. Therefore, my discomfort frequently surfaced in the form of wanting to "rescue" Kim from her own discomfort. Through regularly processing these feelings in supervision, I was reminded that I was learning just as much from Kim as she was from me. The notion that Kim was her own best expert was crucial to the healing process and the ability to create a safe space (Casement, 2013). She was also an active participant, making decisions and working through the process of healing at her own pace. Kim began to open up to the idea of learning about trauma and developing grounding skills to help turn off her fight, flight, and freeze responses. I conducted a thorough clinical assessment in the midst of this first stage of work. The assessment indicated that Kim's narrative included an array of symptoms; she often felt depressed and anxious, states that were marked by suicidal thoughts, irritability, intense shame and guilt, loneliness, difficulty sleeping and concentrating, panic attacks, flashbacks, and cutting herself from a young age. Her spunky energy masked well many of these experiences; however, irritability and self-injury would reveal themselves, often with a wisecrack remark or a pushing up of her sleeves in my warm office.

A TRAUMA LENS FOR HEALING

Trauma training provided a lens for me to work with Kim and to understand depression and anxiety beyond their diagnostic labels and sets of symptoms. A trauma framework holds that, when people experience trauma, their thoughts, emotions, affect regulation, and impulse control are all influenced, manifesting in signs of mental health diagnoses (Acierno et al., 2010; van der Kolk & McFarlane, 1996). In Kim's case, I began to hypothesize that the emotional and behavioral symptoms she was experiencing were not the result of a mental health disorder, but were her response to trauma. A trauma narrative is also a crucial part of trauma treatment. Using a narrative approach, a reconstruction of my work with Kim allowed me to understand just how important it was for her to co-construct her experiences of the trauma, consequent challenges, and learned resilience with me. It was also important for me to make sense of these experiences and our interactions.

The sexual trauma began for Kim when she was a very young girl. She was just three years old, a time when her brain was developing most quickly and she already had well over one hundred trillion learning synapses—half of what are in the adult brain (Shonkoff and Phillips 2000). The rapid brain development at this stage explains why early experiences are so impactful. For Kim, this meant being shackled to the memories. Kim would often exclaim in a frustrated tone, "I am so over this shit from years ago. . . . I don't want it to keep affecting me like this."

The amygdala and hippocampus, which live in the midbrain, are areas significantly affected by ongoing trauma. The hippocampus stores memories and puts memories in their proper place in the lifetime, allowing for a perspective of looking back on a memory rather than reliving it. However, during traumatic experiences, the hippocampus is suppressed, making it difficult for the experiences to be stored as a memory of the past (Nadel & Jacobs, 1996; Siegel, 2011). Often Kim would experience random flashbacks at home, school, or my office. If there was a noise, scent, or sight that reminded her of the abuse, it triggered these memories, and she felt like she was experiencing the violation again in the present moment. She would cry, shake, or stare blankly. These flashbacks caused intense anxiety because she never knew when one might arise. We talked about why this was happening over and over again. We talked about how her brain was responding to the traumatic experiences and we were working to appropriately store these traumatic memories in the past through therapeutic work.

The amygdala determines whether a situation is threatening, and processes and responds to emotions. It can be overactive because of the many years of trauma (Solomon & Siegel, 2003; Schore, 2001). Consequently, Kim intensely felt highly charged emotional memories, such as fear, shame, and anger, even when she was in a safe place with seemingly no threats, such as at home safely in her bedroom (Phelps, 2004). The office was a safe space because there she felt less "crazy" and worked toward a better understanding of why she would get so angry at her mom, feel intensely disappointed in a friend, or become incredibly sad at random times.

As mentioned earlier, Kim suffered abuse during the years when her brain was developing most rapidly. Therefore, neural networks formed in response to the trauma and adaptive networks did not get much reinforcement, which resulted in the presenting mental and behavioral health issues (Perry et al., 1995). This rapid development, along with the developmentally appropriate, self-referencing nature of children to internalize experiences around them, resulted in networks rooted in core negative beliefs, such as "I am not safe" and "It's my fault." These deeply rooted networks were strengthened with time and also elicited corresponding intense emotions of shame, guilt, and fear (Siegel, 2011; Shapiro, 2001; Erikson, 1959).

I used eye movement desensitization and reprocessing (EMDR) in sessions to help Kim process her traumatic experiences and develop more adaptive neural networks to replace the maladaptive trauma-based networks. EMDR is an eight-phase trauma therapy that incorporates many modalities, including cognitive behavioral, psychodynamic, and body-centered therapies (Shapiro, 2001). A major component of the work is identifying trauma-based networks and reprocessing them. Kim's "I am not safe" network manifested in a feeling of intense fear of expressing her truth and using her voice to express emotions or needs or set boundaries. She had difficulty performing daily activities, such as placing an order for a bagel at the local deli or asking her teacher a question in class. As she processed the traumas related to this neural network, the network lost its intensity, and she developed a new, more adaptive network. I recall the pride in her face as she came into session and excitedly shared, "I ordered my bagel for myself this morning!" and on another occasion, "I got an A on my speech in class!" Seemingly unremarkable actions, they were significant accomplishments for Kim. They illustrated that she was developing a more adaptive network along the lines of "I am safe to use my voice." However, aspects of her environment, such as going to a school at which there were frequent physical altercations and having to walk past a street gang on her way home from school, often made it difficult for this safety network to remain strong. These macrolevel traumas and Kim's positionality as a young Latina girl in this community also facilitated a frequent FFF response. Having a safe home to return to and a mother who loved her very much were major resources to counter these stressors and further foster healing.

Another trauma network Kim had developed was that the sexual abuse was her fault, which led to an intense amount of shame and guilt. She stated often, "How could I have let this happen?" and "I should have told someone sooner." The intensity of this network was what often led to the unhealthy coping mechanism of cutting. After processing the traumas as they related to this network, she was able to develop a more adaptive network that revolved around "I was a child and did nothing wrong." This new network also led to building compassion and love for her younger self using powerful ego-state approaches (Paulsen 2009).

Specifically, Kim developed a nurturing resource part (a compassionate aspect of herself) that was able to love her vulnerable, child part that felt incredibly sad and guilty about the abuse (Paulsen, 2009; Schwartz, 1995). Developing this nurturing part was not easy: the urge to blame and get angry at her younger self often surfaced in self-talk such as "I should have known better!" We had to balance making room for that self-blame and resulting feelings while also moving toward practicing self-compassion for her younger self. Over time, Kim got more comfortable with forgiving herself and treating herself with love. Specifically, she learned both to identify when her "hurt child" was present in feelings of intense sadness and fear and to invite the more nurturing part in to comfort her. This skill became an adaptive coping mechanism for Kim. She recognized the importance of practicing these skills, along with breath work and mindfulness, in helping turn off the FFF response and self-soothe.

Kim was suffering in the present because traumas from the past turned on her FFF response. In addition, her hippocampus had not made sense of the fact that the abuse was in the past; her amygdala was in overdrive, signaling intense emotional responses, and adverse neural networks had developed (van der Kolk et al., 2007; Nadel & Jacobs, 1996; Siegel, 2011). These neurobiological processes often caused Kim to experience severe emotional dysregulation, prompting her to respond to seemingly benign situations with an emotional or behavioral "outburst," such as an argument with her mom, a cutting incident, suicidal thoughts, or isolating herself. I worked with Kim on understanding these neurobiological processes, the use of developmentally appropriate language, and the healing capacity of her brain. We moved from psychoeducation into treatment, using mindfulness and grounding techniques, EMDR sessions, and ego-state work to facilitate healing. As she processed the trauma and developed new skills, her storyline became infused with themes of greater resilience. The narrative approach helped me see the power of shifts in her story in a way that I might not have recognized otherwise.

FINDING VOICE, FINDING MEANING

Building on Kim's strengths of creativity and smarts, we used poetry writing as an expressive tool to process her story. The medium of poetry helped Kim feel safe enough to express her truth and feelings while also taking empowered ownership of her story. Narrative reflections in the form of poetry are valuable tools for presenting complex lived experiences and allow for a depth of understanding to occur (Furman, 2004; Baker & Mazza, 2004). This powerful impact of storytelling through poems parallels the strengths of narrative case studies.

As mentioned, Kim wrote the poem "Photos That Cry," when she was looking through a childhood photo album and was feeling intense nostalgia and sadness. She shared this poem in session years into our work together. I was moved deeply by her words and depth of emotion that came through her voice as she spoke them. This poem illustrates that Kim had learned to express her innermost feelings and pain about childhood powerfully. She writes, "I cry just thinking, how you were let down, So many times, from your loved ones." When we began our work together, it was challenging for Kim to identify her feelings, let alone express them. As she learned to let the emotions out and use her voice, the intensity of the sadness, irritability, shame, and guilt subsided. The compassionate relationship that developed between her hurt younger self and wise/nurturing part is apparent in the following lines of the poem: "I wish I would've been there for you. To wipe your tears, and fight your fears." A critical part of her healing was developing a healthy, loving relationship between these two parts of the self. The words, "I don't know when I'll start feeling, More proud than sorry for you, Knowing that you are me," illustrate that this relationship is an ongoing, ever-changing one. She recognizes that she feels sympathy for her younger self and has a desire to turn that sympathy into a more empowered feeling of pride in her strength. The poem also speaks to her knowledge that a resilient spirit lives inside her. As I read the words, "But that never changed you. Never did it make you bitter. Nor hate the world. Just stronger and wiser," I remember the countless times she shared thoughtful insights in a session or showed compassion and kindness.

Another important aspect of trauma work is meaning-making, the process by which people make sense of their life experiences (Frankl, 1962). Frankl, in a manner similar to Jung, explained that constructive meaning can help the individual cope with even the most difficult of circumstances (Frankl, 1962; Jung, 1933). Kim's poem "The Lotus," depicts how she has made meaning of her trauma: "A lotus flower as strong as me, Rises out the ground with layers of mud upon it. But the heavy, brown, nasty, and sloppy mud. Is no challenge for the beautiful, strong, and white flower . . . The only one who may know the struggle of this flower, Can be me." She was determined not to let the trauma in her childhood define her life. I thought of the lotus flower, which has the strength to emerge through the mud and blossom into a beautiful flower. Kim would emerge from the traumas of her past and step into her present and future, stronger and more powerful as a result. This meaning-making is so important to Kim's life because it allows her to write her future life narrative from a place of empowerment and strength, as opposed to powerlessness and pain.

PRESENT DAY

Today, I hear from Kim every six months or so. She will come in for a session when something stressful is going on or when she is working through an important decision. The more Kim processed her experiences, expressed her feelings, and practiced skills to turn off her FFF response and calm her amygdala, the less intense were the uncomfortable feelings of sadness, irritability, guilt, and shame. Healthier, more adaptive responses and behaviors replaced trauma-based networks and coping strategies: the self-injurious behavior and suicidal thoughts subsided. She also was able to engage in school more effectively, graduating from high school and beginning college. Kim learned how to speak with her mother, often expressing her need for one- on-one time with her and frustration about her mother's ongoing relationship with her brother. She also began to set boundaries (healthy limits around acceptable behavior) while dating, with her mom, and with her friends. She was able to express clearly to her mom, "I don't want to hear about how my brother is doing." She communicated to her boyfriend, "I feel disrespected when you flirt with other girls in front of me." Communicating her needs and setting boundaries helped Kim feel empowered and safe.

Today, Kim is a young adult living on her own. She continues to use poetry and art to process her emotions and express her feelings. She struggles with typical developmental issues that are common for the majority of people her age, such as deciding which profession to enter, budgeting, and figuring out her romantic life. When Kim feels overwhelmed with her mood, she is still inclined to isolate herself. However, once she recognizes that she is doing so, she will reach out for support, use her poetry, or read something related to healing to cope.

PRACTICE WISDOM

As I reflect on the therapeutic work Kim and I did together, I feel grateful for having been exposed to the trauma-informed perspective. Before learning this model, I felt like something was missing in my clinical work. In 2007, I was sitting in rounds at a prestigious inpatient psychiatric hospital as a social work graduate student, taking in valuable information from the seasoned professionals in the room. Working on that unit taught me not to fear mental illness; to see the beauty in each adolescent who came into the group as he or she became part of the milieu family; and to treat from a strengths-based perspective, foster resilience, and use evidence-based, short-term interventions. As in the majority of hospitals, the medical model framed the meetings, which focused on symptom presentation, DSM diagnosis, and responses to medication. These aspects were important for communication purposes, treatment planning, and to measure progress (McLeod, 2014). Still, my inner voice resounded, "Something is missing!" At the time I was not sure exactly what it was. But shortly after that when a professor lectured on trauma theory and EMDR, the gap became more evident. The missing puzzle pieces fell into place as she explained the impact that traumatic experiences have on the brain and the body (Shapiro, 2001).

After that lecture on trauma, I began to make sense of my clinical practice in a different way. The commonality of each client whom I had worked with over the past two years was a history of interpersonal trauma, such as sexual abuse, neglect, physical abuse, assault, or abandonment. No matter what the presenting symptoms were—panic attacks, anxiety, depression, mood swings, self-harm, suicidality, substance abuse, and the like—these earlier traumatic experiences affected their neurobiological processes (Herman. 1992; van der Kolk et al. 2007). Research shows us that traumatic stressors, from micro interpersonal traumas to macro oppressions such as poverty and community violence, have a great impact on children's mental, physical, and behavioral well-being: there is a high prevalence of traumatic experiences underlying many mental health diagnoses: Major Depressive

Disorder (MDD),Generalized Anxiety Disorder (GAD), Post Traumatic Stress Disorder (PTSD), and behavioral issues (Felitti et al., 1998; Messina & Grella, 2006; Maschi et al., 2011).

This new understanding inspired me to get trained as an EMDR clinician. Through that process, I learned that to effectively treat children and adolescents we must move beyond symptom presentation and diagnosis and understand the whole client, including their life experiences and how such experiences have informed their neurobiological development. This view reinforced the ecological, person-in-environment perspective that I had learned in social work school, emphasizing the importance of viewing individuals in the context of the whole environment (Bronfenbrenner, 1979). The biopsychosocial assessment stems from this holistic perspective. It fosters understanding of how various systems affect clients, allowing clients to be more central to their healing process (Engel, 1977). Integrating trauma theory and ecological approaches facilitates a recognition of the impact of traumatic experiences on their lives.

The retelling of Kim's story and the retelling of our working together were crucial in recognizing that my narrative and Kim's narrative paralleled each other. We were each able to rewrite our narratives to focus on growth and resilience after learning about trauma.

CASE CONCEPTUALIZATION AND TREATMENT

After conducting a thorough assessment of Kim, I developed a clinical case conceptualization and then co-created a treatment plan with her. Case conceptualization is the clinician's understanding or hypothesis of the client's behavior based on the application of a theoretical approach (Eells, 2015). If I had understood Kim's presentation from a medical model perspective, I would have assessed her emotions and behaviors, labeled them as symptoms, analyzed the cluster of symptoms in the *Diagnostic Statistical Manual*, and diagnosed her with Depression based on that cluster (American Psychiatric Association, 2013). This case conceptualization would have then informed the treatment plan and approach with her. Specifically, I would have set goals to reduce symptoms of depression significantly. To achieve these goals, it is likely that cognitive behavioral therapy (CBT), a standard treatment approach for depression, along with an antidepressant, would be the course of treatment. Using the medical model approach, however, leaves little room for psychological and social dimensions of mental health (Engel, 1977). Further, it is possible for the client to overidentify with the diagnostic label and begin to fully take on the sick role (Parsons, 1951). While the medication and the skills learned from CBT would have likely helped Kim, they would not have resolved or healed the source of the emotional suffering: the years of trauma and its impact on the brain. Since we know the abuse affected Kim's brain development, it is likely that many of her presenting emotions and behaviors would have continued.

In contrast, the trauma-informed perspective allowed me to understand Kim's emotional and behavioral presentation as a manifestation of the trauma and a way to cope with the emotional pain. I was able to conceptualize that the ongoing sexual abuse had resulted in an overactive amygdala, causing intense feelings of shame, guilt, sadness, and irritability. In addition, Kim's FFF was stuck in an activated state since the trauma was continual, leading to difficulty concentrating and an inability to sleep at night. It was also likely that Kim had developed unhealthy coping skills such as self-harm to escape from the emotional dysregulation and physiological discomfort, and she had not yet developed adaptive coping skills. Informed by this conceptualization, we collaborated on a treatment plan based on these goals: calm down the FFF response, develop more adaptive neural networks, heal her younger self, and learn adaptive coping skills.

FROM PARTICULAR TO GENERAL

This chapter illustrates how understanding children's brains helps us better understand their mental and emotional well-being and, ultimately, more efficiently serve their healing. Applying a trauma-informed perspective to Kim's case significantly changed the conceptualization and course of treatment. Her symptoms of depression and anxiety were a manifestation of a "stuck" FFF, an overactive midbrain, and trauma-based neural networks. Psychoeducation, mindfulness approaches, EMDR, and ego-state work helped Kim's nervous system reset and her brain reprocess the traumatic experiences. As a result, the symptoms greatly decreased. The narrative case study approach allows us to see that one story has the power to help make sense of the complex topic of trauma and the brain. Readers are encouraged to determine what from Kim's story applies to their work and to reconstruct it in a way that improves their practice (Erickson, 1986; Stake, 2005).

It is also important to extend beyond micro practice and apply this information to macro systems as well. We must understand all of our children, not only those who wind up in our offices, from this trauma-informed perspective. Race, socioeconomic status, sexual orientation, gender, religion, and multiple other factors affect children's lives. Social stressors can have a significant traumatic effect on children (Greenleaf & Williams, 2009). The intersection between these oppressions and the systems that affect children, including foster care, education, criminal justice, and mental health, must be continually examined and better understood. Human service professionals must take the lead in advocating for implementation of trauma-informed perspectives on both individual and systematic levels to most effectively serve our children. As we continue to better understand the brain, we will be much more equipped to understand and help our children. We also will gain the power to move beyond the individual child and change socially unjust environments and cultures that create and perpetuate trauma, with the goal of creating a less traumatic, more peaceful world—one that is kind, sensitive, empowering, just, equal, connected, and compassionate. When we create our systems in line with these human service values, we will have far fewer traumatized children and less need for this discussion.

QUESTIONS FOR REFLECTION AND GROUP DISCUSSION

1. What feelings surfaced for you as you read the chapter?
2. If the medical model (symptom identification, diagnosis, and medication) was used alone to conceptualize and treat this client, how do you imagine things would have been different for her?
3. What are your ideas about how we can create a more trauma-informed sensitive environment for all children: for example, what would need to change in schools, the juvenile justice system, child welfare system, and mental health system?

REFERENCES

Acierno, R., Hernandez, M. A., Amstadter, A. B., Resnick, H. S., Steve, K., Muzzy, W., & Kilpatrick, D. (2010). Prevalence and correlates of emotional, physical, sexual, and financial abuse and potential neglect in the United States: The National Elder Mistreatment Study. *American Journal of Public Health, 100*(2), 292–297.

American Psychiatric Association. (2013). *Diagnostic and statistical manual of mental disorders* (text rev.). Washington, DC: American Psychiatric Publishing.

Annan, J., Priestley, A., & Phillipson, R. (2006). Narrative psychology: A tool for ecological practice. *Kairaranga, 7*(2), 20–27.

Baker, K. & Mazza, N. (2004). The healing power of writing: Applying expressive/creative component of poetry therapy. *Journal of Poetry Therapy, 17*(3), 141–154.

Bronfenbrenner, U. (1979). *The ecology of human development.* Cambridge, MA: Harvard University Press.

Cannon, W. (1932). *Wisdom of the body.* New York: W. W. Norton.

Casement, P. (2013). *Further learning from the patient.* Abingdon, UK: Routledge.

Eells, T. (2015). *Psychotherapy case formulation.* Washington, DC: American Psychological Association.

Engel, G. (1977). The need for a new medical model: A challenge for biomedicine. *Science, 196*(4286), 129–136.

Erikson, E. (1959). *Identity and the life cycle.* New York: International Universities Press.

Erickson, F. (1986). Qualitative Methods in Research on Teaching. In M. Wittrockk (Ed.), *Handbook of Research on Teaching* (3rd ed., pp. 119–161). New York: MacMillan.

Felitti, V., Anda, R., Nordenberg, D., Williamson, D., Spitz, A., Edwards, V., & Marks, J. (1998). Relationship of childhood abuse and household dysfunction to many of the leading causes of death in adults. *American Journal of Preventive Medicine 14*(4), 245–258.

Frankl, V. (1962). *Man's search for meaning: An introduction to logotherapy.* Boston: Beacon Press.

Furman, R. (2004). Using poetry and narrative as qualitative data: Exploring a father's cancer through poetry. *Family, Systems and Health, 22*(2), 162–170.

Gagnon, M., & Hersen, M. (2000). Unresolved childhood sexual abuse and older adults: Late-life vulnerabilities. *Journal of Clinical Geropsychology, 6*(3), 187–198.

Greenleaf, A. & Williams, J. (2009). Supporting social justice advocacy: A paradigm shift towards an ecological perspective. *Journal for Social Action in Counseling and Psychology 2*(1), 1–14.

Herman, J. (1992). *Trauma and recovery.* New York: Basic Books.

Jansen, A., Nguyen, X., Karpitsky, V. & Mettenleiter, M. (1995). Central command neurons of the sympathetic nervous system: Basis of the fight-or-flight response. *Science, 270*(5236), 644–646.

Jung, C. (1933). *Modern man in search of a soul.* London: Kegan Paul Trench Trubner.

Maschi, T., Morgen, K., Zgoba, K., Courtney, D., & Ristow, J. (2011). Trauma, stressful life events, and post-traumatic stress symptoms: Do subjective experiences matter? *The Gerontologis, 51*(5): 675–686.

McLeod, S. (2014). The medical model. Retrieved from https://www.simplypsychology.org/medical-model.html.

Méndez, M. (2013). Autoethnography as a research method: Advantages, limitations and criticisms. *Colombian Applied Linguistics Journal, 15*(2), 279–287.

Messina, N., & Grella, C. (2006). Childhood trauma and women's health criterions in a California prison population. *American Journal of Public Health, 96*(10), 1842–1848.

Nadel, L. & Jacobs, W. (1996). The role of the hippocampus in PTSD, panic, and phobia. In N. Kato (Ed.), *Hippocampus: Functions and clinical relevance*. Amsterdam:
Elsevier Science.

Padgett, D., & Glasser, R. (2003). How stress influences the immune response. *Trends
in Immunology 24*(8), 444–448.

Page, N. & Czuba, C. (1999), "Empowerment: What Is It?" *Journal of Extension, 37*(5), 5.

Parsons, T. (1951). *The social system*. Glencoe, IL: Free Press.

Paulsen, S. (2009). *Looking through the eyes of trauma and dissociation: An illustrated
guide for EMDR therapists and clients*. Bainbridge Island, WA: Bainbridge Institute
for Integrative Psychology.

Perry, B., Pollard, R., Blakley, T., Baker, W., & Vigilante, D. (1995). Childhood trauma,
the neurobiology of adaptation, and "use-dependent" development of the brain:
How "states" become "traits." *Infant Mental Health Journal, 16*(4), 271–291.

Phelps, E. (2004). Human emotion and memory: Interactions of the amygdala and hip-
pocampal complex. *Current Opinion in Neurobiology, 14*, 198–202.

Reiss, K. (2009). *Qualitative research and case study applications in education*. San Francisco: John Wiley & Sons Inc.

Rothschild, B. (2000). Post-traumatic stress disorder: Identification and diagnosis. *Swiss
Journal of Social Work*. Retrieved from http://www.healing-arts.org/tir/n-r
-rothschild.htm.

Schore, A. (2001). The effects of early relational trauma on right brain development,
affect regulation, and infant mental health. *Infant Mental Health Journal 22*(1),
201–269.

Schwartz, R. (1995). *Internal Family Systems Therapy*. New York: Guilford.

Shapiro, F. (2001). *Eye movement desensitization and reprocessing: Basic principles, protocols and procedures* (2nd ed.). New York: Guilford Press.

Shonkoff, J. & Phillips, D. (2000). *From neurons to neighborhoods: The science of early
childhood development*. Washington, DC: National Academies Press.

Siegel, D. & Bryson, T. (2011). *The whole-brain child: 12 Revolutionary strategies to nur-
ture your child's developing mind, survive everyday parenting struggles, and help your
family thrive*. New York: Delacorte Press.

Solomon, M. & Siegel, D. (2003). *Healing trauma: Attachment, mind, body and brain*.
New York: W. W. Norton.

Stake, R. (2005). Qualitative case studies. In N. K. Denzin & Y. S. Lincoln (Eds.), *The
Sage handbook of qualitative research* (3rd ed.) (pp. 443–466). Thousand Oaks, CA:
Sage.

Substance Abuse and Mental Health Services Administration. (2014). *Leading change:
A plan for SAMHSA's roles and actions*. Retrieved from http://store.samhsa.gov/shin
/content/SMA11-4629/04-TraumaAndJustice.pdf.

van der Kolk, B. & McFarlane, A. (1996). *Psychological stress: The effects of overwhelming experience on mind, body and society*. New York: Guilford Press.

van der Kolk, B., Spinazzola, J., Blaustein, M., Hopper, J., Hopper, E., Korn, D., & Simpson, W. (2007). A randomized clinical trial of eye movement desensitization and
reprocessing (EMDR), fluoxetine, and pill placebo in the treatment of posttraumatic
stress disorder: Treatment effects and long-term maintenance. *Journal of Clinical
Psychiatry, 68*(1), 1–9.

Chapter Fifteen

BEYOND DEFICITS

Shifting Perspectives in Child and Youth Mental Health

MARGOT K. JACKSON

I was at the (inner city hospital) when I was a kid for attempting suicide. Right before I attempted suicide, I was raped when I was thirteen and I really wasn't
getting the right help at all. I was living with my mom and it happened in my
mom's building. I just couldn't be there anymore so they moved me to my Aunties, or my mom's friends, and then they took me camping for a month. I came
back and nothing changed. I went to the psych ward, and they tried to get me
into a center for sexual assault but there was a long waitlist and they couldn't
get me to see anybody. It was stupid. When I started using drugs they would
put me in a secure facility, but I never stayed. I would manipulate the psychologist and say I don't have problems, I ran away from every group home I was
ever in. They tried to put a one-on-one worker on me and I'd just ditch 'em anyways. I've never stayed. I was just like, I didn't really care you know. I had
nothing to lose at that time. (Stephanie, age twenty)

These words were shared by Stephanie, a remarkable young woman who
participated in a research study inquiring into the lived experiences of
youth who were considered at risk or homeless and their encounters with
mental health and mental health services. In related literature, this group
of youth is referred to by many interchangeable names, including the
following: street youth, homeless youth, at-risk youth, high-risk youth,
youth at risk, runaways, throwaways, curbsiders, and children of or on the

streets. The term "at risk" in this inquiry suggests that the youth are exposed to situations that place them in danger of being harmed physically, developmentally, and/or psychologically. These risks include poverty, exposure to violence, living in unsafe communities, substance use, lack of family stability, and inadequate housing. During the ten months over which this research took place, I was able to work closely with six youth ages twelve to twenty-two whom I met through a community agency, the Centre for Arts and Youth (CAY) [a pseudonym]. CAY is in a large western Canadian city in a section of the downtown core where are also located homeless shelters and services to assist socially vulnerable individuals. The youth in this study participated by sharing photographs and participating in conversations about the photos and other issues affecting their lives and experiences. Over time, trusting relationships formed between the youth and me. These relationships were an integral piece of the inquiry, because the youth shared such personal and often emotional experiences. As part of these relationships, I shared part of my life with them, as we grew together and learned from each other. During this inquiry I kept field notes and personal reflections in a journal where I documented my own journey alongside the youth. The ability to share my thoughts, feelings, fears, and questions was a valuable and necessary part of this inquiry: it helped me grow and understand where I stood in relation to the youth with whom I worked.

In this chapter, I share personal stories of my experiences as a nurse and researcher working within the realm of child and youth mental health and provide an intimate look at the life of one young woman, Stephanie, whom I met at CAY. Stephanie had a tremendous impact on my understanding of mental health, of developing personal strength, and of overcoming adversity; her life story is a guide and inspiration for other youth who have shared a similar narrative, as well as those touched by mental health. The narrative approach places personal experience as the focal point to facilitate understanding, insight, and change; it allows individual voices to be heard and places value on all that is shared. Thus, this chapter provides the reader with an understanding of child and youth mental health through a narrative inquiry lens and encourages alternative ways of learning and knowing.

BACKGROUND

In child and youth mental health, there is a dominant narrative that often influences practice and understanding. It emphasizes assessment, diagnosis, categorization, and labeling in order to come to an understanding of illness, the choice of treatment, and the prognosis of recovery—identifying youth by their mental health diagnosis or label, rather than by their experiences or by coming to know them as individuals. This dominant narrative has evolved as the basis for most mental health, psychiatric, social sciences, and social services education and is reliant on the American Psychiatric Association's 2013 *Diagnostic and Statistical Manual of Mental Health Disorders* (DSM-V) as a guide. The DSM-V focuses on signs and symptoms of disorders, as well as guidelines for diagnosis. Reinforced by my professional experiences and training, this dominant narrative shaped my practice and affected how I viewed the field of child and youth mental health.

Yet, little exists in this dominant narrative about the context of people's lives, their individuality, hearing the person's story, attending to people's lives and experiences, or the concept of hope for the future. Recognizing these gaps opened my eyes to a world within myself that I did not know existed. Before becoming aware of the shortcomings of the dominant narrative, my treatment and relationship with clients were influenced by their diagnosis without fully exploring the uniqueness and individuality of their personal experiences.

"WHAT'S HIS DIAGNOSIS?"

As I sat with Stephanie, during one of our conversations I was taken back to an experience I had with Casey, a youth whom I met while working as a nurse at a youth emergency shelter:

What's his diagnosis? I hear these words across the admissions office, and my ears perk up to hear the answer to the question as though the response will provide some great insight into Casey's care and a magical cure for his issues. "He has ODD and ADHD," I recall hearing as the youth shelter worker refers to the Diagnostic and Statistical Manual of Mental Disorders (DSM) diagnoses of Oppositional Defiant Disorder and Attention Deficit Hyperactivity Disorder. "His behavior at home is pretty bad . . . he stays out all night, fights with his mom and sister, and has been kicked out of school. Sounds like he fits the ODD criteria all right"! I am listening intently now, trying to get as much information as I can about this fifteen-year-old boy whom I had just met outside while he was smoking a cigarette. I can't help wonder why the focus became about his diagnosis, rather than his story. (Researcher, reflective journal).

This reflective paragraph shares but one of many personal experiences that I faced as a nurse and mental health therapist working with children and youth. It clearly shows how this teen's life and experiences became lost or overridden by the youth shelter worker's need to diagnose and label the clients. It was easy to get caught up in these diagnoses or labels and lose sight of the human being who existed behind them. These diagnoses provided some sort of safe haven for professionals like myself who were working with youth. They provided a sense of *knowing* that there was something *wrong* with the youth and that having this knowledge could help guide their care. Diagnosis is a common language among health professionals; it can frame thinking in regard to behavior and treatment and can provide a reason for care. It can also allow practitioners to remain *clinically distant* without fear of becoming *emotionally* entrenched in clients' lives.

I do not believe that this framing was done to harm; rather it was a means for the youth shelter workers to organize and focus their thoughts and, ultimately, their potential treatment plan for Casey and other youth; it also reflected a common approach that college and university students are taught when faced with mental health and behavior concerns. The focus becomes a specific diagnosis with corresponding treatments, rather than the individual's story or narrative. It emphasizes deficits and defines the individual as a case, rather than a person with unique traits, resources, possibilities, and talents. Integrating this strengths perspective into health and social service teaching and practice leads to a different way of perceiving those in need and helps one pursue a practice based on resilience, hope, and transformation (Saleeby 1996).

WHAT'S IN A LABEL?

Historically, mental health and psychiatry have invested both in deconstructing people's problems by searching for meaning and engaging in the modernist practices of assessment, diagnosis, and treatment. More recently, with the introduction of the DSM, psychopharmacology, research, and evidenced-based practice, mental health has become dominated by a biologically focused approach to people's problems (Carrey 2006). In a study by Hagen and Nixon (2011) on women's experiences recovering from psychosis, the mental health care system is described as a *label factory* with physicians focused on giving their patients psychiatric labels. They go on to describe the way patients are given mental health labels depending on where they are in the system and whose care they are under. They compared this pattern of activity to that of a *diagnostic slot machine* where a health professional would pull the handle and see what was revealed. So often in the mental health system the meaning and stories of people's lives have been brushed aside and replaced with the categorization and compartmentalizing of mental health concerns. It is as though it is easier for these health professionals to neatly stack and organize people in terms of their behavior or diagnosis than to take the time to learn who they really are. What if we learn something out of the ordinary? What if the person does not exactly fit into a diagnosis? What if we begin to care too much? There are so many dangers to categorization in mental health and of this dominant narrative. Consider the issue of totalizing judgment, where the person with schizophrenia becomes labeled a schizophrenic or where normative judgments of behavior such as normal or abnormal become commonplace (Carrey, 2006). Moreover, as seen with some of the youth at the homeless shelter who called themselves ADHD or ODD, individuals begin to categorize and label themselves, which can lead to a self-fulfilling prophecy in terms of future success and function (Sternberg et al. 2011; Launer 1999).

In the health care and social service professions it is easy to forget that people's stories are their clinical history (Coles 1989) and that what we do is listen to these stories and try to make sense of them as best we can. Robert Coles, a psychiatrist by profession, addresses these issues in his 1989 work, *The Call of Stories: Teaching and the Moral Imagination*. In this influential work, Coles shares his experiences during his psychiatric residency with a mentor who guides him to see more in his patients than their primary diagnosis and clinical assessment history. He recalls a brief lecture by this mentor that influenced his practice for the remainder of his career: "The people who come to see us bring us their stories. They hope they tell them well enough so that we understand the truth of their lives. They hope we know how to interpret their stories correctly. We have to remember that what we hear is *their story*" (1989, 6, emphasis added). How lovely this quotation is. It reminds me both of the privilege of hearing another human's life stories and of how much courage and trust it takes for that person to share his or her experiences with me. Furthermore, it reminds me as a health service provider of how much power and influence we can have over another person's care and success.

Studying children and youth's experiences narratively is, in part, a resistance against the labels, a resistance against organizing people in terms of their diagnosis. In the context of the my initial reflective journal, so much could be missed about an individual if his or her story is overlooked in place of a diagnosis.

LEARNING FROM STEPHANIE AND OTHER YOUTH

During the inquiry, Stephanie and I worked together a scrapbook of her life and on two related projects: a chronological timeline of perceived major events in her life and a river of life. The timeline served as the starting point to the river of life, which was more complex and drawn on a much larger scale. These experiences or exercises were meant as a means for Stephanie to recall her life—her victories, her stumbles, and her path. I hoped that they were a way to celebrate who she is and to provide a vision for the future.

After Stephanie worked on these projects, I took photographs of her work, which are shared in figures 15.1 and 15.2. Writing in the coil-bound journal was the first step in this process: Stephanie wrote down what she viewed as pivotal and influential moments in her life, along with her age at the time of the experience. These life moments were put into a life river she drew on a large roll of paper approximately twenty feet long. Under the river, Stephanie wrote her age when she experienced each event. This river acts as a metaphor to show the flow of her life; transitions, traumas, and events flow through wide and narrow streams, rough waters, and islands of hope or despair. Stephanie's life river spans over four pages (due to the large size of the original drawing) so the writing can be clear and legible. Stephanie writes about this experience of creating this timeline and river:

My name is Stephanie and I am 21 years old. I am Metis. I have two beautiful children. I am also a recovering meth addict with mental health issues. I also

FIGURE 15.1 Stephanie's timeline and images captured from the street.

have been through some trauma and hard times. Here is part of my story and healing journey. This is a timeline of events of my past, some traumatic and life changing. Some of these events lead to alcohol and drug use. Not until recently have begun to heal.

Because I was abused I developed different personalities . . . When I was a little girl I made up this world that only I knew of. A place where I could go and things would happen and I didn't really like sitting in my dark rooms either. What I mean by dark rooms is the things that I was going through, and so I had escaped to this other place that I just basically made up where I knew these positive people and we'd talk and have fun. But really, it was just me going crazy. It's all it was. (Julia, research participant)

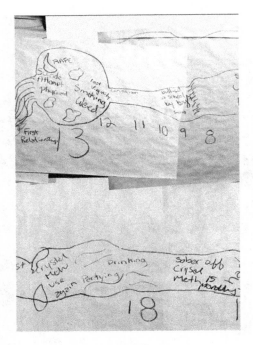

FIGURE 15.2 Stephanie's "river of life."

As the research project unfolded, several of the other youth participants shared that they have received formal psychiatric diagnoses in the past (such as depression, bipolar, anxiety, and psychosis) and had been admitted to both child and adolescent psychiatry and adult psychiatry inpatient units at an inner city hospital. Not one of the youth suggested that these hospital admissions were helpful or provided any long-lasting support. As well, I came to see intergenerational patterns within the youth's families: most youth also shared that their parents, grandparents, or other family members suffered from mental illness and substance abuse issues. I think of a day not so long ago when I was meeting with Stephanie to see a documentary she was making. In her documentary she talks about having been diagnosed with bipolar disorder and borderline personality disorder (BPD). As I heard those words, I told Stephanie that she does not have BPD. Stephanie looked at me and said, "Well, that's what I was told," and I remember telling her that she was informed wrongly. It was kind of a strange moment between us as Stephanie looked at me for some time in wonder and then asked me, "How do you know?" I replied simply with "I know you." I often wonder if my comments challenged Stephanie in some way to re-story herself from a diagnosis to simply a girl; a girl whose experiences have been shaped who she is today.

Stephanie shares:

I went to school when I was in the young offenders program and a little bit after, and I was in grade eight when I was 13 and I finished, but then grade nine I don't know what the hell happened. I completed grade 10 but then that's it.

When I started using drugs they would put me in a secure facility but I never stayed. I would manipulate the psychologist and say I don't have problems, I ran away from every group home I was ever in. They tried to put a one on one worker on me and I'd just ditch 'em anyways. I've never stayed. I was just like, I didn't really care you know. I had nothing to lose at that time.

In the past, if I were to read her history and see her past behavior I would have agreed that Stephanie categorically fit the common description of someone with BPD. She is a female with a family history of neglect, abuse, sexual abuse, defiant behavior, unstable relationships, substance use, and at risk behaviors, all of which tend to diagnostically be associated with BPD. I could have easily labeled her and slotted her into the DSM diagnosis. This is no longer the case: I have come to know Stephanie differently. I have looked into her bright-green eyes and pretty face while she shared pieces of her life. We have spent time together walking in the river valley, drinking coffee, and painting pictures with her children. I have seen her interact with others in relationships and have experienced a relationship with her. I do admit that if I were to assess and diagnose Stephanie in a clinical setting, her history would predispose her toward a diagnosis of borderline personality disorder—but that would be the easy way out. As I think about Stephanie now, I realize that I have formed a relationship with her and have come to experience her as she is: a person with a past, a present, and a future, not a category within a diagnostic manual. Words that I read in Coles's (1989) work entered my mind, and I am reminded that I am hearing Stephanie's *story* without trying to get a *fix* on her.

Throughout this inquiry I often found myself tangled in an internal struggle against the dominant narrative. I would hear the experiences of the youth and their intergenerational stories while I also bumped up against tensions with what I had learned or had been exposed to in the past. Instead of avoiding or resisting these tensions, I attended to them while allowing them to shape my views and experiences. In this way, I moved beyond seeing the youths' stories in negative terms (Huber, Huber, and Clandinin 2004). I choose to follow Stephanie's words that she shared near the ending of our work together; *We as humans are all equal; we all deserve life. Everybody dies but not everyone lives. I will continue to share my story wherever and whenever possible to help and support others.*

NARRATIVE INQUIRY AS A GUIDE

Narrative inquiry is both a way of understanding experience and a methodology that is designed to understand people's storied experiences as embedded within social, cultural, institutional, linguistic, and familial narratives (Clandinin and Connelly 2000). This methodology is relational in nature and enables the formation of intensive relationships with each individual to hear how their lives have unfolded. Stories and narratives are a part of being in the greatest sense as they are part of the human experience and affect us in the past, present, and future. Narrative inquiry differs from other research which incorporates the use of narratives into their methodology as it involves the inquiry into our lived, told, relived and retold experiences. Connelly and Clandinin (2006) define narrative inquiry in the following:

Arguments for the development and use of narrative inquiry come out of a view of human experience in which human, individually and socially, lead storied lives. People shape their daily lives by stories of who they and others are and as they interpret their past in terms of these stories. Story, in the current idiom, is a portal through which a person enters the world and by which their experience of the world in interpreted and made personally meaningful. Viewed this way, narrative is the phenomenon studied in foremost a way of thinking about experience. Narrative inquiry as methodology entails a view of the phenomenon. To use narrative inquiry methodology is to adopt a particular narrative view of experience as phenomena under study. (2006, 479)

The evolution of narrative inquiry as a methodology has been influenced by educational, anthropological, and human science theories. This research methodology is not simply the telling and retelling of stories but "a way of understanding experience. It is a collaboration between researcher and participants, over time, in a place or series of places, and in social interaction with milieus" (Clandinin and Connelly 2000, 20). Narrative inquiry provides an opportunity for individuals to share their stories and life experiences in a way that can be meaningful for them. A large part of narrative inquiry is the mutual sharing of experiences by both participant and researcher and the relationship that grows between them. As such, personal stories, reflections, and experiences are interwoven throughout the inquiry. This interweaving of the participants' experiences with the researchers reflects the relational nature of a narrative inquiry. During this process, participant and researcher learn from each other and grow together over time and place.

The human experience is both individual and social. Lives are composed of stories that are interpreted personally, yet influenced by the surrounding social milieu. In a narrative inquiry, the narratives of individual participants are shared, but there exists an understanding that the context of their experience is grounded in the world in which they live (Clandinin 2007). Clandinin and Connelly's work (2000) is greatly influenced by educational studies and by John Dewey's (1934) views of experience in which there exist two criteria: that the personal and the social always exist together and that of continuity. Continuity is described as "experiences grow out of other experiences, and experiences lead to further experiences" (Clandinin and Connelly 2000, 2). Dewey discusses experiences as occurring continuously, because of the interaction of living creatures and environmental conditions that are involved in this process of living. As such, narrative inquiry researchers are cognizant of the fact that the individual's stories vary depending on where they are in the world and the existence of potential influencing factors. In other words where we live, and what and whom we are exposed to in that living space, are tremendous shaping factors to our lives and our own personal narratives.

Anthropologists Geertz and Bateson were also influential in the development of narrative inquiry as a research methodology by both identifying change as a key factor in understanding the world: "Whereas Geertz emphasizes the changing phenomena, the changing world studied by the anthropologist, Bateson (1994) emphasizes the person, participant sometimes, researcher sometimes, always the inseparability of the two" (Clandinin and

Connelly 2000, 8). Bateson also focused on learning and the importance of the change that emerges from learning in an unpredictable and disordered world.

Coming to narrative inquiry from the sciences and in particular from the field of mental health, I found Polkinghorne's (1988) and Coles's (1989) use of narrative to be the most compelling: both use narrative in their practice, Polkinghorne as a psychotherapist and Coles as a psychiatrist. Coles incorporates narrative into his understanding and way of thinking about patients, their experiences, their behavior, and their stories within his clinical practice. Polkinghorne uses narrative within his clinical practice as does Coles, but also incorporates it into research.

LIVING AMIDST

The relationships built between researcher and participants are the foundation of the narrative inquiry. They are the basis for our trusting and collaborative work and the sharing of lives and experiences. Relationships are central to narrative inquiry on many levels, from participant to researcher, the social to the personal, and narratives to methodology. As well, there exists the important relationship between "narrative as phenomenon and narrative as methodology" (Clandinin et al. 2010, 82), in which the inquirer in relation with the participant examines the participant's relations of the past, present, and future. In narrative inquiry, experiences are the phenomena through which people live and understand their world. This understanding of phenomena is central to narrative inquiry as a methodology. During the inquiry there is a continual journey of moving forward and backward together in which participant and researcher learn from each other. Furthermore, as a narrative inquirer the lives and stories are interwoven and are seen in relation to those of the participant. As researchers we do not stand outside the lives of participants; we place ourselves with them and see ourselves as part of the phenomenon being studied (Clandinin et al. 2010).

As a researcher, I find myself living amidst the participants because of the relationships we have formed and the foundations built throughout the inquiry. This "living amidst" can often evoke emotional reactions within the researcher and stimulate the questioning of personal ideas and beliefs. I often found myself living at the boundaries, caught between my narrative thinking and my earlier experiences (Clandinin and Connelly 2000). Finding myself at these boundaries causes tension as I bounce against different ways of thinking, perceiving, and understanding experience. For example, a tension I experienced during my research with at risk youth and mental health was caused by the existence of the dominant narrative of diagnosis and categorizing. This tension forced me to examine who I am in relation to the youth, as well as who I am personally. Tensions are integral to narrative inquiry as they take the research many steps beyond the single narrative of one person and lead us down a trail of self- discovery. Narrative inquiry is much more than looking for or hearing a story:, it is "a form of living, a way of life . . . it is one of trying to make sense of life as lived" (Clandinin and Connelly 2000, 78).

PROVIDING CARE IN PIECES?

As health care providers there is often pressure to "make a diagnosis," ascertain what "factors" and "variables" have been at work, and decide upon a "therapeutic agenda" (Coles 1989, 7). During my professional career as a nurse in the health care system, I have often seen care provided toward the illness rather than the person. There are several reasons why this may occur, ranging from pure practicality to clinical learning. Patients are divided up into units in acute care based on their medical issue (e.g., a patient with a knee problem is placed on orthopedics, a patient with a head injury will be in neurology). It is simpler to keep patients categorized based on illness or injury. Medical residents, nursing students, and other learners need to focus on the tasks at hand that require their specialization. Furthermore, clinical teaching is primarily centered around illness and injury, with focus paid to disease etiology, epidemiology, signs and symptoms, diagnosis, and treatment. I think about the concept of knowledge and how explicit knowledge (such as that gained through textbooks, lectures, and manuals) and tacit knowledge (knowledge gained from experience and having a sense of what is to be done) are inherent to nurses' ways of knowing (Zander 2007). How explicit knowledge is gained, such as from lectures, textbooks, or memorization, could contribute to patients being labeled and placed into tidy, categorical boxes by symptoms or illness. Tacit knowledge, however, requires living and experiencing; it suggests that learning can take place through being a person. I recall how I felt going into this study armed with a knowledge of narrative inquiry methodology, child and youth mental health, and community health. I was not prepared for how much I still did not know. As this inquiry proceeded, I came to realize I had a lot to learn about myself, the youth with whom I met, and about experience.

CONCLUSION

The social significance of the dominant narrative in mental health is one of particular concern to me and one that has emerged during the course of this narrative inquiry. This dominant narrative, which I have been exposed to while working in the area of child and youth mental health, has been one of diagnosis, assessment, and categorization. An emphasis on using criteria from the *Diagnostic and Statistical Manual of Mental Health Disorders* (DSM) has superseded the individual client's story. There is no room for practitioners to explore the meaning of experiences in patient's lives because of time constraints, the need (or desire) for a quick diagnosis, a focus on psychopharmacology and quick treatment modalities, and an unease about delving into troubled waters that may unbalance the power differential between client and clinician. The work of Coles (1989)—hearing a patient's story rather than getting a fix on him or her—is often forgotten because of these constraints and the dominant narrative prevails. This dominant narrative is evident in health facilities and community agencies where a biologically focused approach to people's problems dominates (Carrey 2006).

During this inquiry I found myself drifting further and further away from the dominant narrative I had learned in the past. This movement can be attributed to my role as inquirer rather than nurse, the removal of expectations from me to provide clinical feedback, and the incorporation of narrative into my philosophy of understanding and being. In addition, meeting with the youth in the community setting at CAY tilted the balance of power I normally would have, because CAY was a place where the youth felt more comfortable than I did; it was a place where they lead the activities and structure of the day. What a change from meeting the youth in a clinical setting! It makes me very aware of the different information obtained while collecting histories and assessment information in settings where youth might feel vulnerable and powerless, such as in hospitals or clinics.

FIGURE 15.3 Stephanie's flowers as signs of "spring and promise."

At times I was reminded of the dominant narrative when the youth identified themselves as their diagnosis. This happened more than once during
this inquiry. As I write this, I am reminded of a time I shared earlier when
Stephanie labeled herself as Borderline Personality Disorder. I found myself jumping in, as if to her defense, by stating frankly, "You do not have
Borderline Personality Disorder." In the past, I can see how I might have
given her this diagnosis, because of her history, but something changed over

the course of this inquiry. I was no longer set on "getting a fix" on her as described by Coles (1989); I was there to share in her stories and understand her view of life and experience. I wanted to hear her story, and I hoped that she trusted me enough to share it.

This experience reminds me of the lessons learned by Coles during his psychiatry residency, and once again, these words play in my mind: "The people who come to see us bring us their stories. They hope they tell them well enough so that we understand the truth of their lives. They hope we know how to interpret their stories correctly. We have to remember that what we hear is their story" (1989, 6). Coles reminds me that life is experience and that both clinician and patient bring their experiences with them when working together. To provide care and support for youth they need to be viewed in a different light, focusing on their strengths and potentials and as always becoming.

I end this chapter with a photograph that Stephanie took in the inner city, on which she placed her writing (figure 15.3). This image shows the beauty and hope that Stephanie represents and captured within a world that could have been seen as oppressive and painful. Stephanie shares the words that inspire and propel her forward. In working with Stephanie, I have learned to see beyond perceived deficits of individuals and focus on their promise and becoming.

QUESTIONS FOR REFLECTION AND GROUP DISCUSSION

1. How do personal experiences shape our world view and understanding of others? Do these experiences affect how health and social service professionals work with clients?
2. What can be done to promote further understanding of mental health as a part of an individual's story or narrative?
3. How can health and social service practitioners avoid the use of mental health diagnosis as a predictor for a client's behavior and future success?

REFERENCES

American Psychiatric Association. 2013. *Diagnostic and Statistical Manual of Mental Disorders* (5th ed.). Arlington, VA: American Psychiatric Publishing.
Bach, Hedy. 2008. "Visual Narrative Inquiry." In *The Sage Encyclopedia of Qualitative Research Methods*, ed. L. M. Given, 934–938. Thousand Oaks, CA: Sage.

Bateson, Mary C. 1994. *Peripheral Visions: Learning Along the Way*. New York: Harper Collins.

Boivin, Jean François, Élise Roy, Nancy Haley, and Guillame G. du Fort. 2005. "The Health of Street Youth: A Canadian Perspective." *Canadian Journal of Public Health* 96, no. 6: 423–437.

Carrey, Normand. 2006. "Practicing Psychiatry Through a Narrative Lens: Working with Children, Youth, and Families." http://www.uk.sagepub.com/upm-data/11228 _Chapter_5.pdf.

Clandinin, D. Jean, and F. Michael Connelly. 2000. *Narrative Inquiry: Experience and Story in Qualitative Research*. San Francisco: Jossey-Bass.

Clandinin, D. Jean, M. Shaun Murphy, Janice Huber, and Anne Murray Orr. 2010. "Negotiating Narrative Inquiries: Living in a Tension-Filled Midst." *Journal of Educational Research* 103, no. 2: 81–90.

Coles, Robert. 1989. "Stories and Theories." In *The Call of Stories: Teaching and the Moral Imagination*, 1–30. Boston: Houghton Mifflin, 1989.

Connelly, F. Michael, and D. Jean Clandinin. 2006. "Narrative Inquiry." In *Handbook of Complementary Methods in Education Research 3rd edition*, ed. J. L. Green, G. Camilli, and P. Elmore, 477–487. Mahwah, NJ: Ehrlbaum.

Dewey, John. 1934. *Art of Experience*. New York: Berkeley Publishing

Hagan, Brad, and Gary Nixon. 2011. "Spider in a Jar: Women Who Have Recovered from Psychosis and Their Experience of the Mental Health Care System." *Ethical Human Psychology and Psychiatry* 13, no. 1: 47–63.

Huber, Marilyn, Janice Huber, and D. Jean Clandinin. 2004. "Moments of Tension: Resistance as Expressions of Narrative Coherence in Stories to Live By." *Reflective Practice* 5: 181–198.

Launer, John. 1999. "A Narrative Approach to Mental Health in General Practice." *British Medical Journal* 319: 117–119.

Polkinghorne, Donald E. 1988. *Narrative Knowing and the Human Sciences*. Albany: State University of New York Press.

Saleeby, Dennis. 1996. "The Strengths Perspective in Social Work Practice: Extensions and Cautions." *Social Work* 41, no. 3: 296–305.

Sternberg, Esther, Simon Critchley, Shaun Gallagher, and Varadaraja V. Raman. 2011. "A Self-Fulfilling Prophecy: Linking Belief to Behavior." *Annals of the New York Academy of Science* 1234, no. 1; 104–107.

Zander, Patricia E. 2007. "Ways of Knowing in Nursing: The Historical Evolution of a Concept." *Journal of Theory Construction and Testing* 11, no. 1: 7–11.

Chapter Sixteen

SHIFTING IDENTITIES, SHIFTING MEANINGS

Adolescent Siblings and Grief

ERICA GOLDBLATT HYATT

I was seven years old when I first became both fascinated with and terrified by what would happen when I died. I cannot pinpoint the exact moment I became aware of my own fragile mortality, but I can still recall the feelings that emerged from that realization: Disgust. Confusion. Curiosity. Nausea. Hopelessness. Helplessness. Terror. Anger. Frustration. Sadness. Anxiety. The intensity of these visceral, fear-driven responses strangled me. As I grew older and wrestled with this phobia, I felt all the more imprisoned beneath a thick layer of shame. I never seemed to encounter anybody else who appreciated that they were, like me, inching closer and closer to the end of life every morning they arose under a shining sun and every night they went to sleep. I did not know anyone I could speak to about this horrific epiphany, a constant reality lurking around every corner. It was only later, during my graduate studies, that I came to appreciate that many children are aware of their mortality at a very early age, though few feel comfortable enough to discuss it.

My early dose of existential awareness was likely rooted in a few variables. The obsessive-compulsive disorder that was diagnosed in my twenties forced my thoughts to be intrusive and ever circling in my mind like a shark zeroing in on wounded prey. In my childhood I was also exposed to the horrors of the Holocaust in Hebrew School, where we were shown sometimes gruesome footage of concentration camps as part of our education *never to forget.* I was proud of my ancestors' struggle to survive against the efforts to exterminate them and felt deeply devoted to the Jewish culture because of it. However, being raised in the narrative of postwar Judaism, the topics of death, struggle, and survival may have played a more prominent role in my upbringing than they did for my non-Jewish peers. My parents, the children of first-generation immigrants, often recounted their impoverished childhoods, and I imagined their experiences bathed in sepia tones: my father said there was a period of months where at least one relative died per week. He noted that the frequent greeting at synagogue was not "How are you?" but "Who died this week?" My mother's father was stricken with polio and imprisoned in an iron lung during the early years of my mother's childhood, his legs so withered by the disease that when he returned home, my mother could not bear to look at the braces and crutches that helped him stay upright. These stories of death, struggle, and hardship combined with a genetic propensity to fixate on the darkness in life, and so I was haunted. The thought, *I will die—someday,* followed me at home, at the movies, at friends' houses, in synagogue, in school. It was a fixture at the forefront of my brain, like a jeering taunt, and I could not escape it. I tried pushing it out with happy songs or arguing with it by beginning to explore different views of the afterlife. My family was culturally Jewish but not particularly observant, and I was not raised with a particular belief about what happens when we die. Thus, for the majority of my childhood, I tried my best to believe that death was not *the* end, though being particularly pragmatic, I could not buy into any other religion's explanation of death and the afterlife because I had no proof. I wanted so badly to believe in any description that provided comfort to so many followers, but I could not will myself to do so.

It was not until I was sixteen years old, tucked into the corner of "The Second Cup" coffee shop at the intersection of Yonge and Eglinton in Toronto, that I confessed to my best friend that I was terrified of death. We were sitting in our usual spot in chairs with spindly, winding metal legs and well-worn checkered brown cushions that were deflated and offered little support for our bony adolescent bottoms.

"Why are you so afraid of death?" she asked.

"Because that's the end. Life just stops." I responded, feeling the old familiar terror begin to rise in my throat.

"That doesn't bug me," my friend responded. "I'm OK with not living forever. I'm glad I get to die one day. What would be the point of life going on and on and on?" She sipped her mocha thoughtfully, tapping her fingers against the ceramic mug as she mulled it over. I was annoyed by her calm, peculiar acceptance of the inevitable while simultaneously feeling like I could not contain my fear any longer. I tried very hard to control the volume and tone of my voice.

"But we're dying, Stella," I retorted in tears. "We're all going to die one day. You, me, everyone. What's the point of it? I don't want to die." I felt my voice rise, despite all attempts to stay calm. "I don't want to die!"

While uncrossing my legs in an attempt to calm myself, I knocked the table with my knee, spilling a bit of coffee from my cup. I kept my eyes fixed on the napkin I used to mop up the small mess. Stella reached across the table and rested her hand on mine, radiating the warmth from her coffee cup into my palms. I saw my white-cold skin grow pink beneath her touch. "Hopefully you won't die, not for a very long time anyway. It'll be OK." She patted my hand gently, and the rhythm of her fingers against the fleshy part of my thumb felt like a comforting lullaby. I was grateful that Stella did not think I was strange for bringing the topic up, but neither did she seem much concerned about it.

I assumed that most people, like Stella, were not worried about the topic of mortality; I did not know that feeling the sensation of falling helplessly into a future marked with eventual death was not unusual for adults: "man's finitude, his dread of death and . . . the overwhelmingness of life" (Becker 1974, 63) have been explored from early psychoanalytic to humanistic to existential and gestalt perspectives. Adolescents often feel invulnerable to death, because during this stage of life they are at their physical peak, though their developing brains may ironically heighten the risk for death because of their decreased impulse control. Still, Becker argues that death can unite us instead of dividing us; if we move beyond denial and repression of the knee-jerk reaction that denies its eventuality, we can acknowledge mortality's effects on human creativity, psychology, sociology, and more. We can create meaning and purpose in our lives by facing the fragility of our existence and live more authentically and altruistically. Somehow, like Becker, I came to understand that I had to do more than just talk about death with other people. I could not swallow my fear and deny that death existed. Instead, I needed to witness it firsthand, study it, and unite with others who were as affected by it as I was. I had never experienced the death of a loved one, beyond my maternal grandmother whom

I deeply missed, but hoped that if I worked professionally with those who had, I might gain some perspective on the matter. I hoped that if death became a colleague instead of a looming threat, I would be able to live with it better. I had to give it a try. As a result, I became a social worker.

NARRATIVES AND REFLEXIVITY

The most poignant clinical experiences I have encountered to date have re-volved around how adolescents cope with the death of a brother or sister. In the early years of my career, I worked as a hospital social worker in multiple oncology units, trying to approach death and its impact on our lives with empathy. Barely out of adolescence then, I explored my self-development and often asked myself, *Who am I?* as I came to appreciate that my own identity was shaped by the foundational relationships in my life, especially with my older brother and sister. I began to understand my burgeoning identity as a healer, clinician, and an individual who still had many questions about the meaning of life. Through brief email and text message interchanges with my brother and sister, I was able to safely estab-lish myself in my new career while maintaining a connection with my home base. My brother and sister were constants in my life, serving multiple roles as confidantes and critics, each offering unapologetic advice or unbridled encouragement when needed. Like most siblings, we danced between un-limited gratitude for each other, sharing a common language of family lore, while also sometimes resenting the other or feeling that this sister or that brother was our parents' favorite. My siblings were my surrogate discipli-narians, enthusiastic cheerleaders, and voices of reality and reason. The more I encountered other sibling relationships at the bedsides of dying children, I began to wonder, *How does identity develop in adolescent sib-lings coping with grief?*

This chapter addresses this question. Reflexivity—thinking through the narratives of clients that profoundly affected my clinical and academic career while situated within the greater context of my own story—is a nec-essary part of my exploratory process. As clinicians, we seek to better understand ourselves as healers when we tell our stories: we weave and some-times stitch our stories together alongside our understanding of our clients. Across disciplines, this happens in supervision, grand rounds, and even the case notes sections of medical journals. We take care to protect the identities of the people we work with, but share our subjective experiences with them to honor their contributions to our work.

My work with the family I describe in this chapter and with others like them raised personal and professional questions about adolescent sibling bereavement. The experiences I depict in this chapter opened the door to an unfolding path of exploration in this field. Hickson notes that critical reflection can be used to deconstruct and reconstruct assumptions, and narrative inquiry depends on the ability for individuals to self-reflect (2015, 380). Reflexivity is a necessity. Furthermore, Witkin emphasizes that the process of narrative in autoethnography provides evidence of the social, cultural, and historical factors that situate an author's relationship with his or her context. He notes that an autoethnography should achieve the goal of "enriching understanding," instead of providing *the* unequivocal truth of a situation (2014, 4). Therefore, in this autoethnographic narrative, I situate myself in the context of work in end-of-life settings as a personal response to an existential fear of death. This fear arose from my individual history as a white, female, culturally Jewish social worker trying her best not to deny, but better understand, death and its influence on life itself.

In this chapter, I share my experiences working with dying youth and their siblings, in particular, my work with Jayla and Bryce.[1] I look at the last moments of Jayla's life and the impact of her death on her brother through an ecological lens. I argue that just as experimentation with substances, clothing styles, and social groups is a common hallmark of adolescence, grieving teens may "try on" a variety of identities to adapt to the loss of a brother or sister. I reflect on emerging interdisciplinary work in the social studies of childhood and use David Balk's discussion of ecological niches to assert that identity development among grieving teens evolves within a context reflective of gender, culture, family norms, resource availability, and more (2014, 31).

The catalyst of sibling loss provides teens with the opportunity to examine different aspects of themselves in their response to this life event. Because teens are developmentally exploring their own identities, the experience of bereavement may be more formative on who they subsequently become than a loss that occurs in adulthood. The more we understand how bereaved teens grieve, the better equipped we are to provide successful interventions with effects that endure as they continue to grow.

THE SETTING

I was twenty-five years old, barely out of adolescence myself, when I began working as a pediatric oncology social worker in one of the nation's foremost children's hospitals. I was assigned to the solid tumor service, working with children diagnosed with brain tumors. I worked long hours performing biopsychosocial assessments, applying for grants, and performing bedside family counseling. I was so exhausted that I often curled up beneath my desk for quick naps during late-night shifts while I waited for patients to die, every now and then grabbing the soft, starched quilts that elderly volunteers knitted for the patients and the bright-yellow pillows with inspirational Bible verses sewn onto the back.

One early Monday morning, I walked into the room of a new patient. Jayla was sixteen years old, newly diagnosed with an aggressive form of cancer. Her family lived several miles away in a different state, but her mother chose our hospital after being told that Jayla would not live to see her seventeenth birthday. Our oncology team offered her an experimental combination of particularly toxic chemotherapy infusions and aggressive radiation as her best shot at living long enough for newer, more successful protocols to be developed, and Jayla's mother was determined to buy her daughter as much time as she possibly could. As I encountered the family, I appreciated what a unique contradiction lay before me: Jayla was walking a line between childhood and adulthood, clad in footie pajamas and clutching what appeared to be a childhood blankie, but her hair was half-shaved in preparation for radiation and streaked with hot-pink highlights. Her eyes were caked with smoky black eyeliner and thick mascara, and at her side was a young man with so many chains attached to his jeans that he made music every time he shifted beside her. I was immediately taken in by the entire scene: Jayla holding the young man's hand, her mother typing furiously on a portable laptop, and her dad asleep in the corner of the room, his trucker hat pulled over his eyes. Another young man—clearly Jayla's brother—stood beside the window, squinting in the streams of sunlight bombarding the room. Jayla was the center of the universe, seated atop her bed, and her family rotated around her.

"Hi," I began. "I'm Erica, and I'm the social worker who'll be working with you while you're here at the hospital."

"Finally, someone who can help!" Jayla's mother replied. "I can't get my laptop to connect to the hospital wireless, and I really need to email my boss."

"Mom—she's not IT . . ." Jayla muttered quietly and flashed me a quick, apologetic smile. Her boyfriend rolled his eyes and looked down at his hands, picking at the black polish on his thumbnails.

"It's OK. I kind of am. I mean—social workers do a lot of things around here, and I can definitely help you with the WiFi."

Jayla laughed quietly. She was pretty and full of life—another contradiction. She did not seem like somebody who had been given less than a year to live. As I crouched over her mother's computer, I noticed a stack of Moleskine notebooks on the end of the bed.

"Do you write?" I asked Jayla.

"Yeah, sort of," she replied. "Weird poems, mostly. I draw, too, and take pictures. But these days I'm kind of in love with Whitman. For a while, I was super into Dylan Thomas, but then he got old."

"Jayla is an amazing artist!" her mother exclaimed, and the boy by the window shuffled uncomfortably. "You should take a look at her stuff sometime."

"I'd like that," I smiled, and I meant it. I felt an immediate connection to both mother and daughter, and I was perplexed by how somebody who was apparently dying could be so full of life.

As the days passed, I grew closer to Jayla and her family. Her mother was a fierce advocate for her daughter, emailing the treatment team so frequently that they were quickly overwhelmed. "She's not our only patient, you know," the neurosurgeon, exasperated, vented to me. "Can I forward you her emails, and you can deal with her?"

"Absolutely. I'll take care of all of it." I was happy to help. I admired this mother's persistence and determination.

While she was an inpatient, Jayla and her boyfriend Cole spent their time writing each other poems, tattooing words in ink pen on their arms, and strolling through the hallways like lovers in Paris. I introduced them to the poetry of Pablo Neruda: I shared with her "Sonnet XVII, one of my favorite Neruda poems celebrating the intimacy of love, something I saw between Jayla and Cole: it includes the line, *I love you as certain dark things are to be loved, in secret, between the shadow and the soul* (Neruda 1986).

On her rougher days, Jayla wore cowboy boots underneath her hospital gown. I never asked her why, but I imagined they helped her feel strong, determined, and in control. She wore those boots when she left the hospital and when she came back for her outpatient infusions. One of the last times I saw her, she was stumbling to the bathroom with the help of her mother. The tumors that were developing and multiplying from the star-shaped cells in Jayla's brain, the astrocytes, were exerting pressure on its ventricles, filling them with excess fluid and causing more and more seizures, loss of balance, an almost complete loss of vision, and slurred speech. The experimental treatment was not slowing the cancer's course. She was so thin I imagined that her bones were hollow like a bird's, and the remnants of her hair fell limply to her shoulders. The cowboy boots clicked against the laminate hospital floors, and she repeatedly slipped, but refused to take them off. Her tiny legs plunged into them like broomsticks rattling around in giant buckets. When she was ready to go home, her father pulled the car up to the hospital entrance, and I helped ease her into the back, where the seats had been folded down and covered with blankets so that Jayla could lie down for the trip. She was so weak that she could not hold herself up.

"Jayla, do you need anything?" I asked tentatively, and she quietly responded, "No." I do not know what I was expecting in that final moment with her. A cathartic monologue about impending death? A plea for me to take care of her family after she was gone? I must have been fantasizing about a far more romantic end of life for her, but she was barely strong enough to answer my question. The edges of her mouth were cracked and burned from vomit and chemo. Her head slumped between her two sharp shoulders, and her clothes appeared to melt off of her body. By that time, I had worked with many dying children. Death, ever unique in its approach, came for each of them in different ways. Some of them became septic and swollen, so much so that their features became unrecognizable on their puffy faces. Some of them became screaming, tangled balls of arms and legs, wild-eyed and frantic. And some of them withdrew into the recesses of disease-ravaged bodies, of whatever skin they had left, and disappeared. I knew that I was witnessing Jayla's final days, and I wanted to give her something, some words to cling to if she was afraid, but of course I came up short. What could I have possibly said to ease her transition, and would I be saying it more for her or for me? Instead, I said nothing more and helped her into the back of the car. Days later she transitioned to hospice and died shortly after her seventeenth birthday, surrounded by family, wearing her cowboy boots.

I did not hear from the family for a long time. Then, a few months later, an email from Jayla's mother appeared in my inbox.

Erica, I don't know what to do about Bryce. He's gone off the rails. Ever since Jayla died, he's been doing stupid, dangerous things. Drinking too much and trying to hide it, like I don't know or can't smell it on him. Smoking weed (I can smell that too). Cutting class. Yesterday I had to pick him up at the police station after he and a friend threw rocks at a car passing by and broke a rear window. I don't know what to do. I know he's hurting, but it's gotten out of hand. He won't talk to anybody and he's about to get kicked out of school. I don't recognize him anymore. I've already lost Jayla and now I think I'm losing Bryce. Can you help?

Bryce was two years younger than Jayla, and they had been close. At the hospital I rarely saw her without him there, walking a few paces behind Cole and her in the hallways. Jayla was especially fond of taking pictures of her brother. She told me, "He's always changing. Just starting to become himself. It's cool to catch it in pictures."

Jayla was not wrong; adolescence and the process of identity development have been explored by many of the "greats" in psychology who have unraveled universal pathways of human development. For Piaget and other developmental psychologists who followed, human development appeared as a sequential trajectory of stages on a continuum from birth to death. These stages are said to be epigenetic, building on each other and requiring skills from earlier stages to create the next ones. Piaget argued that adolescence marks a stage in life when teenagers begin to take the viewpoints of others and to picture themselves in situations they have never encountered; in essence, they become capable of abstract thought (Batten and Oljtenbruns 1999). Furthermore, he postulated that teens are capable of manipulating ideas and thinking relativistically, reflecting on their own life experiences to cognitively explore foreign or unfamiliar terrain, such as death (Brainerd 1978).

Erik Erikson, perhaps one of the most prolific identity theorists of the twentieth century, also applied a sequential, stage-based, epigenetic approach to development. According to Erikson, every stage of human development is marked by a crisis or conflict that must be encountered and overcome as an individual interacts with his or her environment. The result of successfully overcoming the crisis associated with each stage of life is a healthy, integrated personality. Erikson (1964) argued that adolescence begins at age twelve and is marked by the crisis of identity versus role diffusion. Previously integrated into family systems, youth now seek to become independent and are focused on integration with peer groups, instead of the family of origin. If families had successfully performed their jobs up until that point, they will remain the healthy base for teens to return to while exploring new relationships and experiences. Neuropsychological research has supported Erikson's hypothesis that adolescence is a time of social, emotional, and physiological upheaval: with neurotransmitters in flux, teens become sensation-seeking and novelty oriented, because their developing neural systems dictate impulsive behavior (Ernst, Romeo, and Andersen 2009).

The shortcoming of these psychological approaches to identity development is their reliance on the assumption that identity development progresses along a fixed trajectory for all human beings, despite most early theories being founded on theoretical assumptions with little or no clinical research to support these assertions. These stage-based approaches are based on a hierarchical, epigenetic approach to understanding how we become who we are: essentially, there are set phases on the path to becoming ourselves, and we cannot successfully be you, or me, without encountering them. Identity should be consolidated by early adulthood, and adolescents are subjects of external forces such as peer and family acting on them.

Bryce's case, however, was not so neatly black and white: I appreciated as I got to know him that *who* he was appeared highly contextual and rooted in the dynamics, resources, and audience of his current situation. The Bryce whom I encountered at his sister's bedside, who rarely met my gaze, was entirely different from Bryce with his peers, engaging in binge drinking and risk-taking behaviors. According to his mother, another Bryce appeared in the classroom, as teachers reported that he was studious, responsible, and engaged in class work appropriately. So, yes, Bryce was always changing, as his sister noted, but it appeared he demonstrated much more self-agency, determination, and autonomy depending on the variety of actors with whom he came into contact. Bryce was continually constructing and reconstructing himself to better determine who he was and who he wanted to be. As Graham (2011) might argue, Bryce was not a child developing an identity as a passive response to the adults around him, with a fixed path of identity ahead of him. Rather, he was a dynamic, engaged actor navigating various settings and experiences arising in response to the loss of his sister, but situated in a familiar context of family, peers, teachers, and helping professionals. When I interacted with him at Jayla's bedside, I noted his withdrawn, sullen, and even irritable countenance. He was not eager to share information about himself with me, especially under the watchful eyes of his parents. Conversely, he was explosive and expressive with Jayla the very next minute, poking and jostling her, doodling temporary tattoos on her arms with sparkling gel pens. His eyes crinkled with laughter when they recalled an inside joke, and sometimes he appeared downright joyful. He certainly was not seeking to define himself only by the parameters expressed by adults or peers alone: who he was and how he acted were truly dependent on context and relationship.

Children develop an identity and personality partly in a dynamic and active response to a variety of environmental factors that dictate what resources, supports, and behaviors are available to them. In this regard, childhood is defined and redefined by the actors within the group, without external prescriptions asserting an expectation of what is normal behavior (Graham 2011). One might assume, then, that the process of teen grieving would be shaped by the members of the teen's current group, within its context. For example, Bryce was white, middle class, and from a two-parent household. He had access to multiple resources to help support his quest for identity in a variety of environments, including school and his community. As a result, there were few constraints within the environment in which he was growing and grieving. In contrast, a child raised in a single-parent home in an urban environment attending a poorly performing school might not be as free to express different aspects of identity development and grief. And if that child were to engage in petty vandalism, law enforcement might not be as generous and understanding as they were with Bryce, when they called his mother to pick him up, rather than arresting him, and his family had the funds available to cover the cost of the cracked windshield.

Recent literature has reaffirmed the influence of some pre-bereavement factors, such as low socioeconomic status, temperament, and parent–child relationships, on how grieving teens cope with familial bereavement and whether they engage in increased internalizing behaviors such as depression and substance abuse (Martens et al. 2016; Stikkelbroek et al. 2015). Unsurprisingly, because Bryce's family had access to numerous support systems in his community, he was buffered and protected from engaging in coping strategies that would completely derail him, despite his dabbling in drugs, truancy, and petty vandalism. As a middle-class white kid from the suburbs, he was also privileged to come from a family that had an open communication style; by all accounts, although he was quiet, he was a resilient and friendly teenager. Unsurprisingly, after Jayla died, he began to explore questions of identity, undoubtedly asking himself, "Who am I now that my sibling is gone?" perhaps feeling a sense of incompleteness commonly experienced by teens who have lost a brother or sister (Flesner 2015).

Though I was never able to engage in clinical therapy with Bryce, I was able to observe his interactions with his family and speak with him multiple times when I visited them after Jayla's death. I was unable to attend the funeral, but the family held a few charity events to raise money for the children's hospital, and I was also invited to family birthday and holiday celebrations in the first few years after Jayla died. Within his family, personal expressiveness and exploration were encouraged, and I wondered whether the death of his sister had launched Bryce on some quest to find out who he was in the absence of Jayla. Furthermore, was Bryce at risk for becoming rooted, as a person, in the negative coping mechanisms he was using? Would he fall into habitual substance abuse, for example, or drop out of high school? Or would he become more compliant with his parents' expectations over time?

Balk uses the concept of ecological niches to understand how identity develops in adolescence, defining them as "environments in which an organism responds to survival demands and prospects for thriving." He asserts that adolescent behavior cannot develop in isolation; rather, it is woven within a fabric of multiple ecological contexts that are shaped by culture, ethnicity, gender, and more. Teens create and co-create a sense of identity within their relationships as family members, peers, and students, often presenting multiple selves across these settings. Therefore, Balk proposes, "The self an individual puts on display with close friends varies from the self on display with teachers, with a coach, with an employer, and with one's parents" (2014, 31).

Bryce seemed to search for himself in a variety of settings in the wake of his sister's death and displayed multiple identities as he coped. Sometimes, he appeared to feel an increased sense of responsibility for his parents and the other adults around him, who were overwhelmed with grief: he took on new jobs outside the home in an attempt to make money and decrease his parents' overall caregiving burden. Sometimes Bryce appeared to resent his parents' grief, standing by silently while his mother openly expressed her yearning for Jayla, helping his mother sort through and categorize the multiple photos and artwork Jayla left behind, and assisting her to post them on social media. I saw this behavior at charity events when he faded into the shadows at the silent auction table where Jayla's printed artwork and poetry were on display. Other times, Bryce seemed to feel pressure to fulfill the roles Jayla left behind—hanging out with her old friends and tattooing one of her drawings on his bicep as a memorial and reminder of her enduring presence in their lives. Still, there were plenty of occasions where Bryce wanted to remove himself from Jayla's shadow and break free of others' expectations about how he should behave as a bereaved sibling. This happened when he engaged in drinking and substance use with friends after school and on the weekend.

Depending on the context, characters, and what was happening inside of him on any given day, Bryce seemed to be trying to determine who he was by experimenting with multiple coping identities. True to the concept of Balk's ecological niche, Bryce was never the same, but always dynamically changing in response to his environment that, in turn, responded to and shaped him. I hoped that, with time, Bryce would develop resiliently, learning to create meaning from the experience of losing a sibling.

There is little evidence to support major distinctions in the grieving process undergone by boys and girls. However, societal expectations and other research point to differences in coping mechanisms for overall stressors. Research suggest that boys tend to display more externalizing or "acting-out" behaviors, but not to assume roles of hypermaturity in the way girls might. I hope to subvert this stereotypical understanding of grief by honoring the truth of Bryce's experience, which was that his grief *and* self-concept were ever changing depending on his interactions. Ideally, had I become his therapist, I would have wanted to elicit from him a self-narrative in which he could honor his relationship with Jayla and explore the impact of her death on his burgeoning sense of identity, while also honoring the other experiences that shaped him. The search for identity in Bryce involved exploring a variety of interpretations of who he was in a post-Jayla universe and included associated activities and affiliations by which he could create meaning from his loss.

CONCLUSION

Though working with dying children and their families did not initially ease my fear of death, my choice of vocation created a deeper, more nuanced understanding of the purpose of mortality and how as clinicians we can develop an appreciation for what it provides clients and families. Death can be a catalyst for growth and self-exploration among surviving loved ones, and it can inspire helping professionals to challenge how they relate to the bereaved. Through a renewed appreciation of the many factors that influence grief and identity development in adolescents, social workers can begin to view surviving siblings as multifaceted, nuanced actors within larger reciprocal systems that shape and reshape self-understandings. We should therefore seek further narrative self-analysis from bereaved teen siblings to explore whether this group is consciously seeking to define identity after the loss. Autoethnographic exploration with adolescents may help us better understand their processes in coping with the reality of death while maintaining engagement in life. We can better understand the multiple cultures, contexts, and expectations exerting an influence on each teen's lived experience by eliciting, in their voices, their perspectives and their truth of how an understanding of the self develops after the death of a brother or sister. Just as society attempts to exert pressure on how we cope with and deny death, so too does it attempt to dictate norms of bereavement (Becker 1974). I believe that openly confronting death and struggling with its reality have helped me to live life more authentically, even if that means enduring anxiety with the understanding that all of us are born dying. My hope is that, instead of sweeping death under the rug and relegating it to the unconscious, we can work with adolescents in eliciting their autoethnographic narratives to determine how, in the wake of a sibling's death, they have incorporated the eventuality and understanding of the reality of death into their own lives.

QUESTIONS FOR REFLECTION AND GROUP DISCUSSION

1. What makes you the person you are? Your relationships, your achievements, or something else? Are you a different person depending on your environment, friends, and family? How does who you are in one setting relate to the person you are in the next?

2. Do you think the death of a loved one can derail or enhance a person's search for identity?

3. Do you think that a person has to experience the death of a loved one or a major loss in life to create a deep understanding of self?

NOTE

1. This information originates from a real-life case situation. I included composite information and removed any identifying information to protect the identities of the individuals involved.

REFERENCES

Balk, David E. 2014. *Dealing with Death, Dying, and Grief during Adolescence*. New York: Routledge.

Batten, Michelle, and Kevin A. Oltjenbruns. 1999. "Adolescent Sibling Bereavement as a Catalyst for Spiritual Development: A Model for Understanding." *Death Studies* 23, no. 6: 529–546.

Becker, Ernest. 1974. *The Denial of Death*. New York: Simon & Schuster.

Brainerd, Charles J. 1978. *Piaget's Theory of Intelligence*. New Jersey: Prentice-Hall.

Erikson, Erik H. 1964. *Identity, Youth, and Crisis*. New York: Norton.

Ernst, Monique, Russel D. Romeo, and Susan L. Andersen. 2009. "Neurobiology of the Development of Motivated Behaviors in Adolescence: A Window into a Neural Systems Model." *Pharmacology, Biochemistry, and Behavior* 93, no. 3: 199–211.

Flesner, Jodi M. 2015. *Alone in our Grief: Exploring How Surviving Siblings Make Meaning After the Death of a Brother or Sister*. St. Louis: ProQuest Dissertations.

Graham, Makeeda. 2011. "Changing Paradigms and Conditions of Childhood: Implications for the Social Professions and Social Work." *British Journal of Social Work* 41, no. 8: 1532–1547.

Hickson, Helen. 2015. "Becoming a Critical Narrativist: Using Critical Reflection and Narrative Inquiry as Research Methodology." *Qualitative Social Work* 15, no. 3: 380–391.

Neruda, Pablo. 1986. *One Hundred Love Sonnets*. Austin: University of Texas Press.

Stikkelbroek, Yvonne, Denise H. Bodden, Ellen Reitz, Wilma A. Vollebergh, and Annaloes L. van Baar. 2015. "Mental Health of Adolescents Before or After the Death of a Sibling." *European Child and Adolescent Psychiatry* 25, no. 1: 49–59.

Witkin, Stanley L .2014. *Narrating Social Work Through Autoethnography*. New York: Columbia University Press.

Chapter Seventeen

CREATING SPACES FOR SAM

A Story of Healing Trauma Through Narrative Means and Art Therapy

SUSAN MCDONALD AND STEPHANIE WISE

Childhood trauma affects both the child and the entire family system. When preverbal trauma occurs before a child is adopted, the family and the child can experience underlying anxiety and distress that seem to be without explanation. Lacking full knowledge of the trauma, and with a child unable to express his or her feelings, the family is still deeply affected. Direct and indirect exposures to traumatic events adversely affect individual family members, as well as the interpersonal relationships between family members. In this chapter we narrate our collaborative work using narrative theory; we present an adoption narrative and art therapy that we used to create spaces for the story of a child and his family and their healing from early childhood traumatic experiences.

HEALING THROUGH NARRATIVE MEANS

I (Susan) had first learned of narrative therapy as a doctoral student at Fordham University and knew immediately that this was how I wanted to practice as a social worker. Letting go of the dominant pathological perspective that had made up my prior education was freeing. I traveled to Chicago to attend a narrative therapy conference led by Michael White and David Epston, the developers of narrative therapy, which provided the foundation I needed. Soon after, I joined a narrative reflecting team in Philadelphia, which to this day remains the most stimulating work I have ever done. It was during this time that I met the Smiths, Sam's family. Their concerns centered on Mr. Smith's drinking and its subsequent negative impact on Sam. I also learned the story of Sam's adoption from a Russian orphanage and Sam's experience of preverbal trauma during his time there, an area in which I was not trained. As we continued to engage in therapeutic work together, I took a "not knowing stance" with the Smiths, who were the experts in their lives. The "not knowing stance" is one of curiosity, which provides opportunities to ask questions from a position of not knowing. It creates openings for the family to move from a problem-saturated story to one of healing. Using this stance raised the possibility of including art therapy as a means for Sam to tell his story, and they eventually agreed to collaborate with an art therapist trained in trauma.

Trauma is caused by the overwhelming threat or perceived threat to life or the sense of safety in the world (Herman 1992).When childhood trauma is experienced during infancy, parents may be unaware of the severe impact of the traumatic experiences, particularly with cases of adoption. The subsequent adaptive behaviors may be viewed as disruptive, causing problems in school and/or at home. Secondary family trauma can become the impetus that persuades a family to seek therapeutic support (Figley 1988). This is Sam's story of the transformation of his preverbal traumatic experiences and its resultant impact on the healing of his entire family system.

The Smiths

We first get to know Sam through Mr. and Mrs. Smith. They initially sought treatment for marital discord after ten years of marriage. Mrs. Smith was concerned about Mr. Smith's increased drinking and his denial of having an alcohol problem. The initial assessment found that both spouses had a family history of alcoholism. The Smiths had attended the same high school and were high school sweethearts, marrying soon after graduation. They remained in their small, former coal mining town that has a strong Irish and Polish Catholic community identity. During our first meeting they told a story of strengths and resiliency and how family was extremely important to both. I was immediately struck by how in tune they were with each other as they cast agreeing side glances at each other throughout our conversation. The Smiths were very committed to their children and to each other. I was drawn to how openly they shared that from the very first date they had "each other's back." Protection was a major family theme and an important strength.

As a narrative therapist, I took a decentered approach (White 2000), listening to the Smiths' telling of their story of their relationship and what was important to each of them. Rather than taking on the role of the authority on what constitutes a healthy relationship, I used the decentered approach, which is open and nonhierarchical. The Smiths led the discussion, with an occasional "Could you tell me a little more about that?" from me. Listening to their story in this way created a collaborative context in which they were able to identify what had become problematic and share what they preferred for them as a couple. The Smiths were concerned about recent changes in Sam's behavior, his failing grades, and moodiness. We began to talk about possibilities for their preferred crisis-free family life and protecting their children, rather than setting treatment goals.

Mr. and Mrs. Smith have two children: Sam, age seven, and Tim, two years old. The Smiths had adopted Sam from Russia when he was two and a half years old. They quickly developed a close attachment with Sam, but both noted that, almost immediately, he became very attached to Mr. Smith. Mr. Smith in turn was closely bonded with both children, but had a very special bond with Sam. Sam would stand on the back of the couch waiting for his father to come home from work, and that led to Mr. Smith taking him to work as often as possible. He owned his own business, which allowed Sam and his father to spend a great deal of time together. They became inseparable.

"Abandonment and Rescue": An Entrance Story

Sam's birth story began with his birth mother's abandonment and his adoptive family's rescue. The story of Sam's adoption began with the Smith's first trip to the Russian orphanage and continued with the family's entrance story. The entrance story is a type of narrative used to establish legitimacy as to how the child joined the family and became integrated into the family. The conditions in the orphanage were dire, and the Smiths' immediate reaction was a solemn commitment to provide Sam with the best possible life after all he had endured in his first few years. This protection and commitment to Sam became a dominant family theme. Krusiewicz and Wood (2001) identify themes that adoptive families use to construct meaning in the telling of their adoption stories. One common theme is that of rescue, which was woven throughout the Smiths' description of adopting Sam and feeling that they had saved him. This theme became a dominant theme in our narrative work.

The family engaged in family therapy when Sam began to experience difficulties with peers, family relationships, and schoolwork. Four years after Sam was adopted, his father's drinking increased, and he underwent inpatient treatment for alcoholism. Sam's reaction to his father's relapse and inpatient treatment resulted in his self-regulating and self-determining behavior. Sam viewed his father's drinking as problematic, creating instability in the home.

My mother and family met with someone who asked us to talk to dad about his drinking. I didn't want to but when my dad came home, I asked him to stop drinking and he got mad at me. I ran out of the house and didn't want to come home. I didn't want to do things with my dad anymore. I would hide behind the couch when he came home. I didn't want to go to school or play baseball anymore. I was mad at my mom because she was always angry with my dad.

Details of Sam's early childhood before he was adopted were spotty. The Smiths were able to learn that his biological mother was an alcoholic, but were unable to obtain any information about his biological father. They also knew that Sam had been abandoned and found at eighteen months of age weighing only fourteen pounds. He was hospitalized for malnourishment and soon thereafter placed in an orphanage, where he remained for seven months until his adoption. The few details about Sam's beginnings left only questions. His adoptive family did know, or rather felt, that when Sam joined them, he formed a very strong bond with his father, quickly becoming a well- adjusted child for the next four years until Sam's father relapsed.

Childhood Trauma

Untreated or unresolved childhood trauma can potentially create interpersonal, academic, and emotional difficulties throughout one's life (Kaplow et al. 2006). Resolving early childhood trauma is essential if the child is to attain developmental skills, particularly the skills needed to ameliorate the effects of the trauma. There is a dearth of research articles addressing this critical topic, and the effect of trauma on children was not well acknowledged until 1987 (DSM-III-R), resulting from the seminal work of Lenore Terr and others (Adler-Nevo and Manassis 2005). Terr defines childhood trauma is as follows: "the mental result of one sudden, external blow or a series of blows, rendering the young person temporarily helpless and breaking past ordinary coping and defensive operations"; she sees all childhood traumas as externally imposed (1991, 323). She further posits that childhood trauma has four major characteristics: (1) strongly visualized or otherwise repeatedly perceived memories, (2) repetitive behaviors, (3) trauma-specific fears, and (4) changed attitudes about people, aspects of life, and the future. Recognizable symptoms include "thought suppression, sleep problems, exaggerated startle responses, developmental regressions, fears of the mundane, deliberate avoidances, panic, irritability, and hypervigilance" (Terr 2003, 324). These symptoms often continue throughout the child's life and into adulthood.

NARRATIVE FAMILY THERAPY

The use of family therapy in the treatment of traumatic events developed with the work of the family sociologist Reuben Hill, who studied the transmission of traumatic material from one family member to another and wrote about his findings in his classic 1949 book, *Families Under Stress*. Hill (1949, 1958) developed the ABC→X model to describe how families adapt to the separation and reconnection with family members who went to war and returned to the family system. McCubbin and Patterson (1983) expanded Hill's ABC→X Model by creating the double ABC→X model. The double ABC→X model looks at the family's adaption (positive adaptation or maladaptation) and perception of a crisis, taking into consideration family resources, how the family perceives the event, and how the family responds and makes meaning of the experience or the crisis: the x factor (Kropf and Greene 2001; Patterson and Garwick 1998; figure 17.1).

I first met the Smiths when Mr. Smith's drinking became problematic and the family's stress became increasingly difficult to manage. Sam's stress eventually led to failing grades, problems with peers, and isolating himself from Mr. Smith. This crisis motivated them to call me. Mrs. Smith told me

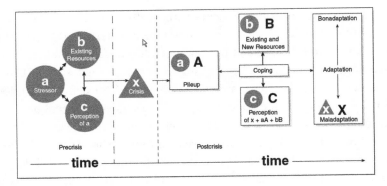

FIGURE 17.1 The double ABC→X model. *Source*: McCubbin and Patterson (1983).

that she did not "rescue" Sam from the orphanage only to have him experience an unstable family life. She felt committed to providing Sam the best life possible, and her husband's drinking was creating family instability. Mr. Smith, although agreeing that Sam's behavior was a concern, was reluctant to talk about his drinking.

In the beginning of our first session, I asked them to tell me the story of how they met. Mr. and Mrs. Smith enjoyed sharing this story, and we immediately felt at ease with each other. Families tell their stories as a means of communicating beliefs, values, and important life lessons of the family system (Fiese and Wamboldt 2003). Listening to and guiding the Smiths as they told their story helped me understand the strengths that they identified. When I asked what helped them to move through tough times, they were able to share how they come from the same place, they see things the same, and they want the same things in life.

Our family sessions worked in tandem with an interventionist who after several tries, finally convinced Mr. Smith to undergo inpatient treatment. The interventionist, a professionally certified drug and alcohol therapist, met with the family several times. Sam, however, was deeply affected by his father's initial rejection of the family's intervention. Sam and I had a good rapport, and he expressed to me his frustration with both parents. His anger with his mom increased as she tried to enforce family rules, and worrying about his dad was stressful. Negotiating quickly became one of my most-used skills. I also knew I had to connect the Smiths with resources to assist them in managing the stressors that led to the crisis (Mr. Smith's relapse), with the understanding that its impact would be different for each individual family member. Mrs. Smith seemed most concerned with not providing Sam with a stable family. Sam's perception of his father's relapse was one of being re-traumatized.

Working with the family and the art therapist evoked in me a sense of sincere care and concern with everyone committed to the same outcome for Sam. Mrs. Smith's commitment to providing Sam with the best possible life was the starting point for many of our sessions. This led to talking about possibilities for a crisis-free family life. As the sessions progressed the family began to enjoy spending time with each other, and as treatment was concluding, they made a family decision to buy a puppy. Shared inside family jokes came easily in our sessions, and there was a sense of ease. I felt that the family was once again in tune with each other. The feeling of mutual protection came back into the life of this family, and a re-storying of the Smiths began to be shared in our sessions. As we neared the end of our sessions, Sam told me:

I started Alateen and have made friends! I am planning on joining the swim team too! I am doing a lot of things with my dad like playing video games.

Narrative Method

People create stories as a means both to understand their experiences and to communicate that understanding. Storytelling is how humans create meaning of their lives; the understanding of these experiences forms one's belief systems about the self and others (Goldenberg and Goldenberg 2000; Williams and Kurtz 2003). Yet the process of creating meanings of our lives through stories, which in turn shape our lives, is itself shaped by the context. Narratives influence how we make meaning of our past, how we experience the present, and how we think about our future (Jenmorri 2006; Polkinghorne 1988). Creating meaning from a family crisis provides family members with an empowering means to bring balance and efficacy into their lives.

When families begin therapy, they begin by telling their story: it is in the storytelling that families apply meaning to their experiences (Epston 2000). They enter therapy when their problem-saturated stories (life story) no longer work for them (White and Epston 1990). Narrative family therapists view the family as the experts in their lives. David Epston, one of the co-founders of narrative therapy, suggests that therapists engage in ethnographic imagination, inquiring as to how "they go about living their lives" (2000, 181). They begin therapy by separating families from the problem: the problem is "the problem" and not the person (Williams and Kurtz 2003). The initial story Sam and his family told to themselves about themselves was the adoption story and Sam's immediate attachment to his dad. This strong bond between them became strained when Sam's dad relapsed. Sam became retraumatized and did not know how to manage the conflicting feelings he was experiencing. They re-story themselves with the prevailing theme of protection and rescue as a means of healing from trauma.

ART THERAPY WITH SAM

As the art therapist for Sam's therapy, I (Stephanie) met with him three times over a period of six weeks. Sam was seven years old, and because of his previous experiences in therapy, he understood he was there to try to explore some of the feelings and issues that had been bothering him. He had not experienced art therapy before, but he articulated that he loved to draw and was very willing to make art with me present.

Sam was a very engaging child. Clearly above average in his capacity to verbalize, he also exuded a kind of charm not typical for his young age. In session, Sam appeared to enjoy adult conversation and the individual attention paid by the therapist. From the outset, it seemed he was going to be able to enjoy and benefit from art therapy.

Sam started right off in the first session telling me about a deer he had seen recently that had been hit and killed by a car on the country road near where he lived. Since this was on his mind, I asked him if he thought he might want to make a drawing about it. Sam was not shy about picking up the markers and creating an image of a deer that was very much alive, whom he named "Bambi." The story of Bambi is about a young fawn whose mother is shot and killed in front of him. How Bambi survives this loss, the lack of food as he wanders the forest, his inexperience, helplessness, and the need to forge relationships to survive create the emotional tension of the story. In the end, Bambi goes on to thrive and ultimately sire his own children that he watches from a great distance to be certain they are protected from the "men with guns."

FIGURE 17.2 Sam's drawing of what stress is to him.

Sam used the word "stress" when describing how he felt a lot of the time. I asked him what he thought was causing this. He could not really pinpoint where the feelings were coming from, but he told me that he hated feeling that way. I asked Sam if he could make marks on the paper that would show us what "stress" looked like to him (figure 17.2). Sam took two markers and, holding them together, began to draw a spiral moving from the outside inward. The drawing was kinetic in nature: it was created through energetic motion. Unlike the symbolic story image previously made of the deer, this expressive image reflected the turmoil of his inner state of mind with no narrative attached to it.

The final drawing of the first session was a free drawing. I invited Sam to create any image that he wished. Sam took his time before taking a black oil pastel and carefully making what he later titled "Broken House" (figure 17.3). When he was finished, he spontaneously began to speak about this house. He did not know where it was located, but was certain it was not his current home. He said it made him very sad to think about it, because it felt dark, threatening, lonely, and from far away.

FIGURE 17.3 Sam's drawing of "Broken House."

We concluded the session with a conversation about continuing to work together for a few more times. Sam was very enthusiastic about coming back. He indicated he had enjoyed sharing with me. I told him I also enjoyed our time together and that I looked forward to seeing him again. I gave Sam a sketch pad and some markers so he could draw on his own in the waiting room while I was to meet with his parents and the primary family therapist.

Before that meeting, I studied Sam's last drawing. Having seen many drawings done by children who have experienced trauma and having witnessed and heard what he said about his own art, my sense was I was looking at a diagrammatic image, which was expressing a core stressor for him. He could not articulate a narrative about the image, but on a sensorial level, it depicted a great deal of pain. My inclination was to assume that in some way, this image was a part of Sam's past, which was outside the realm of his explicit memory. Old trauma seemed to be newly present.

When the parents and primary therapist convened in the room, I shared the morning's experience with them. I took them through the drawings and when we got to "Broken House," Mrs. Smith gasped. She had never seen such an image from her young son. I asked her if she saw something familiar or recognizable in the image. Mrs. Smith stared intently at the drawing, and she teared up. She said, "This really looks a lot like the orphanage in Russia where we got Sam." Mrs. and Mr. Smith were both quite startled by this revelation. Mrs. Smith went on to say that she had "no idea he could remember that place."

This drawing moved the parents deeply. They had believed that, since Sam was so young when he was adopted, he would have very few memories of his early life. As a trauma specialist, it was important for me to help them understand the role of implicit memory as a container for traumatic material. It was virtually certain that Sam could not recollect specific memories about his early life, but yet these traumatic memories were stored on a sensorial level. Somehow, when Sam and I began to explore his understanding of his own "stress," the container opened enough to let this image come forth.

Sam came to his second session eager to talk. He told me he had something to share, but he did not want to get into trouble. I explained to him that as long as he was not in danger or going to put someone else in danger, I felt confident that we could work out whatever he was concerned about. With that, Sam informed me that he does not sleep. He told me that he could not sleep—that sometimes he pretends to sleep so his parents will think he is, but that he is up for hours and hours all night. Sam's father had told him not to turn on the TV in his room, so he would wait until his parents were asleep and then turn it on. He felt sneaky doing this. Sam also wanted a light on in his room, but his father and mother did not think he should need to have it on at his age. He shared that he wandered around the house at night, bypassing the motion sensor alarms and sometimes bringing food back to his bedroom. Sam would hide this food in the clothing drawers. I asked him why he did that and he told me he was "saving it in case I need it." Sam indicated that most of the time he stared at the wall in the dark of his room for hours trying to hypnotize himself, failing to do so, and then getting more and more upset. Sam told me that not sleeping was his biggest stress.

There was such deep suffering in Sam's description of his nightly torment. I asked him how he would feel about making a drawing about what he had shared. Sam said he would prefer to make a list so I could really

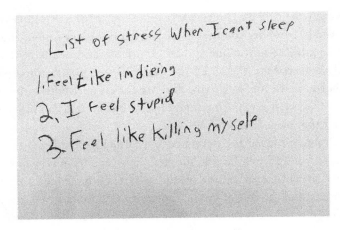

FIGURE 17.4 Sam's "List of Stress When I Cannot Sleep."

understand what he was feeling. The list (figure 17.4), was called, "The List of Stress When I Cannot Sleep." It was heartbreaking to read what he wrote: "1. Feel Like im dieing" (sic). 2. I feel stupid, 3. Feel like Killing myself."

The lengths that Sam had unconsciously gone to try to take care of himself were remarkable. He had even tried to spare his parents from his suffering. There was no doubt in my mind that his intense hypervigilance and inability to sleep were directly connected to his earliest preverbal abandonment. As mentioned, Sam had been "found" at age eighteen months weighing only fourteen pounds. He had been severely neglected and was near death. On every level, he must have felt then like he was dying. Not being able to sleep aroused tremendous self-punishing feelings in him: he "felt stupid." His inability to self-sooth adequately left him with feelings of failure, which aroused such anger at himself—displaced anger at the elusive original parents who had so recklessly abandoned him—that he felt like "killing himself," rather than them. Sam was so ingenious that he even stole food from his own kitchen, hiding it away for the coming time when it might be necessary to stave off starvation.

Not wanting to end the session with much heaviness in his heart, I encouraged Sam to explore a bit about what he would like the "stress" to know about him. He made a simple bubble drawing, much like the type found for the thoughts and words of a comic strip character. Sam wrote, "I am not a Loser" (figure 17.5). He then told me all the ways he feels he is a win-

FIGURE 17.5 Sam's "I'm not a Loser" drawing.

ner! He said he was a good baseball player, a very good student, a good son, kind to people, and funny; the list went on. We agreed that these were qualities that could be a mighty force against his "stress."

Again, Sam went to the waiting room while I shared with the parents and primary therapist how the session went. In this session, the father was visibly shaken. He had no idea what Sam had been going through at night. The father was very compassionate and understood that there might need to be some shifts in response to Sam's needs at this point. We agreed that it should be all right for Sam to keep the TV on low if he needed to watch it. He was also going to be allowed to have the light on if he wished, without any comments about being "too old" for that. The primary therapist and I explained to the parents that Sam could not just "outgrow" or "will away" these defensive strategies. I explained that, to facilitate recovery from trauma, avoiding triggers is paramount. Sam's mother had been aware of the food hoarding, and it had troubled her deeply. Now she understood his fears, and she indicated she was going to find snacks that he could keep in his bedroom all the time.

In our final session, Sam told me that his father was upset with him because they had planned to go to a haunted house weekend, but Sam was too frightened participate. This disappointment left his father annoyed and frustrated. It reinforced feelings of failure in Sam.

Sam made a drawing of a huge volcano in between a giant dinosaur and a tiny little person (figure 17.6). The volcano is erupting, threatening both

FIGURE 17.6 Sam's drawing reflecting scary play with his father.

figures. Feelings can become "volcanic," and so it appeared to me that there were volatile emotions between father and son. As the session went on, Sam shared that his father loves to try to scare him as part of their playing together. Sometimes that is fun, but sometimes it is not. It appeared to be a source of mutual bonding for them, so according to Sam, he has endured the scary behaviors for a lot longer than he has wanted to. The weekend was the culmination of this pattern. For Sam, going near the haunted house was too stressful, and it was disappointing that his father left him in a terrible bind.

I asked Sam if it would be all right for me to discuss this with his father. He appeared relieved and said he wanted me to do that. Thus, we concluded our session, and once again, the adults met for conversation.

Sam's father and mother were surprised to learn that Sam had been merely tolerating the scary playful behaviors of the father. I had learned that sometimes Mr. Smith would hide in Sam's closet and pop out to play a prank on him. This really did scare Sam, but he was reluctant to tell his father that. Again, we went over the concept of triggering and that we should try to avoid it if possible.

When it came to the haunted house, both parents were uncertain why he had resisted so much, given that he had initially said he wanted to go. The primary therapist and I explained that it is not unusual for children to think they want to do something and then change their minds. Adults do that as well. But in this case, Sam's terror of the haunted house may have been triggered on an unconscious level. A dark house with "scary" elements might have been too close to his terrifying, implicit sensorial memories: he just could not tolerate the exposure to it.

Throughout these sessions, it was very clear that this family was loving and supportive. With their new understanding, the parents were willing to adjust the demands they made on their son. And through creating and talking about the art, Sam was better able to express his feelings, which he had hidden from those who loved and cared most about him.

Art Therapy and Trauma Work

Art therapy when doing therapeutic work with children is compelling, using art to provide a space for children to have a voice. It is such a powerful tool because young children generally do not have access to verbal language to work through difficult traumatic material. Memories are often nonverbal and stored through images, which are more readily accessed through art and art making. Children employ imagination naturally in both play and learning. Art permits a safe distancing from traumatic material and is naturally appealing to children.

The art therapist is in the unique position of "giving support on a pre-verbal, essentially symbolic level" (Kramer 2006, 54). Art therapists serve as witnesses to the machinations of the client's inner world expressed through the creation of the art product. The process and the final product represent the internal experience. The art therapist observes the client's affect, behavior, and choices made while in the act of creating. Understanding the interplay between process and product is experienced as support by the client as the art image develops dynamically: "The art therapist is trained to pick up communications of great sensitivity through the process of image making, and more importantly, waiting with holding and containing the anxiety and uncertainty of the child struggling with their unfolding of their deepest difficulties" (Case and Dalley 1990 157).

Art therapist, educator, and writer Shaun McNiff states, "Art heals by activating the medicines of the imagination" (2004, 221). Nowhere is this concept truer than in the visual expression of traumatic material. The child who externalizes terrifying internal images often finds great relief in being able to leave the horror behind in the art room. This can occur without verbally deconstructing the exact meaning of the image.

It is important not to trigger or overwhelm the child. Children often need to "leave the images as images" at an unconscious symbolic level, preferring to leave them behind with the art therapist: the facilitator of the process, witness of traumatic material, and guardian of the product. In cases of preverbal trauma, the "unspeakable" event likely remains elusive and outside the realm of discussion. However, this does not mean that healing has not occurred. In trauma, the capacity for healthy imagination can be deeply compromised and the reengagement of imagination in creative expression becomes a healing force.

Finally, although it may not always be possible or indicated, there may be value in sharing the art work of the traumatized child with supportive parents. In those cases, the deeper understanding and compassion gained by parents after seeing their child's art work can have a positive impact on their relationship to the child. Parents may question their assumptions about the child, and family dynamics may shift for the better. Art can play an enormous role in forging meaningful reconnection within the family.

In this case, therapy began with a family session with both the family therapist and art therapist, during which there was an initial assessment and the art therapist explained the course of treatment. The parents then met with the family therapist while Sam met with the art therapist. At the end of each art session, both therapists met with the Smiths to discuss treatment outcomes and provide continued support to the family. The art therapist provided a supportive context in which to share Sam's art with his parents (with Sam's consent) and engaged the strengths of Sam and his parents. The family therapist and the art therapist provided the parents a safe and empathetic context in which to make meaning of the family trauma, Sam's trauma, and the stressors that affected the family. The parents used this supportive therapeutic context to tell their stories, the therapists provided validation, and the trauma became contained in the narrative. The therapists encouraged Sam and his parents to recognize their strengths and power to engage in self- healing.

CONCLUSION

Creating spaces for Sam's and his family's trauma provided an opportunity for transformation and healing from past trauma stories (White 2000). Being curious, collaborative, and respectful way provided the space for raising questions that generated experiences. The storytelling provided openings for alternate stories to be told and witnessed. Both narrative therapy and art therapy enabled Sam to voice the interpretations of his experiences. Taking a "not knowing stance" created a collaborative process in which the family efficacy led to the parents agreeing for our work to include an art therapist. We were all equally vested in Sam's healing from his early trauma. The prevalent family theme of protection laid the foundation for our work. The postmodern approach's perspective that there is no single objective reality gave space for each family member to tell the story of his or her reality. The transformative process of this family's healing emerged in the safe and open spaces created by the family and art therapist. The collaboration of narrative therapy and art therapy provided Sam and his family a means to re-story their experience.

QUESTIONS FOR REFLECTION AND GROUP DISCUSSION

1. How did the art therapist and the narrative family therapist create spaces for the trauma stories to be told?
2. What was meant by the statement that the trauma became contained in the narrative?
3. In what ways is the McCubbin and Patterson's Double ABC->X model useful in assessing how families experience nonadaptation or maladapation?

REFERENCES

Adler-Nevo, Gili, and Katharina Manassis. 2005. "Psychosocial Treatment of Pediatric Posttraumatic Stress Disorder: The Neglected Field of Single-Incident Trauma." *Depression and Anxiety* 22:177–189.

Case, Caroline, and Tessa Dalley. 1990. *Handbook of Art Therapy*. New York: Routledge.

Epston, David. 2000. "Anthropology, Archives, Co-Research and Narrative Therapy." In *Family Therapy*, ed. David Denborough, 177–182. Adelaide, Australia: Dulwich Centre Publications.

Fiese, Barbara, and Frederick Wamboldt. 2003. "Coherent Accounts of Coping with a Chronic Illness: Convergences and Divergences in Family Measurement Using a Narrative Analysis." *Family Process* 42, no. 4: 439–451.

Figley, Charles. 1988. "Treating Traumatic Stress in Family Therapy." *Journal of Traumatic Stress* 1, no. 1, 3–16.

Goldenberg, Irene, and Herbert Goldenberg. 2000. *Family Therapy: An Overview*, 5th ed. Belmont, CA: Brooks/Cole.

Herman, Judith. 1992. *The Aftermath of Violence: From Domestic Abuse to Political Terror*. New York: Basic Books.

Hill, Reuben. 1949. *Families Under Stress*. New York: Harper & Row.

——. 1958. "Generic Features of Families under Stress." *Families in Society: The Journal of Contemporary Social Service* 39, nos. 2–3: 139–150.

Jenmorri, Katrina. 2006. "Of Rainbows and Tears: Exploring Hope and Despair in Trauma Therapy." *Child & Youth Forum* 35, no. 1: 41–55.

Kaplow, Julie, Glenn Saxe, Frank Putnam, Robert Pynoos, and Alicia Lieberman. 2006. "The Long-Term Consequences of Early Childhood Trauma: A Case Study and Discussion." *Psychiatry: Interpersonal and Biological Processes* 69: 362–375.

Kramer, Edith. 2006. *Art as Therapy: Collected Papers,* edited by Lani Gerity. London: Jessica Kingsley Publishers.

Kropf, Nancy, and Roberta Greene. 2001. "People with Developmental Disabilities." In *Resiliency,* ed. Roberta R. Greene, 293–319. Washington, DC: NASW Press.

Krusiewicz, Erin, and Julia T. Wood. 2001. "'He Was Our Child from the Moment We Walked in That Room': Entrance Stories of Adoptive Parents." *Journal of Social and Personal Relationships* 18, no. 6: 785–803.

McCubbin, Hamilton, and Joan Patterson. 1983. "The Family Stress Process: The Double ABCX Model of Family Adjustment and Adaptation." http://www.hbftpartner ship.com/documents/uploadResources/FamilyStressProcess-McCubbin1983.pdf.

McNiff, Shaun. 2004. *Art Heals: How Creativity Cures the Soul.* Boston: Shambhala.

Patterson, Joan M., and Anne W. Garwick. 1998. *Theoretical Linkages: Family Meanings and Sense of Coherence.* Thousand Oaks, CA: Sage Publishing.

Polkinghorne, Donald. 1988. *Narrative Knowing and the Human Services.* Albany: State University of New York Press.

Terr, Lenore C. 1991. "Childhood Traumas: An Outline and Overview." *The American Journal of Psychiatry,* 48(1), 10–20.

——. 2003. Childhood Traumas: An Outline and Overview. https://doi.org/10.1176 /foc1.3.322.White, Michael. 2000. *Reflections on Narrative Practice: Essays and Interviews.* Adelaide, Australia: Dulwich Centre Publications.

White, Michael, and Epston, David. 1990. *Narrative Means to Therapeutic Ends.* New York: W.W. Norton & Company.

Williams, Nancy, R. and Kurtz, P. David. 2003. "Narrative Family Interventions." In *Working with Families,* ed. Alice C. Kilpatrick and Thomas P. Holland, 174–193. New York: Pearson Education.

Chapter Eighteen

STORIES OF YOUTH AND FAMILY NAVIGATING A NEW FRONTIER OF SOCIAL MEDIA

REBECCA G. JUDD AND BENJAMIN T. MAY

Today, social media is not only a constant presence in the lives of children and adolescents but it is also an ever-changing entity. For adolescents, social media can be a space to shape identity, make connections, and find voice. For parents, who can so often be left behind by the rapid changes on this platform, it can be a source of deep fears of the unknown. As family clinicians, we are privy to the tensions, worries, and conflicts that arise between youth and their families about the use of social media. Social workers are well positioned to mitigate these fears by empowering family members.

Through the stories of Rachel and Amber we share in this chapter, we contextualize the use of social media: how adolescents negotiate and interpret their identities in this space and how they negotiate relationships in and out of its parameters. We discuss our clinical work with their families and outline the use of positive safety support systems as a framework for restoring trust and a new way of engaging youth and their parents around the use of social media. Fear of the unknown, in this case advances in technology, can present challenges in personal and interpersonal growth. Our work with youth and their families, however, also highlights that understanding social media spaces can facilitate positive change as families negotiate this new frontier.

ADOLESCENTS AND SOCIAL MEDIA

Often viewed by adults as a time of unrestrained biological motivation, rebelliousness, and testing value limits, adolescence is also a time of intellectual growth. During this stage youth develop a personal sense of identity, values, and psychological independence from parental figures. Traditionally, adults try to make sense of adolescence, but often forget their own experiences. In addition, contemporary adults have no history to draw on in reference to the internet, the proliferation of social media sites, and the technology that has become an extension of their children's experiences; this lack of knowledge fuels parents' fear of the unknown and need to protect their child. Yet, all humans strive to discover varying skills that give us purpose and motivation.

The contemporary westernized adolescent lifestyle is widely carried out online through chatting, texting, friending, blogging, tweeting, and posting as an extension of physical experiences. Approximately, 92 percent of teens go online daily, of whom 24 percent say they go online almost constantly, with nearly three-quarters of those teens having access to smartphones (Lenhart 2015). The question becomes, not if, but when and how, to address the use of social media with both adolescents and the adults around them.

We know all youth have different experiences on social media platforms. However, there are commonalities. Livingstone (2008) notes that older teens use social media to create a highly ornate identity that is a simple link to peers and should be considered a positive adaptation to modern society. Academic research has focused on the potential positive and negative outcomes of current technologies, especially with regard to social media technologies (SMTs). Of particular interest are social networking sites (SNS), which are defined as "websites which make it possible to form online communities and share user created content" (Kim and Lee 2010, 216). Some studies have found that there are positive psychological outcomes from engaging in social networking on various SNS (Burke, Marlow, and Lento 2010; Ellison, Steinfield, and Lampe 2011; Kim and Lee 2011, 6).

As clinical social workers we grapple with these spaces of modern-day adolescence. Barth (2015) points to the challenges that social workers and other helping professionals encounter in learning about and understanding new forms of communication, human interactions within the cyber-world, and the impact of social media. How do we keep up with the ever-changing platform of social media spaces?

We use a narrative approach that allows us not only to reflect on our practice but also to center on the complexities of our young client's experiences. Storytelling provides a meaningful way to give a different voice to the adolescent who is immersed in a technological space of interactions characterized by emojis, 140-character statements, and abbreviated collo-quialisms unique to social media. We found that social media spaces shift the ways adolescents interact and develop their identity and relationships. We also saw that the outcomes of these interactions were more positive when parents better understood the adolescent's motivation. Once parents came to appreciate that social media could give voice to their children and empower their self-identity, they were able to refocus on their needs and well-being. Moreover, they were able to negotiate boundaries based on an understanding of positive social media use.

Rachel's and Amber's cases can help us understand how youth assimilate into the world of social media, navigating its many paths, and how this new frontier is altering—or not altering—interactional relationships during a complex developmental period in their lives. Making sense of youth experiences can facilitate the development, implementation, and evaluation of educational and therapeutic approaches needed to assist adolescents and young adults. For example, creating a better understanding of social media's positive attributes during family communication sessions lowers the parents' fear of social media and allows them to better understand why the adolescent is constantly motivated to post "all of their situations" online. The goal of family educational sessions is for everyone involved gain a deeper understanding of both sides of every family situation. Following the social work discipline's tenets of practice, this approach would be described as focusing on the *here and now* of adolescent experiences, especially as new scholarship argues that traditional research has focused on children's *becoming*, rather than who they are now and how they experience the world in the present (James, Jenks, and Prout 1998; McNamee, 2016).

While social media has changed the way human relationships develop, many aspects of our interactions remain the same. In her study, boyd (2014) found adolescent development and desires to be relatively unchanged from those of earlier generations. Adolescents today still try to distinguish them-selves from other age groups through fashion, still choose skills to make them powerful, and decide how they spend their money. These motivational factors are part of the stimulus for using social media. However, we found that uneducated users (usually parents), who do not understand the reasons behind adolescent social media use, describe online adolescent interaction as the use of "an unknown expanse with endless borders and supersonic speed at which changes occurs."

A vital developmental task of adolescence is development of a personal sense of identity. Experiencing a sense of autonomy and learning to make choices in one's actions are critical for human growth and optimal func-tioning, as confirmed by studies of these life domains (Deci and Ryan 2000; Vallerand 1997). Clinical social workers have found that adolescents need to be understood throughout the process of change during the teenage years. We have seen this in our practice, and it is evident in the experiences of Rachel and Amber as they struggled for self-expression. Research show, moreover, that self-determined functioning should be promoted within a supportive, noncoercive family environment. These findings confirm the idea that volitional performance—the ability to separate from parents dur-ing times of growth and choice—does not have to worsen the quality of the parent–child relationship (Grolnick 2003; Soenens and Vansteenkiste 2005). Treatment of adolescents should support the positive use of social media to openly express self-determining factors in a safe supportive, non-coercive environment. The tools of self-expression may have changed along with technology, but the motivation to achieve their individual needs have not diminished in today's adolescents.

Psychological independence from parents remains a primary develop-mental task in this space. The transition between childhood and adulthood and the need for independence and individuality, however, often conflict with the need to build a safe, secure support system. As many parents learn the nuances of social media they often must rely on their children to in-struct them in its use, introducing a conundrum for the adolescent—who is often proficient in the use of technology, but whose parents are not and who are unable to provide safety, security, and support as their children ex-plore these constantly changing platforms of interaction. Rachel's experi-ence of this disconnect is evident as she shares:

My mother worries that I am online too much and I don't spend enough time on my school work or hang out with my friends. She told me that being online so much is rotting my brain.

Laughing, Rachel continues,

A couple of hours after she chewed me out about being on online all the time, she asks me to help her create a web page so she can display her art work online. She makes me go to counseling because of what she thinks is happening, but then wants help using the internet. It's okay for her, but not for me. But she couldn't do it without me.

Contemporary forms of communication, including cell phones, SKYPE, FaceTime, online apps, and Instagram, allow teens more independence while also maintaining a strong connection to the eyes and ears of parents (Barth 2015) through mechanisms of parental controls, GPS systems, and monitoring of posts—but only if the teens are connected to their parents through these platforms. Rachel and Amber came to our attention for different reasons. However, both had parents who sought help from a licensed clinical social worker (LCSW). Their social media use evoked fear in their parents, and establishing boundaries and building a positive support system were the goals of therapy.

PARENTAL FEARS

Rachel is a gregarious, charming, and self-confident fourteen-year-old growing up in a southern urban town, who has a close friendship with three girls she has known since childhood. Rachel's parents, both professionals, describe the friendship as inseparable throughout their elementary and middle school years, stating, "It seemed every weekend the girls were spending the night together at one of their homes." All four took gymnastics, softball, and track together; they shared sicknesses, happy and sad events, and at times even conflict. But in the summer before entering high school, her mother described Rachel as becoming moody, isolative, and defensive when questioned about her friends and activities. Rachel's parents report her behavior continued to become emotionally distressing in the first months of high school, and her mother's concern and frustration led to Rachel entering therapy where she was assessed by a clinical social worker recommended by her school. During the intake assessment, Rachel was initially in denial about the behavioral changes reported by her parents and became defensive, reluctant, and then tearful as she explained, "My three so-called best friends joined with other girls new to our class and created a twitter club and didn't include me."

Rachel went on to describe tweets sent "to the whole school" by her friends and the new girls as "mean and saying things about me that are not true." Rachel's mother, concerned about the change in her temperament and increased isolation as she enters her first year of high school, explained observing Rachel "being obsessed" with her smartphone and spending more time on social media, resulting in her spending less and less time with her friends outside of school.

As part of an English assignment last school year, Rachel created a blog and continued to develop it over the summer. She spent many hours on her computer, skipping the usual summer activities she normally enjoyed with her best friends. Rachel's interest in her blog morphed into what she described as her way to

understand me and the world around me. I can express my ideas and feelings creatively, in kind of a disconnected way. You know, I have more time to think about what I want to say before I say it. It's different than when we are sitting around the table at lunch where everyone is talking at once and you can't really stop and think about what you are going to say.

In writing the blog, Rachel did not seem interested in community building or establishing an audience, but found it to be a creative way to express her thoughts and feelings to "have a voice." Rachel's mother's concern may be attributed to her failure to realize that online interactions have become a primary way to engage in a highly structured lifestyle that affords little free time in a real-world environment. Parents often identify new technological behaviors they do not understand as "bad." As a result, they sometimes focus on teaching skills they believe to be beneficial to academic success such as being a *bookworm*, but quickly identify behaviors such as spending hours surfing the web and jumping from website to website as negative (boyd 2014).

While, Rachel saw her online blog as a way to process and sort through her thoughts and feelings in a stress-free social environment, the reality of public sharing can have unforeseen consequences, for which Rachel was unprepared. Angrily, Rachel stated,

> My blog was the best of me, I was really being creative and opening up my feelings. I gave my three best friends permission to see what I had written. I hadn't published any of my posts before and I wanted them to see my work. Next thing I knew they posted my personal stuff on their Facebook in a public forum.

Rachel was devastated, angry, and embarrassed. She had not created her blog to indiscriminately share information with a wide audience and had intentionally set the controls to "not public" so only those who received an invitation could view her postings. Berriman and Thomas (2015) describe this as a form of cultural entrepreneurship, where audience and reputation are carefully built. However, what cannot be managed is information that is passed through the cybernetwork when a friend violates implied privacy by sharing it outside of the group. This can have important ramifications for teens' personal and interpersonal worlds (Shapiro, Spies, and Margolin 2014) and only social norms and social ties can provide some protection.

During adolescence, young people work on establishing positive separation from parents and developing a sense of who they are in the world (Barth 2015). Rachel used her blog to establish a voice independent from that of her parents, but these actions resulted in negative feedback. Rachel was encouraged during family therapy to discuss blog-related activities with her mother along with the therapy she has learned during the process. Furthermore, Rachel was encouraged by her social worker to help her mother better understand the social media spaces, so that her mother could help her make good choices in how she uses this space. This new understanding between the two helped lessened the point of contention and brought them closer in the relationship. We feel that a useful clinical intervention here is one that allows Rachel the opportunity to express herself through her blog, to consider what she shares, and to assist her in processing negative comebacks from friends or others without engaging in impulsive or negative responses.

In helping Rachel recognize and understand her behavioral rehearsal, in therapy we assisted her in shaping the content which she chooses to post in her blog or other social media venue. Behavioral rehearsals are considered positive and are indicative of Facebook use, where adolescents adapt their profiles, read those of their friends, engage in comparison, and then further adapt their profiles to fit in with the norms of the community (boyd 2014; Cingel and Krcmar 2014). An adaptive skill for many adolescents is to view these types of interactions as *drama*. Marwick and boyd (2014) recommend using the term "drama" rather than gossip, bullying, or interactions that could be emotionally devastating or even fun, which enables teens to disengage from adult models of peer aggression, protect themselves from the social and psychological harm involved, and participate in their own narratives. Rachael was motivated to be creative, and we were able to sanction her social media use instead of stifling her imagination and drive. When social media is not demonized, it becomes an angel of creation. Empowerment of the entire family occurred during treatment. That empowerment, creative thought, and using Rachel's strengths were the focus of the positive outcomes achieved.

AMBER: SOCIETAL FEARS

Amber is a fourteen-year-old Hispanic girl and one of five children; when asked to describe herself, she responded, "I guess I am shy, and don't feel comfortable in groups, and I'm an okay student." She lives with her parents in a lower-middle-class neighborhood. Her mom is a homemaker, and her dad is a supervisor at a manufacturing plant. Amber is in her first year of high school, but has missed several days and is struggling academically. Amber's teacher grew concerned about her mental well-being after overhearing a conversation between other students about controversial material Amber posted on her Facebook wall and referred her to an afterschool private practice therapist. Although the Catholic school Amber attends is somewhat progressive, it is not open to discussions of alternative sexual orientation. Amber complained, "Now my parents troll my Facebook postings and are obsessed with knowing everything I post and everyone I chat with. It really makes me mad!" Amber perceived her parents to be controlling her social media use, which caused a disconnect between them. The goals of the first family session were to identify this issue and for the social worker to assist in reestablishing the parent–adolescent bond through helping the adolescent build a positive safe support system. Connection creates trust. Here, the role of the social worker is to help the adolescent find personal answers to questions in a positive manner. Adolescents should be allowed to find their own peaceful self-resolution to sexual orientation.

Adolescents' need to create psychological independence from parental figures is intensified by the need to answer *"Who am I?"* and remains a distinctive step in the transition to adulthood. The digital spaces may inherently be one of the best domains for adolescents' exploration of personal identity as they engage in the quest to define who they are as a person. Amber was able to create different online profiles using various identities, enabling her to discuss alternative lifestyles without fear of discovery. An emerging theory for understanding how social network use may contribute to the development of self-identity is the *hyperpersonal* model that argues adolescents engage in selective self-presentations online. Feedback from these presentations may in turn alter individual self-perceptions (Shapiro et al. 2014, 10; Sherman et al. 2016).

Amber's teacher reported to Amber's parents her concern about her posting and reposting of stories of gay and transgender teens. When asked about her social media postings, Amber told her therapist,

Sure I have been posting, but so what, other students do too. When I get bad comments or slammed because of what I have posted I shut down my account and open a new one." Amber, proudly states, "I can have two online identities if I want to or even more than that. I can be whoever I want to be online. I can meet and chat with others who talk about feeling different, you know because they might be gay or transgendered, and I can share things I think and feel, but no one knows who I really am."

Amber is linking with other like-minded peers, which is something she values, but could not feel free to do in face-to-face interactions because of how her family, friends, or peers may react (Larson et al. 2002; Markstrom et al. 2010). In family therapy Amber felt safe to examine her interest in alternative sexual orientation, and her parents were able to allow the conversation because they were asked to create a safe place for this discourse to happen. In doing so, Amber demonstrated a way to use the technology to explore and construct her identity and voice, trying to make sense of it the best she can. Using technology to interact with others from diverse perspectives and linking with those who are like-minded are valued and widely available in social media, but also may be lacking in face-to-face interactions (Larson et al. 2002; Markstrom et al. 2010). But as research has shown, in the digital world, adolescents are often blamed and shamed for what they do (boyd 2014). During Amber's first few sessions she responded with anger toward her parents and resented being challenged by her teachers on the subject, but once her parents were able to display their concern for her, she responded with open emotion. There exists a need to first address anger and improve communication by the social work practitioners and other helping professionals working with vulnerable adolescents who create a level of privacy and self-development out of the sight of parents and other authority figures (Simpson 2016).

The important processes during Amber's sessions were allowing her parents to show they only wanted her to be happy with whomever she chose to be with and creating a safe space that allowed her to openly express her thoughts. Parents and other adults often mistakenly equate teens' engagement with social media and their willingness to share information online as evidence they do not care about their privacy (Marwick and boyd 2014). Amber has described quite the contrary and is in fact engaged in network privacy, managing hazards and insecurities related to the production of a future-oriented self via social media tools (Wang and Edwards 2016). Adolescents will use social media to discuss their thoughts and challenge a system that seems unreceptive to open discussions. Parents should be encouraged to allow a safe place for these conversations to take place in their own homes.

FIGHTING FEAR BY BUILDING A POSITIVE SUPPORT SYSTEM

Historically, adolescence has been viewed as the developmental period in which establishing friendships and peer relationships is one of the most important tasks for moving into early adulthood (Thomas 1985): that conception remains unchanged today. Online socializing has become a highly visible avenue to manage, reconstruct, and enhance existing close relationships, as well as build new ones (boyd 2014; Cyr, Berman, and Smith 2016; Khan et al. 2016; Wang and Edwards 2016; Weiqin et al. 2016). Building positive support systems for all adolescents is vital to parenting skills and how these skills, when present, allow open communication by parents of social media. This section focuses on how to help youth develop positive interactions in social media with their friends and how to educate parents, professionals, and others working with adolescents and help them build skills that lead to trust in the adolescents' use of social media.

Both Rachel and Amber's mothers had succumbed to the idea that online interactions were dangerous and that participants targeted by mean-spirited postings were at risk for damage to psychosocial health and serious outcomes such as a risk for suicide. Cyberbullying has captured media headlines and has become a significant concern in schools. Bullying and what can be defined as cyberbullying, however, usually peak during middle school. By high school, what is ever present is what teens refer to as *drama* (boyd 2014; Marwick and boyd 2014), which is how Rachel describes the active situation with her friends: *"It's just drama; there isn't a problem."* Rachel and Amber's predicaments demonstrate important aspects of adolescent development in the digital spaces. The acts by adolescents to claim their place in online space and to walk away from or exclude a person from a social group are conducted primarily between existing relationships (Khan et al. 2016, 943; Wang and Edwards 2016; Weiqin et al. 2016). The characteristics of social media—the durability of online expressions (persistence), the potential audience who can hear (visibility), the ease with which content can be shared (spreadability), and the ability to find content (searchability)—also contribute to how quickly relationships can change among adolescents who use social media (boyd 2014).

Amber, like Rachel, is searching for her own identity through communication with other adolescents. She wants to gain acceptance from and use her voice in support of other adolescents who may feel they are outside of the mainstream from peers. Engaging in interactions beyond traditional peer groups may cause concern for Amber's parents and often occurs away from adult prying eyes and ears, but can also be a commendable trait as today's adolescents enter an adult world. The pre-social media interactions among adolescents took place within the confines of a limited geographic area, such as a school or neighborhood, and within a limited peer group. The potential for an audience beyond the immediate was nonexistent or only available to those with the means to travel. However, today teens have the opportunity to quickly connect with others; often creating major fear for parents associated with their adolescents' use of social media.

A combined history of more than thirty-five years' of professional experience in social work has shown us that, no matter how much technology changes our lives, families need to remain connected and communicating. Therefore, the first and most important intervention we used was to educate, followed by helping establish a positive safety support system (May and Quinn forthcoming). After assessing Rachel and Amber we found they both lacked the personal skills to build a positive support system with solid boundaries; we needed to guide them and their parents to a new understanding where everyone felt confident about their safety and their self-reliance. Building a positive support system for the adolescent goes hand in hand with social media use. Every adolescent who has come into our practices has wanted more online time away from what was described as their parents' "controlling eyes." This model was developed after many years of family sessions with the drawing of circles on my note pad and was finally put down as one of five coping skills that adolescents needed to develop with their parents' approval. First, it is important to assess how friendships are made. During years of practice with adolescents we have found that most develop friendships through school acquaintances and family members with whom they consistently interact. These relationships were built with people who were not deserving of friendship or trust. Therefore, most clients were at risk for trusting peers who had not earned the right to be called a true friend. Furthermore, they needed a new way to build a support system that would create more positive relationships. Teaching adolescents to build a safe positive support system also taught them the process of how best to establish healthy relationships. The Support System ring (A) must be established to include people we have learned to trust and who will not lower our self-esteem. Second, we need Our True Friends' ring (B) that includes people we have learned to trust (we usually need at least five good true friends). Finally, we establish the Acquaintance ring (C), which includes people we meet but have not learned to trust yet (May and Quinn forthcoming). There is a reason why so many young people today are infatuated with social media sites, but the adolescent must not claim people they do not trust to be friends, but only acquaintances. Once adolescents establish how best to build a positive support system, parents are less fearful of their child's social media interactions.

In therapy Rachel and Amber were taught how to create this positive support system. Once it was established, they were both able to show their parents the skills they now possessed and that they were capable of sustaining a positive support system of people in the following categories: acquaintances, who would not be trusted but observed; friends, who once were trusted and held an accepted record of trust; and those few who acted as therapist, who would never lower the adolescent's self-esteem. Both adolescents were more self-confident about who was supposed to be part of their support system and furthermore who should be excluded when relationship problems arose.

OTHER INTERVENTIONS APPLIED

The process of "value differentiation"—in which individuals assign varying importance to their values according to the context (Daniel et al. 2012) and prioritize values in a process that is directed by the surrounding environment (where the person is from defines how values are personally prioritized; Schwartz 1992)—is inherent to social media use. This understanding allows adolescents to better appreciate their own personal value differences in an ever changing social media environment, especially when peers possessing a dissimilar self-value criticize their posts. An extensive comparative study of diverse cultural groups demonstrated that adolescents often perceive socialization agents' values to be different or to conflict across contexts (Daniel et al. 2012). Given the role social media and digital technology play in the lives of adolescents, it is important to begin with an understanding of how they perceive the benefits and risks of internet use and how they value its importance. Smith, Hewitt, and Skrbiš (2015) found young people with limited access to the internet learned to view task-oriented use, such as schoolwork, as the only worthwhile reason for access, while those with more access were more confident and pragmatic about its opportunities and risks as they approached early adulthood.

Online socializing has become a highly visible avenue by which to manage, reconstruct, and enhance existing relationships, as well as build new ones (Bohn et al. 2014; Khan et al. 2016; Wang and Edwards 2016; Weigin et al. 2016) but for those adolescents who lack this resource, social media produces negative experiences when they go online. As the literature points out the "Rich-get-Richer" hypothesis (Weigin et al. 2016) postulates that those who have an avid social life offline benefit further from their online social life. This was true of both Rachel and Amber, who were socially oriented user (Smith et al. 2015). Rachel saw social media as a main component of her current life by enabling her to keep in touch with friends, stay informed, and get her voice out to others through her blog site. Amber described the importance of social media as an "escape from the real and a way to connect with others in another place and express myself in a way I can't at home or in school."

Adopting a personal value system continues to be an aspect of adolescent development and one that plays out in the world of social media in ways that can be very visible. As children enter adolescence and begin an individuation process from parental figures, they begin to define what is meant by *being me*. They question their parents' moral landscape, accepting or rejecting the values and mores learned from their parents or parental authorities and beginning to establish their own. Amber's exploration of alternative lifestyles created conflict with her parents. Her mother learned of her postings regarding gay and transgendered lifestyles, which at first caused fear based on the family's religious beliefs. "Someone told my mom I was posting inappropriate material and I could be getting into trouble for it," Amber spoke quietly as she told the school social worker her story. "My mom went crazy; she took away my phone and even took me to our priest for counseling." Her mom was distraught that Amber might be having gender identity issues herself and blamed them on her use of social media. After exploring this issue in family therapy, however, a safe place was established, which allowed Amber to be more at ease when asking questions concerning sexual development.

Transmission of values is often thought of as a one-way street from parents to children. However, children also influence parental values through active or passive means. Simply put, parenting children through their development stage results in the changes of parental values (Knafo and Galansky 2008). Adolescents also actively work to change parental values using the new frontier in social media as one of the most visible methods. This new genre of participation identified by Ito et al. (2009) as "geeking out" incorporates a willingness to challenge established rules and norms and can be seen through the experiences of Rachel and Amber. However, this combination of complexity, novelty, multiplicity, and instantaneousness may naturally breed impulsive behaviors (Hobbs 2011; Wang and Edwards 2016). This is one area of development in which adolescents must learn control skills.

An overemphasis on risk and dangerousness appears to coincide with less nuanced depiction of social media, which induces significant anxiety among the public (Wang and Edwards 2016). Parents, educators, policy makers, and researchers who overtly influence adolescents' online practices can often misinterpret or disregard their views, not recognizing their competence in this environment (Rollins 2015). Rachel's ability to resolve conflicts evolving through social media and put it in a protective perspective is seen in her words: "It's just drama, there isn't a problem." Amber's agency in exploring her sexual identity was not turned inward in shame or guilt when she experienced negative reactions, but instead she created a new identity and continued seeking a place to belong. Digital socialization has been found to involve differing ways of reconciling technological developments with ideas about life, the pathway to maturity, and status recognition (Smith et al. 2015), and adolescents are demonstrating both competence and agency in this process (Bohn et al. 2014; Marwick and boyd 2014; Shapiro et al. 2014).

As they make their way toward adulthood, teens benefit from developing skills to interact positively with others through social media. Enabling self-presentations, managing social relationships, and developing an understanding of the world around them are the goals of social media use (boyd 2014). The possibility of taking a hobby or interest and making it into what is a successful YouTuber is a goal of the younger generation (Berriman and Thomas 2014). The term "playbour," which is an amalgamation of play and labor (Kucklich 2005), is used in the literature to describe the transformation of something that starts out as *just for fun* into something that can generate economic value (Berriman and Thomas 2014). For adolescents, it is not more than an aspiration, and attracting the attention of a wider audience remains a slim possibiity. As such, like the unrealistic goal of becoming a highly paid professional athlete or musician, this group of young media users also represents a generation in which becoming a successful YouTuber and not having to work in a traditional job is the new dream profession. Despite these apparently out-of-reach goals, using social media to find a future career is indeed a positive skill. The Rachels of the world will traverse the online venue and experience detriments, but no more than in the developmental process from child to adulthood. Those who share Amber's penance for exploring alternative, non-normative lifestyles may find that social media can provide a platform to develop confidence and positive self-esteem while advocating for others in vulnerable situations.

CONCLUSION

Our narrative cases illustrate combined experiences of more than thirty-five years of professional social work that began in the 1990s with developing strong assessments skills and knowledge in the traditional model of family therapy. We as practitioners have chosen to work with and empower children and adolescents, and these experiences have taught us to value and improve our methods with changing technology. Social work assessment views individuals and families through an ecological perspective encompassing all domains of the human condition—biological, psychological, social, and environmental—and emphasizing the interaction of social systems for human development. Well established within the social work profession, the ecological perspective is relevant for understanding the current social media domain and adolescent use. Additionally, this orientation helps inform American families how best to adapt to this modern environment through interventions that consider both risk and protective factors for the adolescent (Masten and Telegen 2012).

We explored three factors that led to our outlined interventions: adolescent identity development, how important peer relationships are to adolescents; and parental relationships/boundaries. We further suggested that building positive support systems for all adolescents is vital to parenting skills and how these skills allow open communication by parents for the use of social media. We showed how to help youth develop positive interactions with their friends during social media use and how to educate parents, professionals, and others working with adolescents to help them build skills that lead to trusting its use. Therefore, through our sessions with adolescents, we found they must be empowered and made to feel they are developing maturation skills. By helping adolescents and their parents overcome the typical fear that any new technology brings, we are better able to teach this new generation of teens how to use these new tools to improve skills. Technology has the potential to enhance decision making when open communication leads to better understanding.

The focus of intervention for the profession of social work has been cognitive behavioral theory (CBT), which has been taught to every social work graduate student who sought to help people. Teaching adolescents to use *our way* to change their lives was the focus and was supported by empirical findings. However, adolescents have their own way of adapting to challenges, which often conflict with our therapeutic techniques. Recognizing that an adolescent is the expert in his or her life on social media led to seeing and intervening through their narrative expressions, and through these stories, we learned they changed the environment and the environment changed them.

Initially, we fell into commonly held assumptions that online activity results in poor social skills, decreased problem solving, increased impulsivity, and overall bad behaviors. However, recognizing that social media parallels the physical gathering places of previous generations has allowed us to embrace it as a positive environment for those transitioning from childhood to responsible adulthood. A few of our epiphanies occurring over time included recognizing that adolescents use social media to test and further develop learning skills and use feedback to create psychological independence, support systems, and defining who they are. We also know from experience and research (boyd 2014; Subrahmanyam et al. 2008; Wang and Edwards 2016; Weiqin et al. 2016) that adolescents who develop strong, positive social skills in the face-to-face world will enhance these through social media usage. However, those who have difficulty in face-to-face social interactions or are marginalized in the physical world will experience these same challenges in the world of social media.

When working with adolescents, recognizing the protective factors of opportunities for educational and psychological growth—collective efficacy, the presence of caring adults, and positive peer relationships (Barth 2015; Berriman and Thomas 2014; boyd 2014; Michikyan and Suàrez-Orozco 2016)—helps inform actions to mitigate social media's risk factors pointed out by boyd (2014): the durability of online expressions (persistence), the potential audience who can hear (visibility), the ease with which content can be shared (spreadability), and the ability to find content (searchability).

This chapter recommends an ecological strengths perspective, building a positive support system, and parental education concerning the challenges and opportunities of adolescents on the positive aspects of social media use. It is important to consider the presence or absence of supportive adults who are informed about social media, as well as interaction, and social functioning within the face-to-face world and how this may or may not be replicated in the online world of social media. Narrative accounts in Rachel's and Amber's stories demonstrate both benefits and challenges of the New Frontier in a healthy transition from adolescence to responsible adulthood.

QUESTIONS FOR REFLECTION AND GROUP DISCUSSION

1. Time spent in social face-to-face interactions for adolescents has lessened in recent years. What have you learned from this chapter that helping professionals can do through social media to build skills and connection for effective social relationships when working with adolescents?
2. Information in this chapter outlines the positive effects social media can play in adolescent development, such as testing of parental separation and self-reflection. What exercises do you suggest using with adolescents that promote a positive learning process?
3. Explain how the chapter addresses open discussion of adolescent use of social media and what skills you have learned to improve family fear about levels of social media use.

REFERENCES

Barth, Diane F. 2015. "Social Media and Adolescent Development: Hazards, Pitfalls and Opportunities for Growth." *Clinical Social Work* 43, no. 2: 201–208.
Berriman, Liam, and Rachel Thomas. 2014. "Spectacles of Intimacy? Mapping the Moral Landscape of Teenage Social Media." *Journal of Youth Studies* 18, no. 5: 583–597.
Bohn, Angela, Christian Buchta, Kurt Hornik, and Patrick Mair. 2014. "Making Friends and Communicating on Facebook: Implications for the Access to Social Capital." *Social Networks* 37: 29–41.
boyd, danah. 2014. *It's Complicated: The Social Lives of Networked Teens.* New Haven, CT: Yale University Press.
Burke, Moira, Cameron Marlow, and Thomas Lento. 2010. "Social Network Activity and Social Well-Being." *Proceedings of the 2010 ACM Conference on Human Factors in Computing Systems,* 1909–1912.
Cingel, Drew P., and Marina Krcmar. 2014. "Understanding the Experience of Imaginary Audience in a Social Media Environment." *Journal of Media Psychology* 26, no. 4: 155–160.
Cyr, Betty-Ann, Steven L. Berman, and Megan L .Smith. 2016. "The Role of Communication Technology in Adolescent Relationships and Identity Development." *Child Youth Care Forum* 44: 79–92.
Daniel, Ella, Maya Benish-Weisman, Davis Schiefer, Anna Möllering, and Klaus Bohenke. 2012. "Value Differentiation in Adolescence: The Role of Age and Cultural Complexity." *Child Development* 83, no. 1: 322–336.

Deci, Edward L., and Richard M. Ryan. 2000. "The 'What' and 'Why' of Goal Pursuits: Human Needs and the Self-Determination of Behavior." *Psychological Inquiry* 11, no. 4: 319–338.

Ellison, Nicole B., Charles Steinfield, and Cliff Lampe. 2011. "Connection Strategies: Social Capital Implications of Facebook-Enabled Communication Practices." *New Media & Society* 13, no. 6: 873–892.

Grolnick, Wendy S. 2003. *The Psychology of Parental Control: How Well-Meant Parenting Backfires*. Mahwah, NJ: Erlbaum.

Hobbs, Renee. 2011. *Digital and Media Literacy: Connecting Culture and Classroom*. Thousand Oaks, CA: Corwin.

Ito, Mizuko, et al. 2009. *Hanging out, Messing Around, and Geeking Out: Kids Living and Learning with New Media*. Cambridge, MA: MIT Press.

James, Allison, Chris Jenks, and Alan Prout. 1998. "Theorizing Childhood." Cambridge: Polity Press.

Khan, Shereen, Monique Gagné, Leigh Yang, and Jennifer Shapka. 2016. "Exploring the Relationship Between Adolescents' Self-Concept and Their Offline and Online Social Worlds." *Computers in Human Behavior* 55: 940–945.

Kim, W, O. Jeong, and S. Lee. 2010. "On Social Web Sites." *Information Systems* 35, no. 2: 215–236.

——. 2011. "The Facebook Paths to Happiness: Effects of the Number of Facebook Friends and Self-Presentation on Subjective Well-Being." *Cyberpsychology, Behavior, and Social Networking* 14, no. 6: 359–364.

Knafo, Ariel, and Neta Galansky. 2008. "The Influence of Children on Their Parents' Values." *Social and Personality Psychology Compass* 2/3:1143–1161.

Kucklich, Julian. 2005. "Precarious Playbour: Modders and the Digital Games Industry." *Fibreculture* 5, no. (1). http://five.fibreculturejournal.org/fcj-025-precarious-playbour-modders-and-the-digital-games-industry/.

Larson, Reed W., Suzanne Wilson, B. Bradford Brown, Frank F. Furstenberg Jr., and Surman Verma. 2002. "Changes in Adolescents' Interpersonal Experiences: Are They Being Prepared for Adult Relationships in the Twenty-First Century?" *Journal of Research on Adolescence* 12, no. 1: 31–68.

Lenhart, Amanda. 2015. "Teens, Social Media & Technology Overview 2015." *Pew Research Center: Internet and Technology*. http://www.pewinternet.org/2015/04/09/teens-social-media-technology-2015/.

Livingstone, Sonia. 2008. "Taking Risky Opportunities in Youthful Content Creation: Teenagers' Use of Social Networking Sites for Intimacy, Privacy and Self-Expression." *New Media & Society* 10, no. 3: 393–411.

Markstrom, Carol A., Erron Huey, Bethanie Morris Stiles, and Amanda L. Krause. 2010. "Frameworks of Caring and Helping in Adolescence: Are Empathy, Religiosity, and Spirituality Related Constructs?" *Youth & Society* 41, no. 1: 59–80.

Marwick, Alice, and danah boyd. 2014. "'It's Just Drama': Teen Perspectives on Conflict and Aggression in a Networked Era." *Journal of Youth Studies* 17, no. 9: 1187–1204.

Masten, Ann S., and Auke Tellegan. 2012. "Resilience in Developmental Psychopathology: Contributions of the Project Competence Longitudinal Study." *Developmental Psychopathology* 24, no. 2: 345–361.

May, Benjamin T., and M. Quinn. Forthcoming. "Clinical Practice with U.S. Families and Children in Financial Distress." In *Empowering Clinical Social Work Practice During a Time of Global Economic Distress,* edited by L. Openshaw. Washington, DC: NASW Press.

McNamee, Sally. 2016. *The Social Study of Childhood: An Introduction.* London: Palgrave Macmillan.

Michikyan, Minas, and Carola Suàrez-Orozco. 2016. "Adolescent Media and Social Media Use: Implications for Development." *Journal of Adolescent Research* 31, no. 4: 411–414.

Rollins, Joe. 2015. "Sexting Cyberchildren: Gender, Sexuality, and Childhood in Social Media." *Sexuality & Culture* 19: 57–71.

Schwartz, Shalom H. 1992. "Universals in the Content and Structure of Values: Theoretical Advances and Empirical Tests in 20 Countries." *Advances in Experimental Social Psychology* 25: 1–65.

Shapiro, Lauren, A. Spies, and Gayla Margolin. 2014. "Growing Up Wired: Social Networking Sites and Adolescent Psychosocial Development." *Clinical Child Family Psychological Review* 17, no. 1: 1–18.

Sherman, Lauren, Ashley A. Payton, Leanna M. Hernandez, Patricia M. Greenfield, and Mirella Dapretto. 2016. "The Power of the Like in Adolescence: Effects of Peer Influence on Neural and Behavioral Responses to Social Media." *Psychological Science* 27, no. 7: 1027–1035.

Simpson, Jennifer. 2016. "A Divergence of Opinion: How Those Involved in Child and Family Social Work Are Responding to the Challenges of the Internet and Social Media." *Child and Family Social Work* 21, no. 1: 94–102.

Smith, Jonathan, Belinda Hewitt, and Zlatko Skrbiš. 2015. "Digital Socialization: Young People's Changing Value Orientations Towards Internet Use Between Adolescence and Early Adulthood." *Communication & Society* 18, no. 9: 1022–1038.

Soenens, Bart, and Maarten Vansteenkiste. 2005. "Antecedents and Outcomes of Self-Determination in Three Life Domains: The Role of Parents' and Teachers' Autonomy Support." *Journal of Youth and Adolescence* 34, no. 6: 589–604.

Subrahmanyam, Kaveri, Stephanie M. Reich, Natalia Waechter, and Guadalupe Espinoza. 2008. "Online and Offline Social Networks: Use of Social Networking Sites by Emerging Adults." *Journal of Applied Developmental Psychology* 29: 420–433.

Thomas, Murray R. 1985. *Comparing Theories of Child Development,* 2nd ed. Boston: Wadsworth.

Vallerand, R. J. 1997. "Toward a Hierarchical Model of Intrinsic and Extrinsic Motivation." In *Advances in Experimental Social Psychology,* vol. 29, ed. Mark P. Zanna, 271–360. San Diego: Academic Press.

Wang, Victoria, and Simon Edwards. 2016. "Strangers Are Friends I Haven't Met Yet: A Positive Approach to Young People's Use of Social Media." *Journal of Youth Studies* 19, no. 9: 1204–1219.

Weiqin, Eliza Leong, Marilyn Campbell, Melanie Kimpton, Kelly Wozencroft, and Alexandra Orel. 2016. "Social Capital on Facebook: The Impact of Personality and Online Communication Behaviors." *Journal of Educational Computing Research* 54, no. 6: 747–768.

CONTRIBUTORS

Kristina Baines, PhD, is assistant professor of anthropology at the City University of New York (CUNY), Guttman Community College.

Yasemin Besen-Cassino, PhD, is professor of sociology and distinguished scholar at Montclair State University.

Vera Caine is currently a professor and CIHR New Investigator in the faculty of nursing at the University of Alberta.

Deborah Courtney, PhD, LCSW, is an entrepreneur, psychotherapist, professor, and speaker serving NYC, Westchester, and Fairfield Counties.

Mery F. Diaz, DSW, LCSW, is an assistant professor in human services and CREAR Futuros Peer-Mentoring Program Faculty Liaison at New York City College of Technology/CUNY.

Gretta M. Fernandes, PhD, LCSW, is currently the coordinator of Justice, Peace and Integrity Creation for Holy Spirit Missionary Sisters.

Sabrina Gonzalez, DSW, LCSW, is a mental health clinical assessor and family therapist at Healing Educational Alternatives for Deserving Students (HEADS).

Janice Huber is in the faculty of education, University of Alberta.

Erica Goldblatt Hyatt, DSW, LCSW, MBE, is assistant director of the DSW program at Rutgers University's School of Social Work.

Margot K. Jackson, PhD, MA, BScN, is an assistant professor with the faculty of nursing at the University of Alberta in Edmonton, Alberta, Canada.

Sharon Johnson, PhD, is in the Psychology Faculty of community college Cornerstone Institute, in Cape Town, South Africa. She is a counselor, consultant, post-doctoral researcher, and author.

Rebecca G. Judd, PhD, LMSW-IPR, is department chair and associate professor in the school of social work at Texas A&M University-Commerce.

Susan McDonald, PhD, LSW, is department chair and assistant professor in the department of social work at Misericordia University.

Benjamin T. May, PhD, MSW, is associate professor and BSW director at Texas A&M—Commerce.

Trevor B. Milton is an assistant professor of sociology and criminal justice at Queensborough Community College, CUNY.

Jerry Otero is founder and director of Cre8tive YouTH*ink, a New York City–based nonprofit youth development organization.

Elizabeth Palley, PhD, JD, MSW, is a professor at the Adelphi University School of Social Work and the co-author of *In Our Hands: The Struggle for US Child Care Policy.*

Sherri L. Rings, PhD, is a counselor, associate professor, and chair in the department of SEEK Counseling and Student Support Services at The City College of New York.

Stephen Ruszczyk, PhD, is assistant professor of sociology at Montclair State University.

Benjamin Heim Shepard, PhD, by day is a professor in the human services department at New York City College of Technology/CUNY. By night, he battles to keep New York from becoming a giant shopping mall. He is also the author and editor of ten other books, including *Brooklyn Tides*, *Sustainable Urbanism* (2019), and *Illuminations on Mark Street* (Ibidem, 2019).

Muneerah Amin Vastani is a Ph.D. student in faculty of nursing at the University of Alberta, Canada.

Stephanie Wise ATR-BC, ATCS, is associate professor of practice at Marywood University in Scranton, PA, where she is the director of the Art Therapy Program.

INDEX

abandonment, 315–316

ABC →X model, 317–318, *318*

ableism, 180–184

abuse: brain development and, 270–271; Brooklyn Society for the Prevention of Cruelty to Children, 194; in childcare, 222–223; coping with, 271–275; culture and, 77–78; drugs and, 93–94; in family, 79; gender and, 93; medical model for, 278; neglect and, 37–40; psychology of, 90–92; self-belief and, 271–272. *See also* sexual exploitation

acceptance, 183–186

accomplishments, 60–61

Achieving Independence Center, 55

ACT UP (organization), 188, 194, *194*

adaptation, 68–69, 338

Addams, Jane, 15–16, 22

Adelphi University, 235

Adler, Alfred, 40

adolescents: adults and, 32; brain development in, 270; children and, 23, 107; coping for, 42–43; encouragement for, 40–41; ethnographies for, 311; foster care and, 60–61; heritage traditions for, 102–109,

115–116; hyperpersonal model, 339; identity for, 306–307; leadership for, 258; migration for, 116; narratives and, 1–5, 32, 109–115; for NYPD, 128; part-time work and, 135–136; psychology of, 81; self-belief in, 42–43; social media for, 331–335, 338–340, 343–348. *See also* siblings

adoption, 314–318

adults: adolescents and, 32; children and, 2, 115, 240–241; counseling of, 51–52; after Department of Human Services, 50; love for, 57; motivation from, 54–55; social justice for, 240–241; for vulnerable youth, 48

advocacy, 50–51, 183–186; drugs and, 243–244; for HIV-AIDS Services Administration, 188, 196; for social justice, 234–235; in social work, 188–189, *190*, 191–192, *194*, 194–199, 210

aesthetic labor, 136–140

African Americans, 167n1. *See also* minorities

agency, 3, 11–12, 68–69, 81–82, 185–186, 243

aging out: from foster care, 54; narratives of, 53–54, 61–62; psychology of, 59–60; resiliency after, 55–56; for vulnerable youth, 48–50
Aichhorn, August, 19
AIDS. *See* HIV
alcoholism, 314–318
Ali Forney Center (AFC), 190
alternative schools, 163–164
American Psychiatric Association (APA), 283
Americans with Disabilities Act (ADA), 172, 183
amygdala, 270
analytic third, 13–14
anthropology, 291–292
anxiety, 175–177, 266–269, 275–276, 344–345
apartheid, 34, 37–38
art: at Art School Without Walls, 231–232, 232; art therapy, 320–329, 321–322, 324–326; *ARTnews* (magazine), 238; public, 240–241
assimilation model, 69, 333
at-risk adolescents. *See* vulnerable youth
attendance laws, 7–8
autoethnography. *See* ethnographies

Bantu Education Act, 35
Barnhart, Kate, 188–189, 190, 191–192, 194, 194–199, 210
Bateson, Gregory, 291–292
becoming, 11–12
behavior support, 44, 44–45, 107, 274–277, 337–338
beliefs, 105–106
Belize, 102, 106, 108, 109–111, 113–115
bereavement. *See* grief
Besen-Cassino, Yasemin, 135
Bettelheim, Bruno, 16, 19
bilingual education, 70, 150–151, 154–155, 219
biology, 7
bi-sexuality. *See* LGBTQ
Black children, 167n1. *See also* minorities
Black Lives Matter, 3, 234
blogs, 336–338

bonding, with parents, 315
Borden, William, 15
borderline personality disorder (BPD), 288–289, 295–296
Bowlby, John, 17
brain development, 223, 263–265, 267, 270–271, 277–278
Bratton, William, 122, 125–126
Brooklyn Museum of Art, 238
Brooklyn Society for the Prevention of Cruelty to Children, 194
bullying, 341
Bureau of Labor, 136
Burke, Jocelyn, 216–217

Call of Stories, The (Coles), 285–286
Canada, 93–94, 221, 282, 294
Cape Town, 31–32, 33, 33–34
care policy, 224–226
case conceptualizations, 265, 276–277
caste system, 247–251, 253–259
Centre for Arts and Youth (CAY), 282, 294
Chicago Area Project (CAP), 15–16
Child Care Aware, 217–218
childcare: abuse in, 222–223; cross-national comparisons of, 221–222; ethos of, 36; gender in, 217; policy for, 215–220; politics of, 214–215, 226–227; research on, 222–226
children: ableism for, 180–181; adaptation for, 338; adolescents and, 23, 107; adults and, 2, 115, 240–241; agency for, 185–186; anxiety in, 266–269; art therapy for, 320–329, 321–322, 324–326; behavior support for, 274–275; bilingual education for, 219; biology of, 7; brain development in, 223, 263–264, 277–278; Brooklyn Society for the Prevention of Cruelty to Children, 194; bullying, 341; care policy for, 214–220; Child Protection Services, 266; Children's Act (2005), 36; corporal punishment for, 35–36; counseling with, 265–266; death for, 302; death of, 311; Department of Human Services for, 48–50; with

disabilities, 171–172, 175–177; ecological perspectives for, 8–9; education of, 5–6, 215–216; ethnographies for, 13–14, 215; ex-inmates and, 128–129; family and, 50; gender for, 339; grief in, 178–179; history of, 10–11; with HIV, 33; HR, 232–233, 240–244; imagination of, 327; in India, 250–259; international rights for, 36; intervention for, 153, 302, 343–345; introverted children, 78; knowledge for, 10; labeling for, 281–282; Latin@, 151; LGBTQ for, 165; *The Making and Breaking of Affectional Bonds*, 17; maladaptive behavior in, 7; as minorities, 156–157; motivation for, 52–53; narratives from, 1–5; North Central Children & Youth, 85, 88–89, 94–97; pediatricians and, 216–217; perspectives of, 6; political care and, 214–215; poverty for, 250–259; psychology of, 2, 5–6, 179–180; religion for, 298–299; rescue, 315–316; research on, 3–5, 7–8, 23–24; self-belief, 324–325, *325*; sexual exploitation of, 84–85, 87–92; social justice for, 11, 232; for social sciences, 2–3; in social work, 303–304; socialization for, 343–345; socioeconomics for, 4–5; sociology of, 7, 10; in South Africa, 35–36; stress for, 321, *321*, 323–324, *324*; studies on, 6–8, 12–19; suicide, 323–324, *324*; trauma for, 264–265, 316–317; triggering for, 327–328; universal children, 6–7; violence and, 35, 127, 130–131; well-being for, 9
China, 2
Chomsky, Noam, 130
circle of courage, 37
City College of New York, 235
City University of New York (CUNY), 108
civil disobedience, 3
civil rights laws, 172, 183
class issues, 216–218, 225–226, 249–251
clinical history, 285–286, 295–296
clinical psychology, 171
cognitive behavioral therapy (CBT), 276–277, 347–348

cognitive strategies, 106
coherency, 23, 64
Cohler, Bertram, 16–19
Coles, Robert, 285–286, 292, 296
collaboration, 85–89, 92, 97–99
Common Core, 159
communication, 1–2, 59, 274, 332–333, 335
community: apartheid and, 37–38; community agencies, 84–87, 94–98, 282, 294; education and, 336; encouragement from, 45; Fabulous Independent Radicals for Community Empowerment, 198; family and, 38–40, 161; Gangstas Making Astronomical Community Changes Inc., 126–127; identity and, 314–315; leadership in, 242–243, *243*, 256; for migration, 108; narratives of, 22–23; psychology of, 40–41; relationships from, 209–210; sociology of, 15–16, 255–256; ubuntu, 39–40; for vulnerable youth, 9–11, 35–36; youth care and education center and, 35
compassion, 13–14, 21
complexity, 87–88, 99
confidence, 41, 61
constructive meaning, 273–274
Consuming Work (Besen-Cassino), 135
context, 68–69, 74–75, 81–82
Cooper, Martha, 231–232, *232*
coping, 42–43, 271–275, 277, 309
corporal punishment, 35–36
couch surfing, 59
counseling: of adults, 51–52; for behavior support, 337–338; case conceptualizations, 276–277; with children, 265–266; cognitive behavioral therapy, 276–277; for drugs, 237–238; in education, 59; empathy in, 266–267; ethnographies in, 264; in foster care, 62–63; group counseling, 88–91; intervention in, 99, 337; narratives and, 88–89, 97–99, 234–237; negotiating in, 318–319; psychotherapy, 241; relationships in, 291–293; suicide, 281; youth mental health in, 283–284

counter-stories. *See* narratives
Cre8tive YouTH*ink, 231–232, *232*,
   237–238, 240–242, *243*
credit cards, 139
criminal justice: intervention and, 158;
   John Jay College of Criminal Justice,
   119; for minorities, 123–124, 158; in
   New York City, 121; policy and,
   129–130; socioeconomics in, 131; Urban
   Justice Center, 190; for vulnerable
   youth, 122–123; zero tolerance, 159–160.
   See also prison assembly line
cross-national comparisons, 221–222
culture: abuse and, 77–78; acceptance in,
   183–186; Belize, 102; discrimination
   in, 182, 254; of drugs, 71; gender and,
   110–111, 252–256; identity and, 155;
   India, 247–250; knowledge and,
   20–21; language and, 200; *The Nanny
   Time Bomb*, 216–217; New York City,
   103, 122; of United States, 68–69,
   223–224; violence relating to, 253; of
   writing, 106–107
custodial care, 222–223
cyberbullying, 341

daycare, 220, 223
death, 281, 298–306, 309, 311, 323–324,
   324
debt, 139
Deferred Action for Childhood Arrivals
   (DACA), 72–73, 75, 77–78
Deferred Action for Childhood Arrivals
   program, 2
Deficit and subtractive practices, 157–158
deficit and subtractive practices (Yosso),
   157–158
delinquents. *See* vulnerable youth
democracy, 5, 167
Department of Human Services (DHS),
   48–51
Department of Social Development
   (DSD), 36, 45
Derner Institute, 235
developmental theories: anthropology
   in, 291–292; brain development, 223,
   263–265, 267, 270–271, 277–278; on

childcare, 223; ecological systems,
   8–9, 54–55; for emotions, 236;
   face-to-face interactions, 339–340,
   347–348; on gender, 251–252; HR,
   240–244; identity in, 334; intervention in, 216, 225, 235, 242–243;
   narratives in, 15, 346–348; success in,
   306–307; trauma in, 267; universal
   children, 6–7; youth development
   programs, 231–232, *232*
Devos, Betsy, 158
*Diagnostic and Statistical Manual of
   Mental Health Disorders* (DSM), 275,
   283–285, 289, 295, 317
digital socialization, 343–345, 347
disabilities: children with, 171–172,
   175–177; education with, 177–180;
   intervention for, 174, 178, 180; medical
   model for, 178, 180–181; minorities
   with, 181–183; psychology of, 173–175;
   social justice for, 183–186
discrimination, 182, 186, 193, 254, 255,
   258–259. *See also* gender; inequalities;
   minorities
do-it-yourself (DIY) approach, 200–202
drugs: abuse and, 93–94; advocacy and,
   243–244; counseling for, 237–238;
   culture of, 71; Drug Policy Alliance,
   244; dual frame of reference, 74;
   education and, 231–240, *232*, 242–244,
   243; gangs and, 37–38; mental health
   and, 286–287; needle exchange, 206,
   207; policy for, 232–242; psychology
   of, 241–242; regulation of, 243–244;
   violence and, 126–127; for vulnerable
   youth, 56–58, 97. *See also* wayward
   youth
DuBrul, Sascha Altman, *199*, 200–204,
   201, 208, 210

East Harlem. *See* New York City
ecological systems: developmental
   theories, 8–9, 54–55; ecological
   perspectives, 5, 8–9, 12, 172, 181–182,
   185, 346, 347–348; embodied ecological heritage, 103–106, 116; heritage
   traditions for, 102–109, 115–116;

niches, 309–310; psychology of, 64, 114–115; traditional ecological knowledge, 103–104

education: alternative schools, 163–164; attendance laws in, 7–8; Bantu Education Act, 35; bilingual education, 70, 150–151, 154–155, 219; of children, 5–6, 215–216; City University of New York, 108; class issues in, 250–251; Common Core, 159; community and, 336; counseling in, 59; democracy in, 5, 167; with disabilities, 177–180; drugs and, 231–240, 232, 242–244, 243; Education of the Handicapped Act, 172; ethnographies for, 120–121; evaluations in, 175–176; family for, 56; globalization and, 108–109; higher education, 72–74, 110–111; high-risk schools, 33, 33–34; IDEA, 172; for immigrants, 69; integration in, 165–166; intervention and, 94–95, 342; interviews during, 53–54; labeling in, 153; mainstreaming, 177–180; in Mexico, 73–74, 77; narratives for, 23–24; in New York City, 149–150; for parents, 340–341; philosophy of, 240; policy for, 258–259; Prep, 164–166; psychology and, 32, 293–294; public education, 151–152, 155, 158–159; *The Real School Safety Problem*, 123; research in, 33, 33–34, 223; under resourced urban public schools, 149–150; segregation in, 157–158; sexual exploitation in, 90–91; social justice in, 165; social sciences in, 22, 31–32; social work and, 163–164, 335; socioeconomics of, 3, 76–77, 109–111, 122, 150–151; special education, 177–180; success and, 62–63, 129–130; teachers in, 161–162; travel for, 111–115; in United States, 3, 78–79, 103; for vulnerable youth, 50–51; welfare state and, 23; Western Cape Education Department, 36. *See also* youth care and education center

effort, 40–43

ego state, 272

emancipation, 63

embodied ecological heritage (EEH), 103–106, 116

EMDR, 271

emotions, 141–143, 236, 270, 277

empathy, 266–267

encouragement, 40–42, 45

Epston, David, 313–314, 320

Erikson, Erik, 306–307

ethics, 99

ethnographies: for adolescents, 311; for children, 13–14, 215; in counseling, 264; for education, 120–121; identity and, 64, 113–114; for introverted children, 78; *Narrating Social Work Through Autoethnography*, 4; narratives in, 106–109, 173–175, 215; from New York City, 192; research on, 21–22, 137, 164–165; scrapbooks, 286

ethos, 36, 43–44

evaluations, 175–176

exclusion, from college, 73

ex-inmates, 119–121, 124–126, 128–129

eye movement desensitization and reprocessing (EMDR), 271–272, 275, 277

Fabulous Independent Radicals for Community Empowerment (FIERCE), 198

Facebook, 338–339

face-to-face interactions, 339–340, 347–348

fairness committees, 164

faith, 43, 238

family: abuse in, 79; alcoholism for, 314–316; children and, 50; communication with, 274; community and, 38–40, 161; for confidence, 61; for education, 56; encouragement from, 42; *Families Under Stress*, 317; foster care as, 57; gender and, 325–326, 326; intervention for, 275, 318; marriage and, 110–111; for motivation, 76–77; narratives for, 317–320, 318; narratives of, 301–302, 334–335; psychology

family (*cont.*)
and, 58; religion in, 344; in social
work, 331; socioeconomics of, 215–218;
trauma and, 265–266, 313–314; trust in,
341–343; for vulnerable youth, 58–60,
63–64. *See also* parents; siblings
feedback, 225, 337, 339
Felix, David, 189–190, *190*
feminization, of poverty, 247, 256–259
fight, flight, or freeze (FFF) response,
267–268, 271–272, 274, 277
financial aid, 80–81
first encounters, 86–87
First Information Report (FIR), 254
Fordham University, 313
Forty Years in Hull House (Addams), 22
foster care: adolescents and, 60–61;
aging out from, 54; counseling in,
62–63; as family, 57; narratives about,
57–58; in Philadelphia, 48; psychology of, 51; research and, 50–53; in
United States, 49; for vulnerable
youth, 60–62; wayward youth from,
201–202
Foucault, Michel, 122
France, 221–222
Freud, Sigmund, 17–18, 211
Friends Make the Best Medicine (Icarus
Project), 204
Fromm, Eric, 241

gangs, 37–38, 71–72, 75, 126–127, 239–240
Gangstas Making Astronomical
Community Changes Inc. (GMACC),
126–127
gay (sexual orientation). *See* LGBTQ
Gay Liberation Movement, 13, 17–18
Geertz, Clifford, 291–292
gender, 167n1; abuse and, 93; in childcare, 217; for children, 339; culture
and, 110–111, 252–256; developmental
theories on, 251–252; family and,
325–326, *326*; gender norms, 71, 73, 75,
80–81; gendered narratives, 75–82; in
marriage, 112–113; minorities and,
136–137, 143–145; research on, 310. *See
also* inequalities

General Accounting Office (GAO), 21–22
Generalized Anxiety Disorder (GAD),
275–276
Giuliani, Rudolph, 122, 125–126, 193
globalization: cross-national comparisons, 221–222; education and, 108–109;
neoliberalism and, 11; self-help
financial groups, 247, 252–258; World
Trade Organization, 203–204
Gonzalez, Emma, 3
governmentality, 162–163
grief: death and, 298–306; identity and,
307–308, 311–312; for parents,
309–310; psychology of, 178–179,
308–309; reflexivity and, 301–302; for
siblings, 298–301, 311–312
group counseling, 88–91

Hampshire College, 194–195
harm reduction (HR), 232–233, 240–244
healthcare, 214–215
Hehir, Thomas, 180
heritage traditions, for ecological
systems, 102–109, 115–116
hermeneutic circle, 32
higher education, 72–74, 110–111
high-needs children. *See* school-based
mental health services
high-risk schools, *33*, 33–34
Hill, Reuben, 317
Hinduism, 247–251, 253–259
hippocampus, 270
history: children and, 10–11; clinical
history, 285–286, 295–296; Gay
Liberation Movement, 13; knowledge
in, 34; maltreatment in, 49; of
politics, 224–225; of Preparing
Leaders of Tomorrow, 120; of prison
assembly line, 121–124, 129; of
psychology, 284–285; of sexual
exploitation, 93–94; of social work,
341–342; of vulnerable youth, 54–55;
of youth mental health, 283
HIV: children with, 33; in narratives, 84;
psychology of, 5, 18; for social work,
14–15; for vulnerable youth, 188,
190–192, 195, 197, 205, 210

HIV-AIDS Services Administration (HASA), 188, 196
Hoffman, Amy, 1–2
homeless youth. *See* runaway and homeless youth
homophobia. *See* LGBTQ
Hong Kong, 2
HR. *See* harm reduction
Hughes, Craig, 191
Hull House, 22
human rights, 3, 36
Humanities Prep Academy (Prep), 164–166
hyperpersonal model, 339

Icarus Project, 192, *199*, 199–204, *201*
identity: for adolescents, 306–307; beliefs about, 105–106; community and, 314–315; culture and, 155; in developmental theories, 334; ethnographies and, 64, 113–114; grief and, 307–308, 311–312; intervention and, 346–347; marginalization for, 180–181; narratives and, 1–2, 52, 87–88, 105–106, 114–115, 248; psychology of, 9; self-belief and, 43; social media for, 343–345; sports relating to, 42
imagination, 327
immigrant bargain, 71
immigrant generation, 68
immigrants: agency for, 68–69; assimilation model for, 69; bilingual education for, 154; class issues with, 218; context for, 68; Deferred Action for Childhood Arrivals for, 72–73; education for, 69; financial aid for, 80–81; gangs for, 71–72; higher education for, 72; language for, 76; Latin@ as, 153; from Mexico, 111–113; native-born Americans compared to, 81; New York City and, 66–67, 105–106, 118–119; policy for, 79–80; SIJS, 80–81; socioeconomics for, 67, 78–79; United States for, 77
impulse control, 269–270
In Our Hands (Palley/Shdaimah), 220
independence, 59–60, 95, 332, 334, 339

India: caste system, 247–251, 253–259; children in, 250–259; class issues in, 249–250; culture in, 247–250
Individuals with Disabilities Education Act (IDEA), 172, 183
inequalities: in aesthetic labor, 136–140; emotions and, 141–142; lived experience of, 140–143; in part-time work, 133–135, 143–145; qualitative studies for, 135; from residency, 139–140, 144; segregation, 157–158
integration, 11–12, 165–166
international human rights. *See* human rights
International Labour Organization (ILO), 221
interpretive action, 45n1
intervention, 9, 33, 37, 63; for children, 153, 302, 343–345; for community agencies, 85–86; in counseling, 99, 337; criminal justice and, 158; in developmental theories, 216, 225, 235, 242–243; for disabilities, 174, 178, 180; education and, 94–95, 342; for family, 275, 318; identity and, 346–347; race and, 150; in social work, 160–165
interviews, 34, 37–42, 53–54
introverted children, 78

James, Alice, 17
James, Henry, 17
John Jay College of Criminal Justice, 119
Johnson, Marsha P., 193
"Just Say No" campaign, 232–233

knowledge, 10, 20–21, 34, 103–104
Kohut, Heinz, 16, 19
Kupchik, Aaron, 123

labeling, 153; for children, 281–282; DSM, 275, 283–285, 289, 295, 317; narratives of, 283–284; of youth mental health, 284–286, 293–294
lack of financial aid, 72, 76–77, 80
LaGuardia Community College, 73

language: communication and, 335; culture and, 200; for immigrants, 76; for marginalization, 242; narratives and, 333

Latin@, 151, 153, 167n1. *See also* minorities

Laura and John Arnold Foundation, 119

leadership, 118, 242–243, *243*, 256, 258

lesbians. *See* LGBTQ

LGBTQ, 211n1; for children, 165; Gay Liberation Movement, 13, 17–18; New Alternatives for LGBT Youth, 188, 192–199; for vulnerable youth, 188–190, *191*, 210. *See also* wayward youth

life rivers, 286–290, *287–288*

"Life Story and the Study of Resilience and Response to Adversity, The" (Cohler), 16–17

lived experience: childcare, 226–227; of inequalities, 140–143; of part-time work, 140–143; in poetry, 273; research on, 286, 290–291; of vulnerable youth, 133–134

love, 57, 63–64

mainstreaming, 177–180

Major Depressive Disorder (MDD), 275–276

Making and Breaking of Affectional Bonds, The (Bowlby), 17

maladaptive behavior, 7

maltreatment, 49

managed care, 10

Mandela, Nelson, 40–41

Manjari (India), 250–259

marginalization, 156–157, 180–181, 242

marriage, 110–113

maternity leave, 218–219, 221

Mattachine Society, 193

Mayan people. *See* Belize

McAdams, Dan, 120, 210

McNiff, Shaun, 327

McPhatter, Shanduke, 126–129

media, 185, 189–190, *190*. *See also* social media

medical model, 178, 180–181, 278

memory, 85–89, 92

mental health, 10, *199*, 200–204, *201*, 286–287. *See also* youth mental health

Mexico, 221–222; education in, 73–74, 77; immigrants from, 111–113; narratives of, 103; New York City compared to, 69; United States compared to, 66–67

middle-class, 141–142

migration: adaptation after, 68–69; for adolescents, 116; community for, 108; context for, 81–82; narratives of, 67–68, 70–75, 153–155; psychology and, 75–76; for social work, 82; vulnerable youth from, 66–67. *See also* immigrants

mindfulness, 268, 272

minorities: alternative schools for, 163–164; for Bureau of Labor, 136; children as, 156–157; class issues for, 225–226; criminal justice for, 123–124, 158; with disabilities, 181–183; discrimination for, 186; gender and, 136–137, 143–145; narratives from, 137–143; public education for, 151–152; Race to the Top, 159; school-based mental health services for, 153–158; segregation for, 160; socioeconomics of, 134–135, 151–152, 166; youth of color, 233–234, 240–241, *243*. *See also* inequalities

mortality, 298–301

motivation, 52–55, 76–77, 98–99, 237–238

Nanny Time Bomb, The (Burke), 216–217

narratives: adolescents and, 1–5, 32, 109–115; adoption in, 316–318; agency from, 12; of aging out, 53–54, 61–62; behavior support from, 107; of Belize, 109–111, 113–115; blogs, 336–338; brain development and, 264–265; *The Call of Stories*, 285–286; from children, 1–5; coherency from, 23, 64; collaboration for, 87; of community, 22–23; from community agencies, 95–98; for compassion, 13–14; complexity of, 99; of couch surfing, 59; counseling and, 88–89, 97–99, 234–237; of death,

303–306; in developmental theories, 15, 346–348; of discrimination, 193, 258–259; for education, 23–24; in ethnographies, 106–109, 173–175, 215; of ex-inmates, 124–126; for family, 317–320, *318*; of family, 301–302, 334–335; about foster care, 57–58; gendered narratives, 75–82; HIV in, 84; identity and, 1–2, 52, 87–88, 105–106, 114–115, 248; of labeling, 283–284; language and, 333; of LGBTQ, 194–199; life rivers, 286–290, *287–288*; of marginalization, 156–157; of mental health, *199*, 200–204, *201*; of Mexico, 103; of migration, 67–68, 70–75, 153–155; from minorities, 137–143; *Narrating Social Work Through Autoethnography*, 4; narrative inquiry, 290–294; of New York City, 111–115; outsider narratives, 21; "Personal Narratives and the Life Story," 210; *The Protestant Ethic and the Spirit of Capitalism*, 16; psychology and, 19–23, 104–105, 247–248; of recidivism, 126–129; research and, 67–68, 87–92, 282, 292–293; for restorative care practices, 23–24, 43–45, *44*; for runaway and homeless youth, 210–211; after sexual exploitation, 99; for siblings, 301–302; from social work, 14–15, 62, 160–161, 167n1; societal fears in, 338–340; socioeconomics in, 133–135; sociology and, 105–106; testimonios, 150–151, 166–167; transformative stories, 53–54; for trauma, 269–272, 313–317, 328–329; in treatment, 269; for vulnerable youth, 41–42, 119–121, 140–141; writing of, 276; youth mental health and, 281–282, 286–292, *287–288*, 294–296, *295*
National Center for Juvenile Justice, 130
National Rifle Association (NRA), 3
native-born Americans, 81
needle exchange, 206, *207*
negative feedback, 337
neglect, 37–40

negotiating, 318–319
neighborhood surveillance, 118–121, 124–126, 129–131
neoliberalism, 11, 150–151, 158–163, 224–225
Neruda, Pablo, 304
New Alternatives for LGBT Youth, 188, 192–199
New York City, *189*; Art School Without Walls in, 231–232, *232*; Belize and, 106, 108, 113–115; Brooklyn Society for the Prevention of Cruelty to Children in, 194; criminal justice in, 121; culture, 103, 122; education in, 149–150; ethnographies from, 192; gangs in, 126–127; immigrants and, 66–67, 105–106, 118–119; Mexico compared to, 69; narratives of, 111–115; research from, 119–120; runaway and homeless youth in, 188–189; social justice in, 13; socioeconomics of, 70, 124–125, 156–157, 191, 217–218; Studio Museum of Harlem in, 238; for vulnerable youth, 68. *See also* wayward youth
New York Police Department (NYPD), 125–126, 128, 189–190, *190*
Nixon, Richard, 224
No Child Left Behind Act, 159
nongovernmental organizations (NGOs), 252
North Central Children & Youth, 85, 88–89, 94–97

opportunities, 55–56
oppression, 21
orphanages, 314–318, 323
Otero, Jerry, 237
outreach, 249–250
outsider narratives, 21

Palley, Elizabeth, 220
panic attacks, 267, 275
parents: art therapy for, 322, *322–323*, 326–327; bonding with, 315; education for, 340–341; grief for, 309–310; psychology of, 173–180, 225–227; social media for, 335–338, 340

part-time work: adolescents and, 135–136; aesthetic labor, 136–140; inequalities in, 133–135, 143–145; lived experience of, 140–143

pedagogy, 164–165

pediatricians, 216–217

"Personal Narratives and the Life Story" (McAdams), 210

person-in-environment, 8

perspectives, 6, 11–12

Peter Cicchino Youth Project, 190

Philadelphia, 48, 55

playbour, 345

poetry, 263–264, 273–274

policy: for childcare, 215–220; criminal justice and, 129–130; for Deferred Action for Childhood Arrivals, 77–78; for drugs, 232–242; for education, 258–259; feedback, 225; for immigrants, 79–80; maternity leave, 218–219; for New York Police Department, 125–126; No Child Left Behind Act, 159; *In Our Hands*, 220; public assistance, 155–156; regulation and, 226; social welfare, 215–216, 241; for socioeconomics, 143–145; for United Nations Convention on the Rights of the Child, 11; for vulnerable youth, 94–95; zero tolerance, 159–160

politics: of childcare, 214–215, 226–227; history of, 224–225; of maternity leave, 221; media and, 185

Polkinghorne, John, 292

Post Traumatic Stress Disorder (PTSD), 275–276

poverty, 152–154, 247, 250–259, 256–259

Prep. *See* Humanities Prep Academy

Preparing Leaders of Tomorrow (P.L.O.T.), 118, 120

prison assembly line: history of, 121–124, 129; neighborhood surveillance and, 118–121, 124–126, 129–131; violence and, 126–129

Protestant Ethic and the Spirit of Capitalism, The (Weber), 16

psychology: of abandonment, 315–316; of abuse, 90–92; of acceptance, 183–186;

of accomplishments, 60–61; of adolescents, 81; aging out in, 59–60; American Psychiatric Association, 283; analytic third, 13–14; of anxiety, 175–177; of borderline personality disorder, 288–289, 295–296; of children, 2, 5–6, 179–180; class issues in, 216–217; clinical psychology, 171; cognitive strategies for, 106; of communication, 1–2; of community, 40–41; of complexity, 87–88; of context, 68–69; of death, 298–300; *Diagnostic and Statistical Manual of Mental Health Disorders*, 275, 283–285, 289, 295, 317; of disabilities, 173–175; do-it-yourself approach, 200–202; of drugs, 241–242; DSM, 275, 283–285, 289, 295, 317; of ecological systems, 64, 114–115; education and, 32, 293–294; of effort, 40–42; family and, 58; of foster care, 51; Generalized Anxiety Disorder, 275–276; of grief, 178–179, 308–309; history of, 284–285; of HIV, 5, 18; of identity, 9; of independence, 332, 334, 339; interpretive action, 45n1; of love, 63–64; of Major Depressive Disorder, 275–276; migration and, 75–76; of mortality, 298–301; narratives and, 19–23, 104, 247–248; of parents, 173–180, 225–227; Post Traumatic Stress Disorder, 275–276; psychotherapy, 241, 264, 267–268; of Queerness, 17–18; of racism, 236–237; research and, 99, 116, 171–172; of self-belief, 39–40; of stress, 321, 321, 323–324, 324; of success, 49–50; of vulnerable youth, 265–266; of youth care and education center, 37. *See also* counseling

public art, 240–241

public assistance, 155–156

public education, 151–152, 155, 158–159

public sexuality, 18

public sharing, 337, 344–345

qualitative studies, 21, 135, 214, 249

quantitative analysis, 21, 249

queer. *See* LGBTQ
Queerness, 17–18

race, 33–34, 150, 190. *See also* minorities
Race to the Top, 159
racism, 182, 183–184, 206, 236–237. *See
also* minorities
Reagan, Nancy, 232–233
Real School Safety Problem, The, 123
recidivism, 123–124, 126–129
reentry, for ex-inmates, 119–121
Reflections (journal), 22–23
reflexivity, 301–302
regulation, 220, 226, 243–244
Rehabilitation Act (1973), 172
relationships: from community,
    209–210; confidence from, 41; in
    counseling, 291–293; ethics of, 99;
    face-to-face interactions, 339–340,
    347–348; social justice in, 240–241; on
    social media, 333–334, 339–343; in
    social work, 194–199, 291
religion, 96, 298–299, 344
rescue, 315–316
research: on agency, 11; on anxiety,
    275–276; on becoming, 11–12; in brain
    development, 267; on childcare,
    222–226; on children, 3–4, 7–8, 23–24;
    from collaboration, 97–98; on
    daycare, 223; in education, 33, 33–34,
    223; on emotions, 142–143; on
    ethnographies, 21–22, 137, 164–165;
    foster care and, 50–53; on gender, 310;
    by General Accounting Office, 21–22;
    on life rivers, 286–290, 287–288; on
    lived experience, 286, 290–291; on
    middle-class, 141–142; narratives and,
    67–68, 87–92, 282, 292–293; from
    New York City, 119–120; psychology
    and, 99, 116, 171–172; on public
    sexuality, 18; in qualitative studies,
    214, 249; on segregation, 165–166; on
    siblings, 303–310; social justice and,
    15–16; in United States, 226; writing
    and, 19–20; on youth mental health,
    292–293
residency, 139–140, 144

resiliency: after aging out, 55–56;
    ecological perspectives and, 12; "The
    Life Story and the Study of Resilience
    and Response to Adversity," 16–17; for
    vulnerable youth, 57–58
restorative care practices, 23–24, 31–32,
    43–45, *44*
return migration, 73–74
"Rich-get-Richer" hypothesis, 343–344
right to attend school, 69
Rivera, Sylvia, 193
role modeling, 52–53
runaway and homeless youth (RHY):
    Icarus Project, *199*, 199–204, *201*;
    narratives for, 210–211; in New York
    City, 188–189; vulnerable youth and,
    188–192, *189–191*; wayward youth and,
    192–199, *194*, 205–206, *207*, 208–210

Safe Horizon's Sreetwork Project,
    192–193, 205–206, *207*, 208–210
safe space, 266
St. Germain, Jim, 120–124
school-based mental health (SBMH)
    services: for minorities, 153–158; in
    neoliberalism, 158–163; for social
    justice, 163–166; for success, 166–167;
    for vulnerable youth, 149–152
schools and immigrant students, 69–71,
    76–77, 79–80
scrapbooks, 286
segmented assimilation, 69
segregation, 157–158, 160, 165–166
self-belief, 324–325, *325*; abuse and,
    271–272; in adolescents, 42–43;
    identity and, 43; in interviews, 40–42;
    for opportunities, 55–56; psychology
    of, 39–40; for restorative care
    practices, 31–32, 44–45
self-help financial groups (SHGs), 247,
    252–258
sexism. *See* gender
sexual exploitation: of children, 84–85,
    87–92; in education, 90–91; history
    of, 93–94; memory of, 85–86;
    narratives after, 99; of vulnerable
    youth, 95–97

Shaw, Clifford, 15–16, 22
Shdaimah, Corey, 220, 224
siblings: grief for, 298–301, 311–312;
    narratives for, 301–302; research on,
    303–310
Siciliano, Carl, 190, 193
"Sign Language" (mural), 231–232, 232
Small, Deborah, 234
social justice: for adults, 240–241;
    advocacy for, 234–235; Black Lives
    Matter, 3, 234; for children, 11, 232; for
    disabilities, 183–186; ecological
    perspectives for, 5; in education, 165;
    neoliberalism and, 150–151; in New
    York City, 13; outsider narratives, 21;
    in relationships, 240–241; research
    and, 15–16; school-based mental
    health services for, 163–166; socioeco-
    nomics and, 143; in Sweden, 3; in
    welfare state, 23; for youth of color,
    240–241
social media: for adolescents, 331–335,
    338–340, 343–348; for identity,
    343–345; for parents, 335–338, 340;
    relationships on, 333–334, 339–343
social networking sites (SNS), 332
social sciences, 2–3, 22, 31–32
Social Security, 218
social welfare, 215–216, 241
social work: advocacy in, 188–189, 190,
    191–192, 194, 194–199, 210; bilingual
    education and, 150–151; children in,
    303–304; clinical history in, 285–286;
    clinical psychology, 171; cognitive
    behavioral therapy in, 347–348;
    collaboration in, 98–99; communica-
    tion in, 332–333; education and,
    163–164, 335; family in, 331; fight,
    flight, or freeze response in, 267–268,
    271–272, 274, 277; history of, 341–342;
    HIV for, 14–15; intervention in,
    160–165; migration for, 82; Narrating
    Social Work Through Autoethnogra-
    phy, 4; narratives from, 14–15, 62,
    160–161, 167n1; by nongovernmental
    organizations, 252; outreach in,
    249–250; person-in-environment, 8;

racism for, 206; Reflections, 22–23;
    relationships in, 194–199, 291;
    socioeconomics in, 9; success and, 53;
    trauma and, 278; in United States,
    63–64; University of Chicago, 15;
    vulnerable youth in, 12–13
socialization, 343–345, 347
societal fears, 338–340
socioeconomics: for children, 4–5; in
    criminal justice, 131; debt, 139; of
    disabilities, 177; of education, 3,
    76–77, 109–111, 122, 150–151; of family,
    215–218; of higher education, 73–74;
    for immigrants, 67, 78–79; of
    minorities, 134–135, 151–152, 166; in
    narratives, 133–135; of New York City,
    70, 124–125, 156–157, 191, 217–218; of
    parents, 225–226; policy for, 143–145;
    of poverty, 152–154, 247, 250–259,
    256–259; self-help financial groups,
    247, 252–258; social justice and, 143;
    in social work, 9; in United States,
    153; in violence, 118–119; for vulner-
    able youth, 50, 56, 93–94
sociology: ABC →X model, 317–318, 318;
    of children, 7, 10; of community,
    15–16, 255–256; Families Under Stress,
    317; narratives and, 105–106; on social
    behavior, 20
Sonia Shankman Orthogenic School, 17
"Sonnet XVII" (Neruda), 304
South Africa (SA): apartheid in, 34;
    Bantu Education Act, 35; children in,
    35–36; Children's Act (2005), 36;
    ubuntu, 39–40. See also Cape Town
special education, 177–180
special immigrant juvenile status (SIJS),
    80–81
sports, 42
stories. See narratives
stress, 321, 321, 323–324, 324
studies, 6–8, 12–19
Studio Museum of Harlem, 238
success: bilingual education for, 155; in
    developmental theories, 306–307;
    education and, 62–63, 129–130;
    motivation for, 237–238; psychology

of, 49–50; school-based mental health services for, 166–167; social work and, 53
suicide, 281, 323–324, *324*
Sullivan, Harry Stack, 241
surveillance, 162–163
Swarnjayanthi Gram Swarozgar Yojana, 257–258
Sweden, 3

teachers, 90–91, 161–162
technology. *See* social media
teenagers. *See* adolescents; vulnerable youth
Temple University, 50–51
Terr, Lenore, 317
testimonios, 150–151, 166–167
therapy: in adults, 51–52; art therapy, 320–329, *321–322, 324–326*; for behavior support, 337–338; case conceptualizations, 276–277; with children, 265–266; cognitive behavioral therapy, 276–277; for drugs, 237–238; in education, 59; empathy in, 266–267; ethnographies in, 264; in foster care, 62–63; group counseling, 88–91; intervention in, 99, 337; narratives and, 88–89, 97–99, 234–237; negotiating in, 318–319; psychotherapy, 241, 264, 267–268; relationships in, 291–293; suicide, 281; therapeutic agendas, 293; youth mental health in, 283–284
Thompson, Clara, 241
Thunberg, Greda, 3
traditional ecological knowledge (TEK), 103–104
transformative stories, 53–54
transgender. *See* LGBTQ
transnational context, 74–75
trauma: art therapy for, 320–329, *321–322, 324–326*; for children, 264–265, 316–317; in developmental theories, 267; eye movement desensitization and reprocessing for, 271–272, 275; family and, 265–266, 313–314; fight, flight, or freeze

response, 267–268, 271–272, 274, 277; framework, 269, 275; narratives for, 269–272, 313–317, 328–329; poetry for, 273–274; Post Traumatic Stress Disorder, 275–276; social work and, 278; trauma based case conceptualization, 277; treatment for, 276–277; wisdom and, 275–276
travel, 111–115
Travis, Jeremy, 119
treatment: case conceptualizations and, 265, 276–277; constructive meaning from, 273–274; life rivers, 286–290, *287–288*; narratives in, 269; for trauma, 276–277
triggering, 327–328
trust, 341–343
Twitter, 336

ubuntu, 39–40
under resourced urban public schools, 149–150
undocumented status, 66–67, 69, 73, 76, 78; and representation, 68
United Nations (UN), 221
United Nations Convention on the Rights of the Child (UNCRC), 11, 36, 135
United States (U.S.): Americans with Disabilities Act, 172, 183; childcare in, 221–222; criminal justice in, 121; culture of, 68–69, 223–224; drug education in, 232–240; education in, 3, 78–79, 103; Education of the Handicapped Act, 172; foster care in, 49; General Accounting Office, 21–22; healthcare in, 214–215; for immigrants, 77; Individuals with Disabilities Education Act, 172, 183; "Just Say No" campaign, 232–233; to Mexico, 66–67; neoliberalism in, 224–225; No Child Left Behind Act, 159; *In Our Hands*, 220; poverty in, 152–154; prisons in, 119; public education in, 158–159; recidivism in, 123–124; Rehabilitation Act, 172; research in, 226; Social Security, 218; social work in, 63–64; socioeconomics in, 153; as third world, 130

universal children, 6–7
University of California Berkeley (UCB), 203
University of Chicago, 15
urban decay, 122
Urban Justice Center, 190
U-visa, 78

Vakharia, Sheila, 244
value differentiation, 343
violence: against children, 127; children and, 35, 127, 130–131; discrimination and, 255; drugs and, 126–127; prison assembly line and, 126–129; relating to culture, 253; socioeconomics in, 118–119
vulnerable youth: adults for, 48; aging out for, 48–50; in Canada, 93–94; Cape Town for, 31–32; Chicago Area Project for, 15–16; collaboration for, 85–86; communication for, 59; community agencies for, 84; community for, 9–11, 35–36; *Consuming Work*, 135; criminal justice for, 122–123; drugs for, 56–58, 97; education for, 50–51; emancipation for, 63; faith for, 238; family for, 58–60, 63–64; first encounters with, 86–87; foster care for, 60–62; gangs and, 239–240; governmentality for, 162–163; history of, 54–55; HIV for, 188, 190–192, 195, 197, 205, 210; HR, 232–233, 240–244; independence for, 59–60, 95; international human rights for, 35–36; interviews with, 34, 37–39; LGBTQ for, 188–189, *191*, 210; lived experience of, 133–134; mental health care for, 10; from migration, 66–67; motivation for, 98–99; narratives for, 41–42, 119–121, 140–141; New York City for, 68; pedagogy for, 164–165; Peter Cicchino Youth Project, 190; poetry by, 263–264; policy for, 94–95; psychology of, 265–266; religion for, 96; resiliency for, 57–58; role modeling for, 52–53; runaway and homeless

youth and, 188–192, *189–191*; Safe Horizon's Sreetwork Project for, 205–206, *207*, 208–210; school-based mental health services for, 149–152; sexual exploitation of, 95–97; in social work, 12–13; socioeconomics for, 50, 56, 93–94; Sonia Shankman Orthogenic School, 17; teachers of, 90–91; testimonios for, 166–167; writing for, 4; youth care and education center for, 39. *See also* wayward youth

war on drugs, 233–234
Washington Heights, 153
wayward youth, 192–199, *194*; from foster care, 201–202; Safe Horizon's Sreetwork Project for, 205–206, *207*, 208–210
Wayward Youth (Aichhorn), 18
weathering the storm. *See* resiliency
Weber, Max, 16
Welch, John, 205–206, *207*, 208–210
welfare state, 23
well-being, 9
Western Cape Education Department (WCED), 36, 45
White, Michael, 313–314
White, Ryan, 5
Wicker, Randy, 193
William Allanson White Institute, 19, 241
wisdom, 275–276
Witkin, Stanley, 4
Wolfman (Freud), 17–18
women. *See* gender
World Trade Organization, 203–204
writing: culture of, 106–107; of narratives, 276; research and, 19–20; for vulnerable youth, 4

Yosso, Tara, 157–158
youth care and education center (YCEC), 31–32; behavior support from, *44*, 44–45; community and, 35; Department of Social Development and, 36; for education, 40–41; psychology of,

37; race at, 33–34; for vulnerable youth, 39
Youth Day, 35
youth development programs, 231–232, 232
youth mental health: in counseling, 283–284; history of, 283; labeling of, 284–286, 293–294; narratives and,

281–282, 286–292, 287–288, 294–296, 295; research on, 292–293
youth of color (YOC), 233–234, 240–241, 243
YouTube, 110–111, 345

zero tolerance, 159–160
zoning, in public education, 155